AMPLIFYING
SOUNDWRITING PEDAGOGIES

INTEGRATING SOUND INTO
RHETORIC AND WRITING

PRACTICES & POSSIBILITIES

Series Editors: Aimee McClure, Mike Palmquist, and Aleashia Walton

Series Associate Editor: Jagadish Paudel

The Practices & Possibilities Series addresses the full range of practices within the field of Writing Studies, including teaching, learning, research, and theory. From Richard E. Young's taxonomy of "small genres" to Patricia Freitag Ericsson's edited collection on sexual harassment in the academy to Jessie Borgman and Casey McArdle's considerations of teaching online, the books in this series explore issues and ideas of interest to writers, teachers, researchers, and theorists who share an interest in improving existing practices and exploring new possibilities. The series includes both original and republished books. Works in the series are organized topically.

The WAC Clearinghouse and University Press of Colorado are collaborating so that these books will be widely available through free digital distribution and low-cost print editions. The publishers and the series editors are committed to the principle that knowledge should freely circulate and have embraced the use of technology to support open access to scholarly work.

RECENT BOOKS IN THE SERIES

Crystal VanKooten and Victor Del Hierro (Eds.), *Methods and Methodologies for Research in Digital Writing and Rhetoric: Centering Positionality in Computers and Writing Scholarship, Volumes 1 and 2* (2022)

Heather M. Falconer, *Masking Inequality with Good Intentions: Systemic Bias, Counterspaces, and Discourse Acquisition in STEM Education* (2022)

Jessica Nastal, Mya Poe, and Christie Toth (Eds.), *Writing Placement in Two-Year Colleges: The Pursuit of Equity in Postsecondary Education* (2022)

Natalie M. Dorfeld (Ed.), *The Invisible Professor: The Precarious Lives of the New Faculty Majority* (2022)

Aimée Knight, *Community is the Way: Engaged Writing and Designing for Transformative Change* (2022)

Jennifer Clary-Lemon, Derek Mueller, and Kate Pantelides, *Try This: Research Methods for Writers* (2022)

Jessie Borgman and Casey McArdle (Eds.), *PARS in Practice: More Resources and Strategies for Online Writing Instructors* (2021)

Mary Ann Dellinger and D. Alexis Hart (Eds.), *ePortfolios@edu: What We Know, What We Don't Know, And Everything In-Between* (2020)

Jo-Anne Kerr and Ann N. Amicucci (Eds.), *Stories from First-Year Composition: Pedagogies that Foster Student Agency and Writing Identity* (2020)

AMPLIFYING SOUNDWRITING PEDAGOGIES

INTEGRATING SOUND INTO RHETORIC AND WRITING

Edited by Michael J. Faris, Courtney S. Danforth,
and Kyle D. Stedman

The WAC Clearinghouse
wac.colostate.edu
Fort Collins, Colorado

University Press of Colorado
upcolorado.com
Denver, Colorado

The WAC Clearinghouse, Fort Collins, Colorado 80523

University Press of Colorado, Denver, Colorado 80202

ISBN 978-1-64215-168-8 (PDF) | 978-1-64215-169-5 (ePub) | 978-1-64642-392-7 (pbk.)

DOI 10.37514/PRA-B.2022.1688

Produced in the United States of America

Library of Congress Cataloging-in-Publication Data

Names: Faris, Michael J., editor. | Danforth, Courtney S., 1975– editor. | Stedman, Kyle D., editor.
Title: Amplifying soundwriting pedagogies : integrating sound into rhetoric and writing / edited by Michael J. Faris, Courtney S. Danforth, Kyle D. Stedman.
Description: Fort Collins, Colorado : The WAC Clearinghouse ; Denver, Colorado : University Press of Colorado, [2022] | Series: Practices & possibilities | Includes bibliographical references.
Identifiers: LCCN 2022059660 (print) | LCCN 2022059661 (ebook) | ISBN 9781646423927 (paperback) | ISBN 9781642151688 (adobe pdf) | ISBN 9781642151695 (epub)
Subjects: LCSH: English language—Rhetoric—Study and teaching (Higher). | English language—Composition and exercises—Study and teaching (Higher) | Sound—Recording and reproducing—Digital techniques. | LCGFT: Essays.
Classification: LCC PE1404 .A486 2022 (print) | LCC PE1404 (ebook) | DDC 808/.0420711—dc23/eng/20230309
LC record available at https://lccn.loc.gov/2022059660
LC ebook record available at https://lccn.loc.gov/2022059661

Copyeditor: Tony Magialetti
Designer: Mike Palmquist
Cover Art: Image by Uchechukwu Azubike. Used with permission.
Series Editors: Aimee McClure, Mike Palmquist, and Aleashia Walton
Series Associate Editor: Jagadish Paudel

The WAC Clearinghouse supports teachers of writing across the disciplines. Hosted by Colorado State University, it brings together scholarly journals and book series as well as resources for teachers who use writing in their courses. This book is available in digital formats for free download at wac.colostate.edu.

Founded in 1965, the University Press of Colorado is a nonprofit cooperative publishing enterprise supported, in part, by Adams State University, Colorado State University, Fort Lewis College, Metropolitan State University of Denver, University of Alaska Fairbanks, University of Colorado, University of Denver, University of Northern Colorado, University of Wyoming, Utah State University, and Western Colorado University. For more information, visit upcolorado.com.

Land Acknowledgment. The Colorado State University Land Acknowledgment can be found at https://landacknowledgment.colostate.edu.

Contents

Foreword (and Backward)

Steph Ceraso

University of Virginia

I've always been captivated by sound. I have actual sonic proof of this. After my grandma died in 2017, my dad found a beat-up shoebox of cassette tapes in her attic. Since I'm the only family member that still owns a boombox, he gave the tapes to me.[1]

> *[rattling sound of cassette tape being put into boombox, the click of the pray button, and the warm static-like buzz of the beginning of the tape]*

Strangely, all of the cassettes were blank except for one; it was labeled First Tape December 1984. This was the year my Grandpa Ron bought a portable recorder with a microphone. His first and only audio composition was a variety show of sorts. The tape is a mix of Christmas carols recorded from the radio, *[music: Grandpa Ron's 1984 recording of "The Little Drummer Boy" from an unknown Pittsburgh radio station; the rhythmic plucking of a stringed instrument followed by angelic female voices singing "Come they told me pa rum pum pum pum"]* narrative that sounds a bit like my grandpa impersonating a game show host, *[Grandpa Ron: "OK now Stephanie you listen here" in the style of Bob Barker]* and multiple attempts to "interview" the grandchildren.

> **Grandpa Ron**: Come on let's play, they're waiting for you. Ok, sing from over there.
>
> **Toddler Steph**: NO!
>
> **Grandpa Ron**: We can hear it. Sing from over there.
>
> **Toddler Steph**: NO!

Most of these interview attempts feature the breathy noises of little kids sugared up on holiday treats *[sound of kids' fast, heavy breaths followed by hyper scream-laughing]*, but one particular moment of lucidity made my ears perk up.

> **Grandpa Ron**: Say it, go ahead. Well do you have something to say, Stephanie?
>
> **Toddler Steph**: Nah, I wanna just listen.
>
> **Grandpa Ron**: You wanna just listen?

---

1. The audio version of Steph Ceraso's foreword can be found on the book's companion website.

DOI: https://doi.org/10.37514/PRA-B.2022.1688.1.2

Toddler Steph: Yeah to the music.

Grandpa Ron: Ohhh. To the music.

As a longtime music nerd and someone who has made a career of thinking about sound, "I wanna just listen" could be the thesis statement of my life.

[an exaggerated, cartoonish fast forward sound]

Fast forward ahead, through awkward grade school trumpet lessons, *[two badly played trumpet notes]* angsty teenage years, *[MTV News anchor Kurt Loder: "Kurt Cobain, the leader of one of rock's most gifted and promising bands, Nirvana, is dead and this is the story as we know it so far . . ."]* and that intense Britpop phase in college *[music: "Crazy Beat" by Blur; Damon Albarn sings "They think you're clever/'Cos you've blown up your lungs/But I love to hear that crazy beat (yeah, yeah, yeah, yeah, yeah)"; accompanied by powerful drums, distorted guitars, and electrifying synth sounds]*, to 2008—the year I started graduate school at the University of Pittsburgh. This is when I discovered that multimodal composition was a thing, but also that rhetoric and composition scholars were starting to pay more attention to sound in general.

So when I got to teach my first class at Pitt the next year, I immediately wanted to try out an assignment that required audio editing—a very simple "musical literacy narrative." After taking students through the basics of how to use a digital audio editor, I was walking around the classroom to see if they were getting the hang of it. I went over to a student with his hand raised and asked how it was going. In the most sincere voice, he said: "This feels radical." It really did. It was 2009. While others in the field were incorporating sound into their pedagogies by that point in time, it felt radical for me and for that student to be composing with sound in a writing course—even though neither one of us really knew what we were doing.

[Music: "Happy Soul" by Daniel Johnston; Johnston sings, "I got a mind blowing philosophy/I don't know exactly what it is" to a simple, raw rock rhythm on the electric guitar; music then fades into an exaggerated, cartoonish fast forward sound.]

Here we are, more than a decade later, and teaching with sound no longer feels radical. In fact, it's now commonplace—a standard feature of multimodal composition courses. And that's a good thing. The eclectic range of topics taken up in this collection—soundscapes, voice, hip-hop pedagogy, remix, audio tours, oral histories, archives, listening, access, and more—is a testament to the health and continual growth of sonic work in writing and rhetoric, and in related fields. *Soundwriting*, a concept popularized by the editors of this collection, has become not only accepted, but embraced. We now have the freedom to experiment—to keep pushing the limits of what we can teach and do with sound in the classroom.

[Music: "Brown" by John Oswald; a high energy remix featuring James Brown songs and a range of hip-hop and soul samples.]

Amplifying Soundwriting asks us to turn up the volume and listen to authors who are invested in spreading their bold and dynamic approaches to sonic pedagogy. Relying on both theory and praxis, the authors in this collection offer innovative ways to challenge teachers and students to engage and compose with sound. They invite us to interact with the sonic world in more attuned, expansive, and full-bodied ways.

This collection reverberates with pedagogical potential. The question is, are you ready to listen?

[Toddler Steph: "Nah, I wanna just listen." "Nah, I wanna just listen." "Nah, I wanna just listen.".]

Note

All sound and music clips not included in the references list are from the Ceraso family cassette tape, First Tape December 1984.

References

Blur. (2003). Crazy beat [Song]. On *Think tank*. Parlophone.

Johnston, D. (1991). Happy soul [Song]. On *Artistic vice*. Kramer.

MTG. (2016, September 16). Trumpet single notes (played badly) [Audio file]. *Freesound*. https://freesound.org/people/MTG/sounds/357583/.

Oswald, J. (1989). Brown [Song]. On *Plunderphonics 69/96*. Fony/Seeland.

Pantheon Podcasts. (2020, January 22). Kurt Cobain death MTV News April 8, 1994 [Video file]. *YouTube*. https://youtu.be/cvMlQAVBme8.

Plasterbrain. (2017, September 17). Cartoon fast forward [Audio file]. *Freesound*. https://freesound.org/people/plasterbrain/sounds/402451/.

Saavik. (2012, April 8). ejectinsertplaycassette.aif [Audio file]. *Freesound*. https://freesound.org/people/saavik/sounds/151059/.

AMPLIFYING SOUNDWRITING PEDAGOGIES

INTEGRATING SOUND INTO RHETORIC AND WRITING

Introduction. Why We Teach Soundwriting

Michael J. Faris
TEXAS TECH UNIVERSITY

Courtney S. Danforth
COLLEGE OF SOUTHERN NEVADA

Kyle D. Stedman
ROCKFORD UNIVERSITY

Prelude: How We Came to Sound

Michael's Narrative

When I was growing up on a farm in Iowa, sounds seemed either quiet or loud. There was no nuance to my childhood ears.[1] The quiet: The soft murmur of the high school football game heard from five miles away on a still night. The stillness after a snowstorm, when the sunlight bounced off an expansive sheet of fresh snow, the world only a visual with no discernible sounds. The silence of family members as their eyes were glued to the television (and the loud injunction to be quiet if we children interrupted). The loud: The roar of grain augers and tractor engines you couldn't hear people speak over. The thunderclaps during those awe-inspiring Midwestern storms. *[thunder in background (Fission9, 2020), followed by fading in of cows mooing (kilgore54, 2016)]* The bellowing from weaning calves at night as they huddled together, separated from their mothers for the first time.

It wasn't until I neared my teenage years that sound began to acquire nuance. Watching Reba McEntire on Country Music Television on Sunday mornings before going to church. *[basketball crowd fades in and then out (phillyfan972, 2017)]* Listening to Iowa State men's basketball games on the radio as my family drove home from our junior high games (sometimes held 45 or 75 miles away). Recording country songs from the radio onto my cassette player. (We could, from our farm, really only pick up a few local radio stations, all playing country music, Paul Harvey, and *Trading Post*, in which listeners called in looking to sell or buy an item.) And later, alternative rock (who can ignore or forget the voice of the Cranberries' Dolores O'Riordan?) on my portable CD player or with my best friend

---

1. Audio versions of Michael J. Faris's, Courtney S. Danforth's, and Kyle D. Stedman's opening narratives can be found on the book's companion website.

DOI: https://doi.org/10.37514/PRA-B.2022.1688.1.3

while playing Final Fantasy III on the Super Nintendo *[Final Fantasy III tune plays (DarkEvil, 2006) for a few seconds]*; punk-ska concerts; poetry slams in college; the beats of "Tumbthumping" at high school dances long before I began to drink.

It wasn't until I had been teaching writing for a few years that I began to see sound as a pedagogical and composing tool for college writing. In summer 2009, I assigned my first sound-based assignment. Students had written a literacy narrative that had to question or challenge a common assumption about literacy. I asked them to remediate their essays into audio essays. I remember listening to these audio essays on my blue iPod Mini as I drank coffee outside of a local coffee shop and wrote feedback to the students. It was the most enjoyable grading I've ever experienced. I just sat there and enjoyed student work for three hours as I wrote responses to the students' lovely projects.

I can't claim that assignment was radical or pushed the practices of composing far—either at that time or now. But this moment opened up a world of composing and teaching writing and the power of sound as a mode for student composition. I've later assigned podcast episodes and other soundwriting in my courses, and I've come to see sound as more integral to all composing than I had in the past. In grad school, I wrote best in coffee shops, with ambient sounds helping me to focus on the work in front of me. *[ambient sounds of a bar—talking, music, glasses clinking, door creaking—fade in (BurghRecords, 2018)]* And later, as a professor, I started writing at night at bars (as the day was too packed with teaching and admin work and meetings); I'd occasionally get interrupted by someone who would ask how I could work somewhere so loud: Talking, cheering at the football game on television, the clinking of glasses, the occasional dropped and shattered glass all became part of the ambience of my writing. *[ambience fades out]*

Rhetoric is about movement, and what better way to move than with sound.

[Paul Harvey fades in: ". . . and now you know the rest of the story" (Harvey, n.d.).]

Courtney's Narrative

I lived in Australia as a baby and long-distance phone calls were too expensive, so my parents recorded audio cassettes of me learning to talk and sent those back to family in the States. "G'day, y'all" is my soundbite from that era; I was a soundwriter from the start.

Then I grew up as a cathedral chorister, later a singer in punk and bluegrass bands. I listened to a lot of talk radio—mostly BBC and NPR, but Howard Stern too. This all would have stayed a hobby if it weren't for one fateful Saturday morning in my second year of graduate school.

I was injured by a hit-and-run driver while cycling. My broken neck was terrible, but it was the brain injury that was worse. Physically, I could see (when my eye healed) and I could hold a pen or type (when my arm healed), but the connection between those actions and the meaning of language had evaporated. In the impact or the coma, I lost the ability to read with my eyes or write with my hands. I lost whole languages I had learned, including the language of music. My health insurance (pre-Affordable Care Act) was tied to my employment as a graduate instructor, so my immediate concern was how to keep working while I figured out my recovery. And what I figured out was that I still had access to language through sound. If my first-year writing students read their papers to me out loud, I could give them oral feedback and I could still teach. So that's what we did.

I might have made different decisions had I known then what was ahead. I couldn't get treatment because I could still talk and reason capably. The campus disability office couldn't offer anything without a diagnosis. I couldn't get a diagnosis without insurance approval. My policy didn't cover injuries "resultant of a crime." I couldn't get a different policy with pre-existing conditions. There was no help. Eventually, I taught myself to read and write again, though now, more than ten years later, I don't think I'll ever regain even half the stamina I used to have. But all this time, however burned out my sight-reading gets, I have been able to call on soundwriting as an access point to language. I manage.

My experience prompts me to value sound as access to language for other people too. I show my dyslexic students how to read with voice synthesis. I get my English language learners to use speech-to-text when they're more comfortable speaking than writing. I try to give my blind students an easier time than I had. Soundwriting hasn't helped me teach my Deaf students exactly, but they remind me to be always purposeful about when and how I use sound versus visual versus any other media of composition.

As a student, a teacher, a writer, a reader, and an editor, sound has been a helpful "what about" to help me question my assumptions about language. It checks me and supports me in trying to be inclusive and fair and effective. While it may have begun professionally as a workaround, sound has always been a medium of access for me and I have come to value sound as an important contributor in its own right.

Kyle's Narrative

[Music fades in and plays beneath the following narration. It's rhythmic yet uneven, with airy synthesized notes jolting in and out—both upbeat and odd (Nctrnm, 2017).]

In the early 1990s, my dad brought home an old-school karaoke machine—a heavy box with two tape decks, two mic inputs, and a big speaker. When my middle-school friends came over, we'd grab a tape of old sermons from my parents' reject bin and record over it with jokes and songs, the echo and gain jacked up until feedback screamed.

Two conclusions: For me, soundwriting means cassettes and community.

I wouldn't have called it "community" then, but that's what it was. Sure, I made a lot of recordings by myself—layering kazoo over the instrumental side of Boyz II Men's "End of the Road" cassette single, telling silly stories where I did all the voices—but I mostly remember making tapes with friends. They'd talk into the mic while I recorded, then I'd rearrange what they said and play it back for them later. We'd collaborate on audio dramas made for high school English classes, adding dramatic music and unexpected sounds to "The Masque of the Red Death," a scene from *Antigone*, or a retelling of the myth of Antiope—though we pronounced it an-tee-OH-pee. I was addicted to making something new with someone else (and, sure, for the feeling of pride when I played the finished tape back). Together, we'd scan the shortwave dial for something unusual, tape it, dub it in slow motion, dub it in slow motion again, blend it with sound effects or movie scores, and laugh and laugh and laugh.

[Music fades away.]

In grad school, I didn't initially plan for those sonic games to become part of my scholarly and pedagogical identity. But in 2009, when a professor asked us to read and present on a recent article in the field, I picked Jim Ridolfo and Dànielle Nicole DeVoss's (2009) *Kairos* article "Composing for Recomposition: Rhetorical Velocity and Delivery," mostly because it uses the word *remix* so often. *That's a word I know something about*, I thought. *It reminds me of all those tapes I used to make—remixing old sounds into something new.* By early 2010, I'd started reading and blogging and publishing about remix, but always drawn towards the sonic side of remix studies: how fans and scholars record and remix, together.

And just as my tapes had built community in high school, I found academic communities eager to play and make and listen to sounds together. At my first Computers and Writing conference in 2011, I played audio clips of interviews I had conducted for my dissertation, which I had layered with music and edited for timing to emphasize their emotional impact. That soundwriting led to conversations and friendships with other scholars, which led to more conference presentations, more friendships, and more of the same cycle I remembered from high school: make an audio piece (sometimes alone, sometimes with others), play it for friends, repeat. Presentations, podcasts, and more connections followed. Instead of dubbing a copy of a tape for a friend, I could just upload a sound to Dropbox or Google Drive, but the concept was the same. Even better, these sonic communities affected my teaching, leading me to share more of these playful audio remix skills with students looking for more available means of communication.

[New music fades in and plays until the end: a slow electronic drone, as synthesized notes fade in and out, occasionally with electronic percussive blips (Nctrnm, 2018).]

So when Courtney Danforth emailed me in December 2014 about coediting a journal issue or edited collection on soundwriting pedagogies, it just made sense.

As editors, we'd be connecting in a deeper way to a community that was eager to make and listen and share soundwriting. Our first collection playfully broke boundaries in all the ways that soundwriting communities love to do, but it was smaller than the large vision we began with, with fewer voices featured than we'd hoped to share, so we expanded our work into two projects, then three. This collection thus represents the culmination of a trilogy, but also the ever-growing community of soundwriting teachers. (I wonder if anyone from high school will listen.)

Now we just need to figure out how to release it on cassette.

[Music gets louder for a moment, hits a brief major chord, and fades out.]

Why Soundwriting?

We share these three narratives to help attune you to the affective nature of and possibilities for composing with and in sound in rhetoric and writing courses. Just as we came to sonic rhetoric through our own individualized experiences with sound, our students and colleagues come to sound through the lenses of their own experiences. Our narratives—often invisible and inaudible to outsiders—shape our soundwriting and our approach to the field.

Indeed, in our discipline, sound has until recently been writing studies' invisible (rather than ugly) stepsister. As Cynthia L. Selfe (2009) showed, due to the historical separation of speech from writing in academic settings and due to a desire to "modernize" English studies by moving away from aurality, most writing teachers have focused on the visual, printed word and largely ignored the aural nature of rhetoric and communication. The multimodal turn in rhetoric and writing studies has offered the opportunity to reincorporate sound in rhetoric and writing courses, though sound perhaps at first took a backseat to the visual, which dominated much of the discussion of the turn to multimodality in the late 20th century and early 21st century.

However, the last two decades has seen a sonic turn in rhetoric and writing pedagogy and in the humanities more broadly. Sound studies has become a strong interdisciplinary field in which scholars from a variety of disciplines have studied sound production and reception from a variety of critical perspectives (Gunn et al., 2013; Lingold et al., 2018; Sterne, 2012). And in rhetoric and writing studies, scholars have now argued persuasively that sound deserves our attention for rhetorical analysis and theory (Comstock & Hocks, 2016; Eckstein, 2017; Goodale, 2011; Hawk, 2018a, 2018b; Kjeldsen, 2018; Lambke, 2019; Rickert, 1999; Stone, 2015; Stone & Ceraso, 2013; VanKooten, 2016), scholarly research methods and production (Ball, 2004; Carson, 2017; Detweiler, 2018; Wargo, 2020; Wargo et al., 2021), and, importantly, for this book here, pedagogy (Ahern, 2013, 2018; Alexander, 2015; Ball & Hawk, 2006; Bessette, 2016; Bowie, 2012a, 2012b; Ceraso, 2014, 2018, 2019; Ceraso & Ahern, 2015; Comstock & Hocks, 2006; Danforth et al., 2018; Davis, 2011; Detweiler, 2019; Faris et al., 2020; Folk, 2015; Greene, 2018;

Hawkins, 2018; Hocks & Comstock, 2017; Klein, 2020; Rodrigue et al., 2016; Sady, 2018; Selfe, 2009; Stedman et al., 2021).

There are many reasons to incorporate soundwriting in rhetoric and writing courses—from required first-year writing courses to upper-division classes for majors or as electives to graduate courses, and in all settings, including community colleges, liberal arts colleges, research universities, Historically Black Colleges and Universities, and more. Before addressing these reasons, though, we'd like to address the central term of our collection: *soundwriting*. In our earlier collection's introduction, we take a deep dive into the history and meaning of the word, ultimately defining soundwriting as those practices when rhetors "manipulate recorded sound and make something new from it" (Danforth & Stedman, 2018, Part 5.0 section). What we mean by this is that soundwriting is the action and object created by drafting, revising, and delivering compositions in the aural mode. The term sets a fence around the kinds of assignments explored in this book: those where students actually compose and revise sonic projects (as opposed to listening to someone else's soundwriting, getting feedback through an instructor's soundwriting, or delivering content live without the opportunity to revise). The term *soundwriting* also prominently includes the word *writing*, which emphasizes that much of our disciplinary knowledge about writing—recursive strategies for composing, rhetorical situatedness, multimodality's centrality, and so on—applies to composing with sound as well. Thus, the term soundwriting suggests a disciplinary remix between sound studies and writing studies, but with a focus on the compositional and pedagogical side that terms like "sonic rhetoric" don't necessarily include. (See Katz, 2020, p. 2, for a recent discussion of the multiple terminologies emerging in this subfield.)

So why teach soundwriting? First, sound is rhetorically powerful and should be among the available modes for student composition; thus, including soundwriting in a course with a rhetorical framework helps address a historic and problematic gap in our field. As Selfe (2009) argued, multimodal composing—including in and with sound—is important for students, and

> teachers of composition need to pay attention to, and come to value, the multiple ways in which students compose and communicate meaning, the exciting hybrid, multimodal texts they create—in both nondigital and digital environments—to meet their own needs in a changing world. (p. 642)

Sound, we suggest, circulates in a wide variety of media—from YouTube and TikTok videos, to podcasts, to music on Spotify and (for some) the radio, to the blurps and blips of social media apps and text messaging, to the ambient and environmental sounds of private, public, and work environments.

Soundwriting has the potential to call students' attention to how rhetoric does not solely *mean* but rather engages with affect and sensations (Hawhee, 2015), as our personal narratives above emphasized. Many soundwriting scholars have called attention to the affective, material, and sensuous nature of sound (Alexander, 2015; Anderson, 2014; Comstock & Hocks, 2016; Ceraso, 2018, 2019; Davis, 2011; Harley, 2018). As Byron Hawk (2018b) observed, sound is material "energetic movements," a view that affords teachers and students opportunities to

> feel their bodies vibrate empathetically (embodiment); locate themselves in space via reverberation (spatial orientation in an environment); analyze language as with phonemes (communicate via speech); and capture and distribute sound via technological mediation (produce and circulate music and culture). (p. 315)

A second reason we should teach soundwriting is that sound is ambient and shapes our environments and experiences. That is, since courses in writing and rhetoric should engage in the environments and discourses of particular rhetorical situations, we should teach students to actively understand and participate in soundscapes. The concept of soundscape, most commonly attributed to R. Murray Schafer (1977), has become quite useful across sound studies to help scholars explore how sound shapes our experiences and relationships to environments. In her recent chapter on soundscapes, Kati Fargo Ahern (2021) defined a soundscape as a composition that

> meets the following criteria: 1) it communicates some purpose or potential to an audience, 2) it can be experienced in some multimodal, embodied way, and 3) it includes some aspects of spatialization in addition to sound sources, simultaneity, and arrangement in time, which can be found in soundtracks. (2021, 2. Soundscape Studies section, para. 3)

Drawing from a variety of sound studies scholars, including in rhetoric and writing studies (Ahern, 2018; Ceraso, 2014; Comstock & Hocks, 2006; Rickert, 2013), Ahern suggested that rhetors compose soundscapes through composing with sound sources, temporality, layering of sounds, and spatialization, creating soundscapes that can shape how audiences interact with and understand their environments—whether digital or nondigital. As her chapter argued, students, as rhetors, can design soundscapes in order to create not simply sonic, but fully embodied, experiences for audiences. By asking students to compose with and in sound, we are also asking them to attend to how sound shapes environments, helping students to develop a sensibility or an "attunement between listener, materials, and environment" (Droumeva & Murphy, 2018, 4. Composing with/in Media Texts section, para. 14).

Third, sound is always multimodal and helps attend to materiality, embodiment, and the aesthetics of composition. Sound, like all modes, is material, and thus helps us as rhetoric and writing teachers and researchers attend to how rhetoric and writing is material and embodied. As Lisbeth Lipari (2014) has argued, listening is fully an embodied, multisensory practice: "What if our entire body is one giant listening organ, one great resonating chamber? What if we are, in some sense, all ears?" (p. 30). Sounds, she explained, resonate and vibrate through our bodies, in ways that "we actually touch the sound" (p. 31) and listen with all of our senses. Likewise, Steph Ceraso (2014, 2018) has argued that listening is not simply a matter of our ears but rather a multimodal and multisensory experience. Multimodal listening, she argued, means understanding that listening involves multiple senses and modes simultaneously: "sound is always connected and experienced with multiple senses" (2018, p. 8).

Fourth, sound can be used to disrupt conventions about rhetoric and writing and about learning and teaching. Students often enter rhetoric and writing classes with preconceived notions about and habituated practices of research and writing (for instance, Howard & Jamieson, 2013, showed how students' research habits led to patchwriting and little engagement with arguments), and introducing new and foreign modes can help to defamiliarize research, incorporating research, drafting, revising, arrangement and organization, and style and voice. Christina Sady (2018), for instance, argued that "teaching a multimodal genre encourages transitioning writers to extend beyond standardized genres and formulas learned in high school and to see composing as multimodal, complex, and audience-aware" (p. 256). As she explained, first-year students often carry standardized or formulaic genre conventions with them from high school, and teaching new media, like podcasts, "invites students to see writing in a new way" (p. 259).

Fifth, teaching sound can assist in social justice work. Sound studies scholars have increasingly turned to how sound and oppression are linked. Jennifer Lynn Stoever (2016), for example, has shown how "listening operates as an organ of racial discernment, categorization, and resistance in the shadow of vision's alleged cultural dominance" (p. 4). Sound, she argued, is racialized, creating what she termed the *sonic color line*, and listening practices are sensuously and epistemologically trained to create the *listening ear*, or "dominant listening practices [that] accrue—and change—over time" (p. 7). (See also Burns et al., 2018; Keeling & Kun, 2011; Robinson, 2020; Sano-Franchini, 2018). Ceraso (2018) argued that attending to sound can help us to re-attune to our environments. She called "for a reeducation of our senses—a bodily retraining that can help listeners learn to become more open to the connections among sensory modes, environments and materials" (p. 5)—a call similar to Lipari's (2014), who argued for "an ethics of attunement" (p. 2). Ceraso's and Lipari's projects both call attention to how we have been sensorially trained to listen to or hear certain sounds and ignore others (a notion also advanced by Krista Ratcliffe, 2005). Ceraso (2014) suggested that "through multimodal listening practices we might retrain our bodies to be more aware, alert, and attuned to sonic events in all of their complexity" (p. 103). Indeed, if "listening is guided by positionality as an intersection of perceptual habit, ability, and bias" (Robinson, 2020, p. 37), then rhetoric and writing classes provide opportunities to retrain our listening practices. As Michael Burns et al. (2018) argued, sound can be used in rhetoric and writing classes to "disrupt the circulating rhetorics of multiculturalism and other safe, schooled responses to racism" (Introduction section, para. 10).

Sixth, counterintuitively, soundwriting can be designed for access and accessibility. By using these two terms—*access* and *accessibility*—we have in mind James Porter's (2009) distinction between the two terms. He explained that access is a matter of one's ability to materially access "the necessary hardware, software, and network connectivity" to engage in digital literacy practices (p. 216; see also Banks, 2005, who complicated access as merely material access). Accessibility, however, entails designing for those with disabilities and ensuring that new media compositions are usable by disabled bodies. Regarding the latter, sound composition has been critiqued for its exclusions. Sean Zdenek (2009), for instance, critiqued podcasting for assuming students can hear sound and challenged the field to design sonic compositions for accessibility by considering a variety of embodied engagements with sonic texts, starting with universal design, and including transcripts with rich descriptions for sonic compositions. Many in rhetoric and writing have critiqued the ableist notion of the retrofit (Bose et al., 2021; Buckner & Daley, 2018; Butler, 2016; Dolmage, 2008, 2014; Yergeau et al., 2013). Stephanie Kershbaum defined retrofits as "reactive, responding to situations or problems that arise, rather than seeking to anticipate potential concerns with the design or production of a multimodal text or environment" (Yergeau et al., 2013, "Retrofitting" section).

However, we argue that if designed well, soundwriting assignments can be sites of accessibility and universal design from the beginning. In fact, we argue, designing for accessibility increases usability and accessibility for all users. Even for normative hearing bodies, transcripts or captions can help audiences follow and distinguish aspects of a sonic composition. For instance, well designed captions can help viewers understand the importance of sounds that they might otherwise miss (see Zdenek, 2015, on the rhetoric of captions). Or someone with hearing might be listening to something in public with poor headphones and the ambient sounds make listening difficult; a transcript can help. Or a researcher is returning to a sound composition a second or third time to find a key quotation: A transcript can help them find that quotation quickly, rather than listening around in the sound file. Further, transcripts can do rhetorical work for all listeners/audiences, serving as another version of the text (see Boyle & Rivers, 2016) that can highlight meaning in new and different ways by translating through description and design (Heilig, in Faris et al., 2020). Teaching soundwriting with accessibility and universal design in mind from the get-go is a must.

Regarding access, soundwriting offers the opportunity to value and practice with a democratic ethos and low-fidelity technologies to make the practice materially accessible. Rather than viewing the teaching of soundwriting as "a professionalization of technology" that requires high-tech and expensive recording hardware and software, soundwriting can be produced in rhetoric and writing classes through an ethos of "democratization of practice," as Byron Hawk and Greg Stuart (2019, p. 45) described it. That is, soundwriting teachers in rhetoric and writing classes can value amateur practices and technologies rather than professional audio production by offering students options that include recording with the technologies they already own and using audio-editing software that is free and open source (like Audacity).

Why This Book?

This book showcases 25 chapters that provide soundwriting assignment prompts, context for those prompts, and teachers' (sometimes along with students') reflections on those prompts and context. Additionally, chapters are accompanied by student examples of projects (along with transcripts) and an audio version of authors' reflections on their assignments, hosted on the book's companion website. These multiple ways of accessing our content are an important part of our mission, giving our audience multiple "access points to language," as Courtney put it in her personal narrative above.

As we survey the field, while sonic rhetoric and soundwriting have been topics in scholarly literature for roughly two decades, few examples exist where rhetoric and writing teachers can "steal" assignments and adapt and teach them in their own courses. (As teaching lore goes, good teachers borrow; great teachers steal.) As editors, we wanted to make a resource available for teachers in rhetoric and writing—at all levels and in almost any context—to more easily incorporate soundwriting into their classes. Of course, the field has some wonderful examples from teacher-scholars who have shared their assignments and rationales. Ceraso's (2018) book *Sounding Composition* provided interchapters with assignment prompts and classroom practices on exploring the multimodal and embodied dimensions of composing with and in sound. Eric Detweiler (2019) provided scaffolding activities toward teaching with sound in his article "Sounding Out the *Progymnasmata*." Jeremy Cushman and Shannon Kelly (2018) shared their podcast assignment and scaffolding used in the first-year writing program at Western Washington University, as well as a wonderful podcast that explains how the assignment was received by both teachers and students. Other contributors to our collection *Soundwriting Pedagogies* (Danforth et al., 2018) provided some practical classroom practices as well. Jason Palmeri and Ben McCorkle (2018), for instance, provided a few short example assignments for classes that are "inspired by voices from the past" (Appendix section). And other soundwriting assignments written by those in our discipline can be found in various brief articles and blog posts as well, such as Alison Klein's (2020) "opinion podcast," Ceraso's "sonic object," and Ahern's "embodied soundscape design" (Ceraso & Ahern, 2015).

However, these pedagogical examples are scattered across publications and can be difficult for a teacher new to soundwriting to access and easily incorporate into their classes. By collecting the 25 chapters here, we hope to provide rhetoric and writing teachers—whether new to soundwriting or quite experienced with teaching with sound—with examples they could easily translate into their own classes, with rationales to understand the approaches to the assignments, with teacher reflections to help situate and adjust the assignments to new contexts, and with student examples to share with students as models to provoke creative thinking and creative composing.

An important note here, though: We've asked every contributor to take access into account as they've shared their assignment and reflection. Access is an important aspect of teaching multimodality in general and teaching sound-writing specifically—and for teaching in general. Here, access has two important meanings, as we noted above: access in terms of material access and accessibility in terms of being accessible for students and teachers with a variety of disabilities. Every audio file on the book's companion website includes a transcript that is, to the best of our ability, descriptive of sounds instead of merely a transcript of words. We acknowledge that "the verbal reproduction of sound will necessarily be a metaphorical translation, fundamentally different from the sounds themselves" (Kjeldsen, 2018, p. 367), and so transcripts are never a faithful reproduction of sound (see Zdenek, 2015, on the rhetorical work of captions). However, we have striven to make this book as accessible as possible.

Our hope, then, is that readers can pick up chapters (or the whole collection) to draw inspiration as teachers of soundwriting, and that this collection continues to push the conversation about what it means to teach rhetoric and writing with sound. This collection should be useful to teachers of first-year writing at a variety of institutions. As we know, first-year writing is tasked with doing too much (teach all the things!), so the wide variety of approaches to soundwriting in this collection means that one (or more!) contributor's approach will hopefully be useful to most teachers. Also, as rhetoric and writing majors continue to be developed and grow across the United States, this collection should be useful to teachers of upper-division courses in the major or to teachers of rhetoric and writing courses with broader student audiences. This collection should also be useful for graduate courses in composition studies, multimodal literacies, digital rhetoric or literacies, and sonic rhetoric, or individual chapters could be useful in these courses or a composition practicum course. As graduate students are preparing to teach their own classes, individual chapters can inspire their own approaches to teaching multimodality or teaching soundwriting. Naturally, some assignments will be more or less useful in a particular context, depending on a course's level of study, curricular emphases, access to technology, and instructor preferences. We see this breadth as a strength, and we encourage readers to adapt assignments for their needs.

This Book's Organization

The 25 chapters in this collection bring together a wide variety of student and pedagogical practices related to soundwriting: remix, the use of music, primary research, place-based pedagogy, teaching with stories, collaboration, audience awareness, public engagement, play, reflection, remediating projects, listening practices, and more. There's no right way to organize 25 chapters. We expect many readers will use this book as a reference guide, skimming the table of contents or searching the companion website for what they need. To help readers navigate the rich resources provided by contributors to this collection, we've organized chapters into four sections: Soundwriting Through Remix, Soundwriting with Music, Soundwriting with Primary Research, and Soundwriting with Stories. In the next section, we provide suggestions for other ways to organize chapters based on student practices.

But first, a quick reminder: The "stealing" principle we mentioned above is one of the book's core purposes; we want you to find assignments that work and adapt them to your own classrooms. That's why the student-facing assignment language is presented with an intentionally flexible license (Creative Commons Attribution-NonCommercial 4.0 International) that allows you to legally modify and distribute the assignments you find here without asking permission from the authors, as long as you attribute the authors and use them in noncommercial settings (like your own classroom). All other parts of the book can also be shared without seeking permission, but not in a way that modifies the original language or audio; everything except the assignments is under a Creative Commons Attribution-NonCommerical-NoDerivatives license designed to protect the original work, including the work composed by students.

Soundwriting Through Remix

The book begins with a number of chapters that add nuance to a type of soundwriting assignment that many instructors new to soundwriting begin with: asking students to download or gather recordings and mix them together for a new rhetorical purpose. Logan Middleton's "Mix It Up, Mash It Up: Arrangement, Audio Editing, and the Importance of Sonic Context" especially focuses on this rhetorical transformation of audio's meaning, as he asks his students to engage in "audio trickery" that leads to an audio mashup in a genre of their own choosing and then defending their rhetorical choices in a video reflective statement. Similarly, Crystal VanKooten's "Experimentation, Integration, Play: Developing Digital Voice Through Audio Storytelling" asks students to download and combine audio assets, but this time with a focus on the principles of digital storytelling. VanKooten's scaffolded assignment sequence also teaches students the basics of how copyright law (including fair use and Creative Commons licenses) affects our soundwriting work when we shape assets created by others. Sara Wilder's "Elements of Sound: Three Scaffolded Assignments" focuses less on the genre of the work students create and more on the types of assets students combine (music, voice, and sound effects) that they wield in three subsequent assignments. Like Middleton and VanKooten, Wilder encourages students to reflect on their work, each time writing "artist statements" to accompany their soundwriting.

Many other variations on the collage are featured in the book as well. Chad Iwertz Duffy introduces his students to the concept of "disabling soundwriting," a concept he describes as "fundamentally about centering disability in the production of soundwriting" in his chapter, "Disabling Soundwriting: Sonic Rhetorics Meet Disability Pedagogy." As in the assignments featured in previous chapters, he asks students to find and remix existing sounds and to reflect on that activity, along with a focus on writing rich, complex transcripts. Scott Lunsford's "Sound-Play: A Sonic Experience of Digital Loose Parts" focuses on another angle: His students use recorded and downloaded sounds to create a soundscape that evokes a "play ecology" from their childhood, remediating and reconceptualizing a written play narrative they write first. A similar playful attitude and similar sequence of assignments (from written to sonic work) is present in Thomas M. Geary's "Electrate Anti-Definition Sound Collage and Transduction," in which students are asked to playfully define (or "anti-define") a term through sonic collage. "What does 'freedom' sound like to different people?" he asks his students. "What audio captures 'success' for most?"

Ben Harley's "The Sonic Collage Assignment: Aesthetics, Affect, and Critique in Audio Sampling" transitions the first chapters' focus on remix to a collection of chapters that deal in some way with one of the most ubiquitous forms of audio surrounding us: music. Harley's remix assignments help students investigate music by creating dense, rich mashups, either in the genre of concept art (in his original prompt) or a musical history in which students soundwrite "an audio track composed of short samples from different iconic, important, interesting, or essential songs from within that genre."

Soundwriting with Music

Coming at music from a different angle, Rich Shivener uses his 20 years of experience as a working musician to inspire his students to remediate or "recast" their research into an audio essay that relies on the affective power of music, as described in his chapter "Cultivating Signal, Noise, and Feeling: Songwriting Practices in Digital Rhetoric Courses." Todd Craig also uses his experience as a musician—a hip-hop DJ—to guide his soundwriting pedagogies; in "'How *Eve* Saved My Soul': Sonic Lineage as the Prequel to the Playlist Project," he invites students to investigate the deep impact hip-hop albums have across decades, as they sample the past and influence the future. Justin Young's assignments are also inspired by DJ practices; "Sampling Sound, Text, and Praxis: Student and Teacher as Producer in a (Somewhat) Open-Source Course" describes how students move through a series of assignments asking them to analyze how musical remixes work before collaboratively creating a sonic remix of their own.

Music is a central part of Doyuen Ko and Joel Overall's chapter, "Audio Engineering and Soundwriting in an Interdisciplinary Course," yet in a different key from the chapters preceding it. Ko (professor of audio engineering technology) and Overall (professor of English) teach linked courses at their university that introduce students to terminology for understanding sound and music from both audio engineering and rhetorical contexts, ultimately asking students to share what they've learned in a group podcast series. Students collaborated in a very different way in Trey Conner's "The Resonance Is the Composer: Students Soundwriting Together," a chapter he cowrote with students Emma Hamilton, Amber Nicol, Chris Burton, Kathleen Olinger, Alyssa Harmon, and Ivan Jones. Their chapter describes an inquiry-based, experimental course where students remixed downloaded sounds, improvised in the classroom with "noisemakers" of all kinds, and brought their listening and songwriting skills to a Tampa Bay harbor, where they reflected on (and recorded) the sounds around them. The next chapter also features unexpected sounds and student involvement, in a way: In "The Sound of Type: Multimodal Aesthetics," Helen J. Burgess describes how her assignment asking students to explore typography through a multimodal lens led her student (and coauthor) Travis Harrington to compose a multipart musical work by "isolating qualities of type and mapping them onto similar qualities of sound." The chapter features Burgess's reworked version of the assignment, which invites students to make sonic choices as Harrington did, along with Harrington's reflections on his musical composition process.

Soundwriting with Primary Research

As described in "From Cylinders to WordPress: Using Digital Sound Archives for Short-Form Radio Programs," Jason Luther's students might listen to music, but they might also listen to any other audio genre housed in the massive archives of digitized recordings available online. His chapter begins a series of chapters that ask students to use soundwriting as part of research projects, often using sonic materials and archives to create a sonic composition that helps audiences experience those materials in new ways. For instance, Luther's students create 90-second radio spots that explain, contextualize, and share an archived, digitized recording. Brandee Easter and Meg M. Marquardt frame research as part of a feminist act of listening in their chapter, "Toward a Feminist Sonic Pedagogy: Research as Listening." Their students research and share real-world "mysteries" in a series of podcast episodes, using the physical act of listening to introduce ideas of embodiment and rhetorical listening to their students. Instead of seeking out local stories as Easter and Marquardt's students did, Timothy R. Amidon's students composed soundwriting based on the words that came to them: In "From Postcards to PSAs: Activist Soundwriting," he describes how his students collected postcards from their campus from members of the community that described "stories about their experiences with online privacy and security." Those written experiences from the community were then performed aloud in a public space and remediated into public service announcements for the campus radio station.

Many of the research-based soundwriting assignments in this book led students to learn more about their local communities. Jennifer J. Buckner's students explored specific discourse communities through interviews, composing discourse ethnographies in the form of audio essays, as explained in her chapter cowritten with students Benjamin Flournoy, Katie Furr, Sarah Johnson, Katie Lewis, Angela Meade, Hannah Ray, Garrett Simpson, Kate Vriesema, and Ally Ward, "Research Remix: Soundwriting Studies of the English Language." Lance Cummings's students, including student coauthors Hannah Lane Kendrick and Devon Peterson, created audio tours to help introduce guests to a local historic home and museum, as described in "If These Walls Had Ears: Applying Sound Rhetorics Through Audio Tours." L. Jill Lamberton's students walked through a lengthy, scaffolded series of assignments that introduce them to methodologies for recording interviews with members of their local community and then editing that interview recording into a final, shareable form, as she explains in "Engaging and Amplifying Community Voices: An Interview Assignment Sequence." Janice W. Fernheimer's students, including student coauthors Madison Cissell, Hannah Thompson, Hannah Newberry, and Laura Will, collaborate with the Jewish Heritage Fund for Excellence (JHFE) and Jewish Kentucky Oral History Collection. Their chapter, "The Sound(s) of Sustainable Stewardship: Indexing and Composing Audio Essays with the JHFE," details how students interview community members and edit those recordings into shareable audio formats—in their case, collaboratively authored audio essays. Mariana Grohowski's students research the spaces and stories of their local community, allowing them to record brief audio stories and required transcripts designed to be uploaded to the mobile app and website VoiceMap, as she writes in "Producing Community Audio Tours."

Soundwriting with Stories

Daniel P. Richards's students also research their community, collaboratively creating publicly accessible podcast episodes about their city for a show called *Of Norfolk*. In "Place-Based Podcasting: From Orality to Electracy in Norfolk, Virginia," he describes how his assignment relies on the affordances of orality and a focus on storytelling to keep the attention of listeners. That focus on stories weaves through many of the chapters in this collection, but especially in the chapters that deal more explicitly with fiction. For example, Jasmine Lee and Jennifer Geraci's "YA On the Air: A Scaffolded Podcast Assignment on YA Literature" describes an assignment that asks students to use the power of soundwriting to creatively respond to or review a work of young adult literature, always focusing on using the affordances of audio to achieve their rhetorical purposes. Jennifer Ware and Ashley Hall's "Let's Get Technical: Scaffolding Form, Content, and Assessment of Audio Projects" also relies on stories but more as a way to introduce students to the technical skills needed for any soundwriting work. Their students brainstorm creative things that could have led to the "audio capture of a strange sound" and "unexplained disruption to the broadcast" at a real shortwave radio numbers station. By creating soundscapes that explain this unexplainable phenomenon, they learn basic skills such as working with tracks, loops, field recording, vocal recording, and audio editing.

Tanya K. Rodrigue's "Speech, Invention, and Reflection: The Composing Process of Soundwriting" closes the collection by focusing exclusively on reflection, a metacognitive activity that has been heard through the entire book. Instead of giving her graduate students a specific task, she instead asks them to choose an audio genre and compose something effective within that rhetorical situation. This focuses her chapter instead on the reflections students make, both along the way in a series of "audio process notes" and in a final reflection.

Alternative Organizations

Of course, the collection could have been organized in many other ways as well. Below are just a few alternative ways to organize chapters to help readers looking for particular kinds of activities or focuses. These lists are of course imperfect as well; they attempt to pull together major focuses of chapters for generalized broad swaths, not respond to every little detail of every chapter.

- **Collaborative Work**: Many chapters in this collection encourage or require collaborative work as students compose with and in sound. Readers interested in teaching collaborative soundwriting projects should consult chapters by Amidon, Conner et al., Cummings, Easter and Marquardt, Fernheimer, Ko and Overall, Lee and Geraci, and Young.
- **Podcasts**: The popularity of podcasting naturally leads to many assignments that ask students to create episodic compositions that are part of a larger podcast show. For examples of podcasting pedagogies, see Easter and Marquardt, Ko and Overall, Lee and Geraci, and Richards.
- **Public-Facing Deliverables and Public Engagement**: The following chapters detail pedagogies that ask students to create deliverables to be experienced beyond the classroom itself, including radio shows, museums, audio tours, and public SoundCloud accounts: Amidon, Cummings, Fernheimer, Grohowski, Lamberton, Lee and Geraci, Luther, Richards.
- **Remediations of Other Texts**: Rhetoric classes commonly ask students to transform content experienced primarily through one mode into another in a process often called "remediation." Examples in this collection are found in chapters by Burgess and Harrington, Geary, Iwertz Duffy, and Shivener.
- **Listening Practices**: Good soundwriters are also good listeners. Instructors who emphasize listening in their pedagogies include Easter and Marquardt, Grohowski, Ko and Overall, and Shivener.
- **Place-Based Research**: As scholars of soundscapes have taught us, sounds are intimately tied to the places where they're experienced. Chapters that ask students to emphasize and engage in local places include Cummings, Fernheimer, Grohowski, Lamberton, and Richards.

- **Play**: Soundwriting is an inherently playful activity, as rhetors test audio assets against each other, serendipitously finding connections that can reach audiences effectively. Chapters by Conner et al., Geary, and Lunsford emphasize a play angle.
- **Storytelling**: The word story is used in many different soundwriting genres, from fiction and drama to journalism. An emphasis on effective storytelling in one or more of its many forms appears in chapters by Easter and Marquardt, Lee and Geraci, Richards, Rodrigue, VanKooten, Ware and Hall, and Wilder.
- **Scaffolded Practices**: Many of our chapters highlight assignments that were part of a scaffolded series of course activities, from early low-stakes assignments to final reflections. While these contexts are mentioned in many chapters, readers will find the most support for a series of pedagogical practices in chapters by Cummings, Easter and Marquardt, Fernheimer, Grohowski, Ko and Overall, Lamberton, Lee and Geraci, Middleton, Richards, Rodrigue, VanKooten, Ware and Hall, Wilder, and Young.
- **Student Reflection**: A hallmark of multimodal composition is a focus on student reflection, allowing them to share their rhetorical purposes and strategies developed along the way and after sharing a finished project. Those reflection activities are available in chapters by Fernheimer, Grohowski, Iwertz Duffy, Ko and Overall, Lamberton, Middleton, Rodrigue, and Wilder.
- **Technical Practice and Guidance**: One of the challenges for students and teachers new to soundwriting is understanding and practicing using audio-recording hardware and audio-editing software. Some chapters in this collection provide guidance for students and teachers to navigate these functional literacy practices. Readers might consult chapters by VanKooten and Ware and Hall.

Outro

It seems impossible—and irresponsible—not to acknowledge the larger cultural and political context of this book's publication. Though many chapters in this collection were begun much earlier, many of them were revised and rewritten during the global coronavirus pandemic that began in 2020, during an increased demand for antiracist action across the United States, and during the last few years of the Trump presidency, which instigated crises of democratic and institutional norms. We suggest that these crises—a global pandemic, ongoing systemic oppression, and assaults on democracy—are sonic events, warranting our and our students' attention as soundwriters and as citizens.

As colleges and universities rapidly moved online in March 2020, rhetoric and writing teachers quickly adjusted their pedagogies for online instruction. And as we write this in summer 2021, many colleges and universities are still swimming through the uncertainties of the next academic year, including what policies they'll devise about in-person learning and vaccination requirements. The pandemic brought many problems to the forefront: disparities in access to health care, how systemic racism is a public health issue, disparities in access to learning technologies for remote learning, the challenges (especially for parents and especially gendered) of working from home, and more. The sonic aspect of teaching and learning became quite apparent as many moved to teaching online and holding meetings via Zoom (the challenges of reminding people to mute themselves, or to unmute when they speak, comes to mind). And for in-person instruction, many teachers and students worked through the challenges of being heard while wearing facial coverings.

In August 2019, the *New York Times Magazine* published "The 1619 Project" (Silverstein, 2019), reminding (sometimes informing) readers just how long and how inextricable the legacy of racial violence is in America. In May 2020, George Floyd was lynched by police in Minneapolis on video, sparking stunning daily protests about the individual deaths of George Floyd, Ahmaud Arbery, Tony McDade, Trayvon Martin, Laquan McDonald, Freddie Gray, Eric Garner, Aiyana Stanley-Jones, Botham Jean, Michael Brown, Sandra Bland, Yvette Smith, Alton Sterling, David McAtee, Walter Scott, Breonna Taylor, Tamir Rice, Philando Castile, Stephon Clark, and legion unnamed others (see Kadir Nelson's "Say Their Names," 2020) at the hands of police (see also Ore, 2019, on lynching and anti-Black violence). Protests addressed both the individual victims and institutional injustices at blame. In September 2020, after 118 straight days of protest in Louisville, the state of Kentucky declined to bring charges against any of Breonna Taylor's executioners in alignment with the president's vision of "law & order." Among the further chants amplified by marchers have been "No justice, no peace," "I can't breathe," and "Whose streets? Our streets." Led by #BLM activists, protestors call to "defund the police" and reallocate funds to public works less prone to immediate racial violence like social work, schools, and libraries.

The chant/command/plea to "say their names" directs witnesses to, literally, say the names of victims of racial violence. Fundamentally, it is a sound action. Through *elocutio, pronuntiato*, we commemorate. While epideixis has been largely ceded to the speech side of rhetoric, 2020's summer of #BLM protests offers an opportunity to renew our dedication to this skillset in the writing classroom too. Marching matters, art matters, song matters, banners matter, chants matter. Sound matters. Both participation and receptivity to these methods matter. Black lives matter. (See Richardson & Ragland, 2018, on the literacy practices of the #BlackLivesMatter movement, which includes a discussion of their use of sound.)

In addition to the crises of the global coronavirus pandemic and the long history of systemic racism is a current crisis in democracy. This crisis is multifaceted: the demagoguery of the Trump presidency (Mercieca, 2020), the breakdown of the norms of democratic institutions, the rise of post-truth rhetoric (McComiskey, 2017), the increased spread of conspiracy theories, and more. These events are thoroughly sonic, from the cadence and rhythm of Trump's rhetoric to the demagogic chants at rallies to aesthetic qualities of conspiratorial rhetoric. And responses to these crises have also been thoroughly sonic. For instance, the U.S. presidential inauguration of 2017 began with one of the largest international, protests in history (Wikipedia says up to 5,246,670 in the United States ["2017 Women's March," 2021]): the "Women's March." From chants to musical performances, protestors engaged in an affective politics that worked, in part, through the agonism of sound (see Tausig et al., 2019, and hear the sounds of the march in Rodrigue, 2017).

Admittedly, the chapters in this collection do not directly address these contexts—though some student examples do. For example, Carmen Greiner's soundwriting project commemorates Black lives lost to police brutality (Iwertz Duffy's chapter); Lesley M. Rodriguez and Christian Nevarez-Camacho's soundwriting project responds to protests against police brutality and Trump's responses to those protests (Middleton's chapter); and Abby's project responds to and critiques Trump's hateful rhetoric by remixing it with hip-hop and the opening from *The Twilight Zone* (Harley's chapter). What these and other student projects show us, we believe, is that students are aware of the sounds of the world around them, and that by incorporating soundwriting into rhetoric and writing classes, teachers can help students develop their awareness and their rhetorical agency in using soundwriting to address and respond to problems.

We hope this book gives you some new ideas to engage soundwriting in your own rhetoric and writing pedagogy. Thanks for reading (and listening).

References

2017 Women's March. (2021, May 18). *Wikipedia*. Retrieved May 25, 2021, from https://en.wikipedia.org/wiki/2017_Women%27s_March.

Ahern, K. F. (2013). Tuning the sonic playing field: Teaching ways of knowing sound in first year writing. *Computers and Composition, 30*(2), 75–86. https://doi.org/10.1016/j.compcom.2013.03.001.

Ahern, K. F. (2018). Understanding learning spaces sonically, soundscaping evaluations of place. *Computers and Composition, 48*, 22–33. https://doi.org/10.1016/j.compcom.2018.03.007.

Ahern, K. F. (2021). Soundscapes: Rhetorical entwinements for composing sound in four dimensions. In K. D. Stedman, C. S. Danforth & M. J. Faris (Eds.), *Tuning in to soundwriting*. enculturation | Intermezzo. http://intermezzo.enculturation.net/14-stedman-et-al/ahern.html.

Alexander, J. (2015). Glenn Gould and the rhetorics of sound. *Computers and Composition, 37*, 73–89. https://doi.org/10.1016/j.compcom.2015.06.004.

Anderson, E. (2014). Toward a resonant material vocality for digital composition. *Enculturation: A Journal of Rhetoric, Writing, and Culture, 18*. http://enculturation.net/materialvocality.

Ball, C. E. (2004). Show, not tell: The value of new media scholarship. *Computers and Composition, 21*(4), 403–425. https://doi.org/10.1016/j.compcom.2004.08.001.

Ball, C. E. & Hawk, B. (Eds.). (2006). Sound in/as composition space [Special issue]. *Computers and Composition, 23*(3).

Banks, A. J. (2005). *Race, rhetoric, and technology: Searching for higher ground.* Routledge.

Bessette, J. (2016). Audio, archives, and the affordance of listening in a pedagogy of "difference." *Computers and Composition, 39,* 71–82. https://www.doi.org/10.1016 /j.compcom.2015.11.004.

Bose, D. K., Zdenek, S., Markussen, P., Wallace, H. & Giannone, A. (2021). Sound and access: Attuned to disability in the writing classroom. In K. D. Stedman, C. S. Danforth & M. J. Faris (Eds.), *Tuning in to soundwriting.* enculturation | Intermezzo. http://intermezzo.enculturation.net/14-stedman-et-al/bose.html.

Bowie, J. L. (2012a). Podcasting in a writing class? Considering the possibilities. *Kairos: A Journal of Rhetoric, Technology, and Pedagogy, 16*(2). http://technorhetoric .net/16.2/praxis/bowie/index.html.

Bowie, J. L. (2012b). Rhetorical roots and media future: How podcasting fits into the computers and writing classroom. *Kairos: A Journal of Rhetoric, Technology, and Pedagogy, 16*(2). http://technorhetoric.net/16.2/topoi/bowie/index.html.

Boyle, C. & Rivers, N. A. (2016). A version of access. *Technical Communication Quarterly, 25*(1), 29–47. https://doi.org/10.1080/10572252.2016.1113702.

Buckner, J. J. & Daley, K. (2018). Do you hear what I hear? A hearing teacher and a deaf student negotiate sound. In C. S. Danforth, K. D. Stedman & M. J. Faris (Eds.), *Soundwriting pedagogies.* Computers and Composition Digital Press. https://ccdigitalpress.org/book/soundwriting/buckner-daley/index.html.

BurghRecords. (2018, January 20). Bar ambience, talking, music, glasses, door creaking [Audio file]. *Freesound.* https://freesound.org/people/BurghRecords/sounds/415974/.

Burns, M., Dougherty, T. R., Keubrich, B. & Rodríguez, Y. (2018). Soundwriing and resistance: Toward a pedagogy of liberation. In C. S. Danforth, K. D. Stedman & M. J. Faris (Eds.), *Soundwriting pedagogies.* Computers and Composition Digital Press. https://ccdigitalpress.org/book/soundwriting/burns-et-al/index.html.

Butler, J. (2016). Where access meets multimodality: The case of ASL music videos. *Kairos: A Journal of Rhetoric, Technology, and Pedagogy, 21*(1). https://kairos .technorhetoric.net/21.1/topoi/butler/index.html.

Carson, A. D. (2017). *Owning my masters: The rhetorics of rhymes and revolutions* [Doctoral dissertation, Clemson University]. http://phd.aydeethegreat.com /dissertation-part-i-the-introduction/.

Ceraso, S. (2014). (Re)educating the senses: Multimodal listening, bodily learning, and the composition of sonic experiences. *College English, 77*(2), 102–123.

Ceraso, S. (2018). *Sounding composition: Multimodal pedagogies for embodied listening.* University of Pittsburgh Press.

Ceraso, S. (2019). *Sound never tasted so good: "Teaching" sensory rhetorics.* enculturation | Intermezzo. http://intermezzo.enculturation.net/11-ceraso.htm.

Ceraso, S. & Ahern, K. F. (2015). Composing with sound. *Composition Studies, 43*(2), 13–18.

Comstock, M. & Hocks, M. E. (2006). Voice in the cultural soundscape: Sonic literacy in composition studies. *Computers and Composition Online.* http:// cconlinejournal.org/comstock_hocks/index.htm.

Comstock, M. & Hocks, M. E. (2016). The sounds of climate change: Sonic rhetoric in the Anthropocene, the age of human impact. *Rhetoric Review, 35*(2), 165–175. https://doi.org/10.1080/07350198.2016.1142854.

Cushman, J. & Kelly, S. (2018). Recasting writing, voicing bodies: Podcasts across a writing curriculum. In C. S. Danforth, K. D. Stedman & M. J. Faris (Eds.), *Soundwriting pedagogies.* Computers and Composition Digital Press. https://ccdigitalpress.org/book/soundwriting/cushman-kelly/index.html.

Danforth, C. S. & Stedman, K. D. (2018). Introduction. In C. S. Danforth, K. D. Stedman & M. J. Faris (Eds.), *Soundwriting pedagogies.* Computers and Composition Digital Press. https://ccdigitalpress.org/book/soundwriting/introduction/index.html.

Danforth, C. S., Stedman, K. D. & Faris, M. J. (Eds.). (2018). *Soundwriting pedagogies.* Computers and Composition Digital Press. https://ccdigitalpress.org/soundwriting.

DarkEvil. (2006, May 22). Final fantasy III: Original sound version mix [Music remix]. *Wikipedia.* (Original work composed by Nobuo Uematsu). https://en.wikipedia.org/wiki/File:Final_Fantasy_III_-_Original_Sound_Version_mix.ogg.

Davis, D. (Ed.). (2011). Writing with sound [Special issue]. *Currents in Electronic Literacy.* http://currents.dwrl.utexas.edu/2011.html.

Detweiler, E. (2018). A podcast?! Whatever gave you that idea? Some reverberations from Walter Benjamin's radio plays. In J. Rice, C. Graham & E. Detweiler (Eds.), *Rhetorics change/Rhetoric's change.* Intermezzo; Parlor Press. http://intermezzo.enculturation.net/07-rsa-2016-proceedings.htm.

Detweiler, E. (2019). Sounding out the *progymnasmata. Rhetoric Review, 38*(2), 205–218. https://doi.org/10.1080/07350198.2019.1588567.

Dolmage, J. (2008). Mapping composition: Inviting disability in the front door. In C. Lewiecki-Wilson & B. J. Brueggemann (Eds.), *Disability and the teaching of writing: A critical sourcebook* (pp. 14–27). Bedford/St. Martin's.

Dolmage, J. T. (2014). *Disability rhetoric.* Syracuse University Press.

Droumeva, M. & Murphy, D. (2018). A pedagogy of listening: Composing with/in new media texts. In C. S. Danforth, K. D. Stedman & M. J. Faris (Eds.), *Soundwriting Pedagogies.* Computers and Composition Digital Press. https://ccdigitalpress.org/book/soundwriting/droumeva-murphy/index.html.

Eckstein, J. (2017). Sound arguments. *Argumentation and Advocacy, 53*(3), 163–180. https://doi.org/10.1080/00028533.2017.1337328.

Faris, M. J., Kostelich, C. F., Walsh, T., Sinor, S., Flahive, M. & Heilig, L. (2020). 3,000 podcasts a year: Teaching and administering new media composition in a first-year writing program. In C. Chen & L. Wilkes (Eds.), *The proceedings of the Computers and Writing annual conference, 2019* (pp. 71–82). The WAC Clearinghouse. https://wac.colostate.edu/docs/proceedings/cw2019/chapter6.pdf.

Fission9. (2020, September 5). Thunderclap [Audio file]. *Freesound.* https://freesound.org/people/Fission9/sounds/534023/.

Folk, M. (2015). Making waves: Voiceless audio essays & the visual rhetoric of aural rhetoric. *Computers and Composition Online.* http://cconlinejournal.org/Folk/.

Goodale, G. (2011). *Sonic persuasion: Reading sound in the recorded age.* University of Illinois Press.

Greene, J. (2018). Advanced exposition: Writing through podcasts. *Composition Studies, 46*(2), 137–162.

Gunn, J., Goodale, G., Hall, M. & Eberly, R. A. (2013). Ausculating again: Rhetoric and sound studies. *Rhetoric Society Quarterly, 43*(5), 475–489. https://doi.org/10.1080/02773945.2013.851581.

Harley, B. (2018). Sounding intimacy. *The Journal of Multimodal Rhetorics, 2*(2). http://journalofmultimodalrhetorics.com/2-2-harley.

Harvey, P. (n.d.). Abraham Lincoln (Kidnapped after death) [Audio file]. *Paul Harvey Archives.* http://www.paulharveyarchives.com/trots/a/.

Hawhee, D. (2015). Rhetoric's sensorium. *Quarterly Journal of Speech, 101*(1), 2–17. https://doi.org/10.1080/00335630.2015.995925.

Hawk, B. (2018a). *Resounding the rhetorical: Composition as a quasi-object.* University of Pittsburgh Press.

Hawk, B. (2018b). Sound: Resonance as rhetorical. *Rhetoric Society Quarterly, 48*(3), 315–323. https://doi.org/10.1080/02773945.2018.1454219.

Hawk, B. & Stuart, G. (2018). English composition as a sonic practice. In J. Alexander & J. Rhodes (Eds.), *The Routledge handbook of digital writing and rhetoric* (pp. 38–47). Routledge.

Hawkins, A. (2018). Soundwriting, feminist pedagogy, and the vox pop as transgressive form. In K. Sawchuk, O. Ursulesku & E.-M. Trinkaus (Eds.), *Transformation, transgressions, and trust* (pp. 17–26). Grazer Universitätsverlag.

Hocks, M. E. & Comstock, M. (2017). Composing for sound: Sonic rhetoric as resonance. *Computers and Composition, 43*, 135–146. https://doi.org/10.1016/j.compcom.2016.11.006.

Howard, R. M. & Jamieson, S. (2013). Researched writing. In G. Tate, A. R. Taggart, K. Schick & H. B. Hessler (Eds.), *A guide to composition pedagogies* (2nd ed., pp. 231–247). Oxford University Press.

Katz, S. B. (2020). Sonic rhetorics as ethics in action: Hidden temporalities of sound in language(s). *Humanities, 9*(1), 13. https://doi.org/10.3390/h9010013.

Keeling, K. & Kun, J. (Eds.). (2011). Sound clash: Listening to American studies [Special issue]. *American Quarterly, 63*(3).

kilgore54. (2016, September 7). Mournful cows [Audio file]. *Freesound.* https://freesound.org/people/kilgore54/sounds/353682/.

Kjeldsen, J. E. (2018). The rhetoric of sound, the sound of arguments. Three propositions, three questions, and an afterthought for the study of sonic and multimodal argumentation. *Argumentation and Advocacy, 54*(4), 364–371. https://doi.org/10.1080/10511431.2018.1525013.

Klein, A. (2020). The opinion podcast: A visceral form of persuasion. *Prompt: A Journal of Academic Writing Assignments, 4*(1), 29–40. https://doi.org/10.31719/pjaw.v4i1.55.

Lambke, A. (2019). Arranging delivery, delivering arrangement: An ecological sonic rhetoric of podcasting. *Kairos: A Journal of Rhetoric, Technology, and Pedagogy, 23*(2). http://kairos.technorhetoric.net/23.2/topoi/lambke/index.html.

Lingold, M. C., Mueller, D. & Trettien, W. (Eds.). (2018). *Digital sound studies.* Duke University Press.

Lipari, L. (2014). *Listening, thinking, being: Toward an ethics of attunement*. The University of Pennsylvania State University Press.

McComiskey, B. (2017). *Post-truth rhetoric and composition*. Utah State University Press.

Mercieca, J. (2020). *Demagogue for president: The rhetorical genius of Donald Trump*. Texas A&M University Press.

Nctrnm. (2017, December 31). Xenon [Song]. *SoundCloud*. https://soundcloud.com/nctrnm/xenon.

Nctrnm. (2018, October 12). Flight [Song]. *SoundCloud*. https://soundcloud.com/nctrnm/flight.

Nelson, K. (2020, June 14). Say their names. *The New Yorker*. https://www.newyorker.com/culture/cover-story/cover-story-2020-06-22.

Ore, E. J. (2019). *Lynching: Violence, rhetoric, and American identity*. University Press of Mississippi.

phillyfan972. (2017, November 29). Fans at basketball game (crowd) [Audio file]. *Freesound*. https://freesound.org/people/phillyfan972/sounds/412160/.

Palmeri, J. & McCorkle, B. (2018). English via the airwaves: Recovering 1930s radio pedagogies. In C. S. Danforth, K. D. Stedman & M. J. Faris (Eds.), *Soundwriting pedagogies*. Computers and Composition Digital Press. https://ccdigitalpress.org/book/soundwriting/palmeri-mccorkle/index.html.

Porter, J. E. (2009). Recovering delivery for digital rhetoric. *Computers and Composition, 26*(4), 207–224. https://doi.org/10.1016/j.compcom.2009.09.004.

Ratcliffe, K. (2005). *Rhetorical listening: Identification, gender, whiteness*. Southern Illinois University Press.

Richardson, E. & Ragland, A. (2018). #StayWoke: The language and literacies of the #BlackLivesMatter movement. *Community Literacy Journal, 12*(2), 27–56. https://doi.org/10.1353/clj.2018.0003.

Rickert, T. (Ed.). (1999). Writing/music/culture [Special issue]. *Enculturation, 2*(2). http://www.enculturation.net/2_2/toc.html.

Rickert, T. (2013). *Ambient rhetoric: The attunements of rhetorical being*. University of Pittsburgh Press.

Ridolfo, J. & DeVoss, D. N. (2009). Composing for recomposition: Rhetorical velocity and delivery. *Kairos: A Journal of Rhetoric, Technology, and Pedagogy, 13*(2). https://kairos.technorhetoric.net/13.2/topoi/ridolfo_devoss/index.html.

Robinson, D. (2020). *Hungry listening: Resonant theory for Indigenous sound studies*. University of Minnesota Press.

Rodrigue, T. (2017, June 12). Peaceful warriors (No. 50) [Audio podcast episode]. In *Rocky Mountain revival*. https://rockymtnrevival.libsyn.com/50-peaceful-warriors.

Rodrigue, T. K., Artz, K., Bennett, J., Carver, M. P., Grandmont, M., Harris, D., Hashem, D., Mooney, A., Rand, M. & Zimmerman, A. (2016). Navigating the soundscape, composing with audio. *Kairos: A Journal of Rhetoric, Technology, and Pedagogy, 21*(1). http://kairos.technorhetoric.net/21.1/praxis/rodrigue/index.html.

Sady, C. (2018). Beyond words on the page: Using multimodal composing to aid in the transition to first-year writing. *Teaching English in the Two-Year College, 45*(3), 255–273.

Sano-Franchini, J. (2018). Sounding Asian/America: Asian/American sonic rhetorics, multimodal orientalism, and digital composition. *Enculturation: A Journal of Rhetoric, Writing, and Culture, 27.* http://www.enculturation.net/sounding-Asian-America.

Schafer, R. M. (1977). *The tuning of the world.* Alfred Knopf.

Selfe, C. L. (2009). The movement of air, the breath of meaning: Aurality and multimodal compositing. *College Composition and Communication, 60*(4), 616–663.

Silverstein, J. (2019, December 20). Why we published The 1619 Project. *New York Times Magazine.* https://www.nytimes.com/interactive/2019/12/20/magazine/1619-intro.html.

Stedman, K. D., Danforth, C. S. & Faris, M. J. (Eds.). (2021). *Tuning in to soundwriting.* enculturation | Intermezzo. http://intermezzo.enculturation.net/14-stedman-et-al/index.html.

Sterne, J. (Ed.). (2012). *The sound studies reader.* Routledge.

Stoever, J. L. (2016). *The sonic color line: Race and the cultural politics of listening.* New York University Press.

Stone, J. W. (2015). Listening to the sonic archive: Rhetoric, representation, and race in the Lomax prison recordings. *Enculturation: A Journal of Rhetoric, Writing, and Culture, 19.* http://enculturation.net/listening-to-the-sonic-archive.

Stone, J. & Ceraso, S. (Eds.). (2013). Sonic rhetorics [Special issue]. *Harlot: A Revealing Look at the Arts of Persuasion, 9.* https://harlotofthearts.org/ojs-3.3.0-11/index.php/harlot/issue/view/9.

Tausig, B., Sonevytsky, M., Silverstein, S., Harbert, B. & Manabe, N. (2019). Colloquy: This is what democracy sounds like: Sound, music, and performance at the Women's March and beyond. *Music & Politics, 13*(1), https://doi.org/10.3998/mp.9460447.0013.100.

VanKooten, C. (2016). Singer, writer: A choric explanation of sound and writing. *Kairos: A Journal of Rhetoric, Technology, and Pedagogy, 21*(1). http://kairos.technorhetoric.net/21.1/inventio/vankooten/index.html.

Wargo, J. M. (2020). Be(com)ing "in-resonance-with" research: Improvising a postintentional phenomenology through sound and sonic composition. *Qualitative Inquiry, 26*(5): 440–446. https://doi.org/10.1177/1077800418819612.

Wargo, J. M., Brownell, C. J. & Oliveira, G. (2021). Sound, sentience, and schooling: Writing the field recording in educational ethnography. *Anthropology & Education Quarterly, 52*(3), 315–334. https://doi.org/10.1111/aeq.12365.

Yergeau, M. R., Brewer, E., Kerschbaum, S., Oswal, S. K., Price, M., Salvo, M. J., Selfe, C. L. & Howes, F. (2013). Multimodality in motion: Disability and kairotic spaces. *Kairos: A Journal of Rhetoric, Technology, and Pedagogy, 18*(1). http://kairos.technorhetoric.net/18.1/coverweb/yergeau-et-al/index.html.

Zdenek, S. (2009). Accessible podcasting: College students on the margins in the new media classroom. *Computers and Composition Online.* https://seanzdenek.com/article-accessible-podcasting/.

Zdenek, S. (2015). *Reading sounds: Closed-captioned media and popular culture.* University of Chicago Press.

Part One. Soundwriting Through Remix

Chapter 1. Mix It Up, Mash It Up: Arrangement, Audio Editing, and the Importance of Sonic Context

Logan Middleton

UNIVERSITY OF DENVER

While soundwriting presents countless pedagogical opportunities for invention—recording music, voice, and sound effects among other possibilities—so too does it lend itself to exploring the rhetorical canon of arrangement. Thanks to open-source audio-editing technologies, sound files ranging from music tracks to speeches can be easily cut up and recombined to create new meaning.

It's this affordance of audio composition that informs the assignment at the heart of this chapter. In the Audio Manipulation Project, students work to sample, decontextualize, and distort existing audio files and stitch them back together to produce a unique composition. While this assignment can be completed in any genre, be it a mock dialogue or musical remix, the end result must be a "lie" created through editing—a recording with some sort of central message that's been fabricated through the magic of audio editing. As composers cut, arrange, and rearrange the audio files they work with, they wind up transforming the meaning of these clips. This process of audio trickery obscures, covers up, and/or erases the original text and context of each sound file while also creating new circuits of meaning through the creation of a new composition. In listening to projects whose core messages aren't created through recording or invention but rather from digital editing and manipulation, audiences make connections they'd not thought of before; reconsider familiar songs, voices, or sound effects in new ways; or just ask themselves, "Did what I just heard *really* happen?" As one Writing Across Media student who reflected on this assignment put it, "We can't always trust what we hear."

Additionally, I ask students to account for their rhetorical decision-making processes in a reflective video statement where they articulate goals for their work, speak to their composing process, and connect key concepts from class readings to their projects. This reflective statement provides an explicit opportunity for individuals to engage in metacognitive reflection about their learning. On the whole, then, this audio manipulation project helps students more fully understand how soundwriting operates from foundational issues of arrangement and context just as much as invention and recording audio content. Whether through rearranging an interview to allow for the interjection of different voices or clipping five seconds of a song to highlight lyrical meaning, this assignment helps students see how a few simple keystrokes on their computer can transform sonic meaning and context.

DOI: https://doi.org/10.37514/PRA-B.2022.1688.2.01

To better comprehend how this assignment is working pedagogically, it's important to situate it within the overarching course to which it belongs. I developed and taught this audio project as a part of my Writing Across Media (WAM) class, an advanced composition course at the University of Illinois. Cross-listed between informatics and writing studies, the class attracts students from a range of disciplinary backgrounds. Through prompts that require students to create video documentaries, podcasts, physical artifacts, comics, or other mixed media projects, WAM asks participants to engage with theories that guide multimodal composition. Students demonstrate their knowledge of these concepts by showcasing the affordances and constraints of these media through their own multimodal creations.

As students typically enter WAM with little audio-editing experience, my audio unit privileges both practical and theoretical work. I pair Erin Anderson's (2014) "Toward a Resonant Material Vocality for Digital Composition" with an in-class Audacity workshop to bring together theory and hands-on editing. It's helpful to discuss principles of how digital audio technologies allow us to "compose with the voices of *others*" (Anderson, 2014) and to provide students with a chance to put these concepts into practice. In the following class, we explore two concepts from a pair of posts from *Sounding Out!*, an online sound studies publication venue. In connecting Christina Giacona's (2014) "A Tribe Called Red Remixes Sonic Stereotypes" with Aram Sinnreich's (2011) "Remixing Girl Talk: The Poetics and Aesthetics of Mashups," we synthesize issues of sonic appropriation, context, and mashup-as-genre to examine the politics and power dynamics of sampling. As you'll hear in the sample audio projects in this chapter, these concepts provide a sound foundation for student work that takes up injustice, racism, and identity.

This audio manipulation project, however, is not without limitations and exclusions. Critically, d/Deaf and/or hard-of-hearing students are excluded from this assignment in its current iteration. While I touch on potential redesigns in this chapter's audio reflection, this assignment requires production through multiple modes to be more accessible. As my former students have suggested, this assignment could easily be reworked into a "media manipulation project," in which participants could mash-up more diverse pieces of media: video clips, sound files, and so on. These revisions would shift the focus of the project away from audio, but this redesign would ultimately result in a more inclusive, modally rich prompt.

More specific to the technological dimensions of this assignment, many students communicated that they would have liked to receive more explicit instruction in audio editing. While I provided an introduction to Audacity, students reported that they needed to spend much more time outside of class to familiarize themselves with the software. While I directed students toward Audacity for this assignment because it's free, many groups found it confusing and unintuitive. In future versions of this assignment, then, I would facilitate class breakout sessions that ask students to play with a range of audio-editing tools to find software that'd work best for them.

Though audio composition always involves some sort of editing, privileging this aspect of soundwriting in assignments provides an openness that enables students to experiment with, hybridize, and even invent new sonic genres. More importantly, it illustrates how soundwriting can serve as a vehicle for demonstrating how messages take on new or revised meanings when placed in different contexts. As students begin to see how frighteningly easy it is to manipulate texts—and often to great rhetorical effect—this work is not only central to our understandings of sonic pedagogy, but also essential to our work as rhetoricians, compositionists, and committed teacher-scholars.

Assignments and Sequencing

Audio Manipulation Project

Though it's the case with all media, audio is especially subject to manipulation: cutting it up, stitching it back together, sampling from existing sources, layering track over track, etc. Given these affordances of audio, what sorts of new possibilities arise for constructing meaning in this medium?

This project will require you to take advantage of digital audio technologies to create a 3–4-minute audio manipulation piece. You'll need to edit, re-edit, distort, take out of context, and/or alter existing audio files in order to produce an audio composition that's a "lie." That is to say, your goal here is to reassemble and rearrange existing recordings to compose something that didn't really happen.

You're welcome to do so through any genre you like. For instance, you could create a dialogue comprised of audio snippets between people who've never spoken before in real life. Or alternatively, you could take an audio recording of a public event and edit in new words, voices, and sounds to create a different effect. Whatever you decide to do, you should be able to articulate why you selected your subject matter. In addition, you'll need to justify why your composition matters and why it's important.

On the whole, this assignment will help you better comprehend how composing with sound can function as an act of writing and remix. In addition, you stand to gain a more critical and nuanced understanding of how digital technologies enable you to process and repurpose sound to create new meaning.

Note: You may either work with a partner or individually on this assignment. For those of you working together, you each still need to produce your own reflective statements.

(Video) Reflective Statement

You will each need to compose a reflective statement about your experiences creating your project. Yet, instead of writing this document in alphabetic text, I'm asking you to complete your reflective statement as a video text. This can be something along the lines of a vlog or something more experimental in nature. All I ask is that you answer the same questions—and document your sources in the same way that you would in an alphabetic text statement—with the same amount of precision and depth that you'd normally include in a "written" statement. I won't specify a length/time requirement for these multimodal rationales so long as you answer all the necessary parts listed above.

Composing your statement in this manner will help you understand connections between forms of multimodal composition: (moving) image, alphabetic text, and sound. Doing so will also help you cultivate an awareness and appreciation for how composition process shapes—and in turn is shaped by—the tools, goals, and contexts with/in which you create.

While you won't need a thesis statement or argument for this statement, you should address all of the following questions/requirements:

- What goal(s) is your audio manipulation file trying to accomplish? What does your piece get people to do, or what might it get people to do? For whom?

- What rhetorical and material choices did you make to fulfill the goals of your audio manipulation file? In other words, what affordances and constraints were already decided for you in terms of working within this particular medium, genre, and context?

- Explain why you pursued this composition plan of action as opposed to others you might have considered. Refer to any ideas you came up with on the road to your audio file. How did the rhetorical and material choices you described above help you accomplish things that other combinations of choices would not have?

- A list of who and what assisted you in the creation of this piece (human and nonhuman). Think of this like the credits at the end of a movie.

In the process of completing this reflective statement, you'll need to explicitly draw in at least two audio-related course texts that we've read this semester. How have these authors' ideas influenced, challenged, and/or complicated your composing process for this assignment? Be sure to engage with and analyze the main ideas of these texts as opposed to citing peripheral details.

All sources, including course texts, should be cited in your reflective statement whenever you analyze, quote, or paraphrase someone else's ideas or works. Your work should also include a works cited portion of your text that includes all (re) sources referred to in your statement. MLA, APA, or Chicago style is fine.

Scaffolded Course Schedule: Audio Manipulation Project Unit

Here's how this audio manipulation project fits into the sound unit in this partic-ular multimodal composition course. Hopefully, the schedule below provides a sense of what readings and tasks students are simultaneously working on at the same time as their audio work.

Table 1.1. Schedule

Topics Covered	Reading	Assignments Due
Day 1 • Introduction to Audio	- - -	Bring in a podcast of your choosing.
Day 2 • Sound, Voice, and Digital Manipulation • In-class Audacity Tutorial	Anderson (2014), "Toward a Resonant Material Vocality for Digital Composition" (excerpts)	- - -
Day 3 • Remixing (Aural) Meaning and Rhetorical Arrangement	Giacona (2014), "A Tribe Called Red Remixes Stereotypes" (*Sounding Out!* blog post) Sinnreich (2011), "Remixing Girl Talk" (*Sounding Out!* blog post)	Blog Post: Mashup and Sonic Reappropriation
Day 4 • Proposal Workshop: Audio Manipulation Project	- - -	Blog Post: Audio manipulation proposal. We'll use this post for an in-class workshop
Day 5 • Audio Formatting, Glitch, and Disruption	Hammer (2014), "WR1T1NG (D1RT¥) NEW MED1Δ/ GL1TCH CoMPoS1TIoN" Sterne (2006), "The MP3 as Cultural Artifact"	- - -
Day 6 • Presenting Audio Manipulation Assignments and Audio Wrap-Up	- - -	Audio manipulation assignment/reflective statement due. Be prepared to talk about your projects in class.

Sample Student Projects

1. "American," composed by Writing Across Media students Edgar Madrigal, Donna Dimitrova, and Saul Rivera, centers around immigration. The students edit together samples from Rihanna's "American Oxygen," Portugal the Man's "So American," and John Lennon's "Imagine" to reimagine what it means to be an immigrant in 21st-century America. Throughout their work, they place these musical refrains into conversation with xenophobic immigration discourse—and later on, Barack Obama's thoughts on immigration reform—to demonstrate tensions in how Americans think about immigrants.[1]

---

1. Two student examples (audio or video files and descriptive transcripts) can be found on the book's companion website.

2. In "Bend the Knee," Writing Across Media students Lesley M. Rodriguez and Christian Nevarez-Camacho reframe recent U.S. National Anthem protests against police brutality and systemic racism as patriotic. Through juxtaposing sound clips of Donald Trump's reactions to these protests with repositioned news coverage of these events, the composers make a case in their project for continuing conversations about free speech, race, and inequality.

Reflection

[An acoustic guitar strums in the background.]

Logan Middleton: Welcome to . . . not NPR.[2]

[Record scratch followed by a slow, industrial drumbeat; drums continue to loop in background.]

This is *Amplifying Soundwriting*, more specifically the praxis chapter "Mix It Up, Mash It Up: Arrangement, Audio Editing, and the Importance of Sonic Context." My name is Logan Middleton. I am a Ph.D. student in English studying writing studies at the University of Illinois at Urbana–Champaign. And this is probably the tenth or so time *[laughing]* I've tried to record this introduction.

So as I'm editing together this reflection, I'm looking at my workspace, and I see all of these attempts at introductions just stacked one on top of the other. And in recording this particular introduction that you're listening to, I went back and listened to bits and pieces *[edits of the speaker's voice, layered on top of each other, simultaneously cut in and out of the background]* and parts from the attempts that I had made before, saying, you know, "I like this, I don't like that. I'm gonna say this, I better avoid that." So while you're listening to one voice right now, mine, it's really a conglomeration of many voices that came before it that is a response to all of these other attempts.

I'm choosing to begin this reflection the way I am to illustrate what it is that I ask students to do in the project I talk about in this praxis chapter—the audio manipulation project. Each vocal recording, background music track, and sound effect I've used so far in this introduction is coming from a different context.

[Acoustic music from beginning plays in background.]

I selected the acoustic music you hear at the beginning to suggest something along the lines of an NPR program, something you might tune into on public radio or hear in a podcast.

---

2. The audio version of Logan Middleton's reflection can be found on the book's companion website.

*[A DJ connects consecutive record scratches, followed by an "Oh yeah!"
looped twice, played concurrently with narration below.]*

The record scratch carries a number of connotations whether from scratch-
ing, turntabling, or transitions between records when you're listening to music.

*[A polyphony of the speaker's voice recordings sound in the background;
his words are incomprehensible.]*

And, of course, the recordings of myself talking that I layered and edited in
were never intended to be used in that particular context. They were my attempts
at starting this reflection that didn't work out.

All of this is to say that, whenever we listen to an edited audio composition,
each of the component parts is bringing with it its own social, historical, cultural,
and experiential meanings. And each of those meanings comes to bear in the
overall meaning of the audio text itself. So whenever we're editing together audio
files, we're not only manipulating or distorting the files, but we're also playing with
or experimenting with the contexts of each of those files. When we mash them up
to create new meaning or take them out of context to alter existing meaning, we're
doing quite a bit of work that goes unnoticed.

*[A feedback-amplified voice loudly proclaims "The assignment!"
followed by the looped sound of glass breaking.]*

And so all of this comes to inform the project at the heart of this chapter—the
audio manipulation project.

*[A downtempo, synth-heavy track begins playing; it persists throughout
the next section.]*

I teach this project as part of a multimodal composition class called Writing Across Media. And this audio manipulation project is largely concerned
with ideas of audio editing, context, and arrangement. For this assignment,
then, students work either on their own or in pairs in order to create a unique,
3-to–4-minute audio composition of their own. The trick is that this composition must consist primarily of edited, repurposed, and recontextualized audio
files. Students are welcome to use any combination of music, speech, interviews,
what have you, to create something that didn't really happen. So whether students
want to create some sort of audio collage or medley that combines content from
political speeches—

John F. Kennedy (excerpt from 1962 Space Race Speech): We
meet in an hour of change.

Logan: —and political songs to mock dialogues between two celebrities
that might have never happened to something entirely else, the genre for this

assignment is wide open. And that's an intentional decision on my behalf so that students get some experience with creating their own genre conventions or working within forms that don't necessarily have limits or prescribed boundaries as to what they should look and sound like. And finally, I ask students to compose a video reflection that explains their rhetorical decision-making processes. Primarily, I find this helpful because it allows students to participate in metacognitive reflection. So when they need to think about what they're doing and why they're doing it, and how their choices are working to create meaning in accordance with the assignment, this generally produces not only stronger texts, but encourages deeper thinking about the decisions that go into multimodal composition, particularly in this project.

[Glass breaks; record scratch. Slower-paced, dreamy electronic music plays in the background; the artist in the track occasionally sings "Destination Unknown" in a whispery voice.]

So in the latter half of this audio reflection, I want to talk a little about how this assignment actually unfolded in the classroom: what I thought, what my students thought, and where I might consider taking this in the future if I were to teach it again.

What I like about this project conceptually is how students made use of the core concepts that animate this audio manipulation project. So in the unit itself, I spend some time talking about reappropriation and mashup—

[Splat!]

—and these are concepts and genres students are familiar with already, that they encounter whether in news, in their own personal or social lives, or in what they listen to. So as far as the first concept goes, we talk a little bit about appropriation and where students might hear this term or where they might see it, you know, culturally, and so on. And students are often surprised to hear that appropriation and reappropriation can work sonically. I find that something similar happens with mashup.

[Splat!]

Students often can point to a number of remix tracks or mashups that they listen to in their own experiences, but translating this to their own practice is not only more challenging but something that students can feel accomplished when they can point to their own work and say, "Hey, I made something that is working in the same way as this thing that I listened to from Girl Talk." And on a final conceptual note here, in reappropriating and taking out of context audio files, students begin to see how this is working in the real world and how it shapes how we consume and process information.

Practically, I was pleased that this project zoomed in on editing as a tangible, foundational skillset for students to develop and put in their arsenal of tools in terms of multimodal composition. So, in making editing and arrangement the primary focus of this assignment, the way clips are repurposed, recontextualized, and taken out of context, I felt as if these emphases lent themselves very well to topics that were oftentimes quite political.

[A protestor yells, high-pitched, "Not my president!"]

As savvy and sophisticated consumers of media and information, students recognize how things are packaged and processed and taken out of context in the media they listen to. And so that awareness makes its way into this project with students doing similar things in order to bend messages to their will and to craft really compelling statements about topics such as immigration, topics such as racism, and so on and so forth.

[Record scratch; background music transitions to a hip-hop, drum machine beat that loops.]

As far as student perceptions for this project goes, the reception was mostly positive. Many did comment that they found difficulties working with Audacity—

[A deep, distorted voice interjects "Audacity!"]

—other similar audio-editing programs and that they would have liked a little more scaffolding and practice working with these programs so that they could spend less time on the how-to, nuts and bolts of audio editing and more time working with actual, conceptual material for their projects. But I did want to read off some responses from students in terms of what kinds of takeaways they came away with regard to this audio manipulation project and the audio unit as a whole.

One student wrote *[pen scribbling noise]* in a reflection for the class, "Recording, editing, and recombining audio reinforces the fact that meaning can be made by taking lots of different things that already have meaning, to make a new, possible more powerful meaning. It tells me that when it comes to writing, literacy, and rhetoric at large, a piece might never be 'done.'"

And similarly, other students spoke to how manipulation is working with regard to this project. They wrote that *[pen scribbling noise]*, "In order to spot a lie in audio, one must have a ton of prior knowledge and context of the piece to spot the lies within the piece."

And another spoke to larger considerations of media and lies and manipulation when they wrote *[pen scribbling noise]*, "While this is probably one of the easiest ways to manipulate a media and change it into something that it maybe wasn't intended to be, we can take the principles of telling a 'lie' with audio into our other forms of media as well. We can't always trust what we hear or what we see."

[A high-pitched voice yells, "You lie! You lie!"]

And so judging from student responses—and granted, this is just a sample—it seems to me that the goals of the assignment are consistent with what students are taking up from the project at large.

[Record scratch; music transitions to electronic, futuristic, synth-heavy track with a robotic voice that interjects "How?"]

And so the final part of this audio reflection will be concerned with a few preliminary, exploratory thoughts on moving forward with this assignment, where it needs to go, and what changes can be made to it in the future.

[loud laser sound]

On a small-scale level—and this is something I reflected upon a bit in the introduction to this chapter—is the need for more in-class time and more support for audio-editing programs.

More pressingly, though, are considerations of access, disability, deafness, and hard-of-hearing people. Later in the course, I run a small unit on disability, access, and media. And as part of this unit, students are asked to reimagine and redesign a part of the course—whether that's an assignment, a policy, or something else—to be more accessible. And a handful of our discussions obviously revolved around the audio manipulation project. As I noted in my introduction to the chapter, this is an assignment that's not accessible in its current state, and it needs some considerable reimagining in order to do so.

Some of my students suggested making this less of an audio manipulation project and more of a media manipulation project, and this is something I'm inclined to do in future versions of this assignment. While opening this project up so that students can manipulate and take out of context any media shifts the focus away from soundwriting at large, I do believe it's important to consider how modes are working together, and if that requires incorporation of visuals *[sound of film reel spinning]*, then so be it. And while we can talk about radio *[sound of high-pitched radio tuning]* and podcasts and other forms of aural communication, it's important to observe that media and modes are always integrated. So in accordance with a few student suggestions, I believe that I would redesign this project to be more accessible by making it less of an audio manipulation project and more of a media manipulation project. That way, students could use any number of resources, technologies, media, and modes to complete their project in a way that's not only more accessible but more accurate to how we produce and consume media generally.

That about does it for this audio reflection. Thanks so much for listening, and I wish you the best in all of your audio-editing and soundwriting endeavors in the classroom and beyond.

[Music fades out.]

References

.Andre_Onate. (2015, April 10). Ah yeah scratch things w eko 2 [Audio file]. *Freesound*. http://freesound.org/people/AndreOnate/sounds/269488/.

Airflow. (2016, February 11). All is gone [Audio file]. *CCmixter*. http://beta.ccmixter.org/files/AirFlow/53025.

Anderson, E. (2014). Toward a resonant material vocality for digital composition. *Enculturation: A Journal of Rhetoric, Writing, and Culture, 18*. http://www.enculturation.net/materialvocality.

cdiaz. (2013, April 23). Radio tuning [Audio file]. *Freesound*. https://freesound.org/people/cdiaz/sounds/185704/.

DJ Vadim. (2012, November 7). Lemon haze [Song]. *CCmixter*. http://beta.ccmixter.org/files/djvadim/39854.

filmsndfx. (2016, December 1). Record scratches [Audio file]. *Freesound*. https://freesound.org/people/filmsndfx/sounds/369673/.

fluffy. (2016, April 19). Or die trying OST: sweetness [Song]. *CCmixter*. http://beta.ccmixter.org/files/fluffy/53632.

FoolBoyMedia. (2014, May 16). Splat and crunch [Audio file]. *Freesound*. https://freesound.org/people/FoolBoyMedia/sounds/237924/.

Giacona, C. (2014, February 13). A Tribe Called Red remixes sonic stereotypes. *Sounding out!* https://soundstudiesblog.com/2014/02/13/a-tribe-called-red-remixes-sonic-stereotypes/.

Hammer, S. (2014). WR1T1NG (D1RT¥) NEW MED1Δ/GL1TCH CoMPoS1TIoN. *Technoculture: An Online Journal of Technology in Society, 4*. https://tcjournal.org/vol4/hammer.

InspectorJ. (2016, April 26). Glass smash, bottle, f [Audio file]. *Freesound*. https://freesound.org/people/InspectorJ/sounds/344271/.

JasonElrod. (2009, December 16). Writing with pen [Audio file]. *Freesound*. https://freesound.org/people/JasonElrod/sounds/85484/.

junggle. (2007, January 28). Scratch01 [Audio file]. *Freesound*. https://freesound.org/people/junggle/sounds/29940/.

Kennedy, J. F. (1962). JFK Space race speech [Speech audio recording]. *Freesound*. https://freesound.org/people/cityrocker/sounds/322026/.

mloveless89. (2017, May 13). Trumpprotest_110917 [Audio file]. *Freesound*. https://freesound.org/people/mloveless89/sounds/392343/.

Ozone, D. (2012, November 14). 1986 [Audio file]. *CCmixter*. http://beta.ccmixter.org/files/donnieozone/39971.

Ozone, D. (2013, February 23). Destination unknown. [Song]. *CCmixter*. http://beta.ccmixter.org/files/donnieozone/41408.

Ozone, D. (2017). Return of the gucci ghost [Song]. *CCmixter*. http://beta.ccmixter.org/files/donnieozone/56686.

Reitanna. (2016, July 29). you lie! [Audio file]. *Freesound*. https://freesound.org/people/Reitanna/sounds/351172/.

Sinnreich, A. (2011, May 2). Remixing Girl Talk: The poetics and aesthetics of mash-ups. *Sounding out!* https://soundstudiesblog.com/2011/05/02/remixing-girl-talk-the-poetics-and-aesthetics-of-mashups/.

Stefano21. (2017, November 29). Film projector—long run with finish [Audio file]. *Freesound.* https://freesound.org/people/Stefano21/sounds/412145/.

Sterne, J. (2006). The mp3 as cultural artifact. *New Media & Society, 8*(5), 825–842. https://doi.org/10.1177/1461444806067737.

tjcason. (2017). ShortLaserSound [Audio file]. *Freesound.* https://freesound.org/people/tjcason/sounds/390474/.

Chapter 2. Experimentation, Integration, Play: Developing Digital Voice Through Audio Storytelling

Crystal VanKooten
OAKLAND UNIVERSITY

This chapter provides an instructional sequence for an Audio Story assignment, originally situated within the 200-level writing course Digital Storytelling that I taught in 2016. I also provide three student sample projects that were composed in response to this assignment, along with my own audio reflections on what I learned as an instructor through working with students on this assignment. Overall, I learned that experimentation and play, scaffolding, and the integration and manipulation of sounds were important for student authors as they worked toward developing a robust digital voice. Some useful ways of enacting and practicing these composing concepts included written and spoken reflection, low-stakes online discussions, and using models.

The Audio Story assignment asks students to compose a short audio story in a digital format, and its purpose is to give students an opportunity to practice storytelling techniques through the use of legally publishable sound materials such as voices, music, sound effects, ambient sounds, and/or silence. Specifically, the learning goals for this assignment include the following:

1. Students will consider and use storytelling techniques from course readings.
2. Students will edit and combine at least three different kinds of sounds with audio-editing software.
3. Students will follow copyright laws and produce a legally publishable audio file.

These learning goals focused first on storytelling techniques that lined up with broader course objectives to explore the rhetoric, ethics, styles, and technicalities involved with telling personal, observational, and ethnographic digital narratives. These techniques involved, for example, giving attention to purpose and meaning, tapping into emotions, and exploring a moment of change. Using such storytelling techniques through sound was our second goal as we had previously focused on visuals and were building our way to composing a video story that would use images, sounds, and written words together. Audio-only composing required students to tune their ears and bodies to words, music, silence, and sounds, and they had to learn audio-editing moves that they needed later on for video. Finally, requiring students to produce a legally publishable file that did not break copyright laws was a challenge, but this goal offered students power: At the end of the assignment, they were entirely free to publish their audio story (or not) without restrictions or worry. This requirement also asked students to learn about and explore how to find, make, and/or use legally publishable materials, which further prepared them (1) for a project at the end of the term where they could decide whether to abide by copyright laws or break them on purpose and (2) for their lives as digital authors beyond the course.[1]

The Digital Storytelling course that this Audio Story assignment was situated within was full of low-stakes, small composing assignments designed to get students familiar with digital composition through image and audio-editing tools, and small assignments led to a larger research-based digital story due at the end of the semester. The Audio Story came after students had composed and turned in a proposal and research plan for their large digital story project, as well as an Image Story that asked students to tell a story using only visual media. Early in the course, students also learned about copyright law, Creative Commons, fair use, and searching online for legally publishable materials through several readings and completing an activity using the handout provided on the book's companion website. For the Audio Story, I assumed that students had no prior experience with audio composition or editing.

The Assignment Sequence

Lesson One: An Introduction to Audio Editing with Audacity

This lesson asked students to use the free, open-source audio editor Audacity to compose a practice audio file in class.[2] Students used the handout provided on the book's companion website to orient themselves to Audacity's interface and to compose a practice file due by the end of the class period.

Lesson Two: The Audio Story Assignment, Analysis of Serial, and Searching for Sound Assets

During this lesson, we first went over the prompt for the Audio Story assignment. The main requirements of the assignment were to tell an interesting story with a purpose, meaning, emotion, or a moment of change; to use only sound to tell the story; to use at least three different kinds of sound within the story; and to compose a "copyright-free" story that was legally publishable online.

---

1. Crystal VanKooten's handout "Educating Yourself on Copyright Laws and Fair Use" can be found on the book's companion website.

2. Crystal VanKooten's handout "Audacity Workshop" can be found on the book's companion website.

Audio Story Assignment

For this assignment, you will use audio and audio-editing software to create a short audio story in a digital format. You may choose how long your audio story is, but this assignment is meant to be short, so aim for between 0–2 minutes if you can.

Requirements

You must tell an interesting story. Think about the elements of story that we've read about in *The Digital Storytelling Cookbook* (Lambert, 2010)—your story should have a purpose or a meaning, tap into emotions, and have a moment or moments of change.

You may only use sound to tell the story—no written text or images allowed.

You must use at least three different kinds of sounds within the story: your own voice, other voice(s), music, sound effects, ambient sounds, or silence.

Your audio story must follow copyright laws and be legally publishable online (whether you choose to publish it or not). That means that you need to use sounds and music that you have created yourself, that you have permission to use, that are available for reuse and modification under Creative Commons, or that are in the public domain.

Your audio story must be presented in MP3 or WAV format. You can hand in an MP3 or WAV file directly or you can upload the file to a hosting service like soundcloud.com and hand in the link.

Timeline

Wednesday, March 2: Rough draft due to Moodle and bring digital copy or link to class for workshop

Monday, March 7: Final draft due to Moodle

After discussing the assignment, we moved into an analysis of popular podcast *Serial*, Season 1, Episodes 1 and 2 (Koenig, 2014). Students had listened to the episodes before class. In class, we used the following discussion questions to analyze how the podcast used different kinds of sounds, layering, a narrator's voice, and story.

1. What sound assets are used? How are the assets layered (or not layered)? Which sound assets are the most compelling for you as a listener, and why?
2. What do you hear in the sequence? *Describe* the sounds that you hear. Describe the *effect* of the sounds that you hear.
3. What is the role of Sarah Koenig's voice in the story?
4. Did you find *Serial* a compelling story, and why or why not?
5. Why do you think *Serial* is so popular?
6. What can you take from *Serial* and apply to your own use of audio?

After discussing *Serial*, we used the following prompt and spent about 15 minutes searching online for different kinds of music and/or sound effects that had a suspicious, triumphant, or remorseful tone.

Search for music or sound effects on the web that could be used to set the following tones:

- suspicious
- triumphant
- remorseful

Lesson Three: Combining Sounds

This lesson was conducted online. Using the following prompt, students were asked to compose a 30-second audio file that combined at least three sound assets, post the audio file to the class forum in Moodle, and comment on two classmates' posts.

Combining Sounds

Using Audacity or another sound editor (GarageBand, TwistedWave, etc.), create a 30-second audio file that combines at least three sound assets. The sound assets you use are up to you—they might include, for example, your own recorded voice, the voice(s) of others, original music, music from others, sound effects, and more.

For this Create and Share assignment, don't worry about copyright—you can use any sound or piece of music, as long as you cite it. You can place citations written out in the forum, or you can speak your citations as part of your audio file.

Post your file as an MP3 in the forum below, and provide comments on what works and what might be revised in your classmates' work.

Lesson Four: Analysis and Discussion of Barber and Dorwick

During this lesson, we used the following prompt to discuss two sound articles published online: John F. Barber's (2013) "Audiobiography of the 1960s" and Keith Dorwick's (2013) "Two Sound Pieces."

Discussion Prompt: Barber and Dorwick

Topic 1: Barber's "Audiobiography of the 1960s." What kinds of sounds does Barber include in his article "Audiobiography"? What was the effect for you as a reader getting to hear the sounds versus reading the words about the historical events? What sound or sounds was most powerful for you as a reader of the piece?

Topic 2: Dorwick's "Two Sound Pieces." What is your reaction to Dorwick's experimental sound work? Would you consider this work digital storytelling, and why or why not?

Lesson Five: Audio Story Workshop

For workshop, students brought a rough draft of their Audio Story to class. They were placed in groups of three to four students and asked to follow this protocol for workshopping their drafts:

1. Author introduce the story (1 minute)
2. All: listen the story—use headphones if necessary (2–3 mins.)
3. All: take notes on the handout (3 mins.)
4. Discuss the notes and have a back-and-forth conversation (5–10 mins.)

The handout students used during the workshop asked them to answer a series of questions to guide their small group discussion of the drafts:

1. What story does the audio tell? What is the story's meaning? Does the story tap into emotions, and how? What is the moment or moments of change in the story?
2. How is the story organized? What organizational revisions might the author consider?
3. Discuss the composition of the sounds. How are they layered (or not)? How does the author use voice, music, sound effects, and/or silence? How might the author consider further editing or composing the sounds?
4. Does the author use only sound? Are the sounds legally publishable online? If attribution is used, is it done clearly and effectively?
5. What other ideas for revision can you offer the author?

Lesson Six: Distorting Sounds

This lesson was conducted online through Moodle. Using the following prompt, students were asked to record an ordinary sound, use audio-editing software to distort the sound for an alternate meaning, post the audio file to the class forum, and comment on two classmates' posts.

Distorting Sounds

Find or record an ordinary sound, and use sound-editing software to distort the sound in a noticeable way for an alternate meaning. You might slow the sound down, speed it up, change the pitch, or do other kinds of distortions. Post both the original sound and the distorted sound to the forum, along with a paragraph describing what you hope the new meaning for the distorted sound might be.

Sample Student Projects

1. Audio Story by Audrey Downs: Audrey tells the story of how she met her best friend Alex using music and narration.[3]
2. "The Empty Barn" by Paige Efting: Paige tells the story of showing and selling animals at a 4-H fair using music, poetic narration, animal sound effects, and silence.

---

3. Three student examples (audio files and descriptive transcripts) can be found on the book's companion website.

3. Audio Story by Mandy Olejnik: Using narration and self-recorded sound effects and music, Mandy tells the story of the initial confusion of studying abroad in Montreal.

Reflection on Teaching the Audio Story Assignment

Crystal VanKooten: *[Music plays: bass guitar and drums.]* This is Crystal Van-Kooten, Assistant Professor of Writing and Rhetoric at Oakland University in Rochester, Michigan.[4] I taught the Audio Story assignment that I'm highlighting in this chapter in 2016 in a 200-level writing course that was called Digital Storytelling, and I learned a lot as an instructor about how to support students in developing a robust digital voice through audio storytelling, a voice that included not only the human voice but also other sound elements. And in particular, I learned about three concepts that I want to reflect on today:

- number one: the role of experimentation and play in students' composition processes;
- number two: composing with the support of scaffolds and composing in small pieces;
- and number three: the integration and manipulation of sounds. *[Music fades.]*

First, though, what is digital voice? What is digital voice?
[voice slowed and distorted] What is digital voice?
[Music plays with electronic beat and sound effects.] Erin Anderson's 2014 piece in *Enculturation*, "Toward a Resonant Material Vocality for Digital Composition," has really helped me to think about voice as much more than tethered to language or in service of language only. And it's really helped me to think about voice as something we need to pay more attention to because of the role of technologies in manipulating voice now. And she states that voice sits "at the intersection between language and body." This to me means that voice involves both words *and* the physicality of experience. And thus digital voice becomes a resource: "a performative material with potential to act and to affect in its own right" (Anderson, 2014). So what all might be involved in digital voice if it's not just limited to language? Certainly, I think the sounds of the human voice, but also sounds—other sounds like music, notes, sound effects—these are all part of voice.

And this is something that Kyle Stedman explores in his piece that was published in 2011 in *Currents in Electronic Literacy* called "How Music Speaks." *[Super Mario Bros. theme music plays.]* For Stedman (2011), music is both discursive—through lyrics—and nondiscursive, through instruments, rhythms, tempo, recognizability, association. . . . And he states that "Music has both its inherent

---

4. The audio version of Crystal VanKooten's reflection can be found on the book's companion website.

meaning for an audience *and* the meanings it creates when affecting everything around it. Music is like a virus of meaning. And that shifting meaning is worthy of playful experimentation." So I say yes—voice is both tied to language and to the body, and it can and should include music and other sounds. *[Super Mario Bros. theme ends on ascending phrase.]*

So, where does all this leave us? Erin Anderson (2014) suggests that voice going digital is an invitation to create new texts *[music plays with a gradually ascending phrase]*, and to weave, to play, to disrupt, to experiment, to weave, to play, to disrupt, to experiment *[voice overlaps and repeats].* And she concludes her article with this statement: "Perhaps what emerges, then, is an opportunity to reorient our approach to voice in digital rhetoric away from time-honored models of delivery and toward alternative possibilities of invention."

These alternate possibilities of invention with voice are what I think we as computers and writing scholars and teachers need to be exploring more in our own scholarship, but also in our classrooms with students. Which brings me back to the audio story. *[Music crescendos and lyrics state, "They don't care, just cutting through the barbed wire fence. . . ."]*

So we start this assignment with a getting-to-know Audacity, low-stakes, practice audio-file activity. And this is done in class. *[Music plays with electronic sound effects.]* Students don't receive a grade for their work, they just, you know, get credit for doing it. Students can work at their own pace, which is why I make a checklist and have students check off tasks as they make their practice file. And students can get some help, and some scaffolded help to start building their functional literacies with the Audacity software.

Another thing I wanted them to do through this assignment was to play around a little bit *[bass beat begins to play within music]* and to start enacting some of those principles that Anderson and others talk about of experimentation with audio. However, the way that I encouraged experimentation here was fairly open and wasn't as effective as some other measures that I'll talk about in a minute. So, as you can see on the handout, I had things like, "record or import any other sounds or words you'd like to add to your exploration." Or "play around with the effects menu to manipulate your sounds." And this is all under Phase 5, which I entitled "Play Around." However, when I actually went and listened to the files that students created for this practice activity, not many students were really playing around. They were really just concerned with getting their song in there, getting it clipped, getting it the right length, and then actually exporting the file in a format where they could hand it in.

[Serial music plays, high piano chords.] Another thing we did through this assignment sequence was to listen to models and to discuss and analyze these models and to do a little bit of emulation as we went to do our own composing. So we listened to a couple of episodes from Season 1 of the podcast *Serial* (Koenig, 2014), and we discussed them in class and picked apart a couple sections. We listened to John F. Barber's (2013) piece "Audiobiography of the 1960s."

[Barber's piece plays, reporter states: "From Dallas, Texas, the flash apparently official, President Kennedy died. . . ."]

And we listened to Keith Dorwick's (2013) "Two Sound Pieces."

[Dorwick's piece plays: low, sustained notes crescendo; insect-like clicks continue; a bell chimes.]

So we listened to these pieces, we discussed them, we talked about what they say, how they say it, what their voice was, and then students actually talked about these pieces in their reflections as they looked back at their Audio Stories and thought about how they decided to create meaning. *[Dorwick's piece continues to play.]* So one student really fixed in on the narrator of *Serial* as being an inspiration. Another student really liked the Dorwick piece, the experimental piece, and liked the weirdness of it and tried to do some of her own recording of everyday sounds and distorting of them in her own piece. *[Music fades.]*

A third activity that we did which really helped students to integrate and manipulate sounds was to do these low-stakes online forums. And so we did two of these while students were working on their Audio Story. The first one was called Combining Sounds and the second one was called Distorting Sounds.

[Audrey Downs's Combining Sounds audio file plays: high, echoing notes crescendo and then quickly fade. The sound repeats several times.]

And I think these worked really well to do all three of the concepts that I'm reflecting on today. To have students experiment and play around, but to scaffold their composing. And then also to force them to integrate sounds and manipulate sounds in a way that they may or may not have done on their own. So the first forum asked students to combine three sounds together and post the file, and then comment on each other's compositions.

[Audrey Downs's composition continues to play: low piano notes play and an echoing voice states, "Run like your life depends on it, because it does."]

And the second forum asked them to record an everyday sound *[Mandy Ole-jnik's "Snaps" plays]* and then distort it to get a different meaning, to post the file and then to comment on each other's work. And so there were so many cool things that students put in the forum. One student recorded a microwave beeping and then distorted that sound. *[Audrey Downs's microwave beeping recording plays.]* One student recorded a toilet flushing, which was funny to everyone in the class, and distorted that sound. Students put different kinds of music together and different sound effects that they found on different websites with different kinds of music. So it was a really fruitful place for them to play, to be able to do these small moves, like juxtaposing two or three things, two or three sounds, or distorting one sound for a purpose. And to be forced to do some of the playing and the integrating and the manipulating that they were reticent to do or that they just ran out of time to do in other activities. *[Microwave beeps.]*

[Music plays, bass guitar and drums.] Overall, I just really think I learned to not be so product-based through this assignment. And so if I was valuing experimentation, and valuing integrating and manipulating and having students do new things, try new things, play around with software in ways that they'd never done before, you know, valuing a really polished product in the end wasn't the most important thing, is what I ended up coming to. Instead, I looked to their reflections along the way, that they did in the forums, that we did in class, that they turned in at the end of the assignment and at the end of the course. I looked to elements of story that we'd been talking about in the class. And I looked to how they went out, found the sound assets that they used, and that's the way that I ended up assessing the assignment. And it was great fun, and as you can see by some of the samples, even though I didn't emphasize product, the products came out pretty great too. *[Music fades.]*

References

Anderson, E. R. (2014). Toward a resonant material vocality for digital composition. *Enculturation: A Journal of Rhetoric, Writing, and Culture, 18.* http://encultura tion.net/materialvocality.

Barber, J. F. (2013). Audiobiography: A sonic memoir of the 1960s. *Harlot: A Revealing Look at the Arts of Persuasion, 9.* https://harlotofthearts.org/ojs-3.3.0-11/index .php/harlot/article/view/156.

Dorwick, K. (2013). Two sound pieces. *Harlot: A Revealing Look at the Arts of Persuasion, 9.* https://harlotofthearts.org/ojs-3.3.0-11/index.php/harlot/article/view/154.

Koenig, S. (Host). (2014). *Serial* [Audio podcast]. Serial Productions. https://serial podcast.org/.

Kondo, K. (Composer). (2010, October 13). Super mario bros. music—ground theme [Video file]. *YouTube.* https://youtu.be/wGX4obVl64w (Original work published 1985).

Lambert, J. (2010). *The digital storytelling cookbook.* Digital Diner Press. .

Mana Junkie. (n.d.). Digital revolution [Song]. *digccmixter.* http://dig.ccmixter.org /files/mana_junkie/28611.

markobango. (n.d.). Arrogalla riddim [Song]. *digccmixter.* http://dig.ccmixter.org /files/markobango/30259.

misterC. (n.d.). Digital revolution (status quo mix) [Song]. *digccmixter.* http://dig .ccmixter.org/files/misterC/10479.

PorchCat. (n.d.). Burn the fence [Song]. *digccmixter.* http://dig.ccmixter.org/files /PorchCat/55420.

Stedman, K. D. (2011). How music speaks: In the background, in the remix, in the city. *Currents in Electronic Literacy.* https://currents.dwrl.utexas.edu/2011 /howmusicspeaks.html.

Thorburn, N. (2014). Bad dream (the theme) [Song]. On *Music for Serial.* https:// soundcloud.com/islands/01-bad-dream-the-theme-1?in=islands/sets /music-for-serial.

Chapter 3. Elements of Sound: Three Scaffolded Assignments

Sara Wilder

University of Maryland, College Park

Featuring the Work of Averi Ager, D'Arcee Neal, and Dorian Blue

This chapter presents assignments from an upper-level undergraduate course in digital rhetoric and audio composition. In this course, students explore theories of digital and sonic rhetorics through reading, listening, and composing with sound. I had two major goals when I began this class: (1) I wanted students to develop strong listening practices that allowed them to listen to, analyze, and critique sound, and (2) I wanted students to develop their rhetorical abilities to compose with sound. In approaching this course, I aimed to scaffold student work, to give students opportunities to play with sound on small, specific tasks that they could build from over time. Taking inspiration from scholarship by Tanya K. Rodrigue et al. (2016) and Heidi McKee (2006), I decided to structure the body of my course around four, 2–3-week units, each devoted to one of McKee's elements of sound: music, voice, sound effects, and silence. My units on music, voice, and sound effects were each anchored by one major assignment featuring that sound element. Together, these assignments offer students the opportunity to gradually develop listening and composing practices by focusing their attention on particular elements and asking them to reflect on their compositional choices and their learning throughout the course.

Heidi McKee's 2006 article "Sound Matters: Notes Toward the Analysis and Design of Sound in Multimodal Webtexts" provided a framework that helped students understand sound as rhetorical and cultural artifact. Faced with the complex field of sound studies, McKee drew on a variety of disciplines to present a framework that breaks sound down into four elements: vocal delivery, music, sound effects, and silence. I found her article especially useful in conceptualizing my course because it would allow students to focus their attention on one particular element of sound at a time. They could practice listening with especial focus to an element, read pieces theorizing that particular element, consider how the element worked in concert with other sound elements, and finally practice working with that element.

Within each unit, I used McKee's work as a starting point for developing a class vocabulary for talking about each element. For example, McKee drew on Aaron Copland's framework for listening to music on three planes: the sensuous, the expressive, and the sheerly musical. This gave students a place to start, and we listened to musical pieces to practice hearing and naming these elements. To supplement McKee, I asked students to read the introduction to Daniel J. Levitin's (2007) *This Is Your Brain on Music*, which gave them yet more terms for describing the musical sounds that they heard (pitch, timbre, instrumentation, etc.). Beyond this descriptive work, I wanted students to understand music, like writing, as a socially situated and ideologically weighted practice. Although they can articulate basic genre distinctions and values associated with, say, hip-hop as opposed to classical music, students still often have an idea of music as a "universal language." I wanted to trouble this idea and get students thinking about the relationship between music and power. To that end, we explored histories of American protest music and read pieces like Jonathan W. Stone's (2015) "Listening to the Sonic Archive: Rhetoric, Representation, and Race in the Lomax Prison Recordings." My goal, for music as for the other units, was to help students think about the sound element from both a compositional and analytic perspective, understanding how sound works as compositional element and as cultural artifact.

Although I asked students to complete focused assignments on music, voice, and sound effects, I chose not to do a specific assignment focused on silence. As we neared the end of the term, I wanted to give students the opportunity to revise earlier assignments for a bigger final project. Students had the choice of revising two pieces for a portfolio or more extensively revising and expanding one single piece for their final project. As students revised their earlier work, they would incorporate their growing understanding of silence into their revision. Giving students more time to work on final projects allowed them to thoughtfully revise and to learn from the experiences they had with earlier assignments.

Students came into this course with varied soundwriting experience. A few had done some basic audio work, and others were complete novices. I included a series of workshops and minor assignments to help students develop their listening practices and to practice recording and editing sound. We began the first week with a low-stakes "audio journal" assignment in which they recorded sound from their daily activities and wrote about what they heard, how they heard it, and how they recorded it. I encouraged them to use various methods for recording (phones, laptops, microphones checked out from the library, etc.) and to record a variety of types of sound in a variety of spaces. I led in-class workshops on Adobe Audition, which students could get for free through the university, and included at least one peer-workshop day and one studio work day for each unit. This gave students ample time to get feedback from me and their peers and to get help with any technical issues they were having.

In what follows, I share my Elements of Sound assignments: a remix assignment featuring music, an audio narrative featuring voice, and a Concept in 60 Seconds assignment, featuring sound effects. Although each of these assignments has been part of other digital media composing courses (DeWitt et al., 2015), they are designed in this course to function together. Each Elements of Sound assignment is paired with an artist statement in which students communicate their artistic choices and goals. Artist statements gave students the opportunity to reflect on their composing choices in a recognizable, real-world genre.

This chapter provides writing instructors with an assignment sequence that helps students to gradually develop their listening and composing practices and encourages student reflection. The student examples, including artist statements, demonstrate how students might respond to individual assignments and the challenges they encountered completing the assignments. The reflection that follows provides insight into the challenges that I encountered supporting and, especially, assessing student work throughout the sequence.

Assignment Prompts

Audio Remix: Elements of Sound Assignment #1: Music

Assignment Description and Goals

This is the first of our series of Elements of Sound Assignments. For these assignments, I encourage you to choose a theme, topic, or question that you can explore in various ways. This might be a topic directly related to our course content (for example, uses of particular types of sound or how sounds are linked to places or identities), or it might be a personal or academic interest that you can explore using sound as a medium (for example, a particular cause that matters to you, or a theme, like childhood). While you don't have to stick to the same topic all semester, choosing one may help give you some ideas for these projects and for the final project later on.

Remix, broadly defined, is combining multiple things to make something new. The best remixes bring together old material in a way that lends it new understanding or power. This assignment is designed to engage you in remix as a rhetorical practice while also exploring music as a powerful sound element. Finally, it will help you develop your skills in digital audio editing.

For our music-focused project, you will create a 3–5-minute audio piece that incorporates various pieces of sound. Your piece should combine and juxtapose at least two different sound objects, remixing or mashing them up to create a new piece with a new purpose. Your project should also include a musical element (song(s), instrumental samples, etc.).

As part of this assignment, you will also write a 200–250-word artist statement describing your goals for this piece and your choices in composing (see below for more detail).

Please submit your assignment in the form of an MP3 file and Word document or PDF via our course website.

Assignment Evaluation

This assignment is worth 15% of your final course grade.

We will further discuss evaluation criteria together in class, but generally, I will ask the following questions as I evaluate your piece:

- Is there a purpose or central idea unifying the piece?
- How does the remix or mashup amplify or alter the meaning, tone, or message of the original pieces of sound in a way that furthers the overall goal of YOUR piece?
- Does the arrangement (structural design) further your rhetorical purpose?
- Did you experiment with different techniques or ideas to creatively use the affordances of audio?
- Does your piece creatively or purposefully use music as a key element?
- Do you carefully edit the audio, using control over volume, various effects, etc. to further your rhetorical purpose?
- Does your artist statement thoughtfully reflect on your composing choices?

Audio Narrative: Elements of Sound
Assignment #2: Voice and Narration

Assignment Description and Goals

For our voice-focused project, you will create a 3–5-minute audio narrative that incorporates your own and/or others' voices. You may also choose to use other types of recorded sound (music, recordings of events or spaces, sound effects, etc.). The goal of this assignment is to help you put into practice some of the principles we've learned regarding voice in sonic compositions.

Audio narratives, like written narratives, are driven by their story. You should think about what story you want to tell and why; your story should have a clear purpose or argument. Remember that compelling stories establish character and setting, center around a key problem or conflict, and resolve that conflict, often showing character growth. Strong stories that stick with you include concrete details. Audio narratives harness the power of sound to fill in some of these details. Many audio narratives include both story and reflection, helping guide listeners to the overall argument of the piece.

As part of this assignment, you will also write a 200–250-word artist statement describing your goals for this piece and your choices in composing (see below for more detail).

Please turn in your assignment in the form of an MP3 file and Word document or PDF via our course website.

Assignment Evaluation

This assignment is worth 15% of your final course grade.

We will further discuss evaluation criteria together in class, but generally, I will ask the following questions when I evaluate your project:

- Does the audio narrative have a clear purpose or argument?
- Does the narrative effectively structure the story and organize the piece?
- How does the narrative make use of sounds other than the main voices of the story (such as music or sound effects)? Do these sounds enhance

the story and contribute to the overall purpose? For example, do sounds illustrate what's happening in the narrative, provide details about the setting, transition from one part of the story to another, or emphasize particular aspects of the narration?

- How well have you edited the voice(s) in this piece? Are there unnecessary ums and uhs or are there places where we need a bit of silence?
- Does your artist statement thoughtfully reflect on your composing choices?

Concept in 60: Elements of Sound Assignment #3: Sound Effects

Assignment Description and Goals

For our sound effects project, you will create a 60-second piece that illustrates a concept using sound effects. This piece ought to be conceptual—if you choose the concept "school," for example, you should critically explore the concept of school rather than illustrate the sounds of a particular school.

Although the piece may include voices, it should not rely primarily on narration to explore the concept. For example, you want to avoid a speaker explaining a concept with the occasional sound effect thrown in. Rather, integrate the sounds so that they are featured significantly in the piece and do much of the rhetorical work. The goal is to practice the principles we've learned regarding sound effects in audio compositions.

As part of this assignment, you will also write a 200–250-word artist statement describing your goals for this piece and your choices in composing (see below for more detail).

Please turn in your assignment in the form of an MP3 file and Word document or PDF via our course website.

Assignment Evaluation

This assignment is worth 15% of your final course grade.

We will further discuss evaluation criteria together in class, but generally, I will ask the following questions when I evaluate your project:

- Does the piece critically and creatively illustrate or interrogate a single concept?
- Is it no longer than 1 minute?
- How does the Concept in 60 make use of sound? Does it foreground sound effects or "noise"? Does it integrate these sounds to contribute to the meaning of the overall piece?
- Does the artist statement thoughtfully reflect on composing choices?

On Artist Statements

Artists often use written statements to communicate about their art, including their process, ideas, and their place in their chosen field. Artist statements can vary based on purpose and audience. A statement for a grant proposal, for example, might focus on the identity of the artist and the overall purpose or interest of their work. An artist statement for a show or even for a particular piece will tend to be more focused on the choices the artist made in composing that particular piece or show.

For the purposes of this assignment, you'll take the latter approach, focusing specifically on your composition. In your statement of 200–250 words, address the following sets of questions:

- What is your overall purpose for the piece? What goal did you have in putting it together? What is your piece about? Why do you think it is significant or interesting?
- How did you go about designing and completing your audio project? What choices did you make in order to further your goals? How did the piece change as you continued working on it?
- What do you hope listeners will understand about your work? What has your work helped you to understand?

Sample Student Projects

1. "Prelude to a Dream" by Dorian Blue. In this audio remix (Elements of Sound Assignment 1), Dorian uses musical elements and voices to explore a separation between sound and subject, creating a sense of disembodiment and unease.[1]
2. "The Execution" by D'Arcee Neal. In this audio narrative (Elements of Sound Assignment 2), D'Arcee remediates one of his poems, using sound effects and music to illustrate the story told by the poem's speaker.
3. "Alien Abduction Concept in 60" by Averi Ager. In this Concept in 60 (Elements of Sound Assignment 3), Averi tells the story of an alien abduction by creating a soundscape and making use of recognizable genre conventions.

Reflection

[Ethereal chimes musical introduction.]

Sara Wilder: When I designed my advanced writing course focused on digital rhetoric and audio composition, I knew I wanted students to strengthen their practice in both listening to and composing with sound.[2]

I decided to draw upon Heidi McKee's (2006) framework for analyzing and teaching audio in multimodal compositions to help structure my course. McKee

---

1. Three student examples (audio files and descriptive transcripts) can be found on the book's companion website.

2. The audio version of Sara Wilder's reflection can be found on the book's companion website.

breaks sound down into four elements: music, voice, sound effects, and silence. I structured the bulk of my course around these four elements, anchoring them in three soundwriting assignments: a remix (focusing on music), a narrative (focusing on voice), and a concept in 60 seconds (focusing on sound effects and soundscapes). These three assignments formed my Elements of Sound assignment sequence. Students then chose one or more of these pieces to revise and expand for a final project of their choosing.

[Chimes fade in.]

In this reflective piece, I address each assignment from the sequence in turn, first describing my approach to teaching the element and then giving examples from student work to explain how students took up that assignment. Along the way, I will address how these assignments challenged me as a teacher and what I think students ultimately learned from the experience.

[Musical interlude: chimes.]

Unit 1: Music

[Chimes fade out.]

By the end of this unit, I wanted students to be able to listen to a piece of music, describe what they heard with some specificity and depth, and to be able to manipulate music to suit their compositional needs. Further, I wanted students to interrogate music as a cultural artifact. To that end, we read pieces like Levitin's (2007) introduction to *This Is Your Brain on Music* that introduced students to terms that would help them describe what they heard. To deepen understanding of music as a rhetorical practice, we discussed musical genres and remix, grounding those discussions by watching videos like Ferguson's (2016) *Everything Is a Remix* and Vox's recent short documentary on the history of protest music (Henwood, 2017). We listened to podcasts about music, like *Switched on Pop*'s episode comparing Toby Keith's "Made in America" with Jay-Z's song of the same name (Sloan & Harding, 2016).

To help students put what they were learning into practice not only as critical listeners, but also as producers, I tasked them with making a remix.

[Chimes begin again, quietly under voice.]

Students were to manipulate music by remixing it with another piece of sound, whether another piece of music, a narrative voice, or some other element. My overall goals for the assignment were for students to manipulate music to make something new, to demonstrate engagement with concepts from our reading, to demonstrate reflective and purposeful use of sound, and to simply gain facility with the technology, to learn to use the programs for soundwriting.

Students responded to the remix prompt in a variety of ways, some choosing to remediate creative writing pieces, some choosing to reflect on their own music literacy, and still others doing more conceptual pieces, exploring, through sound, a concept that interested them.

[Music stops.]

The variety of pieces I received speaks to both a strength and a weakness of this assignment. This sequence is fairly flexible; it allows students to pursue their own interests and make their own decisions about the genre their piece might most fit. This flexibility allowed students the creative freedom to meet their own goals for their projects. But it also led to problems for me as I responded to and assessed their work. It was difficult to compare students' pieces. I wanted to reward students for taking creative risks. I didn't want to mark them down for trying something new that ultimately failed, as long as they were learning something from the process.

Take Blue's remix as an example.

[Eerie music from remix starts and then continues as background.]

Blue's piece, titled "Prelude to a Dream," included a variety of music and other elements that were purposefully interwoven to evoke a feeling of unease and detachment. That purpose isn't explicitly in the piece itself exactly, but it is developed in their artist statement.

Blue's piece, experimental as it was, was one of the more difficult for me to assess. Were I to listen to this with a rubric in hand that, for instance, designated clarity as an important factor, I'm not sure how well Blue would have done. And yet clarity was not one of my goals for this particular piece. Blue demonstrated a sense of purpose in their artist statement and drew on specifics from the piece to show how they tried to achieve that purpose. Although my feedback to Blue asked for a bit more development of the artist statement, it seemed to me that they had begun to play with sound; they'd manipulated music from various sources (some originally recorded, some found online); and they'd done so with a sense of rhetorical purpose. And for this assignment, that's exactly what I wanted to see.

[Eerie music stops.]

To try to account for the various goals and projects, I ended up working with students to develop a rubric. During an in-class workshop, we collaboratively designed and tested an assessment rubric. Once students turned in their piece, I gave them feedback in two stages. I first listened to their piece and wrote a response detailing my listening experience. I then read their artist statement, listened again, and used the rubric to write another brief response justifying the grade.

Especially for this first assignment in the sequence, I think that this kind of transparency and collaboration in the assessment was crucial to creating an atmosphere in which students felt they could push boundaries and play with sound.

[Musical interlude: chimes.]

Unit 2: Voice and Narration

As we transitioned into the next unit on voice, we listened to podcasts and other pieces that featured voices prominently. In addition to reading pieces theorizing voice, we also took the opportunity to focus on storytelling.

In the anchoring assignment for this unit, students composed an audio narrative. Many students began to build from the skills they started to develop with the first assignment, choosing to use music or other sounds that would help them illustrate a scene, convey a particular mood, or emphasize particular elements of the piece. While some students started by simply adding music to a narrative, I encouraged them—through in-class workshops and mini-conferences—to use music or other sounds to enhance, extend, or change meaning, in particular focusing on using music for emphasis.

D'Arcee's poem, which he remediated for my class, gives us several examples of how students used music and other elements to foreground and emphasize particular parts of a vocal track. In this piece, titled "The Execution," D'Arcee uses sound effects for illustration, as he writes, to create "a mini movie."

For example, he illustrates the speaker's descriptions with the whispers of voices:

[Metallic drone, quiet voice, underplayed with whispering sounds: I heard from my neighbor, who told her cousin who whispered to her boss.]

and the crunch of gravel.

[Metallic drone, crunching footsteps.]

Further, though, he uses musical elements to evoke the sense of anxiety and impending doom, he also uses music to create emphasis.

The metallic drone sound that repeats throughout is silenced just as we reach the climax of the plot. Listen:

> *[narrative voice over crickets, wind, and metallic drone]* Every-one is silent. *[swirl of wind]* She says one word and the village stops.

[silence]

Ultimately, it is the voice of the poem's speaker that drives the piece, but the use of music and the use of silence helps emphasize important parts of the poem.

As you'll see in his artist statement, D'Arcee actually completed this piece in response to the remix assignment, but I include it here as an example of how a student might respond to the narrative assignment because I think it fits this prompt just as well, if not better, than it fits the remix because it is driven by vocals. What we also see in D'Arcee's artist statement, however, is a reflection on the composing process that helped him to approach later assignments with a better sense of the amount of time involved.

One of the key takeaways that many students learned from these first two assignments was how long it takes to complete a piece of soundwriting. They learned that the process of planning, organizing, recording and collecting sound, drafting, mixing, and editing took much longer than they might have expected. In this second assignment, students were a little less ambitious in their plans than they were in the remix assignment. I also worked with them to think about how they could use the narrative as a small piece of a larger final project. For example, several students interviewed family members, ultimately expanding their audio narratives for longer podcast-style audio essays. For these students, this was just the start of what would become a longer piece for the final project.

[Musical interlude: chimes.]

Unit Three: Sound Effects

As we moved into our unit on sound effects, we returned to some of our readings from earlier in the term, revisiting concepts from McKee but also our experience of sounds in everyday life, this time from the perspective of producers of sound as much as listeners. We focused the unit on soundscapes, listening to pieces such as the *Sound Matters* podcast episode "The Sound of Life Itself" (Hinman, 2016). We listened to Stedman and Stone's (2014) sonic review of Rickert's *Ambient Rhetoric*, returning again to rhetorical principles to understand sound. To anchor this unit, I assigned students an audio Concept in 60 project, adapted from a video concept in 60 assignment I had been introduced to through the Digital Media and Composition institute at Ohio State several years before. Students had 60 seconds in which to convey or interrogate a concept, primarily through using sounds other than music or voice.

Perhaps because it followed our narrative projects, many of my students—like Averi's example demonstrates—chose to tell stories or evoke characters with their 60 seconds. Averi's 60-second piece about an alien abduction also provides us a strong example of how students could build on earlier work, expanding their repertoire and putting concepts from the course into practice.

Averi's initial remix piece (the first piece they wrote for me) combined a poem, told in first person, with music that played up less obvious themes in the poem and with sounds like the opening of a door and chatter in a café.

[Door opens, bell rings, background voices.]

And these sounds told us that we, as listeners, were walking along with the poem's speaker.

In Averi's Concept in 60 piece, they again put listeners in the position of walking with the main character, this time a hiker in the woods who is abducted by aliens. In workshopping Averi's 60-second piece in class, we focused on feedback that would make this feel "realistic,"

[Owl hooting, footsteps, crickets.]

such as making an owl hooting sound further away than the crackle of twigs underfoot. The result was a piece that made use of genre conventions (a hiker, nighttime noises, alien sounds) to tell a story with no narration. In their artist statement, Averi reflected on these choices and eventually built on this idea even more, making their final project into an audio essay on subject position and sound.

Averi's experience of figuring out how to convey subject position through multiple pieces and then using that experience to drive their final project was one ideal outcome for the way a student might experience this assignment sequence. I hoped that this sequence gave students flexibility to pursue subjects of interest, as Blue did in exploring embodiment, D'Arcee did in remediating creative work, and Averi did by exploring how to account for subject position in designing sonic experiences.

[Background music: chimes.]

As students completed these three projects, they became more adept at both listening and producing sound that made use of music, sound effects, and voice. Along the way, they learned key rhetorical concepts that would help them with a variety of multimodal projects.

[Music fades.]

References

amholma. (2016, April 26). Door open close [Audio file]. *Freesound*. https://free sound.org/people/amholma/sounds/344360/.

bastardwrio. (2017, September 10). wild calls [Audio file]. *Freesound*. https://free sound.org/people/bastardwrio/sounds/401826/.

DeWitt, S. L., Harmon, B., Lackey, D. & LaVecchia, C. M. (2015). Techne in 60: The history and practice of the Concept in 60. *Showcasing the Best of CIWIC/DMAC: Approaches to Teaching and Learning in Digital Environments*. http://www.dmac institute.com/showcase/issues/no1/dewitt-techne-60-context.

Ferguson, K. (2016, May 16). Everything is a remix remastered (2015 HD) [Video file]. *YouTube*. https://youtu.be/nJPERZDfyWc.

gurdonark. (n.d.). Ravine [Audio file]. *digccmixter*. http://dig.ccmixter.org/files /gurdonark/34368.

Henwood, B. (2017, May 22). The history of American protest music, from "Yankee Doodle" to Kendrick Lamar: How protest music evolved from Civil War refrains to viral Trump videos. *Vox*. https://www.vox.com/culture/2017/4/12/14462948 /protest-music-history-america-trump-beyonce-dylan-misty.

Hinmann, T. (Producer). (2016, January). The sound of life itself (No. 1) [Audio podcast episode]. In *Sound matters*. Tim Hinmann with Bang & Olufsen. https:// soundcloud.com/sound_matters.

Leafs67. (2012, May 12). Walking in long grass [Audio file]. *Freesound.* https://free sound.org/people/Leafs67/sounds/155589/.

Levitin, D. J. (2007). *This is your brain on music: The science of a human obsession.* Plume.

limwei. (2010, June 26). Up stairs [Audio file]. *Freesound.* https://freesound.org /people/limwei/sounds/100025/.

lunchmoney. (2017, February 8). Cafe restaurant/ambience [Audio file]. *Freesound.* https://freesound.org/people/lunchmoney/sounds/380201/.

McKee, H. (2006). Sound matters: Notes toward the analysis and design of sound in multimodal webtexts. *Computers and Composition, 23*(3), 335–354. https://doi .org/10.1016/j.compcom.2006.06.003.

Rodrigue, T. K., Artz, K., Bennett, J., Carver, M. P., Grandmont, M., Harris, D., Hashem, D., Mooney, A., Rand, M. & Zimmerman, A. (2016). Navigating the soundscape, composing with audio. *Kairos: A Journal of Rhetoric, Technology, and Pedagogy, 21*(1). http://kairos.technorhetoric.net/21.1/praxis/rodrigue/index.html.

shall555. (2009, May 5). Shop doorbell [Audio file]. *Freesound.* https://freesound.org /people/shall555/sounds/72197/.

Sloan, N. & Harding, C. (Hosts). (November 4, 2016). Made in America: Toby Keith & Jay-Z (No. 48) [Audio podcast episode]. In *Switched on pop.* Rock Ridge Productions LLC. http://www.switchedonpop.com/48-made-in-america-toby-keith -jay-z/.

Stedman, K. D. & Stone, J. (2014). Experiencing ambience together: A sonic review of Thomas Rickert's *Ambient rhetoric: The attunements of rhetorical being. Composition Forum, 30.* http://compositionforum.com/issue/30/stedman-stone -rickert-review.php.

Stone, J. W. (2015). Listening to the sonic archive: Rhetoric, representation, and race in the Lomax prison recordings. *Enculturation: A Journal of Writing, Rhetoric, and Culture, 19.* http://enculturation.net/listening-to-the-sonic-archive.

Taylor, D. (Host). (2016). NBC chimes (No. 2) [Audio podcast episode]. In *Twenty thousand hertz.* Defacto Sound. https://twentythousandhertz.squarespace.com /episodes/nbc.

Chapter 4. The Sonic Collage Assignment: Aesthetics, Affect, and Critique in Audio Sampling

Ben Harley

NORTHERN STATE UNIVERSITY

I developed the sonic collage assignment in the fall of 2015 while teaching a first-year composition course called Writing about Popular Music. The course asked students to create, brand, and maintain independent music blogs where they would critique albums, artists, and tracks using a variety of analytical frames. I encouraged students to develop their own voices, styles, topics, and approaches within the parameters of each task I gave them, and each assignment attempted to provide students with an opportunity to express their ideas about culture and art in ways that felt authentic and important to them. However, since neither music nor writing are exclusively personal, I also encouraged students to collectively act as a subpublic that cocreates new ideas and knowledges through composing, distributing, circulating, reading, remixing, and responding to each other's texts. The class blog I created helped to facilitate these kinds of interactions by acting as a hub that linked all of the students' individual blogs together, while also functioning as a space for me to post articles, instructions, and videos to which students could directly respond.

Despite the emphasis on music, creativity, and collaboration, I had not thought to develop any assignments that asked students to create original sonic compositions until the class read Mark Katz's (2010) *Capturing Sound*. Katz's book focused on phonograph effects—how a culture's musical practices (writing, performance, distribution, circulation, etc.) are influenced by its recording technologies. In the seventh chapter, Katz explained that for millennia composers have quoted each other within their original compositions, and he argued that digital sampling is a continuation of this practice. As far as Katz was concerned, the primary difference between notated allusions and digital samples is the specificity enabled by the latter. While composers working with musical notation are limited in how specific they can be in recreating another composer's work, composers working with digitized musical samples can almost exactly recreate any specific recorded performance of whatever work they want. In both cases, musicians are bringing the works of others into their original compositions; one method is simply more exact.

My students and I were intrigued by the comparison between quoting, a practice with which we were all familiar, and sampling, a practice none of us had tried before; we realized that in order to truly understand the similarities and differences between these two practices, we would need to go beyond discussion and engage in what Mark Amerika has referred to as "practice-based research" (CU Boulder

DOI: https://doi.org/10.37514/PRA-B.2022.1688.2.04

Libraries, 2014). We would need to make our own compositions out of sampled sounds. Since the course was already underway, I offered the sonic collage assignment as extra credit. There were very few parameters: Students were simply asked to create a 3-minute audio track using ten samples and four audio effects. They were instructed to use one of the three compositions Katz (2010) critiqued in chapter seven of *Capturing Sound* (Paul Lansky's *Notjustmoreidlechatter*, Fatboy Slim's "Praise You," and Public Enemy's "Fight the Power") as a model for their own work. Following these models was largely arbitrary, but they each asked students to focus on a different way sound can be used—aesthetically, affectively, or critically. For technical instruction, I decided only to help students if they came to see me. Otherwise, I let them learn to use sound-editing tools by engaging with the tutorials created by the sound-editing community itself because this community is the type of subpublic after which I had been modelling the class.

In the end, I was glad the assignment was not required and that I took a hands-off approach to teaching digital sampling because the ad hoc nature of the whole experience emboldened students to experiment and take risks, which led to compositions that were not only interesting but also prompted productive class conversations about the ethics surrounding appropriation, citation, creation, culture, identity, homage, manipulation, originality, ownership, sampling, and the inherently personal, social, and material nature of both sonic and written composition. My students and I never established definitive stances on these topics, but we did learn to ask better questions through our engagement with soundwriting.

The next academic year, I remixed the sonic collage assignment for another first-year composition course focused on writing blogs about popular music. For this iteration, I asked students to create audio histories of musical genres—to sample performances that were instrumental to fashioning a particular genre and put them into conversation with one another so that listeners could hear the evolution of a musical tradition. The class discussed how historical narratives are creative compositions that demand their authors make rhetorical choices, but despite these discussions, the assignment fell flat and felt lifeless. It was clear that the students were not engaging in playful practiced-based research about a method of sonic composition; rather, they were composing linear histories for a grade. The compositions were still interesting, but they were more reserved and less experimental.

When I assign this project in the future, I will be going back to the original structure, asking students to create digitally sampled sonic collages based on loosely constructed categories in which they can experiment and play with bringing other voices into their original compositions, but I want to make some modifications. Since first assigning this project, I have read work by Jean Bessette (2016), Jared Sterling Colton (2016), Dylan Robinson (2016), and Jennifer Lynn Stoever (2016) that highlights the risks of appropriation, colonial violence, and misunderstanding that accompany remix, and I want my students to be aware of these issues. When they sample and remix, I want students to be thinking about community (Banks, 2011), and I want them to be thinking about care (Persaud, 2018). I want my courses to be subpublics that cocreate knowledge through play and invention, and that requires students to think about their compositional practices and how these practices affect others.

Assignment Prompt (2015)

For this assignment, you will create a 3-minute audio track in the style of either Paul Lansky's *Notjustmoreidlechatter*, which mixes up voices to create concept art; Fatboy Slim's "Praise You," which samples and manipulates music to create a dance track; or Public Enemy's "Fight the Power," the introduction to which functions as a sonic collage expressing the group's political beliefs and shared cultural background. After you have created the piece, post it online (using Google Drive or a similar cloud storage platform) and comment on the class blog with both a link to the audio file (either MP3 or OGG) and a link to an MLA works cited page of the samples you used. To receive full credit for this assignment, you must use at least ten samples and four audio manipulation effects.

Some resources you might find useful for completing this assignment:

- Audio-Editing Software
- A YouTube-to-MP3 Converter

Assignment Prompt (2017)

This assignment asks you to research a musical genre and create an audio history that describes how it has changed through time by creating an audio track composed of short samples from different iconic, important, interesting, or essential songs from within that genre. You can add more depth to your audio history by layering tracks, looping tracks, applying effects, or adding non-musical audio samples that are evocative of the various time periods and important figures associated with the history you are creating.

To successfully complete this assignment, you must use at least 15 different audio samples and three different effects. You can create your audio history manually or digitally, but I must be able to access the final product via computer. Feel free to use whatever sound-editing technology you are comfortable with.

To submit the audio history, please save it to a cloud storage platform (I suggest Google Drive), make the file accessible to the public, and post a shareable link to the class blog in two weeks.

Sample Student Projects

1. "Trump Trap Mix" by Abby: In this mix, Abby provides a critique of Donald Trump and his then current Republican primary campaign. As a traditional conservative who also values diversity and inclusivity, Abby was baffled and upset by how Trump's hateful rhetoric was bringing him success in the polls. This anger and confusion are most clearly present in Abby's use of the Blind

Witness sample that screams, "What the fuck is going on?" Overall, Abby's critique is much more nuanced and subtle than this lyric. The track begins with *The Twilight Zone* theme song and ends with applause and game show music that express the ways in which the campaign capitalized on entertainment. The use of screaming fans, Kanye West lyrics, and Lil Wayne hooks are juxtaposed to quotes demonstrating Trump's ignorance and vitriol in order to elucidate how Trump uses American society's infatuation with celebrity culture and excess in order to compensate for his deficiencies as a politician. What emerges from this remix is a portrait of Trump as a showman who uses fanfare, excitement, and humor to deflect from his ignorance and bigotry.[1]

2. "Sonic Collage" by Anthony: The background of Anthony's "Sonic Collage" is Gary Jules and Michael Andrews's soft and melancholy song "Mad World," and the foreground is a series of quotes responding to the increasing influence of evangelical Christianity within United States law and policy. Each of the speakers advocates for secular governance grounded in data-based science, implying that decisions based on biblical teachings are not only misinformed but also cruel in that they lead to policies that are homophobic, misogynistic, oppressive, regressive, and reactionary. The highly emotional music and logical quotations work well together, with the former adding affect to the latter by highlighting the emotion in each speaker's embodied voice and the latter providing a sense of justification for the ennui of the former. This track invited important classroom discussion about both inclusivity (because the composition critiqued masculine power but failed to include women's voices) and audience interpretation (because several conservative students thought the composition was a lamentation on how liberal values in education were leading to the creation of ungodly governance in the United States rather than a critique of religion in government).

3. "Beyoncé Mess" by Logan: "Beyoncé Mess" was an appropriate track for Logan, whose work all semester had focused on Queen Bey's discography. This is a dance track composed solely of Beyoncé songs cut up, spliced, layered on top of one another, distorted, reworked, and remixed. The track lacks the type of consistent beat that generally defines the dance genre, but the author does an excellent job using backbeats to connect the different sections of the episodic to create some sense of cohesion. Similarly, Logan manages to create a few genuinely danceable moments where she briefly captures a groove, though whether those moments were created by Logan, the samples she was using, or the interactions between the two was actively debated in class. Surprisingly, this track opened up very little discussion about appropriation and citation because the class unequivocally agreed that it was a respectful homage to an artist Logan clearly admired.

---

1. Five student examples (audio files and descriptive transcripts) can be found on the book's companion website.

4. "Enlgish [sic] Assignment" by Megan: Megan's "Enlgish [sic] Assignment" begins simply as a series of samples from contemporary pop and dance songs lined up one behind the other, only really notable because of the rapidity of its transitions. However, the track soon becomes much more interesting as individual samples interrupt, layer over, and compete with one another for attention. Sound effects add to the maelstrom to create a disorienting experience that is only partially counteracted by the recurrence of several samples. Despite some musical motifs, the most coherent aspect of the track is its lyrical theme, with all the vocalists expressing cynical views of romantic love as they tepidly enter into new relationships. Students responded positively to Megan's track but were unable to express why, providing us with an opportunity to discuss the importance of affective and bodily responses to sound even if those responses are not "danceable" in the conventional sense of the term.

5. "English E. C." by Rachel: Rachel's "English E. C." plays the music of Ellie Goulding underneath quotes taken from interviews with Payton Head, the University of Missouri student body president who led protests leading to the resignation of University System President Tim Wolf in 2015, and Jonathan Butler, the student activist whose hunger strike initially sparked the protests that would unite students across the Mizzou campus, including the university's football team. Goulding's feminine voice is mournful, supportive, and uplifting under the voices of the two young Black men who are discussing the issues of systematic racism on their campus, the lack of institutional leadership, and their own actions to bring about a more equitable and just future. Several of my students who had been paying attention to the story on the news found this depiction of events illuminating because it invited them to empathize with the students in a way traditional media stories did not; however, the use of a white British female musician whose songs focus on romantic relationships combined with the heavy-handed editing of Black male voices did invite questions of appropriation and cultural stereotyping for some students already invested in the unfolding events.

Reflection

Figure 4.1. Visual collage created by the author, in the spirit of the soundwriting assignment discussed in this chapter.

[A funky electronic beat composed of The Avalanches' (2009) "Frontier Psychiatry"; I Monster's "Daydream in Blue" (Dharma Records, 2013); GRiZ's "Hard Times" (HeadyTunes.co, 2013); and Girl Talk's "Smash Your Head" (Negyxo, 2007).]

Ben Harley: I originally developed the digitally sampled audio assignment as part of a Writing about Popular Music class in which students created music blogs where they wrote reviews of albums that they chose based on their own personal branding.[2] Developing these music blogs invoked a rich rhetorical ecology that asked students to continually consider their voices, their topics, the voices and topics of other reviewers, the genre of the review, and the needs of their intended audiences in order to create new and impactful writing.

To help students with this work, the class read album reviews, rhetorical analyses of music, and cultural studies articles that served as models for student writing. In addition to these texts, the class read Mark Katz's (2010) book *Capturing Sound*, which explains the ways in which recording technologies throughout history have influenced the ways in which music is composed, performed, distributed, circulated, and listened to. I had hoped that Katz's book would provide students with a basic introduction to musicology, a few in-depth genre histories, and a way of considering music-making as a rhetorical act. I was not, however, expecting the book to change how students thought about their own writing by making direct connections between their compositional practices and those Katz ascribes to musicians. Ultimately, it was this connection between the composing practices of musicians and those of alphabetic writers that became the primary value of Katz's book within the class. This was particularly true in regards to our discussion of engaging and integrating source material.

In Chapter Seven of the book, Katz claims,

> **Mark Katz:** "the roots of digital sampling reach back more than a millennium" (2010, p. 148)

[Josquin Des Prez's "Missa L'Homme Armé Sexti Toni 5. Agnus Dei" (micrologus2, 2009), an ecclesiastic chant.]

Ben: —and he cites medieval chants, Renaissance masses, and the allusive practices of classical composers to demonstrate a long tradition of what he refers to as musical quoting. Katz claims that digital musical quoting is an extension of its analog predecessors with the primary difference being that the notational method of analog quoting cites a musical work whereas the splicing method of digital quoting cites a particular performance of a musical work.

[Clyde Stubblefield "Funky Drummer," a funky drum solo, plays over the chanting (Armando Drum Breaks, 2016).]

---

2. The audio version of Ben Harley's reflection can be found on the book's companion website.

Despite this important difference, both quoting practices involve taking aspects of previous compositions and manipulating them to create something new.

To explain what kinds of new things can be generated from the assembled fragments of digitized musical samples, Katz provides four examples:

1. The art piece that *[Paul Lansky* Notjustmoreidlechatter, *a disorienting jumble of speaking voices (Romański, 2013)]* **Katz:** "transforms the ordinary into the precious" (2010, p. 153) **Ben:** —and questions the border between sound, technology, and music in the example of Paul Lansky's *Notjustmoreidlechatter*;

2. the dance song with *[Fatboy Slim's (2010) "Praise You," a peppy dance song]* **Katz:** "a subtlety that rewards close listening" (2010, p. 156), **Ben:** while also opening up issues of creativity, identity, appropriation, and power in the example of Fatboy Slim's "Praise You";

3. the political hip-hop track that is *[Public Enemy "Fight the Power," a hip-hop song composed of densely layered samples (Channel ZERO, 2020)]* **Katz:** "dizzying, exhilarating, and tantalizing" (2010, p. 161), **Ben:** as it quotes, loops, celebrates, and participates in Black traditions of rhetoric, politics, and music in the example of Public Enemy's "Fight the Power"; and finally,

4. the music of hobbyists that *[The Freelance Hellraiser's "Stroke of Genius," a pop rock combination of Christina Aguilera's "Genie in Bottle" and The Strokes' "Hard to Explain" (Mazzarella, 2007)]* **Katz:** "exists outside the traditions, practices, and institutions we typically associate with composition" (2010, p. 172), **Ben:** while opening up questions of musicianship, participation, and community in the example of mashup artists such as The Freelance Hellraiser.

In his book, Katz provides generous readings of art objects within these four groups, but he does not shy away from the difficult questions they raise about appropriation, meaning, community, identity, creativity, and the responsibilities of composition. Each analysis demonstrates that sampling is both a valid form of engagement and a problematic practice.

The chapter ends with a discussion of how sampling is the art of transformation:

> **Katz:** "a rich and complex practice, one that challenges our notions of originality, of borrowing, of craft, and even of composition itself" (2010, p. 176).

Ben: Based on this statement, I asked students, who had already connected the quoting they did with the musical quoting Katz writes about, to discuss how sampling invites them to rethink how the composer should engage her sources; I received a wide variety of answers:

Paraphrase performed by Austin Davis: Source material needs to be attributed out of respect for the original author.

Paraphrase performed by Sandra Kolder: Source material is merely raw data to be manipulated to the whims of those who sample and quote it.

Paraphrase performed by Joe Eckman: Sampling is okay as long as the aggregated samples make something original.

Paraphrase performed by Elizabeth Harley: The concept of originality is itself a myth.

Paraphrase performed by Regina Wilkerson: Anything an author makes will inherently be original because no two people are the same.

Paraphrase performed by Emma Harley: Quotes need to build to something beyond the source material in order to be useful.

Paraphrase performed by Patricia Harley: Ethical sampling is not appropriation if it creates a conversation between the author, the sources, and the audience.

Ben: It was clear that investigating the similarities between sampling and quoting was helping students reconsider how they interact with sources, and I wondered if having hands-on practice with musical quoting might help them to think further about how they choose their sources, how sources can be manipulated, and the ways in which those manipulations have ramifications for the source, the source author, the quoting composer, the quoting composer's composition, and other external audiences. In other words, I wondered if providing students with an opportunity to engage in what Mark Amerika refers to as

Mark Amerika: "practice-based research"

Ben: would enable students to understand the subtleties of source engagement and the inherently social aspects of composition (quoted in CU Boulder Libraries, 2014). I hoped that digital audio sampling would help to teach how authors engage others socially through their writing practices. I hoped this experience would make clear the ways in which all writers are always relying on others to help them generate the perhaps-not-so-original ideas they coproduce.

[The Avalanches' (2009) "Frontier Psychiatry," a haunting, horn-heavy electronic song.]

By the time I had this idea, the course was underway. I had already outlined all the assignments, and it would have been unfair of me to require a new one. In response to this problem, I decided to offer students the opportunity to create a digitally sampled audio composition as extra credit. Because I wanted to see what students would produce, I offered a lot of extra credit. The instructions were vague:

> **Paraphrase performed by Marc Walls**: Create a 3-minute audio track that includes ten digital samples and four sound effects.

Ben: I assumed students might want an example, so I followed Katz's lead and instructed them to either create an art piece like Paul Lansky's *Notjustmore-idlechatter*,

> [Paul Lansky's Notjustmoreidlechatter, *a disorienting jumble of speaking voices (Romański, 2013).*]

a dance song like Fatboy Slim's "Praise You,"

> [Fatboy Slim's (2010)"Praise You," *a peppy dance song.*]

or a densely packed sonic collage like the first forty-five seconds of Public Enemy's "Fight the Power."

> [Public Enemy's "Fight the Power," *a hip-hop song composed of densely layered samples (Channel ZERO, 2020).*]

Students were quick to point out that the distinctions between the genres were blurry because each of the models were simultaneously art, music, and collage, and though I agreed with the critique, I kept the arbitrary taxonomy as a way to help students focus their energies towards aesthetics, affect, or critique.

Aside from the assignment prompt, I didn't provide much guidance on how to create these tracks and instead encouraged students to download the free sound-editing software Audacity and learn to use it through online instructions, tutorials, and message boards created either by the production team or by its community of users. I chose such a lax method of instruction not only because this was an extra-credit assignment that not everyone was doing but also because moving the onus of expertise from myself as the instructor to the organic intellectuals within Audacity's sound-editing community demonstrated another social aspect of writing: the creation, distribution, and circulation of instructional tools. Students not only found and used these kinds of resources, but they also shared them among each other, creating their own social learning community that extended beyond the borders of the physical and digital classroom environment I had designed for them.

On the day the assignment was due, I blocked off the entire 50-minute class for sharing and discussing the compositions. Though students were initially reticent to share their experiments with a new medium, presenting work in progress had become a regular part of the course, and I soon had volunteers. Some students shared social critiques—like Abby . . .

> [Abby's "Trump Trap Mix," *a combination a Lil Wayne's bass heavy*

rap track "A Milli" with Donald Trump saying, "I'm really rich," once normally and once with deep distortion.]

. . . Anthony . . .

[Anthony's "Sonic Collage," which combines Gary Jules's melancholy song "Mad World" with the celebrity scientist Bill Nye saying, "just a reflection of a deep scientific lack of understanding."]

. . . and Rachel.

[Rachel's "English E. C.," which combines Ellie Goulding's soft, pop-electronic track "Burn" with John Butler, the University of Missouri student who went on a hunger strike to protest the university's failure to handle racial harassment on campus, saying, "I had someone write the N-word on my wall."]

Some students shared dance tracks—like Megan . . .

[Megan's "Enlgish [Sic.] Assignment," a rather cut-up and aggressive electronic song.]

. . . and Logan.

[Logan's "Beyoncé Mess," which combines Beyoncé angrily saying, "Where the hell you at?" from "Jealous" with the soft and melodic music from "Pretty Hurts."]

No one created something they were comfortable referring to as art, but many had expanded beyond the prompt to create narratives, hype tracks, and experiments.

All of the compositions my students produced sparked conversations between authors and listeners about the composing process, the affective dimension of sound, the politics of citation, and how to ethically create something using borrowed material. Overall, the assignment went well. Students gained nuanced understandings of source engagement through practice, they raised important questions about appropriation and subjectivity, they felt empowered by having taught themselves to compose in a new medium and genre, they came to understand writing as a social process that affects other humans in specific ways, and they had a lot of fun doing it.

The next year, I tried adding more structure to the assignment and giving it to another Writing about Popular Music class that had not read the Katz book. Specifically, I asked these new students to gather samples and create audio histories of a genre they were planning on writing about. In hindsight, I think the combination of the strict parameters and the grading encouraged students to take less risks than the previous group. For instance, I asked students to learn Audacity for themselves again, but they asked me to give a lecture. I asked students to remix and reimagine genre histories, but they chose to organize their tracks linearly.

These second-generation compositions pale in comparison to their first-generation counterparts, and when I give this assignment again, I will make sure to include the Mark Katz reading, abandon any rigid guidelines, and keep the emphasis on creative source use.

Thank you.

[Goblins from Mars's (2017) "Super Mario—Overworld Theme (GFM Remix)."]

Copyright Statement

In "The Sonic Collage Assignment: Aesthetics, Affect, and Critique in Audio Sampling," I use clips from 14 audio works and eight visual images that are protected by U.S. copyright law. However, I believe I have a fair use defense to use all of these works without permission for these reasons:

1. The purpose and character of my use is for these clips to be part of my scholarly project, which transforms their character from the purpose for which their creator originally made them. Six of the audio files and all of images are used to give voice to works that are alluded to either explicitly or implicitly in texts from which I have taught and on which my assignment is based. The other eight samples are famous examples of remix culture that explain the types of composition practices I am discussing. Further, I intentionally pulled all of the audio samples from YouTube, many of which were posted by someone other than the copyright holder in order to demonstrate the ease with which remixes can be made and to inhabit the composition practices I am discussing. Similarly, I pulled all of the images directly from Google image searches, pulling images from sites that mostly also did not own the original copyright. This practice, made salient by the messy citations, makes clear the regularity with which works are incorporated and remixed into new compositions.

2. The nature of the copyrighted pieces is musical and visual.

3. I only used a small amount of each clip, usually played softly in the background. Further, when possible in the context of my argument, I used clips that did not represent the core, most substantial part of the original copyrighted work. Similarly, I never used the whole of any visual image. Instead of privileging any image, my header demonstrates the variety of the texts being remixed and the ways in which they both enhance and obscure one another.

4. As an audio clip repurposed for purposes of teaching and scholarship, there is no chance that my use will infringe on the potential market for

these copyrighted works. To encourage others to understand the networks in which these samples exist, I include full citation information that others can follow if they want to hear the full works that I sample.

References

Armando Drum Breaks. (2016, July 18). James Brown—Funky drummer (drum break—loop) [Video file]. *YouTube*. https://youtu.be/jOCNmimkFTs.

The Avalanches. (2009, November 30). The Avalanches—Frontier psychiatrist (official video) [Video file]. *YouTube*. https://youtu.be/eS3AZ12xf6s.

Banks, A. J. (2011). *Digital griots: African American rhetoric in a multimedia age.* Southern Illinois University Press.

Bessette, J. (2016). Audio, archives, and the affordance of listening in a pedagogy of "difference." *Computers and Composition, 39*, 71–82. https://doi.org/10.1016/j .compcom.2015.11.004.

Colton, J. S. (2016). Revisiting digital sampling rhetorics with an ethics of care. *Computers and Composition, 40*, 19–31. https://doi.org/10.1016/j.compcom.2016 .03.006.

CU Boulder Libraries. (2014, June 3). Mark Amerika: Practice-based research in the digital arts and humanities [Video file]. *YouTube*. https://youtu.be/BoK76 vICVC8.

Channel ZERO. (2020, July 2). Public Enemy—Fight the power [Video file]. *YouTube*. https://youtu.be/mmo3HFa2vjg.

Dharma Records. (2013, March 3). I MONSTER—Daydream in blue [Video file]. *YouTube*. https://youtu.be/BhB6Lb7_kN8.

Fatboy Slim. (1998). *Praise you (vinyl)* [Album art]. https://www.discogs.com/Fatboy -Slim-Praise-You/release/524351.

Fatboy Slim. (2010, March 21). Fatboy Slim—Praise you [official video] [Video file]. *YouTube*. https://youtu.be/ruAi4VBoBSM.

Goblins from Mars. (2017, August 25). Super Mario—Overworld theme (GFM trap remix) [Video file]. *YouTube*. https://youtu.be/-GNMe6kFojo.

Harley, B. (2016, December 7). Syllabus and calendar [Screen shot]. Researching and writing about popular music: The official class blog for ENGL 102-A81 spring 2017 University of South Carolina. Retrieved September 23, 2018, from http:// engl102a81.blogspot.com/2016/12/syllabus-and-calendar_7.html.

Harris, M. (2019, December 13). *Audacity-save-to-mp3* [Image]. How to convert WAV to MP3 using LAME. *Lifewire*. https://www.lifewire.com/audacity-tutorial -how-to-convert-wav-to-mp3-using-lame-2438749.

HeadyTunes.co. (2013, October 14). GRiZ—Hard times [Video file]. *YouTube*. https://youtu.be/ouOrw8zDYns.

Hill, H. (2021, August 7). *Sound wave free download* [Illustration]. FreePNGimg. com. https://freepngimg.com/png/27504-sound-wave-free-download.

James Brown—Funky drummer (vinyl) [Album art]. (1970). https://www.discogs .com/James-Brown-Funky-Drummer/release/4490154.

Katz, M. (2010). *Capturing sound: How technology has changed music.* University of California Press.

L'homme arme agnus dei [Image]. (1502). Wikipedia. https://en.wikipedia.org/wiki/Missa_L%27homme_arm%C3%A9_super_voces_musicales#/media/File:L%27homme_arme_agnus_dei.jpg.

Mazzarella, B. (2007, September 18). The Strokes vs. Christian Aguilera—A stroke of genie-us. [Video file]. *YouTube.* https://youtu.be/ShPPbT3svAw.

micrologus2. (2009, July 25). Josquin Des Prez: Missa l'homme armé sexti toni 5. Agnus Dei [Video file]. *YouTube.* https://youtu.be/7yEZwpANUOo.

Negyxo. (2007, November 27). Girl Talk—Smash your head [Video file]. *YouTube.* https://youtu.be/iDDdpxEf9hM.

Persaud, C. (Host). (2018, May 16). Imagining otherwise: Tina Campt on listening to images [Audio podcast episode]. In *Ideas on Fire.* https://ideasonfire.net/63-tina-campt/.

[Photograph of Mark Katz, Ph.D.]. (n.d.). Mark Katz, Ph.D. Retrieved January 18, 2015, from https://expertfile.com/experts/mark.katzphd.

Public Enemy—Fear of a Black planet [Album art]. https://genius.com/Public-enemy-fear-of-a-black-planet-lyrics.

Robinson, D. (2020). *Hungry listening: Resonant theory for Indigenous sound studies.* University of Minnesota Press.

Romański, J. (2013, February 22). Notjustmoreidlechatter by Paul Lansky [Video file]. *YouTube.* https://youtu.be/HYvCkfLjQFQ.

Russell, P. C. (1992). [Painting album art for Paul Lansky's CD Homebrew]. https://bridgerecords.com/products/9035.

Stoever, J. L. (2016). *The sonic color line: Race and the cultural politics of listening.* New York University Press.

sweatybeard. (2013, May 16). You're a nut!!! You're crazy in the coconut! *Imgur.* https://imgur.com/gallery/SQYbMTF.

Walls, M. (2018). *Ben 29(2)* [Photograph].

Chapter 5. Disabling Soundwriting: Sonic Rhetorics Meet Disability Pedagogy

Chad Iwertz Duffy

PEPPERDINE UNIVERSITY

Transcript writing *is* soundwriting. Caption writing *is* soundwriting. This is what I impress upon my students when I teach audio composition in digital media composing courses. The materials in this chapter take that claim seriously and work toward imagining what it means to *disable* soundwriting.

I do not use the term *disabling* to mean a lack or deficiency—as it has historically been used as an adjective such as in "she has a disabling condition." Instead, I mean to use *disabling* as a transitive verb, a strategic and intentional method for taking pride in productively disabling something else, centering disability experience in the creation of audio. *Disabling* soundwriting means making audio more accessible while simultaneously drawing attention to the ways it can and has been used to exclude disabled audiences from soundwriting processes and products. It means breaking down the oppressive structures that have removed disabled people from the soundwriting process and rebuilding sonic rhetorics and digital media pedagogy to not only offer ways for including disabled experience—but also to celebrate and accept disabled ways of soundwriting as a gain to the digital media composing process.

The assignments, examples, reflection, and readings shared in this chapter work to move students and instructors in digital media composing courses closer to *disabling* their soundwriting. They are designed to be presented over the course of at least a five-week unit on soundwriting in an introductory digital media composing course. The suggested readings are included to help supplement the technical soundwriting texts or samples an instructor may use in their course in order to help the class prioritize transcribing or captioning as a central, rhetorical element of the soundwriting process. They can be used to "add on" a disability unit in any digital composing course, but they work best if disability and *disabling*, as a method for soundwriting, are highlighted and prioritized throughout the unit. The point of the sequence of assignments—which include a Soundscape Remix Assignment and a Final Sound Project—is to both offer students space to practice soundwriting, supporting the use of tools and skills in the technical production of sound, and offer students time to interrogate and explore soundwriting from different angles, prioritizing diverse experiences with sound by transmediating soundwriting across aural and textual environments.

The objective of the first assignment—the Soundscape Remix—is to introduce students to soundwriting, the ethics of remix culture, and the technical

DOI: https://doi.org/10.37514/PRA-B.2022.1688.2.05

skills used in producing soundwriting. In class, we consider current and historical implications and examples of sound remix culture and question its ethical use and relationship to cultural appropriation. From these discussions, students begin exploring and producing a remix of their choosing as a way to practice soundwriting skills, generic conventions of citing audio, and developing an artist statement. I like this assignment because it allows students to jump into soundwriting without having a strong catalog of originally produced materials from the start. They can begin thinking globally about the rhetoric of soundwriting without getting too bogged down at the start with the lengthy process of collecting and producing their own assets.

The final unit assignment—the Final Sound Project—builds upon the remix assignment by then focusing on the objective of disabling soundwriting. In class, we reflect on the Soundscape Remix and the stories students worked to achieve with their remixes. We then work to break these open—analyzing the messages these and other soundwritings tell to specific, as well as exclusionary, audiences. Working with the texts like those included as suggested readings in this chapter, the class shifts to consider how soundwriting might be rebuilt with access and disability in mind. Then, working primarily from material recorded or produced on their own, students craft their Final Sound Projects.

I like this assignment because inevitably we come to a point in class when someone asks, "Who is responsible for making soundwriting accessible?" I like to expand on that question to ask, "What affordances do producers of soundwriting have when making their work accessible?" Because producers of soundwriting are so often *not* asked to make their work accessible, I flip this question to make students consider what is lost when access is not situated as an essential part of the soundwriting process. Whose experience gets to count when soundwriting? And who gets to have access to the stories and messages—the rich rhetorical environments—that soundwriting creates?

I ground a conversation on disabling soundwriting as one that is fundamentally about centering disability in the production of soundwriting, and I use these assignments to highlight that message. Because captioning and transcribing are as rhetorical and complex as the other elements of soundwriting, producers of sound should likewise be prepared to transmediate the emotion and messages of their sounds into text. Not only because it's the right thing to do. But also because teaching students to produce sound without teaching them how to transcribe or caption can miss the forest for the trees. It's not only that students can produce compelling stories and arguments through sound, but also that they can articulate why and how those stories and arguments work. Effective captions convey both the heard elements of a sound and are crafted in such a way as to convey an effect as well. When captions and sounds support each other, that is truly effective soundwriting.

A quick note on how I use the terms *captioning* and *transcribing*: In my research, which investigates the composing practices of disability service speech-to-text writers, I tend to find professionals use the term *transcript* to mean something that works toward a different rhetorical goal than the sound(s) it translates. A transcript, for example, is usually crafted to be experienced separately from the context in which the sounds it translates are originally performed. A *caption*, by contrast, articulates the pressing need to perform sounds and alphabetic text together in real time. Because I view them as integral to the kind of soundwriting I teach, I use the term *captions* here and with my students to impress a political orientation toward the relationship that exists between sounds and captions which support each other toward a shared rhetorical goal.

Assignments and Assignment Sequence

The following material is introduced over a five-week unit on soundwriting. I start the unit with a mix of theoretical discussion of soundwriting with instruction in the practical use of an audio editor. I demo a couple different tools, like Audacity (because it's free) and GarageBand (because my department has access to iPads that students can check out without paying for the hardware or software), but the assignments are adaptable to a range of scenarios in which students can use any audio creation and editing tools to compose aurally. For departments without access to these resources, for example, the assignment could be adjusted to have students use smart phones and the app Anchor.

The first assignment, the Soundscape Remix, is due in week 3 of the unit. A draft of the Sound Project is due in week 4, and the final Sound Project is due in week 5. Readings, instruction in soundwriting software, and discussion of captioning are interspersed with studio hours that allow students to work on their projects in class. I have provided some suggested readings in the chapter's appendix.

Soundscape Remix Assignment

The Soundscape Remix is a project in which you will demonstrate your developing skill in editing audio using Audacity. For full points for the project, you will clip, layer, trim, amplify, and/or otherwise alter in some meaningful way one found or existing sound. This "found or existing sound" could be a song, podcast clip, speech, announcement, or any other existing aural artifact.

Submit your project as a finished MP3, WAV, or AAC file, not an AUD file or other software-specific file type that requires use of sound-editing software to open. An overview of exporting files to MP3 in Audacity, as well as links to downloading the LAME file required to do so, are available in the online Audacity manual.

With your uploaded remixed sound file, also include a very brief (at least 100 words, though more if you choose) artist statement that explains the changes you made to your soundscape and why you were interested in making these changes or what effect you feel the added changes has on the original sound.

You will also use your artist statement to appropriately cite the source(s) you've used in your remix.

Sound Project Assignment

For this project, you will draw upon your skills and understanding of composing with sound to answer the question: "What digitally created sound do I need to make?" This differs from the question of what you want to make in that it asks you to apply your developing skills in digital media production to a current topic or issue of importance to you and/or the communities of which you are a part. This project will have you seek out, with the aid of the journal of audio and visual assets you have been keeping all semester, elements of your surroundings that you want to explore in more depth through the remixing, editing, and creation of digital sound. You may choose, but do not need, to use this project to extend or transmediate other projects completed in this class, including the Soundscape Remix.

Directions

For this project, you will submit three items:

- your digitally created sound,
- captions/a transcript for your sound, and
- an accompanying artist statement of 100–250 words.

Your digital sound may be a single created sound production, an extended remixed work, or a collection of sound productions that connect in some meaningful way. Submit your sound(s) as MP3, WAV, MIDI, or AAC files.

Your artist statement should address how you approached the question of what digitally created sound you needed to make, what tools you used to create and edit your sound production, and what decisions related to sonic rhetoric you explored and employed when crafting your sound. In other words, your artist statement will act as your description of what you hoped to achieve with the creation of your sound and what elements of your process and crafting of your sound help you to achieve it. Some sample artist statements (and some guidelines you may find helpful) can be found on this list of eight sample artist statements.

Your transcript, on the other hand, should be viewed as an extension of your sound production and a translation of it as an aural production into captions. As the composer of your sound(s), you are especially empowered to craft a transmediation of your work that is as artistic, factual, or experimental as your aural sound(s). The goal of transcription is to translate the aural, hearing setting of a production into a visual, textual environment in order to make it more accessible to people who would otherwise have little to no access to it. Its goal is not necessarily to capture in detail all of the elements of a soundscape but rather to bring attention to the important or salient rhetorical and narrative moves of a soundscape, what makes it interesting, what's important about it, and/or what it conveys. Some additional tips for transcription, as well as some examples, can be found on this starter kit for creating captions.

Sample Student Projects

1. Untitled Project by Courtney Anderson: In this first example, Courtney Anderson explores creating music and creatively captioning her produced sounds.[1]
2. "Welcome to OSU" by Joe Matts: Joe Matts similarly explores tools for music creation, setting a different mood and exploring diverse ways to caption those sounds.
3. Untitled Project by Bryant Cauley. In this next example, Bryant Cauley explores mixing together sound effects to simulate the sounds of drinking while driving.
4. "Virginia Woolf as an EDM Song" by Kristen Cerne: Kristen Cerne explores vocal manipulation tools to convey a new take on a classic poem.
5. "Dayton" by Cat Dotson: Cat Dotson shares her literacy narrative, focusing on the power of her own voice in both the audio and transcript. The narrative was created as part of a larger project focusing on her experiences growing up and living in Dayton, Ohio.
6. Untitled Project by Carmen Greiner: Finally, Carmen Greiner creates a powerful mashup of vocal performance and spoken word commemorating Black lives lost to police brutality.

Reflection

[Introduction sounds of voices echoing in a classroom. It's difficult to pick out what anyone is saying, as if the cacophony of sounds is heard while walking down a hallway, and the classroom is only just heard while passing by. Suddenly, a voice carries over the others while the room quiets down. It speaks: "Morning, everyone. Happy Tuesday. Our main objective for today is to talk more about your sound projects and mixing audio layers." The sound fades out as it leads into main narration.]

Chad Iwertz Duffy: These are the sounds of my class. I'm Chad Iwertz Duffy, and that was me teaching at Ohio State, where I completed my Ph.D. in rhetoric, composition, and literacy.[2] I study the rhetoric of transcription, the composing practices of disability service transcribers, and I bring that background into the assignment I'm giving students in that audio clip and that I've shared with you in this chapter. That assignment is all about getting my students to think about

---

1. Six student examples (audio files and descriptive transcripts) can be found on the book's companion website.

2. The audio version of Chad Iwertz Duffy's reflection can be found on the book's companion website.

how captioning is a deeply rhetorical and artistic process. Just like soundwriting is. Crafting captions is also about creating access to multimodal work, and the assignment I give students teaches access in a way that I hope helps students see that accessible captions are complex and beautiful—kind of like their audio projects. Captions have an aesthetic of their own, and I want to stress that it's important for composers of audio to participate in the process of crafting captions. Because they know best what the purpose, audience, meaning, and significance of that audio is—and captions need that kind of expertise to influence their creation, too.

I first assigned the audio project in a digital media composing class. I had previously had a couple years of experience working for Ohio State University's Digital Media Project and Digital Media and Composition Institute. In those positions, I taught a lot of Audacity. A lot of Audacity. But I noticed that a lot of the complex multimodal composing processes that I'd teach using Audacity were ones that were not always easy to translate into a caption. How might you caption the following audio, for example?

[A student sample is played. The student wrote these captions as follows.]

Virginia Woolf as an EDM Song

Clear, distant voice: And then the body, who had been silent up to now, began its song almost at first as low as the rush of the wheels.

[Drumbeat begins.]

Deep voice: Eggs and bacon toast and tea

High-pitched voice: And red currant jelly

Deep voice: Eggs and bacon toast and tea

Clear voice with slight echo: With coffee to follow with coffee to follow

[Second drumbeat is added.]

Fuzzy voice: Fire and a bath fire and a bath

Deep voice: Eggs and bacon toast and tea

High-pitched voice: And red currant jelly

Fuzzy voice: Fire and a bath Fire and a bath

High-pitched voice: And red currant jelly

Deep voice: Eggs and bacon toast and tea

Echoed voice: And then to bed

[Both drumbeats end.]

Clear, distant voice: And the rest of the journey was performed in the delicious society of my own body.

There are layered tracks here, sounds and distortions that need representation, changes in pitch and tempo, echo—overall what feels to me to be a playfulness in expression that just wouldn't come across without similarly creative captions. The audio is dynamic. Doesn't it also seem like it should have dynamically written or expressed captions?

I wanted to focus my assignment on that process of writing captions as dynamic. You might be thinking at this point, "Well, aren't captions all written the same way? There are standards for writing captions that can be taught and standardized and regulated." And that's true—there are several standardized methods for writing quality captions. And that has an important purpose. Regulating methods and methodologies for writing captions (which I study in depth in my dissertation—*[an almost humorous echo effect is added for the following phrase:]* coming out soon!—can ensure that disabled people who depend on captions for access in otherwise inaccessible environments (including audio-rich or complex environments) receive a quality of access that can be the difference between inclusion and exclusion. And that's important.

But I want to play around in this assignment with imagining not just what disability inclusion would look like when captions are provided by a service provider. I want composers of audio to accept disability as a gain to their composing process. What story is being told with their audio? What arguments are they making? What does that soundwriting do? Captions shouldn't just be routes to access the "true" (and I'm using air quotes there) soundwriting artifact. They can also be used to translate and participate in those quintessential soundwriting questions as well. Multimodal means many, varied ways of effectively communicating. Sound is one mode, and captioning is another. Both are valid in this assignment as multimodal ways of composing soundwriting. That's right—captioning *is* soundwriting. I want students to take that seriously and consider—both theoretically and practically—what composing captions can mean to the rhetorical and artistic processes of composing with sound.

So this assignment is a place to start on that big quest of having students use captions to center and pride disability as part of their effective soundwriting practice. Some scholars, like M. Remi Yergeau (2014), Amy Vidali (2015), and Elizabeth Brewer (2016) might call this practice *disabling*.

[A new voice is heard, slightly distorted from its recording in a large lecture space.]

M. Remi Yergeau: So I want to disable all things, but I want us to really consider to whom are we writing, for whom are we coding and tagging and passing legislation, and where are the disabled people? (Yergeau, 2014)

Chad: That's Yergeau giving a keynote at the 2014 Computers and Writing conference in Pullman, Washington. The presentation is called "Disable All the Things," and in that talk Yergeau argues that, taking a *[Yergeau's voice is layered into the following, which is also spoken by Chad]* "cue from Mia Mingus, disabling all the things involves toppling myriad oppressive structures. It involves more than retrofitting, or applying metaphorical band-aids. It involves catapulting like a velociraptor through a Lego tower. Knock all that shit over, and then maybe melt it in your backyard with a blowtorch" (Yergeau, 2014).

As I continue to teach captioning and access in digital media classes and assign projects like the ones I'm sharing with you, I want to emphasize—maybe even more—captioning as a way of world building and world destroying. Captions have often been situated as a way to build bridges to original content. They're retroffited onto existing soundwriting to make them more accessible. But I want my students to use them like Yergeau imagines a dinosaur in the backyard. How can captions explode a composer's soundwriting? How can they draw out what's important about composing with sound and be the center of our attention—be made so important and participatory to the product that they are essential—not retrofitted—in the composing process?

I don't know if my assignment does all that yet, and actually I'm pretty sure it doesn't yet. But I think it's starting to get close, especially in how is forces student composers to think about artist statements and captions differently. Some of what I've argued for here may be important to include in an artist statement, but I think it's essential to distinguish the two. I encourage students to see artist statements as describing what they hoped to achieve with the creation of their soundwriting and what elements of their process helped them achieve it. Captions, on the other hand, should be viewed as an extension and participation in the effectiveness of their sound production—a way of translating or transmediating (and not just describing) their work that is as artistic, factual, or experimental as the audio portion of their soundwriting.

[Light, airy music begins to play, which signals the reflection is coming to an end (JekK, 2014).]

So that is one way I'm intervening into this larger conversation with this assignment. I hope that it may be helpful to you as you continue to intervene with me more.

[Music continues for a few second, and then fades out.]

Acknowledgment

JekK's (2014) "First" was used with a license purchased through Jamendo.

References

Brewer, E. (2016, July 14–17). Interdisciplinary ways to move: Enabling, disabling, and cripping writing program administration [Paper presentation]. Council of Writing Program Administrators Conference, Raleigh, NC, United States.

JekK. (2014). First [Song]. On *Dear dreams*. https://www.jamendo.com/track/1157362/first.

Vidali, A. (2015). Disabling writing program administration. *WPA: Writing Program Administration, 38*(2), 32–55. http://associationdatabase.co/archives/38n2/38n2vidali.pdf .

Yergeau, M. R. (2014, June 5–8). Disable all the things [Video] [Paper presentation]. Computers and Writing Conference, Pullman, WA, United States. https://vimeo.com/97721996.

Appendix: Some Suggested Readings

Brueggemann, B. J. (2013). *Articulating betweenity: Literacy, language, identity, and technology in the deaf/hard-of-hearing collection*. In H. L. Ulman, S. L. DeWitt & C. L. Selfe (Eds.), *Stories that speak to us: Exhibits from the Digital Archives of Literacy Narratives*. Computers and Composition Digital Press. http://ccdigitalpress.org/book/stories/brueggemann.html.

Corners, B. (2015). Verbatim vs. non-verbatim transcription: What is the difference? *Transcribe*. https://www.transcribe.com/verbatim-vs-non-verbatim-transcription-what-is-the-difference/.

Iwertz, C. & Osario, R. (2016). Composing captions: A starter kit for accessible media. *Peitho, 19*(1). http://cwshrc.org/actionhour2016/osorio.html.

Hitt, A. & Rosinksi, J. (Hosts). (2015, April 25). Transcription//translation [Audio podcast episode]. In *This rhetorical life*. http://thisrhetoricallife.syr.edu/episode-28-transcription-translation/.

Zdenek, S. (2011). Which sounds are significant? Towards a rhetoric of closed captioning. *Disability Studies Quarterly, 31*(3). http://dsq-sds.org/article/view/1667/1604.

Chapter 6. SoundPlay: A Sonic Experience of Digital Loose Parts

Scott Lunsford

JAMES MADISON UNIVERSITY

This project captures in part a sequence of two assignments exploring childhood play in a first-year writing course. The first assignment, Play Narrative, asked students to follow an object, place, or experience of play they could deeply describe and re-enact through text. The second assignment, Digital Loose Parts (DLP) Soundscape, challenged teams of three students to bring their play narratives together in a sonic experience, discovering connections among their words and ideas to develop an audio project.

Context: Playing with (Digital) Loose Parts

Creativity, said play theorist Simon Nicholson (1972), is "the playing around with the components and variables of the world in order to make experiments and discover new things and form new concepts" (p. 5). He calls these variables "loose parts": "In any environment, both the degree of inventiveness and creativity, and the possibility of discovery, are directly proportional to the number and kind of variables in it" (p. 6). Environmental psychologist Leanne Rivlin (2007) added that "these are elements within a site that are amenable to manipulation and change" as well as having "the potential to lead to creativity and discovery" (p. 40).

Through this series of assignments, I played with these notions of loose parts and amenable sites to ask students to construct their own Digital Loose Parts (DLP) Soundscape, the second assignment in a series of explorations into childhood play. The first assignment in the series asked students to individually write a narrative about a single play ecology. Three of these first-person essays explore a backyard trampoline, a tennis court, and a forest stream—each featured in the companion website for this book.

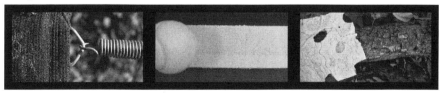

Figure 6.1. A trampoline spring, a tennis ball, and a forest scene

For the DLP Soundscape, students worked together to find connections among ideas in their narratives—loose parts themselves. For example, would students find connections in their relationships to their play environments (like the back-yard trampoline, the school tennis court, a home's neighboring forest)? Would they find connections in sound, like to trampoline springs, tennis ball bounces, and leaves crunching underfoot? Might these sounds come together at any point to create a single soundscape? Students then remediated those combined narratives and other loose parts into a single audio project by revising through sound they recorded themselves or found online, invoking audio research from NPR as well as having other voices record additional source material, and including appropriate music.

Rationale: PlayWriting

Reconciling my life as a parent-scholar has encouraged me to look at the ways my own children learn literacies through play. Much of their earliest literacy practices began on the walls of their bedroom, as they scribbled representative images, such as a "circus" (see Fig. 6.2) and, eventually, communicative, rhetorical symbols (see Fig. 6.3).

Allowing my children to play along the walls of their bedroom seemingly permitted them to do so through the rest of the house: on walls, on furniture, on themselves.

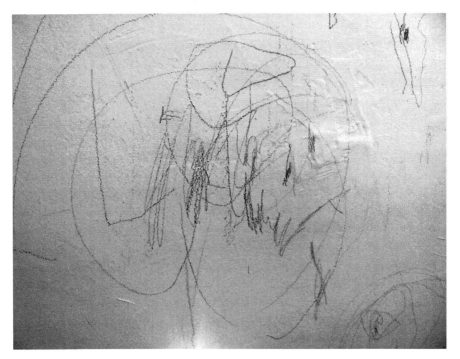

Figure 6.2. My daughter's drawing of a "circus." Photo by author.

*Figure 6.3. My daughter's recording of her own height
on her bedroom wall. Photo by author.*

Now playing as a parent-scholar, my own digital scholarship and teaching answered a call from Bre Garrett, Denise Landrum-Geyer, and Jason Palmeri (2012). I saw the DLP project as a way for students to engage creative juxtaposition:

> Composing is a process of making connections, rearranging materials (words, images, concepts) in unexpected ways. The first words, images, and concepts that come to our minds are often the most obvious/the most expected/the most banal. Thus, if we wish to be creative, we can benefit greatly by gathering a wide array of disparate materials and then taking the time to experiment with combining and re-arranging these materials in novel ways. (Garrett et al., 2012, Act I, Scene 1 section, para. 1, citing Hogan, 2003)

I saw disparate materials manifesting themselves as a way to understand the nature of embodied knowledge and rhetoric. My single body as a scholar and teacher is certainly made up of disparate materials themselves, and, following Garrett et al., we must re-member these kinds of embodied interactions. That is, even as researchers and teachers, we must remember that we are bodies, that our/selves inherently engage with ecologies of other bodies—in classrooms, within institutions, with colleagues and, of course, with students: "We tend to erase the body despite its corporeal presence, and we must re-remember that such erasures are not neutrally enacted, but that the body is always already a politicized identity-space" (Garrett et al., 2012, Act 1, Scene 2 section, para. 4). Students will be very aware of their own voices—*hating to hear* their own voices, they say, but not hating their own voices in the long run.

With re-membering our voices in a digital mode, we should also consider the fact that multimodality extends past the digital, re-membering the body as a mode of analog sound production itself. If, for example, classes of students are unable to use sound recording equipment, the assignment below can easily be reframed for live performance, bringing in materials that would create the sounds live or using their own bodies to create the sounds. This approach, then, would also give student musicians the chance to play along.

The playful nature of such projects should encourage us to see how play is inherently inclusive. A part of my own audio reflection heard later in this chapter is set in a universal-designed playground, where kids of all abilities can play. But in a classroom-sandbox of playing with sound, how do we—and more specifically, the following assignment—invite those who are Deaf and hard of hearing to play as well? Looking through the lens of loose parts, consider the pieces of sound and its synesthetic materiality: the feel of reverberations, the peaks and valleys of sound waves, the colors of three-dimensional sonograms. Can, for example, the aforementioned re-envisioned sound assignment for a live classroom performance benefit those who rely on feeling reverberations? Can those students work together to perform sounds that reverberate across a table where all students can feel the sounds as well as hear them? Embodied knowledge and rhetorics play a part in these scenarios as well, drawing together questions that all bodies experience: Though our bodies are made up of rather tight parts, how can we loosen them to demonstrate their potential in composing in different ways? How can we see the body as one more part negotiating and traveling and reverberating among seemingly other disparate bodies—other parts—coming together to make new meaning?

Assignment Prompts

Play Narrative

In this short paper, you'll explore play through an event/object(s)/journey that you've experienced as a child. We'll use Lindsey Campbell's (2015–16) "Ek Stasis" as a model for your own, even though you may have a different approach, style, and experience that will influence your narrative. We will conduct a number of workshops through this process, so don't worry that the following guidelines are minimal.

Think about your purpose: Why write about this experience? Why is this a good story to tell—out all the stories you have to tell? What do you want your audience to walk away thinking or feeling or doing? It isn't important to explicitly address the purpose in your paper, but we should be able to say by the end of it, "I got it."

Who's your audience? Is it a general reader? Or do you have a group of people in mind? Who might benefit from your story? Don't write as if you're responding to an assignment. Don't assume I know what you're talking about.

Give your story a good title—not "Play Narrative." At least 750 words.

Criteria

The instructions for this assignment are purposefully vague to allow you to discover your own topics and directions. But there are some elements that you'll want to demonstrate:

Tell a compelling story that has a clear point/purpose. ____/60 pts.

Is it clear that you are invested in your own story, providing detail about the play event. Don't simply tell us you had an experience—show us how the experience played out (so to speak).

Use appropriate style and conventions. ____/30 pts.

You should demonstrate appropriate rhetorical choices in style—such as present tense—grammar, punctuation, and organization.

Share insight. ____/8 pts.

This is the infamous So what? question. Show that you've gotten something out of your experience. I do not, however, want to see conclusions that go like this: "What I learned from this experience was . . ." or anything remotely like that.

Total ____/98 pts.

Digital Loose Parts (DLP) Soundscape

The purpose of this project is to encourage you to make and articulate connections among

- some of the ideas you and your classmates wrote about in the first major assignment, the play narrative;
- external research you conduct through the library databases or Google Scholar and through audio sources such as NPR; and
- music and sounds you either record or find royalty free online.

You are engaging what play theorists call loose parts: "found objects and materials that children can move, manipulate, control, and change while they play. . . . The materials come with no specific set of directions, and they can be used alone or combined with other materials. . . . These objects invite conversations and interactions, and they encourage collaboration and cooperation. Put another way, loose parts promote social competence because they support creativity and innovation" (Daly & Beloglovsky, 2014, p. 3).

With other classmates, you'll develop an aural narrative—or soundscape—that engages various loose parts:

- classmates' play narratives
- sounds
- music
- audio/textual research

You'll write, record, edit, and bring together these elements into one innovative sound experience that explores the connections you make among ideas in your play narratives.

Context

You'll produce a 4-minute soundscape using **original and/or found sounds and music** and **voiceovers** (your own and your research sources) to tell a story that incorporates **aspects of each of your own play narratives**. To help you further develop the narrative, you'll conduct **research** into some of its aspects.

Process

Bringing your voices together. Share your personal narratives with each other during the first day of the project. Just like any other assignment, you'll develop a purpose you want to explore or point that you want to make. As you read the narratives, discover things that might lend themselves well to the content of your soundscape:

- Do you notice shared experiences?
- Do you notice shared aspects of the events/places/objects you wrote about?
- How does your writing style compare to the others?

Explore. What ideas might be best to explore in the soundscape? What stories do you tell? What ideas lend themselves well to an aural experience for your listener? What questions or thoughts come up that might lead you to conduct research?

Sketch. You might find yourself sketching out a script before you do anything else, or you might start recording things, or reading research first—more than likely you'll be doing all of this at the same time. You'll probably revise as you start editing the audio. However you go about it, you'll have some idea of the story you're wanting to tell early on.

Capture sound. Keep your ears open for the sonic samples you'll need. You can stage recordings, create the sounds you need to record, or just capture them naturally happening. You can also manipulate sounds to make them sound like you need them to.

Put it together. Undoubtedly this is the most challenging part of the process. You'll find that your script needs reworking, or you need additional audio, or the quality of the sound is not great, or you need to find a different soundtrack.

Criteria for Soundscape

Though I'll look at the soundscape holistically, you must demonstrate effectiveness in several areas. There are, though, some specific criteria to attend to: overall time; minimum times for certain elements; purpose; research; and rhetorical choices in the technical and creative aspects.

Overall Time: Is it between 3:30–4:00 minutes long?

Aural Components: As this is a sound project, the choices you make for a meaningful sonic experience should guide you, but here are some criteria to help you along:

Voiceover. Your own voices should make up most of the soundscape, but it's hard to assign a solid timeframe on how long you should talk. The voice-over might last the whole 3:30–4:00 minutes with sounds and soundtrack underscoring it, or you may pause and let the music or sounds do the work.

Sounds. Determining the number of sounds you use can be challenging too: How do you count sounds? Is the sound of a bouncing tennis ball one sound? Is the sound of a tennis ball being hit by a racket and then bouncing on a tennis court count as two sounds? Or is that one mixed sound? The answers aren't easy, and I don't want you to fret over whether you have one very layered sound made up of six individual sounds, or you have one very distinct, countable sound. You're shooting for quality, not quantity.

Soundtrack. Choose appropriate music for the project, but do not let it overwhelm your narrative. Shoot for no more than 30 seconds total throughout the whole project.

Source. As noted above, you'll engage some form of sonic research; that is, you'll engage at least two sources that are spoken, not written. You might record a friend reading some text-based research that you're engaging in the project. Or you might find appropriate research in an NPR story that you download, edit, and mix into your project.

Purpose: Is it clear that the author is demonstrating a focused purpose?

Research: Is the research appropriate for the purpose and topic?

Rhetorical Choices:

Writing

- Is there a clear purpose or point being made?
- How effectively do the writers engage the research?
- Is the writing equitable for each team member?
- How effectively do the writers transition from one element to the next?
- How well do the authors make connections among their ideas?
- How effective is the overall quality of writing expressed through the voiceover?

Aural

- Is the voiceover understandable?
- Are the soundtrack and sounds appropriate for the story?
- How's the quality of the sound elements?

Editing

- Are the transitions from scene to scene appropriate to the story?

Overall

- How do all of these elements contribute to an overall purposeful experience?

Sample Student Projects

The Play Narrative assignment asked students to individually write a narrative about a single play ecology.[1] The following student samples respectively focus on a backyard trampoline, a tennis court, and a forest stream. Their authors later came together to find connections among various aspects of their narratives and create a 4-minute sound project.

1. "Jump for Joy" by Jessica Maroney (a Play Narrative)
2. "Concrete Cloud Nine" by David Shull (a Play Narrative)
3. "Burnt Out" by Stan Bottcher (a Play Narrative)
4. "Boundaries" by Jessica Maroney, David Shull, and Stan Bottcher: In this audio project, three students discuss the idea of boundaries around playing: in the woods, on a tennis court, and on a trampoline.

Reflection

[A two-by-four bats rocks through the air.]

Scott Lunsford: The neighborhood kids would come over and we'd take two-by-fours and bat rocks across the dirt lot that made up most of my grandparents' backyard.[2] My mom and I were living with my grandparents at the time, in this small town in southeast New Mexico on West Texas Street. There is no East Texas Street, oddly enough. It just starts West.

[running and jumping along junk: old wooden boards, metal materials]

Piles of rusted car fenders, old railway ties, a concrete slab of something sat out behind two sheds my grandfather had built himself many years before, providing enough platforms and roofs to climb on and loose materials to balance and jump from. You weren't supposed to go into the sheds, one full of old tools that my grandfather used when he was a young farmer—when they called him "Bean Picker"—and another shed for stuff Bean Picker didn't want in the house anymore. He'd keep the keys to the sheds on top of the fridge so little ones like me couldn't reach them.

The house is now abandoned, No Trespassing signs attached to a number of its exterior walls. At least that's what Google Earth shows. I zoom in . . .

[walking across a street and through a yard]

. . . and trace the path I used to walk to school, going across 9th Street to stop by my friend Raulito's house and pick him up.

---

1. Four student examples (text and audio files and descriptive transcripts) can be found on the book's companion website.

2. The audio version of Scott Lunsford's reflection can be found on the book's companion website.

[A car passes by.]

We'd cut through his backyard and into the alley, across a dusty vacant lot that parked tractor trailers full of hay bales, and stop long enough to throw rocks into the bales to see if they'd stick. The owner's wife would come out in her house-coat and yell at us, threatening to call our moms. So we'd run down the street to school, Hillcrest Elementary, which is now also empty. Along with three other schools in town, Hillcrest closed in 2017 because of poor performance. All of the students were consolidated into two brand-new, better-performing schools.

My name is Scott Lunsford. I'm an associate professor of writing, rhetoric, and technical communication at James Madison University. I teach courses in genre theory, editing, contemporary rhetorical theory, and first-year writing. I also produce multimodal forms of scholarship, particularly videos.

Much of my current research explores graffiti . . .

[A freight train passes by, its wheels scraping against the rails and horn blowing.]

. . . and other types of counter-rhetorics in unsanctioned spaces. I am particularly drawn to the backs of buildings, and alleyways, and underpasses, and train yards, to be in the places where graffiti writers find their own solace.

It's a profession that I have only recently realized extends from West Texas Street, decades ago.

My teaching over the past couple of years has reached back to that house, to that street, and the desert-tanned neighborhood, and I bring my own experiences from them into the classroom, where I encourage students to write through their own childhood experiences in a variety of modes, including video and audio.

One assignment in a first-year writing class asked students to write a play narrative. They were simply to write about a play event that they could deeply describe, perhaps even re-enact through dialogue they may have had with other kids they were playing with—just tell the story. Now, many students find it challenging to write about themselves, as many of them in previous years of education haven't had the opportunity to reflect much and articulate their own experiences as part of primary research. Depending upon the genre, I advocate researchers inserting their own experiences into their work. Doing so further makes us and our readers aware that research and writing are not disembodied, that it isn't magic and immaterial. Writing and rhetoric are of course always material. And that's what I hope to bring to students' attention, which can be rather frustrating for them because they're not used to it but eventually liberating for some because it gives them permission to play.

[Children play in a playground, a girl squeals and laughs, being spun around on some of the play equipment. A child's voice says, "You've got to hold on." Scott, in the scene, says, "Hold on real tight! You ready?" Another child: "It's not even . . . FAST," laughing, squealing.]

I'm at a playground with my own kids. It's a universal-designed playground, with accessible equipment, stationary but fun nonetheless. There are swings, and slides, and a synthetic rock wall, musical instruments . . .

[Kids drum on the instruments.]

. . . a chalkboard built into a concrete sculpture of a horse. Everything has its definition, everything is used based on its purpose, but every now and then, children will climb on top of the chalkboard wall and walk rope across, and of course the favorite thing to do, walking up the slide to slide back down. With this, kids are attempting to loosen the space in order to appropriate it for themselves.

And I think this is what I'm asking my own students to do with their writing, as they come in from years of using other models that have worked for them in their situations and then venture into a classroom where I encourage them to reflect on their lives as writers. That means tearing apart their assumptions about what it means to be a writer, what *writing* means. They find that they must loosen those tight spaces, those tight approaches, those tight assumptions to writing in order to find room for playing with writing, which of course means writing through modes other than the traditional alphabetic text. This is particularly important for a second assignment that I have this same class of students perform. I group them into teams of three and ask them to share their original play narratives with each other and begin to find aspects of each of them that have some connections among them. They are then to conduct research into the connections they discover and produce a 4-minute audio project, something I call a Digital Loose Parts Soundscape. The idea behind loose parts comes from a play theorist named Simon Nicholson (1972), who back in the early 1970s defined a loose parts theory, which essentially says the less defined or structured an object may be within a certain context, the more opportunity it has to take on other purposes. So, a two-by-four outside the context of carpentry, for example, can become a bat that you hit rocks with. And so some play theorists have taken issue with the design of playgrounds with equipment that have purposefully limited use: for example, a swing is a swing and you can swing on it; you can't take it apart and create something new from it.

This is what I'm asking students to do with each other's narratives: rip them apart, find something new about them, pull in other parts, such as research and sound effects and music, and create something new.

Now, there are challenges to this. One is if I'm expecting my students to take as much agency as possible to find connections on their own, essentially giving them permission to play without supervision, where do I come in as a teacher? How do I teach someone to find connections among disparate things, connections that sometimes simply aren't there? Do I let students play and whatever comes out is what comes out? And do I let them be okay with that, because they might not be okay with it? Sometimes the connections among narratives were contrived, stretched, and made no sense. Others had to revise extensively their original narratives in order to create connections.

One of the other challenges stems from my requiring audio research or audio-recorded research in the soundscape. It's easy to search library databases and Google Scholar for the research you need. You can of course skim parts of alphabetic texts to find what you might be looking for. Much harder to search for research that comes in audio form, such as NPR articles, and then to skim through such audio pieces in order to see if that particular research might be appropriate. You sometimes have to listen to the whole thing in order to see if it works. NPR's website thankfully has a search function, so you can search for various stories on, say, free-range parenting or how play has an effect on the brain. There are also transcripts for many of the audio articles, so anyone can scan the text before actually having to listen to the whole audio piece just to see if it's appropriate. NPR also allows you to download audio articles, which you can bring into audio-editing software.

All in all, though, I've let it be okay that these projects are seemingly messy at the end, because if I am to advocate a notion of play throughout the course, where I must allow for as much agency as I can—that is after all a necessity for playing—the objects of that play become in themselves loose parts, not tightly packaged, tightly controlled, tightly produced artifacts. But manifestations of play themselves, of voices who are re-taking ownership of play that they had left in their childhood.

Note

All sound recordings in this reflection were by the author.

References

Campbell, L. (2015–16). Ek stasis. *Lexia: Undergraduate Journal in Writing, Rhetoric & Technical Communication, 4.* https://www.jmu.edu/lexia/stories/volume4/Campbell_Lexia_IV.pdf.

Daly, L. & Beloglovsky, M. (2014). *Loose parts: Inspiring play in young children.* Red Leaf Press.

Garrett, B., Landrum-Geyer, D. & Palmeri, J. (2012). Re-inventing invention: A performance in three acts. In D. Journet, C. E. Ball & R. Trauman (Eds.), *The new work of composing.* Computers and Composition Digital Press. https://ccdigitalpress.org/book/nwc/chapters/garrett-et-al/.

Hogan, P. C. (2003). *Cognitive science, literature, and the arts.* Routledge.

Nicholson, S. (1972). The theory of loose parts: An important principle for design methodology. *Studies in Design Education Craft & Technology, 4*(2), 5–14. https://ojs.lboro.ac.uk/SDEC/article/view/1204.

Rivlin, L. (2007). Found spaces: Freedom of choice in public life. In K. A. Franck & Q. Stevens (Eds.), *Loose space: Possibility and diversity in urban life* (pp. 38–53). Routledge.

Chapter 7. Electrate Anti-Definition Sound Collage and Transduction

Thomas M. Geary
Tidewater Community College, Virginia Beach, VA

Introduction: Electracy and Sound Collage

For nearly two decades, scholars have reimagined traditional, literate writing for the digital and new media (Selfe, 2004; Writing in Digital Environments Research Center Collective, 2005; Wysocki, 2004), the network (Yancey, 2009), the postmodern (Dobrin, 2011; Johnson-Eilola, 2004), and the participatory (Arroyo, 2013). Perhaps the best realization of postmodern composition, Gregory Ulmer's (2003) electracy theory operates in a third apparatus—an alternative to orality and literacy—that values associative logic, juxtaposition, and appropriation and functions as a "digital prosthesis," opening up communicative possibilities in electronic spaces (p. 145). Electracy embraces fragmentation, multiplicity of meaning, and remix culture and clashes with the traditional hallmarks of literacy: certainty, clarity, and linearity. It promotes playful experimentation as we think and compose through new media rather than with it. Electracy, continually in a state of being invented in theory and praxis, provides composition and rhetoric instructors a framework for modern writing, one that can be fragmented, multimodal, and nonlinear. Yet few pedagogical applications exist, particularly at the first-year and community college levels. In this chapter of *Amplifying Soundwriting*, I share my Electrate Anti-Definition Sound Collage and Transduction assignment to bridge the wide gap in the composition classroom between the literate and electrate while welcoming a new, sonic composition. This electrate sound assignment asks students to gather audio fragments that collectively capture the many perspectives of an abstract word; the resulting collage serves as a springboard for their literate definition essays. Thinking through sound with a playful, electrate approach promotes creativity and a diversity of perspectives as students brainstorm their own definitions.

In "A New Composition, a 21st Century Pedagogy, and the Rhetoric of Music," Crystal VanKooten (2011) proposed, "Composition instructors [should] adopt a new definition of composition that is characterized by multiplicity, participation, and convergence, a definition that foregrounds *all* rhetorical choices available to 21st century composers, but in particular the rhetoric of music" ("New Terminologies" section). VanKooten's call for a postmodern, sonic approach to writing that is suitable for today's students with the affordances of composing audio advances many of the goals of electracy theory. The texts begin to look less like

DOI: https://doi.org/10.37514/PRA-B.2022.1688.2.07

literate creations in the verbal with certainty, directness, and originality as central hallmarks. VanKooten's new composition—with a focus on sound—privileges the student experimenting as DJ or rapper, splicing and cutting, remixing and reimagining, embracing rupture and plurality of meaning, fitting Michael Jarrett's (2007) "rapsthetic" (p. 74). The Electrate Anti-Definition Sound Collage and Transduction exercise grants students the ability to enter that mindset as composers while still working toward literate course competencies; it encourages the remix and plurality of meaning by taking the opposite approach to the standard first stasis assignment: the definition essay.

In writing definitions of debatable, abstract terms, students inevitably consult dictionaries and authoritative voices to set parameters and purge what a term is not. They practice brevity and craft concise statements confirming the aspects and qualities of their topic. In the literate apparatus and rhetorical practice, this activity satisfies the first category of stasis theory, as per the modern adaptation by Jeanne Fahnestock and Marie Secor (1985). Though the definition essay remains in my composition class, students prepare for it by seeking many different voices and sounds related to that term; they develop a collage rather than an argument. In the electrate apparatus and new composition, definitions are inverted and ambiguity is foregrounded. In *Internet Invention*, Ulmer (2003) encouraged multiplicity and open-endedness of meaning, articulation instead of straightforward composition. Jeff Rice (2007) converted the anti-definition into an exercise that turns to other disciplines and reviews how the initial area of study changes based on different meanings.

My Electrate Anti-Definition Sound Collage and Transduction explores how the anti-definition fits in VanKooten's (2011) new, sound-based definition of composition. Students are asked as listeners/composers to work with a plurality of meanings and privilege no single definition, "voice," or mood more than another. In doing so, they might recover what is usually purged when defining in the literate apparatus. Students are encouraged to manipulate, experiment, and play with sounds to gain an understanding of nuance, juxtaposition, and articulation in the digital age. Their choices of fragments that represent and/or evoke all that a term can mean vary greatly, from the straightforward (e.g., verbal definitions from news clips or interviews, excerpts from readings) to the implied (e.g., clips of songs, television shows) to the abstract (e.g., noise, ambience). Rather than limit students, I supported the inclusion of any and all sounds that connect to their terms. As students gather fragments, stitch together and juxtapose the parts, and thinking through and with sound, they push themselves outside of their comfort zones and experience a new composition.

A central assumption made in designing this activity is that it requires minimal technical skill and no inclusion of students' own perspectives. Students are encouraged to compose their collages, consisting entirely of others' definitions, using free software like Audacity, but those who are not comfortable or unable to craft a sound collage are provided visual and multimodal alternatives that still fall within the electrate apparatus. The conscious decision to remain flexible in this assignment was made with accessibility concerns and my target audience of community college students—often low-income, minority, and/or first-generation students, many of whom are food insecure, housing insecure, or even homeless ("Community College Facts," n.d.)—in mind. The assignment is not weighted heavily in the course, and ample workshop time is provided in class.

The next activity in the sequence, prior to the literate definition essay, is an act of transduction, Gunther Kress and Theo Van Leeuwen's (2006) term for a translation of material between semiotic modes (e.g., video to text, audio to image). Students transform their sonic electrate collages to another mode, such as writing, justifying their choices of modal translation and analyzing the affordances and limitations of sound. This activity serves as brainstorming for the literate definition essay and guides students to reflect on their choices in any modality when communicating, either in the literate or electrate apparatus.

Assignment: Anti-Definition Sound Collage and Transduction

Length: 15 seconds to 3 minutes

File type: WAV or MP3 preferred; any form accepted

(Anti-)Definitions

Our first instinct when looking up a word's definition is to turn to authoritative written sources like dictionaries and textbooks or collaborative websites like Wikipedia. We trust that these definitions are correct and accepted by others as they have been standardized by a consensus of experts. Definitions serve an important role in communication as they help us understand new ideas and ensure we're on the same page with each other.

However, these established parameters to a term ultimately purge voices and perspectives that might otherwise fit a broader or different definition of that abstract term or concept. Definitions can serve as the foundation of arguments; we cannot agree to actions to solve a problem if we do not agree on what something is. For example, when a life begins differs greatly depending on whom you ask: it varies from conception to first brain activity to birth. Without considering the variety of perspectives, we might not have a complete understanding of the term.

In this activity, we're going to embrace uncertainty and try to complicate the definition of an abstract term through anti-definition. Your goal will be to promote a plurality of meaning rather than one of certainty.

Sound Collage

Though you might associate writing with verbal texts, composition takes many forms, including audio, video, oral, and visual. We engage various forms of composition on a daily basis: watching TV, engaging social media, and listening to the radio. Later this semester, you will craft a multimodal digital storytelling project.

But first, we'll start with sounds. In this activity, you're going to create a sound collage, a blend of sounds and audio clips that evoke or speak to your term. What does "freedom" sound like to different people? What audio captures "success" for most?

Overview of Assignment

In your two-page definition essay (Essay #1), you are writing a compelling and unique argument for your own definition of a debatable, abstract term. You'll use negation, comparison, and contrast as definition tactics to shape your own term. Here, you'll discover the parameters of your own definition by searching for others.

For this invention activity, you will gather a variety of sound fragments that represent your abstract word. Consider these the "other voices" that define the term. The sounds could be straightforward (e.g., verbal definitions from interviews, friends and family, or news clips, excerpts from texts), implied (e.g., parts of songs, TV, or movies, everyday conversation), or abstract (e.g., noise, ambience).

How to Proceed

This assignment requires no inclusion of your own perspective or composition in your own words; look for OTHERS' representations of your abstract term for Essay #1. However, you might creatively and playfully juxtapose definitions or test the limits of a sound collage by experimenting with editing. Aim not to privilege any voice over another.

I recommend using the free, open-source software Audacity to piece together your sound clips, but you're welcome to utilize any software with which you feel comfortable. Most smartphones allow for voice memo recording, and you could simply record video if you'd like.

Your sound collage can be anywhere from 15 seconds to 3 minutes. Files types WAV and MP3 are preferred, but any format will be accepted.

NOTE: If you are not comfortable or unable to use audio software, you are welcome to complete this collage as a visual one through Microsoft Word, PowerPoint, Prezi, Pinterest, a poster board, or any form that you please. The central idea here still applies: you're looking for various images or written passages that define the same term.

Transduction

Once sound collages are completed, I would like for you to reflect on the affordances and limitations of using audio to capture meaning. Try to recreate your collage in another modality (writing, visuals). You might, for example, create a visual collage of images that best capture the sounds in your project. We will discuss in class what is gained and what is lost in this act of transduction, a translation of material between modes of communication.

Examples

Because of the nascency of this project, only a few examples exist. We will, however, listen to a few in class as inspiration for how you might tackle the project. We will also have workshop time in class to gather sounds and explore the Audacity program.

Sample Student Projects

1. "Family" by Ryan Jamerson: In the first example, Ryan Jamerson contrasts a popular 1970s song with her own version of family at home: her seven dogs.[3]

2. "Love" by Kyleigh Klima: The second example, a lengthy mashup of voices from coworkers, children, friends, and family with Ed Sheeran's "Give Me Love" in the background, Kyleigh Klima shows the many perspectives of love.

3. "Success" by Rachael Gauley. This unorthodox third example, Rachael Gauley's blend of sounds relating to "success," looks to videogames, champagne, and nature.

4. "Art" by Francesa "Chris" Laverghetta: In her 2.5-minute collage of voices discussing artistry, Francesca "Chris" Laverghetta blends a variety of confident definitions and inquiries regarding the boundaries of art.

5. "Accomplishment" by Cristina Babiuc: Though brief, Cristina Babiuc's 46-second project becomes increasingly abstract: from a comedic take on making the bed to police sirens, a grocery checkout, and birds chirping.

6. "Happiness" by Katelyn Gable: Demonstrating the various sounds of success, Katelyn Gable contrasts the abstract—seagulls at the beach—with the overt—Pharrell Williams's smash hit "Happy."

Reflection

[Instrumental excerpt of Sonic Youth's 2004 track "I Love You Golden Blue." A blend of different sounds and effects created by guitars, bass, and percussion simultaneously create an insect swarm-like effect. Fades to background.]

A cacophonous swarm of insects and annoying noises or a symphony of hypnotic bliss?[4] The fluttering, droning noises at the start of Sonic Youth's 2004 track

---

3. Six student examples (audio files and descriptive transcripts) can be found on the book's companion website.

4. The audio version of Thomas M. Geary's reflection can be found on the book's companion website.

"I Love You Golden Blue" encapsulate the band's proclivity for dissonance and multiple voices emerging at once while capturing what so many love—and hate—about their music.

This shroud of sound also serves as the inspiration for my Electrate Anti-Definition Sound Collage assignment.

["I Love You Golden Blue" returns to forefront briefly and fades out.]

["Electronic Music Track X1" by frankum (2018) enters in background. Soft jazzy notes accompany an insistent bass synth and a steady drumbeat with cymbals.]

My name is Tom Geary, and I'm a full professor of English at Tidewater Community College in Virginia Beach. For several years now, I've experimented with blending Gregory Ulmer's (2003) electracy theory into my instruction. Electracy, which Ulmer refers to as a third communicative apparatus to orality and literacy, embraces fragmentation, multiplicity of meaning, remix culture, and associative logic. It promotes playful experimentation as we think and compose through new media rather than with it.

In many ways, however, it clashes with the traditional hallmarks of the literate apparatus: certainty, clarity, and linearity. It runs counter to some course learning outcomes in my first-year composition course. Electracy is also perhaps a bit complicated for the first-year student, particularly at the community college level where questions about access are more prominent.

To blend the electrate with the literate—a soft transition of sorts that introduces students to the key qualities of electrate thinking while still satisfying literate course competencies—I developed an Electrate Anti-Definition Sound Collage project: an invention exercise that builds upon Ulmer's (2003) and Jeff Rice's (2007) anti-definition activities. This sound collage project promotes plurality of meaning—an inversion of the same definition essay assignment in the same class—and exposes students to a different approach to finding sources, including what some might consider noise.

["Electronic Music Track X1" by frankum fades out.]

[a glitching, chaotic computer sound while the user is attempting to stream video (toiletrolltube, 2008)]

In this reflection, I will share the purpose of the assignment, analyze a couple of student collages, discuss how the assignment benefitted those students, identify challenges in implementing a sound collage assignment, and share further inquiries regarding the future of the assignment.

["Ambient Wave 3—(Harmonics)" by deleted_user_2731495 (2018a) enters in background. Droning notes with subtle variations whoosh at what sounds like a slow-motion pace.]

"I Love You Golden Blue"—and in particular the 2-minute instrumental opening—has always stuck with me. Like so many other Sonic Youth songs and other sound artists like Brian Eno and Crys Cole, this excerpt contains a multiplicity of voices—a collection of sounds and noises simultaneously working in unison to build an alarm-like effect. It feels electrate, or at least approaching that apparatus. And it seems like it's trying to define something or capture a mood: an awakening, or perhaps an epiphany. It's an annoying ringing but also one that is comforting. It's ambiguous and multivalent. Though it contrasts with the rest of the song's love elegy whispered by Kim Gordon, the track's opening is a wall of sound that pulls in—or perhaps pushes away—the listener while constructing multiple moods at the same time.

In designing the Electrate Anti-Definition Sound Collage project, I wanted students to seek that essence: ambiguity, plurality of voices, and open-endedness instead of one definitive, literate meaning. Their collages could take the abstract approach with noises alone or blend in any number of sounds: people's voices, excerpts of songs, dogs barking—really, whatever ways others might define the term of their choice. I wanted them to find the other definitions that would establish the parameters of their own in their literate definition essay assignment, but I wanted those to be in a different mode than they're used to researching.

["Ambient Wave 3—(Harmonics)" by deleted_user_2731495 ends.]

The assignment is simple, really. Students gather sounds that evoke a term. Then they compile, remix, or contrast those sounds creatively. It's a low-stakes, playful exploration meant to serve as an invention exercise for the essay, in which students define that same abstract term uniquely to them. The collage can take many forms, and in two semesters of teaching the assignment, I've received projects with a range from *[a woman saying "wow" (yugi16dm, 2015)]* to *[a horn sound that typically signals failure in a game show (TaranP, 2016)]*. Yet all avoid one clear definition and aim for the electrate.

Here's one student project that juxtaposes various types of sounds related to her term "good person." Cristina Babiuc's collage becomes increasingly abstract: from a comedic take on making the bed to police sirens, a grocery checkout, and birds chirping.

["Accomplishment" inserted here.]

> **Man** (perhaps Admiral William H. McRaven): If you want to change the world, start off by making your bed. *[Audience laughs]* If you make your bed every morning, you will have accomplished the first task of the day. It will give you a small sense of pride, and it will encourage you to do another task. And another. And another . . .

[police sirens]

[Unintelligible brief phrase from a woman on an intercom radio— possibly "Here, here."]

[slapping noise of object striking a surface]

[regularly timed beeps with background talking from an employee at a grocery store]

> **Clerk**: Price on three.

[birds chirping]

["Filtered Piano Looped 1 – (90bpm)" by deleted_user_2731495 (2018b) enters. A piano loop of very few notes rises and falls in a consistent pattern.]

In this collage, Cristina forgoes direct definition and truly captures the spirit of the assignment. She shows instead of tells and engages the listener with sounds that vaguely capture what it sounds like to hear a "good person": a policewoman, a grocery store clerk assisting a customer. The opening advice taken from Admiral William H. McRaven doesn't directly speak to goodness in humanity, but it emphasizes the small things in life making a difference. This quotation sets the tone for the rest of the collage. Caring for animals and nature in general can be a "small thing" but it makes someone a good person. Assisting a customer or co-worker is a "small thing" but it makes a difference.

Though Cristina found a thematic thread for each of her sounds and didn't include examples contrary to it, her sound collage served as a springboard to a successful definition essay. Her argument about good people used some of these examples but added components of selflessness and sacrifice. Her sound fragments functioned as other views of "good person" that closely contrasted with her own definition.

Other student projects looked to establish the complexity of a term through primarily verbal descriptions. Chris Laverghetta blends a variety of confident definitions and inquiries regarding the boundaries of art, artists, and artistry with sounds made in the process of creating art.

["Filtered Piano Looped 1 – (90bpm)" by deleted_user_2731495 ends.]

["Art" excerpt inserted here.]

> **Man**: *[fades in]* And here, colors to do everything. And by its simplification, a grander style to things, is to be suggestive here first of rest, or of sleep in general. In a word, looking at the picture ought to rest the brain or rather the imagination. *[fades out]*

[pencil quickly and rigorously striking paper or canvas]

> **Man**: *[fades in]* Art flows from the soul, twists through the consciousness, and decorates life with its beauty.

Woman: It's this object, and you can lose yourself in the won-derfulness of the object, but then the object goes away and stops being an object. It just becomes a window, or a mirror. And that's what, uh, work has become gradually. *[slowly fades out]* It's changed.

[erasing from a paper or canvas]

["Cosmic Glow" by Andrewkn (2017) enters. A pattern of electronic beep-and-boop sounds steadily pace a track that has flourishes of synth in the background.]

Unlike the previous example, which felt like a collection of loosely related sounds, Chris's collage is like entering a Burkean parlor room: The variety of voices—none weighted more than another—pull the listener in different directions before she enters her own opinion. Here, art rests the brain. It twists the conscious-ness. It becomes the object. It emerges from our soul. In her collage, Chris illus-trates the profound nature of art but also the varying descriptions and purposes.

Chris's anti-definition collage resulted not only in a thoughtful positioning of her voice in the larger debate about how to define artist but sparked her interest in narrating a powerful digital story animated project on underrepresentation of women, minorities, and LGBTQA in the film industry. Her confidence in com-posing with sound gained in this collage assignment resulted in an interest in fur-ther explorations of audio projects, particularly animated stories and podcasts.

Though these two student samples were successful immersions into electrate sound composition, the assignment was not always well received or met with enthusiasm and interest. Obstacles preventing students from completing the assignment became apparent in its very first planned iteration as I had a deaf student enrolled in my class and another student without access to the internet except when on campus. Accessibility concerns were certainly in mind when I designed the assignment, but I had not anticipated that an entire lesson on sound-writing would be scrapped to ensure awareness of all students' needs so early. It was the right choice, and it led to further contemplation of the assignment.

To accommodate students with accessibility, access, or comfort concerns, I offer an alternative multimodal or visual collage that follows the same process but replaces sound with images, video, text, or any other modality. The principles of the assignment remain the same, but sound is replaced with whatever the student prefers: a PowerPoint, a poster board, a website.

This flexibility is also of the utmost importance for my student population. Community college students are more likely to deal with food and housing inse-curity, be first generation college students, and struggle with access to the most up-to-date hardware and software. While this sort of flexibility in curricular design may be a necessity for community college students, it should also be con-sidered a best practice for instruction in any context.

Other alterations made to the assignment include making it a minor part of the overall class grade—freeing any expectations or stress accompanying a potentially confusing, new form of composition—and minimizing or eliminating any references to electracy altogether. So long as the principles are foregrounded, students can skip reading dense theoretical work.

["Cosmic Glow" by Andrewkn ends.]

["Electronic Dance Loop 02" by frankum (2015) enters. An upbeat dance track with the repeated vocal "Dancing" chugs along.]

Further inquiries regarding the future of the assignment include how to dive into questions of bodily affect and sound without losing focus of the definition essay assignment, how to properly tie in electracy without overwhelming first-year students, and how to tackle questions of copyright and citation, especially as I encourage more remixing of material. Ulmer promotes free exploration of experimental work and remix in the electrate apparatus without concerns about plagiarism, but that could be a problem for students new to the college experience.

With further refinement and attention to students' needs, I hope the sound collage opens students' ears to the planet of sound and broadens their perspective. I hope that it eases in electracy and introduces what Crystal VanKooten (2011) refers to as a "new composition" that foregrounds music and sound. It's just a first step, but I hope it results in a successful move toward soundwriting.

["Electronic Dance Loop 02" by frankum ends.]

["Success" excerpt inserted here]

[cut to champagne bottle popping open]

[champagne being poured]

[clink of glasses]

[Nature sounds. Birds sing in background as a helicopter flies by.]

Fair Use Statement

In this project, I use clips from one audio work—Sonic Youth's (2004) "I Love You Golden Blue"—that is protected by U.S. copyright law. However, I believe I have a fair use defense to use those works without permission for these reasons:

1. The purpose and character of my use is to use these clips as part of my scholarly project, transforming their character from the purpose for which their creator originally made them.
2. The nature of the copyrighted pieces is more "creative" or artistic, in which case this factor could weigh against me.

3. I only used a small amount of each clip, and when possible in the context of my argument, I used clips that did not represent the core, most substantial part of the original copyrighted work.

4. As an audio clip repurposed for teaching and scholarship purposes, there is no chance that my use will infringe on the potential market for this copyrighted work. To encourage others to legally purchase the original work, I include full citation information that others can follow if they want to buy it.

References

Andrewkn. (2017). Cosmic glow [Audio file]. *Freesound.* https://freesound.org/people/Andrewkn/sounds/391438/.

Arroyo, S. (2013). *Participatory culture: Video culture, writing, and electracy.* Southern Illinois University Press.

Community college FAQs. (n.d.). Community College Research Center. https://ccrc.tc.columbia.edu/Community-College-FAQs.html.

deleted_user_2731495. (2018a). Ambient wave 3—(Harmonics) [Audio file]. *Freesound.* https://freesound.org/people/deleted_user_2731495/sounds/432500/.

deleted_user_2731495. (2018b). Filtered piano looped 1—(90bpm) [Audio file]. *Freesound.* https://freesound.org/people/deleted_user_2731495/sounds/424154/.

Dobrin, S. (2011). *Postcomposition.* Southern Illinois University Press.

Fahnestock, J. & Secor, M. (1985). Toward a modern version of stasis theory. In C. W. Kneupper (Ed.), *Oldspeak/newspeak: Rhetorical transformations* (pp. 217–226). National Council of Teachers of English.

frankum. (2015, November 10). Electronic dance loop 02 [Audio file]. *Freesound.* https://freesound.org/people/frankum/sounds/328366/.

frankum. (2018, April 25). Electronic music track X1 [Audio file]. *Freesound.* https://freesound.org/people/frankum/sounds/426470/.

GowlerMusic. (2015, January 22). Broken violin [Audio file]. *Freesound.* https://freesound.org/people/GowlerMusic/sounds/262264/.

Kress, G. & Van Leeuwen, T. (2006). *Reading images: The grammar of visual design* (2nd ed.). Routledge.

Jarrett, M. (2007). On hip-hop, a rhapsody. In D. Tofts & L. Gye (Eds.), *Illogic of sense: The Gregory L. Ulmer remix* (pp. 68–76). AltX Press. http://www.altx.com/ebooks/pdfs/ulmer.pdf.

Johnson-Eilola, J. (2004). The database and the essay: Understanding composition as articulation. In A. F. Wysocki, J. Johnson-Eilola, C. L. Selfe & G. Sirc, *Writing new media: Theory and applications for expanding the teaching of composition* (pp. 199–236). Utah State University Press.

Rice, J. (2007). *The rhetoric of cool: Composition studies and new media.* Southern Illinois University Press.

Selfe, C. L. (2004). Toward new media texts: Taking up the challenges of visual literacy. In A. F. Wysocki, J. Johnson-Eilola, C. L. Selfe & G. Sirc, *Writing new media:*

Theory and applications for expanding the teaching of composition (pp. 67–110). Utah State University Press.

Sonic Youth (Performer). (2004). I love you golden blue [Song]. On *Sonic nurse*. Geffen Records.

toiletrolltube. (2018). Error noise (input) 180611_0744.wav [Audio file]. *Freesound*. https://freesound.org/people/toiletrolltube/sounds/432283/.

TaranP. (2016, October 11). horn_fail_wahwah_3.wav [Audio file]. *Freesound*. https://freesound.org/people/TaranP/sounds/362204/.

Ulmer, G. L. (2003). *Internet invention: From literacy to electracy*. Longman.

VanKooten, C. (2011). A new composition, a 21st century pedagogy, and the rhetoric of music. *Currents in Electronic Literacy*. https://currents.dwrl.utexas.edu/2011/anewcomposition.html.

Writing in Digital Environments (WIDE) Research Center Collective. (2005). Why teach digital writing? *Kairos: A Journal of Rhetoric, Technology, and Pedagogy, 10*(1). http://kairos.technorhetoric.net/10.1/binder2.html?coverweb/wide/index.html.

Wysocki, A. F. (2004). Opening new media to writing: Openings and justifications. In A. F. Wysocki, J. Johnson-Eilola, C. L. Selfe & G. Sirc, *Writing new media: Theory and applications for expanding the teaching of composition* (pp. 1–42). Utah State University Press.

Yancey, K. B. (2009). *Writing in the 21st century: A report from the National Council of Teachers of English*. National Council of Teachers of English. http://www.ncte.org/library/NCTEFiles/Press/Yancey_final.pdf.

yugi16dm. (2015, September 29). wow/whoa [MP3 file]. *Freesound*. https://freesound.org/people/yugi16dm/sounds/323438/.

Part Two. Soundwriting with Music

Chapter 8. Cultivating Signal, Noise, and Feeling: Songwriting Practices in Digital Rhetoric Courses

Rich Shivener

YORK UNIVERSITY

As a working musician for more than 20 years (and that includes my punk rawk garage days in the 'burbs), I find that songwriting helps me attune to and make sense of pain and emotions—and in some cases, to express the sensations and emotions of another. It's not exactly a new insight among musicians, given that a range of genres and songs evoke felt memories and affective encounters.

In this chapter, I put such an insight to work by arguing for an assignment that teaches and samples songwriting practices in digital rhetoric courses, from introductory to advanced-level sections. Let me be clear: Students aren't required to learn or play an instrument, let alone write a song, but they are required to embody some important practices of a songwriter who composes in a studio. My assignment samples three practices of songwriting: recording, arranging, and "thick listening" (Krukowski, 2017, p. 119) to signal and noise. The assignment is based on a first-year composition course in which students had written researched arguments. After paring their essays down to 500 words, students then recorded vocal tracks, arranged Creative Commons sounds and musical samples, and thought critically about emotions that surfaced in their recordings. My framework for the assignment is based on Damon Krukowski's ideas in his 2017 book *The New Analog*.

This sonic assignment meets the goals of many first-year composition and rhetoric courses that encourage students to expand their digital media literacies while reflecting on rhetorical appeals (ethos, logos, pathos, kairos). When I first delivered this assignment, it was a variation on University of Cincinnati's FYC assignment Recasting for a Public Audience, which asks students to remediate an argument and "explore different genres as possibilities for your writing" (Malek et al., 2017, p. 54). For this assignment, my position was, and still is, that songwriting practices—including arranging tonal signals to represent moods and emotions, and dwelling in ambient noises that stem from recording materials and environments—enrich digital compositions and cultivate feelings through and outside composers. Put differently, students are encouraged to think about the layers of emotion embedded in a sonic composition that integrates voices, songs, and sounds.

Recording, arranging, and thick listening to sonic compositions are common practices among songwriters when they work with engineers and producers,

DOI: https://doi.org/10.37514/PRA-B.2022.1688.2.08

according to Krukowski. In *The New Analog*, Krukowski (2017) examined digital recording devices and formats that have at once sped up and diminished production quality, replaying analog recording productions circa 1965 and those with his band Galaxie 500. "Signal" and "noise" bookended his arguments. As defined by audiophiles like Krukowski, thick listening goes beyond signal—the final, seemingly polished composition—and seeks out the noise—ambient sounds from a room, singer hesitations, band outtakes, vocal miscues, conversations entangled with tracks. "When we listen to noise [via analog productions]," Krukowski wrote, "we listen to the space around us and to the distance between us" (2017, p. 197). In rhetorical contexts, we often think of this stuff as context rather than "noise." Noise is a useful metaphor for context, though, as Krukowski went on to note that noise also includes liner notes and materials (e.g., acknowledgments, background stories, cover images, and advertisements) that are omitted, in part, by digital distribution and formats. Without noise, a song loses depth and feeling, Krukowski posited. Inspired by his claim, my assignment, based on a songwriter's theory, asks students to do some recording, arranging and thick listening with signal, noise, and feeling.

Beyond *The New Analog*, my songwriting assignment indeed implicates rhetoric and composition's loud history of studying and practicing songwriting and music. While some scholars have analyzed songwriting and musical rhetorics (Alexander, 2015; Ceraso, 2014; Hawk, 2010; Rickert, 2013; VanKooten, 2016) as a means of inflecting rhetorical theory and enriching it, others have drawn on musical approaches to frame research agendas and composition pedagogies (Banks, 2010; Palmeri, 2012; Rice, 2003; Sirc, 2005; Stedman, 2013). After reading (and listening to) these scholars' arguments, I imagined an assignment for my students in hopes of joining this scholarly super-group. I wanted to call more attention to songwriting as a viable sonic art in digital rhetoric courses, even first-year composition sections, such as mine, that have privileged digital composing with music. Rickert's and VanKooten's works were particularly insightful in terms of recognizing sensations and emotions that accompany musical composing, whether Led Zeppelin drummer John Bonham's takes at Headley Grange (Rickert, 2015) or Brian Eno's Microsoft Windows startup music (Rickert, 2015). Rickert and VanKooten have banded with scholars who value the *chora*, or a space in which "we compose and feel out meanings from diverse materials, patterns, emotions, bodies, and memories" (VanKooten, 2016, chora section). I was *moved* by VanKooten's choric composing practices that layered a video montage with samples of a choir singing Brahms's *Requiem*. In other words, recent meditations on the chora were useful to me because they unflattened rhetorical activity, especially that of the sonic variety. Paying attention to the chora means composing and feeling out the dynamic surround of a text, or what Krukowski (2017) called the space, the noise. It means if we ask a student to record their voice for an audio essay, then we also need to ask her to consider the context that intentionally and unintentionally accompanies it.

In the assignment section, you will notice I integrate songwriting and musical thinking through in-class activities and the major assignment, an audio essay that stems from a larger researched argument. You will also notice that I use Krukowski's terms in my own audio reflection essay as well as my response letter template to students. While it might seem like a familiar multimodal project contingent on podcasting, I argue that its turn to a musical framework is unique. By and large, I hope the songwriting practices this assignment encourages give ways to exciting projects by students. I'm sounding out what I hope is a significant contribution to digital rhetoric scholarship because it responds to the field's melodic interests and explores pedagogical possibilities that draw on songwriting theory and praxis.

Accessibility Interlude

The assignment I present below embraces two accessibility practices in relation to sonic composing. First, by composing 500-word essays based on longer researched arguments, students are in fact composing transcripts for their future audio essays. The transcript, that is, precedes the sonic composition rather than serving as an add-on. This transcript priority means that students who are hard of hearing might work with a partner to distill one or both of their researched arguments and compose transcripts.

Second, this assignment is achievable with open-access and free software for PC and Apple devices. Take note that I asked students to compose with the open-access recording software Audacity or the baked-in Apple recording program GarageBand. Students should be able to compose audio essays without spending a penny. If students lack a personal computer that can install and handle such software, they might again work with a partner. Instructors might also introduce students to on-campus media resources well before the assignment begins.

Assignments and Schedule

Recasting for a Public Audience: The Signal, Noise, and Feeling of Your Research (20% of course grade)

Assignment Overview and Purpose

A recast involves taking an object and remodeling or reconstructing it. For this assignment, you'll take the essence of your research argument essay on digital devices and writing and "recast" it into an audio essay, complete with music and sounds. The goals of this project are to share your work with more people than your instructor and to be aware of the various decisions that you need to make when working with different audiences, genres, and media. Another goal is to think about songwriting practices and ways in which sound composing—from recording your voice and others, to mixing and writing music—affects your research argument essay.

Resources You'll Need

1. Your research argument

2. Voice recorder (preferably on your phone): In class, we covered Apple's Voice Memo application and free recorders from Android Marketplace.

3. Computer, plus and music or podcasting software:

   a. PC and Mac users, try Audacity (link available on blog).

   b. Mac users, try Garageband (link available on blog).

4. Alternatively, you might use a music/podcast-recording app on your phone (GarageBand, Spreaker, etc.).

Instructions for Producing an Audio Essay [The Simple Version, with More Steps to be Discussed in Class]

1. Revise your research argument into a 500-word piece. This is basically your transcript for the production.

2. Are you interested in working with a classmate on this assignment? You can do that! If so, let me know. You'll need to decide whose argument you will recast. Or perhaps you'd like to mix the two arguments?

3. Re-record yourself (or your collaborator) speaking a 500-word argument, as if you are imitating a transcript from storytelling podcasts such as Lore or Snap Judgment. You might want to record it in sections, or 100 words at a time.

4. Save the files and get it ready for sound-editing software.

5. Load your voice recording files into the editing software and piece it together.

6. Include with your voice recording various sounds and music, either with sounds and music you create, or those you sample with fair use permissions.

7. When ready, export and upload to Dropbox.

Submitting a Rationale

Write a two- to three-page rationale where you have the opportunity to reflect on the choices that went into your recast and discuss the ways your argument has grown or changed in light of those choices. In the rationale, you'll discuss the form (medium or genre) of your project (i.e., the audio essay), the audience your recast project is directed toward, and the technical and rhetorical choices you made in creating your recast.

Sample Lesson Plan

Below, I provide a sample lesson plan in which students search for and incorporate music and other sounds for their projects.

Lesson Subject: Music's Role in Digital Composing

Related Learning Outcomes

- Recognize that different writing situations call for different strategies.
- Understand the complexity of different kinds of arguments/issues.

Instructional Materials
- Laptop and charger
- Sound for music
- Extra sheets of paper
- Phone and charger
- Class website

Pre-meeting Materials/Student Assignments for Class (Homework)
- Through GarageBand, Audacity, or another app, assemble a complete recording of your 500-word argument.
- Finish reading passages from Damon Krukowski's *The New Analog*.
- Check out the range of free music and sounds available at Freesound.org.

Lesson Outline/Activities

Lesson Themes—Music Workshopping, Voice Polishing

1. Short writing quiz related to Krukowski's *The New Analog*
    ◦ Name one example of an analog technology and one example of a digital technology.
    ◦ True or False: Digital media has ruined music.
    ◦ What does Krukowski mean when he discusses "thick listening"?
    ◦ How does Krukowski differentiate signal and noise? Think about what he discusses when he mentions "surface noise"?
2. Discuss answers with class.
3. For follow-up discussion:
    ◦ What sources and kinds of "noise" then would be appropriate in your podcast? How could you incorporate that into your drafted podcast?
    ◦ Some thoughts for you: In a sense, it is ok that your voice recording may not be the most polished. Perhaps we need to embrace the hiss of digital media; we need to hear those ambient sounds, like firetrucks and construction cranes you hear outside your dorm room. Ambient sounds root us in time and place.
4. Turn to Freesound.org for potential noises worthwhile. Noise is sound, usually ambient sound.

    For the next few minutes, I'd like for you to investigate some musical sounds and background noises that might work for your audio essay. We'll come back as a group and discuss these. Use Freesound, but also feel welcome to make and record your own music and sounds if you wish.

    You'll most likely use the same drag-and-drop method as you did with your voice recordings.

5. Students work with sounds and music.

6. Students work with Creative Commons music.

7. Let's listen back to the *Snap Judgment* segment "Brain in a Box" (Washington, 2017) and recount the number of music and noise tracks that go with the story.

Some notes we made as a class on *Snap Judgment*:

Music: 1) Hip-hop instrumental beat, R&B; 2) Blues; 3) Ambient, electronic; 4) Mysterious, sci-fi, almost atonal; 5) Lush jazz vibes; 6) Astro-soul?; 7) Video game-related, techno

Sounds and sound effects: 1) Chime; 2) Angelic sound; 3) Zip-zap; 4) Kid sounds; 5) Computer sounds; 6) Crashing sounds; 7) Computer dying

Homework

Using Freesound.org or another service, pick a range of musical tracks you are thinking about including along with your voice recording. Send along three musical files you are thinking about, with a brief discussion of each (one to two sentences). You can email me links or upload them to Dropbox.

Audio Essay Response Template

> . . . noise is as communicative as signal.
>
> – *Damon Krukowski,* The New Analog

Here, I provide a template for how I respond to students' drafts of their audio essays.

Dear [Student],

Here are my comments on your audio essay draft. I have grouped my comments by three categories discussed in Damon Krukowski's book *The New Analog*. Keep these in mind as you work on your revisions before the final podcast episode is due [insert date]. I look forward to seeing you in next class to talk about any pressing comments and concerns you have!

Signal: "If the voice on a phone is intended to communicate words, why not narrow the definition of signal to just the words in order to improve the accuracy of their transmission?" (Krukowski, p. 75).

[Insert comments based on reading excerpt above.]

Noise: "We might call it thick listening, alert to the depth of the many layers [and noises] in multitrack recording. [Reviewers] listen through the surface noise of the LP, through the hiss of the master tape, through the layers of the music itself all the way back to the room in which it was played" (Krukowski, p. 119).

[Insert comments based on reading excerpt above.]

Feeling: "Digital signal processing places the speaker always in the same non-space: neither near nor far, neither intimate nor distant. The resulting flatness not only isolates the voice but removes affect. The data is intelligible, but the voice that is produced it can only be heard, never felt" (Krukowski, p. 84).

[Insert comments based on reading excerpt above.]

Sample Student Projects

In these sample audio essays, you will hear works by two students: Martha Reifenberg and Trinity.[1] The songwriting practices of recording, arranging, and thick listening to signal and noise show up across the texts. In their rationales regarding their audio essays, Martha and Trinity make sense of these practices and the feelings they evoke. Please see the students' references list for all music and sounds included in their audio essays.

1. In the first example, Martha discusses the impact of social media on literature. Her rationale includes a discussion of her musical choice that runs counter to the revolutionary nature of social media.
2. In the second example, Trinity discusses a hot-button issue—texting while driving. Her rationale concerns her use of stats and the idea that "dark classical music adds a sense of eeriness to the podcast and thus strengths [sic] my message."

Reflection

[The ambient sounds of a band warming up in a club. All the music samples that follow are performed by the band Sweet and the Sweet Sweets.]

Rich Shivener: Hi, this is Rich Shivener, and you're listening to my audio reflection for my chapter on songwriting and emotions.[2] I'm recording this from my basement at home, and the music you hear is from my band.

I demonstrate teaching and sampling songwriting practices in digital rhetoric courses, from introductory to advanced-level sections. My assignment covers three practices of songwriting: recording, arranging, and "thick listening," or a technique that embraces signal and noise. The assignment is based on a first-year composition course in which students had written researched arguments on digital writing and devices. After editing their arguments down to 500 words, they produced audio essays; they recorded vocal tracks, arranged Creative Commons sounds and musical samples, and made sense of ambient noises that found their way into their recordings. Episodes from podcasts such as *Lore* and *Snap Judgment* were useful examples of telling stories, generating atmospheres, and

---

1. Two student examples (audio files and descriptive transcripts) can be found on the book's companion website.

2. The audio version of Rich Shivener's reflection can be found on the book's companion website.

integrating music. Along with my interest in podcasts, my assignment is based on Damon Krukowski's theories in his 2017 book *The New Analog.*

[Live band music fades up for a moment before getting quieter again.]

My assignment is also based on my 20 years as a working musician. I find that songwriting helps me attune to and make sense of pain and emotions—and in some cases, to represent the sensations and emotions of others. That's not exactly a new insight among musicians, given that a range of genres and visceral songs reflect felt memories and affective encounters. I feel the affectivity of songwriting is thickened when musicians, as the saying goes, "play to the space," or embrace the environmental surround of a recording.

[A doo-wop song plays.]

The environmental surround is noise; it might be a room's natural reverb, its hums and creaks, its occupants who aren't involved in the recording session. Thomas Rickert (2013) brought up such an idea in his book *Ambient Rhetoric: The Attunements of Rhetorical Being*. With signal and noise, with ambience, feeling is thickened in varying ways.

[A rock'n'roll song plays.]

Signal, noise, and feeling are three ideas I want students thinking about as they record, arrange, and listen to their audio essays. You can hear students' audio essays in another section of this chapter. For the rest of this reflection, I'd like to make three points about the assignment, looking back on a recent version of the assignment and toward future possibilities.

Let's Start with Point One: Songwriting.

Here's the strange part of this assignment.

[Another rock song plays.]

It doesn't require students to write songs.

You heard that right. It doesn't require students to write songs. So is it a songwriting assignment?

Yes, because the assignment embraces songwriting practices. As I mentioned earlier, those practices are recording vocal tracks, arranging sounds and music, and doing some thick listening. Now, those techniques are also found in podcasting. However, as the title of this chapter suggests, I'm trying to cultivate songwriting, whether in theory or praxis. Damon Krukowski's ideas struck me as a good, introductory framework for students in a first-year composition course themed on digital writing and rhetoric. In other words, I thought a songwriter's theories of signal, noise, and feeling would be a useful framework for students who have little experience producing audio essays, let alone songs. After reading about recording techniques and sampling songwriting practices for an audio essay, they seemed to be in a better position to think about ways in which music and noise amplify the emotional appeals of a written or spoken text.

And This Brings Me to Point Two: Responding to the Students.

[Another rock song plays in the background.]

In this chapter, you will notice that I don't have a rubric. Instead, I have included a response sheet based on signal, noise, and feeling. From experience, I can say with certainty that musicians and bandmates rarely grade each other; however, they talk through ideas, critique each other, encourage each other, and collaborate often in recording sessions. As a means to reflecting songwriting approaches, then, I opted to complete responses rather than complete a rubric. If students didn't complete in-class activities, produce drafts, and present a version of their audio essays to the class during finals week, their grade suffered. As I explained to students, missing out on process work is like missing a recording session, a time to dwell on and try out ideas.

[A faster rocking, soulful song plays with some fake horns.]

You'll have to take my word for it that nearly all students in my recent course completed all facets of the assignment, producing interesting audio essays. I think the sample audio essays you'll hear reflect that.

As a rhetoric and composition teacher, you might wish to integrate a rubric into my sample response sheet, especially if your institution requires it. You might translate the term "signal" to a term like "clarity"; you might change "noise" to "background sounds"; and you might change "feeling" to "emotional appeals."

And Last but Not Least Point Three: More Songwriting?

[the ambient sounds of a band warming up in a club]

I want to come back to my first point in this audio reflection. Beyond first-year courses, more advanced digital composition courses might lend themselves to more intense songwriting practices—including writing songs. In an upcoming semester, I'm teaching a more craft-oriented course on producing digital texts. One idea is to have students work with a prefabricated vocal track, perhaps one from a podcast producer willing to submit it. Students might have more time to focus on writing musical passages and ambient sounds designed to surround a vocal track. We might focus more on the extent to which Garage-Band and other programs help producers compose songs with samples and the like. There might be interesting collaborations between students whose musical literacies and resources vary. Even failed experiments with songwriting might happen.

Another idea is to reverse-engineer a song—from its distribution and back to the room and resources on which it was recorded.

[a sample of a quiet auto-tuned voice singing without words, composed by Rich]

We might need something simple and approachable. I keep thinking about B.o.B.'s (BobbyRaySimmons, 2008) "Auto Tune——-Spoof (Funny)" video on YouTube. In the song, he goes meta by using the auto-tune technique of musical recording programs as a basis for satirizing the technique. We see the musician's recording space, his vocal mics, and the auto-tune technique in question. The YouTube page, for which the song was created, has the song lyrics. Asking students to recompose the auto-tune song might surround discussions of programs and platforms that have helped aspiring songwriters compose and distribute content to public audiences. Public composition and distribution are indeed loud themes in the field of rhetoric and composition. Songwriting practices play out those themes.

So, in Closing . . .

I hope songwriting gives way to exciting projects by students. I'm sounding out what I hope is a significant contribution to digital rhetoric scholarship because it responds to the field's melodic interests and explores pedagogical possibilities that draw on songwriting theory and praxis. It might serve well as an introduction to more robust assignments about devices and materials, music and its genres, and materials and tones that cultivate emotions.

[Live, upbeat, bluesy rock band fades up for a few seconds before fading out.]

References

Alexander, J. (2015). Glenn Gould and the rhetorics of sound. *Computers and Composition, 37,* 73–89. https://doi.org/10.1016/j.compcom.2015.06.004.

Banks, A. (2010). *Digital griots: African American rhetoric in a multimedia age.* Southern Illinois University Press.

BobbyRaySimmons. (2008, December 3). B.o.B——-auto tune——-spoof (funny) [Video file]. *YouTube.* https://youtu.be/IBaXwRQQciI.

Ceraso, S. (2014). (Re) Educating the senses: Multimodal listening, bodily learning, and the composition of sonic experiences. *College English, 77*(2), 102–123.

Hawk, B. (2010). The shape of rhetoric to come: Musical worlding as public rhetoric. *Pre/Text, 20,* 7–42.

Krukowski, D. (2017). *The new analog: Listening and reconnecting in a digital world.* MIT Press.

Malek, J., Carter, C., Shivener, R. & Blewett, K. (Eds.). (2017). *Student guide to English composition 1001.* Hayden-McNeil.

Rice, J. (2003). The 1963 hip-hop machine: Hip-hop pedagogy as composition. *College Composition and Communication, 54*(3), 453–471.

Rickert, T. (2013). *Ambient rhetoric: The attunements of rhetorical being.* University of Pittsburgh Press.

Sirc, G. (2005). Composition's eye/Orpheus's gaze/Cobain's *Journals. Composition Studies, 33*(1), 11–30.

Squareal. (2014, 11 May). Car crash [Audio file]. *Freesound.* https://freesound.org /people/squareal/sounds/237375/.

Stedman, K. D. (2013). Making meaning in musical mixes. *Harlot: A Revealing Look at the Arts of Persuasion, 9.* https://harlotofthearts.org/ojs-3.3.0-11/index.php /harlot/article/view/167/124.

VanKooten, C. (2016). Singer, writer: A choric explanation of sound and writing. *Kairos: A Journal of Rhetoric, Technology, and Pedagogy, 21*(1). https://kairos.tech norhetoric.net/21.1/inventio/vankooten/index.html.

Washington, G. (Host). (2017, July 20). Brain in a box (No. 501) [Audio podcast episode]. In *Snap judgment.* https://snapjudgment.org/story/brain-in-a-box-snap -501-artificial-intelligence/.

Chapter 9. "How *Eve* Saved My Soul": Sonic Lineage as the Prequel to the Playlist Project

Todd Craig

THE GRADUATE CENTER, CUNY, AND MEDGAR EVERS COLLEGE

My mom departed from this physical plane called life on July 27, 2019. It was easily the most devastating blow of my life. My mom was one of those old-school Black women; she raised her three children, then raised me (I'm technically her great nephew), her three grandchildren, and one more of my cousins. They just don't make the cloth humans like my mom was stitched from, simple and plain. She was a miracle worker, moving mountains while here on Earth, and continuing such feats on the next part of her journey. I say this because I got a call to teach my first college-level hip-hop class immediately after her passing. A good colleague and better friend was serving as deputy chair; when she called, she basically said, "I have to call you because I know you would NOT be okay if I didn't. And I know you just lost your mom. But I have to tell you this: Our Hip-Hop Worldview class needs an instructor—and everyone is wondering where you are and if you can teach it. . . ."

As you can imagine, this moment didn't strike me as sheer coincidence. I found it to be kairos: the perfect moment where space, time, and location intersected. I also saw this as my mom's blessing. After being on the tenure track for five years in a retrograde department that rejects contemporary scholarship, rebukes the field of comp/rhet writ large, diminishes my own research, and had relegated my expertise to only teaching sections of first-year writing, teaching Hip-Hop Worldview was a dream come true. This dream, however, did not erase the sheer pain that comes with losing a parent. And in the midst of my mother's death, I was simply trying to put the pieces of my life back together and find my way back through and into my life's requirements.

Enter *Eve*—The Makings of Healing Through Sonics

I share these very raw life moments as integral points of context. At the nexus where my mother's passing and the beginning stages of this class meet, I found myself entrenched in a piece of art-turned-sonic therapy: Rapsody's (2019) album *Eve*. This brilliant musical project highlights Rapsody taking a sonic journey through the evolution and iconic nature of Black women. Each song is named after a significant and charismatic Black woman throughout global culture who has achieved great success in her life—a success that speaks to the radiance and resilience we

DOI: https://doi.org/10.37514/PRA-B.2022.1688.2.09

now call #BlackGirlMagic. An ode to Black women in its totality, each song sonically evokes and symbolizes Rapsody's chosen subject. This album was nominated for a 2020 Grammy award (the nomination sans victory is another conversation by itself). I deemed this album therapeutic because while listening, I could see and hear my mom at every turn; each song presented me with a facet of her being. And every day I waded through the listening of it, trying to make sense of how to persevere and honor the legacy of a woman who raised me when she didn't have to.

The centerpiece of this album for me was "Ibtihaj." The beat, produced by 9th Wonder, is a remix/reproduction of the GZA's song entitled "Liquid Swords," which makes it a fitting tribute to Olympic fencing bronze medalist Ibtihaj Muhammad. "Ibtihaj" features R&B enigma D'Angelo on the chorus, with GZA providing a guest verse. Besides the fact this song slaps stupid, what struck me most was that Rapsody's 2019 lyrical content was evoking the sonic textures and sentiments of 1995 Wu-Tang sonics. Set in Harlem, New York (Rapsody is from North Carolina), the video also evokes the legacy of fashion icon Dapper Dan, with the 1980s and early 1990s luxury clothing wraps, (re)purposings, and (re)envisionings (Day, 2019). Thinking about how this song and accompanying video stretched between decades and sonic sentiments, it helped me create a new assignment: the Sonic Lineage project.

Sitting with Sonic Lineage in Theory to Create Sonic Lineage in Practice

Sonic lineage (Craig, in press) is a term that builds upon Alfred Tatum's work on "textual lineage" through the prism of Dr. Bilal Polson's Instagram framework of #literacylineage and #textual-lineage (Polson, 2019). Sonic lineage functions based on the sounds, sights, and visuals that inform how one engages with historical musical trajectories, as well as ways that "readers" (or listeners) engage in the learning that comes from the sonic. Sonic lineage is not only a list of auditory or musical sources that share the same sentiment, but in some cases, it's an earlier source that predicates the existence of the newer source. Think of it as a "soundline" of sorts: the lineage, the bloodline, and the family tree.

The Sonic Lineage project asks students to choose an album and document its sonic/textual lineage over the course of at least three decades of their choice (1970s, 1980s, 1990s, 2000s, and 2010s). In mapping out the album's sonic/textual lineage, students are asked to tell the story of the album and the significant hip-hop (or hip-hop-connected) "texts" that contribute to the album's sonic literacy. This project focuses on students' discovery through research, creating a heuristic vis-à-vis the insight that comes from how they envision an album's sonic lineage.

This project serves as the prequel to a mixtape assignment I do with students entitled Heavy Airplay, All Day with No Chorus (Craig, 2019). Its overarching intention is to prepare students to delve into strictly composing with sound via mixtapes and playlists by asking them to submerge themselves in sound based upon someone else's sonic sensibilities, and then connect those choices to at least three decades. It is a reflective assignment that forces students to write about sound so they can have the necessary tools to write with sound. The goal here is to situate the soundwriting and composing that comes out with the mixtape project by allowing students the space to engage in their mental and auditory discussions around sound via writing.

Yet, as I mention in my audio reflection, I want to get students past the apprehension around "more beats and sounds in the air" in lieu of "more words on the page." Thus, I envision a final project (project #3 below) where students create a sonic metatext and reflect on how they have engaged in theorizing and wrestling with sonic compositions. The submitted 3–10-minute sound file can allow for a moment of praxis, where students can live, stretch, and grow in a space that privileges sound as the only communicative medium to capture a sentiment that alphanumeric textual production simply cannot.

Assignments

Course Project #1: Sonic Lineage Project

For Course Project #1, you are required to choose an album and document its sonic lineage over the course of at least three decades (choose between the 1970s, 1980s, 1990s, 2000s, and 2010s). In thinking about mapping out the album's sonic lineage, you should tell the story about the album as well as the significant hip-hop (or hip-hop-connected) texts that contribute to the album's sonic literacy. This project should focus on your own learning process and the insight that comes from how you envision the album's sonic lineage. Some questions you may want to ask yourself in completing this project are:

1. What are the significant "texts" that were influential in creating your album's literacy?

2. Describe the "texts" that contribute to your album's sonic literacy.

3. How did you identify these "texts"? Did someone point them out to you, or did you discover them on your own?

4. How is each sonic "text" significant to the album's creation?

This project should be submitted as either a Prezi, PowerPoint, or Google Slides presentation.

Course Project #3: The Sounding Board (Sonic Reflection Project)

For Course Project #3, you are required to reflect on how you have approached using sound/sonic elements throughout the semester. Because we are discussing sonics, this reflection must be a sound recording, and cannot be written. Your recording can be between 3–10 minutes long and should include your voice alongside at least three other sound/sonic elements. Some questions you might think about when composing your reflection include the following:

- Describe your experiences with sound this semester. What sonic sources have you chosen and how have you interrogated those sources this semester?
- What were your apprehensions or fears about working with sound-only sources/artifacts?
- Were you able to communicate specific thoughts and ideas through sound that you could not communicate with alphanumeric textual writing? What were those ideas? Explain your thinking fully.
- If you could revise any of your assignments based on revisiting your sonic sources, what are some revision choices you would make?

This project should be submitted as either a WAV or MP3 file.

Sample Student Projects

1. Hamed Afastu, "*Straight Outta Compton*: N.W.A.'s Influential Album": Afastu discusses the album's influence on contemporary protests and fashion, as well as how it's been sampled by and has influenced three decades of hip-hop.[1]
2. Alyse Ahmide, "*Enter the Wu-Tang (36 Chambers)* Review": Ahmide takes a deep dive into the cultural influences on Wu-Tang Clan's first album and touches on the later careers of some of its members and its ongoing influence today.
3. Perry Stephano, "Textual Lineage of 'Some Rap Songs'": Stephano focuses on the history and meaning of the samples used by Earl Sweatshirt on his third and final album with Columbia Records.
4. Garrison Johanson, "*Everything Is Love*: A Connection to the Decades": Johanson's analysis of The Carters' collaborative album focuses on its reinterpretation of the styles and sounds of the 1960s and 1990s in a way that speaks to the present day.

Reflection

Todd Craig: Check, one, two—what's good everybody?[2] Todd Craig here, aka T. O. Double D on certain days, aka, the Diggy-Diggy-Doctor on other days; there's other "akas" that I can run through, but that's all we need for right now. You're listening to the audio reflection of "How *Eve* Saved My Soul": aka the "Sonic Lineage Project—the Prequel to the Playlist Project."

So, the Sonic Lineage project comes out of, you know, a very interesting time in my life.

---

1. Four student examples of the Sonic Lineage Project (PowerPoint slides) can be found on the book's companion website.
2. The audio version of Todd Craig's reflection can be found on the book's companion website.

[Music: the instrumental to "Hatshepsut" by Rapsody featuring Queen Latifah fades in and continues beneath the following narration. It features prominent hip-hop beats and a walking bass line along with positive, major-key melodies played on a piano.]

I lost my mother right before I started teaching my first college-level hip-hop class. So first and foremost, shout out to Ruth Muchita: Thanks for everything, Mom, appreciate you. I was asked to teach my first college-level hip-hop course days after my mother's passing. And so it was a class that I took on specifically because my research is in . . . rooted in hip-hop, rooted in the hip-hop DJ. And so it just made sense. It was obviously a natural sort of evolution in what my teaching practice was. And so you can imagine what it was like trying to teach a class you've always wanted to teach for the first time, on one hand, and on the other hand, having lost a parent. You know, it was definitely a difficult moment. And what I found through this moment is the thing that got me through this, this period of mourning and grieving, was literally an album from a hip-hop artist named Rapsody (2019). The name of the album is *Eve*, and what Rapsody was able to do with that album was incredible.

Clearly a concept album, where each song is dedicated to sort of an ode or an homage to a particular Black woman, who has, you know, done extraordinary work, you know, in the country, and the globe, in whatever it is that they do. And each of those songs kind of embodies and evokes that woman sonically, in ways where Rapsody just really nailed it. And what became interesting for me about this album was I could hear my mother in every single song. I could see her, hear her, you know, I could feel her presence. And every facet of her kind of came out in Rapsody sort of evoking these different Black women.

[Music slowly fades out as Craig continues speaking.]

And so, as I was listening to the Rapsody album, one of the songs that really just caught my attention straight away was "Ibtihaj." And that is a song named after Ibtihaj Muhammad, who was the first Muslim American woman to win a medal in an Olympics—she was a bronze medalist.

[Music: the instrumental to "Ibtihaj" by Rapsody featuring GZA and D'Angelo fades in and continues below the continuing narration. We can hear organ, beats, and eventually a group singing indistinct words.]

But she's also the first Muslim American woman to wear a hijab while fencing. And what struck me about this song in particular is that "Ibtihaj" as a song is a remix, or an interpolation of sorts, of a song by the GZA, or the Genius, from the Wu-Tang Clan, from his solo album, entitled *Liquid Swords* (1995). The name of the song is "Liquid Swords." So there's already this interesting relation between Rapsody using "Liquid Swords," and then naming that song "Ibtihaj," given that she was a fencer. Rapsody has GZA come and do a guest verse, and there is also guest vocalist, R&B, you know, legend D'Angelo, who also sings the hook on the song.

And so the song is pretty significant because the Rapsody album came out in 2019. This song reaches back to the GZA's album in 1995, but also includes GZA on the record, you know, twenty-some-odd . . . yeah, twenty-some-odd years later.

[Music slowly fades out as Craig continues speaking.]

And what became even more incredible for me was the video to "Ibtihaj," and what I immediately noticed in the video was, you know, there was this—it's a video that's set in Harlem.

[Music: the instrumental to "Liquid Swords" by the GZA fades in; this is the song that Rapsody samples from for "Ibtihaj." It features repeated, rhythmic keyboard chords played one after the other over a beat, playing one chord eight times and then another chord eight times before repeating.]

Rapsody's from North Carolina, so it's interesting that she would bring a video up to be set in Harlem. A number of different Black women, Muslim women in hijabs of various just colors and designs (see Thompson, 2019). There was also a number of different moments where there are different cars and different elements of the video that are wrapped in MCM, which is a sort of designer bag company. But the wrap comes from Dapper Dan, who is—I want to say Dapper Dan is currently with Gucci. But early on in the 1980s and 1990s, Dapper Dan was based in Harlem, and was this incredible fashion designer who would take all of these luxury bags and sort of re-envision them and make clothes, car seats, all sorts of different things for hip-hop culture at the time. And it became super interesting to me that Rapsody in 2019 was reaching back to 1995 and the GZA, was reaching back into the 1980s and early 1990s with Dapper Dan. And that kind of spawned how this idea of sonic lineage comes—this kind of thinking around what different elements sonically, visually connect to a song in the present day. And how far back does that lineage travel? You know, sonic lineage is very reminiscent to Alfred Tatum's (2009) idea of textual lineage.

And one of the people who really, really helped me to kind of spark and envision what sonic lineage looks like, was Dr. Bilal Polson, who . . . Dr. Polson did a year's worth of IG posts (Polson, 2020), where he would post different songs daily, kind of evoking the lineage that other people had based on the song. He would just post an image of a 45, maybe it's a YouTube video, maybe it's a 12-inch, just so people could begin to then have conversations around what that song meant to them, what that song evoked from them. And so in looking at this moment, with Rapsody, "Ibtihaj," and understanding "Liquid Swords," and understanding all of the complexities that Rapsody was weaving throughout the song, and then also the album, that brought me to wanting to do an assignment with students called the Sonic Lineage assignment, where I wanted students to identify an album that they related to. And then I wanted them to connect different routes and different streams of thought that appear in that present-day album, at whatever time it was, but then connect it to three different decades.

[Music slowly fades out as Craig continues speaking.]

Those decades could have been the 1970s, the 1980s, the 1990s, 2000s, or the 2010s.

[Music: the song "Mercy, Mercy, Mercy" by Willie Mitchell fades in; this is the song that is sampled for the opening of "Liquid Swords." It's a positive soul track with lots of horns and bass.]

So giving students about half a century to think about how they are seeing the strands that run through an album in different timeframes. And the idea was to really get students to begin to think about how they would address the sonic, think about how they would address writing about music, thinking about music, and re-envisioning music so that music is the primary text and is not a secondary, tertiary, or even a source that is unacceptable unless it is beefed up by a bunch of other sources. So that's where this idea of the Sonic Lineage project came from. It's also a project that I would do with students before it . . . this project is the first project, the next project they do is a mixtape project, which I call Heavy Airplay, All Day With No Chorus. The mixtape project of course asked students to create a mixtape or a playlist.

[Music slowly fades out as Craig continues speaking.]

So they're really sort of composing with different songs and sounds and ideas that they have around the music.

[Music: "Groovin'" by Willie Mitchell fades in; this is the song that is sampled for the beat of both "Liquid Swords" and "Ibtihaj." It's positive, happy soul music, with a very prominent organ.]

But what the Sonic Lineage project . . . what it aimed to do was to get students to begin to think about what it meant to address music and how you think and write about music, so that you can then begin to write with music.

In terms of reflections, I think the assignment went okay. One of the things I would definitely consider doing, as I continue to do this assignment with other students, is really pushing students to think outside of the box in terms of making their assignments or their projects way more multimodal. I asked that students did this in PowerPoint or Prezi or Google Slides. I didn't want it to be a Microsoft Word document with words on the page. And I was really envisioning that students would have hyperlinks to different songs, and kind of make those connections, maybe do some audio. And what I found was that students were really, really apprehensive about kind of going "all the way there" and pushing the envelope in terms of sound. And in terms of really, really incorporating sound, they still weren't really trusting in the fact that that's what I wanted. And they were kind of leaning on their collegiate, academic sensibilities of, "I need to have more words on the page than I need to have beats in the air."

[Music slowly fades out as Craig continues speaking.]

So that is something I think that I would really push students towards, is really trying to do a little less of the literal writing and more thinking about making these connections sonically, using different audio, using different images and video links, to really give them the sense of creating a sonic lineage and a sonic roadmap and a family tree of sorts when they are addressing this project.

[Music: the instrumental to "Believe Me" by Rapsody fades in; with its modern hip-hop beats, bass, and keyboard lines, it's a striking contrast to the music that's been playing.]

So those are my thoughts. That's where I'm at with this project. And I'm looking forward to continuing to push forward with this project and have students push the envelope. I hope this project is helpful to you to get your students to kind of push the envelope in thinking about how they are beginning to address sound so that they're able to then write *with* sound. So that is it for me. I want to, again, give a shout out to, give a shout out to Rapsody, because the *Eve* album is absolutely crazy. And you know, the fact that she didn't win a Grammy for that one is a whole different conversation in and of itself, but we won't talk about that. But shouts to Rapsody, shouts to the *Eve* album. And that is it. Thank you for listening. Thank you for tuning in.

Also, really quick before I go, I definitely want to shout out Courtney and Michael and Kyle, all the other contributors. Thanks for making this *Amplifying Soundwriting* project possible. We definitely all appreciate it; salutes to you as editors.

And with that, I'm gone! Todd Craig, T. O. Double D: I will see you on the next go-round.

Peace!

[Music slowly fades out.]

References

Craig, T. (2019, October 14). "Heavy airplay, all day with no chorus": Classroom sonic consciousness in the playlist project. *Sounding out!* https://soundstudies blog.com/2019/10/14/heavy-airplay-all-day-with-no-chorus-classroom-sonic -consciousness-in-the-playlist-project/.

Craig, T. (in press). Stacks, sounds and a record a day: An introduction to DJ rhetoric and sonic lineage in praxis. *Rhetoric, Politics, and Culture.*

Day, D. (2019). *Dapper Dan: Made in Harlem: A memoir.* Random House.

Genius/GZA. (1995). Liquid swords [Song]. On *Liquid swords.* Geffen Records.

Mitchell, W. (1967). Groovin' [Song]. On *Solid soul*. Hi Records.

Mitchell, W. (1968). Mercy, mercy, mercy [Song]. Hi Records.

Polson, B. [@bilalpolson]. (2019, August 12). *Literacy-lineage: #literacy #literacylives #textual-lineage #JamesBrown #AlfredTatum* [Photograph]. Instagram. https://www.instagram.com/p/B1D_wLxgvf1/.

Rapsody. (2012). Believe me [Song]. On *The idea of beautiful*. Jamla Records.

Rapsody. (2019). *Eve* [Album]. Jamla/RocNation Records.

Rapsody, featuring GZA & D'Angelo. (2019). Ibtihaj [Song]. On *Eve*. Jamla/RocNation Records.

Rapsody, featuring Queen Latifah. (2019). Hatshepsut [Song]. On *Eve*. Jamla/RocNation Records.

Tatum, A. W. (2009). *Reading for their life: (Re)building the textual lineages of African American adolescent males*. Heinemann.

Thompson, D. (2019, August 6). The 9 best Black Girl Magic moments in Rapsody's "Ibtihaj" video. *Vibe*. https://www.vibe.com/music/music-news/the-9-best-black-girl-magic-moments-in-rapsodys-ibtihaj-video-659516/.

Chapter 10. Sampling Sound, Text, and Praxis: Student and Teacher as Producer in a (Somewhat) Open-Source Course

Justin Young
EASTERN WASHINGTON UNIVERSITY

This chapter describes the assignment sequence for a soundwriting course focused on remix, framing the role of the composition student and instructor as that of the hip-hop producer and breaking down its praxis into the components of theory, pedagogy, and curricula. Remix is a natural fit with soundwriting because at its start, remix was all about sound. Jamaican dance hall and hip-hop DJs from the 1970s were the first remixers, although the term remix is now used to denote everything from the interactive nature of digital cultural production to the process of writing in the field of composition. In the soundwriting course described in this chapter, students learned how to sample and remix in order to design and produce both new soundwriting texts, as well as with more traditional academic texts. Likewise, the teacher produced the course by sampling open educational resources (OER) in order to design and implement the course's pedagogy, syllabus, readings, and soundwriting assignments.

Remix culture has already been the focus of much theoretical scholarship in composition and rhetoric, as well as more generally in fields like design and cultural studies. However, as I began designing this course, I learned that there is little available on the processes and practices of remix and how these might be applied to pedagogy generally and composition and soundwriting specifically. This fact became clear to me as I prepared to teach this course: Plenty was available if I wanted to teach a graduate level cultural studies course on remix theory; very little was available on how one might go about actually teaching first-year college students to use remix practices as means of multimodal text production.

This chapter aims to help address this gap by providing a sequence of assignments that enable students to apply the strategies of remix to a range of composing tasks, including, of course, soundwriting assignments. For the purposes of this chapter, the term soundwriting refers to writing for sound and about sound. I will detail how Kirby Ferguson's (2016) formula for the practice of remix—copy, transform, and combine—can be used as the basis for student production of audio and alphabetic texts, and how the concept of remix can help students reflect upon and refine their own soundwriting processes.

Remix isn't new to composition scholarship and pedagogy. The concept of remix, most generally, has been examined as a framework for understanding the process of composing in digital environments (Davis et al., 2010; Walker & Cox,

DOI: https://doi.org/10.37514/PRA-B.2022.1688.2.10

2013; Williams, 2012). Further, scholars like Mickey Hess (2006) and Martin Courant Rife and Dànielle Nicole DeVoss (2013) have examined how remix complicates traditional notions of plagiarism. Recent research has focused on more practical applications of remix to the classroom. For example, Dustin W. Edwards (2016) worked to "map the many ways that remix writers accomplish their rhetorical goals" (p. 41) by developing a four-part typology of remix. And Abby M. Dubisar et al. (2017) demonstrated how to use remix for the production of feminist rhetorical criticism in a multimodal writing classroom. Despite this work, there still exists a research gap in the field of composition: scholarship focused on remix pedagogy. To help fill this gap, this chapter provides an assignment sequence that exemplifies teaching the remix process in the writing classroom, and specifically, how it can be applied to soundwriting. Below is a description of this assignment sequence.

> **Assignment One: Responding to Sound and Soundwriting.** For this online gateway assignment, students read Greg Tate's (2016) "Why Jazz Will Always Be Relevant" (on music and remix) and listen to a related playlist. They then respond to a writing prompt that includes "embodied" questions that focus on students' feeling about what they listened to, in order to enhance engagement and investment.

> **Assignment Two: Team Presentation of Remix Analysis.** For this collaborative assignment, introducing analytic, remix, and soundwriting strategies, teams write and record a sound presentation or multimodal (sound + video) presentation that provides an analysis of a text that has been remixed. This presentation should identify the texts that were "sampled, transformed and combined," and analyze how remix methods were used to create a new text; it should also examine the purpose and audience of the remix.

> **Assignment Three: Analysis Essay.** Next, students write about a remixed text, relating it to a topic of debate in remix studies. Students produce an academically appropriate essay that "samples, transforms, and combines," primary and secondary sources with their own writing, using remix theory as their analytic framework.

> **Assignment Four: Audio/Video Remix.** Finally, students work in teams to collaboratively produce a remixed sound text, which can include a range of multimodal elements (e.g., sound, video, alphabetic text). For another soundwriting component of the assignment, students will record an audio presentation on the processes they used to plan and produce the remixed text, reflecting on the team's approach to remixing and soundwriting.

I also consider the benefits and challenges of teaching soundwriting as a form of participation in student-relevant, but legally fraught, remix culture. In my audio reflection, I will argue that connecting the practice of soundwriting to remix is ideal for fostering a classroom culture of engagement: Students are affectively invested in the work of the classroom when they write about and produce new sound texts by remixing the cultural texts they are personally invested in outside of the classroom. Essentially, soundwriting, at its best, is a process of remix, per Ferguson's (2016) formula: The soundwriter samples or "copies" a variety of recorded (often copyrighted) sounds and recontextualizes or "transforms" them by combining the sounds with original written then recorded content, which results in an audio remix. But while the process of soundwriting through copying, transforming, and combining found and original content may be technically easier than ever given our rapidly advancing digital ecosystem, teaching and learning it in the classroom is complicated by copyright laws that have not evolved at the same pace.

Assignments & Assignment Sequences

A note about this sequence: Assignments were designed to follow the template developed by the Transparency in Teaching and Learning institute (TILT). This approach to assignment design has been demonstrated to impact student learning and retention via the clear articulation of assignment purpose, task, and evaluative criteria (Winkelmes, 2013).

Assignment One: Responding to Sound & Soundwriting (A Gateway Activity)

You've now read the article "Why Jazz Will Always Be Relevant" by Greg Tate and listened to/viewed the playlist based on some of the artists/songs noted in the article. Now it's time to compose your response!

Your task is to produce an (approximately) 200-word written online response to what you read/heard/watched. Remember, remix is about selections and connections: Your job as the producer of this post is to select a piece (or pieces) of the article and connect them to selections from the related playlist, along with the concept of remix. (You can select keywords or ideas from our remix glossary or any of the other readings we've done to help you make the connection to remix theory.)

You have a choice: You can accomplish this in two different ways:

1. Focus on the article by writing about a story or idea in the reading that really stuck with you—discuss something you found cool or interesting, moving, or even difficult. Why did you connect with this particular part of what the author had to say?

   ◦ You should directly quote (in remix terms, copy & paste) from the article a sentence or two related to the story/idea you select.

○ Try to relate this piece (sample) of the article to at least one of the songs or videos in the playlist and to the concept of remix in any way you like.

2. Focus on a song/video by writing about a part (lyric, beat, melody, image, sample) in the playlist that really stuck with you—something you found cool or interesting, moving, or even strange. Why did you "feel" this song or video? What kind of impact did it have on you and why?

○ You should describe (with a sentence or two) sound or image you select.

○ Select and quote a line or two from the article that relates to the song or video and connect all of this to the concept of remix in any way you like.

Playlist (all selections available on YouTube)

- "Jazz (We've Got)" (1991) – A Tribe Called Quest
- "Passing Me By" (1992) – The Pharcyde
- "Bitches Brew (Live)" (1970) – Miles Davis
- "Manage Bitches Brew–Remix" (2007) – Yesterdays New Quintet/Madlib
- "Alright" (2015) – Kendrick Lamar, featuring Terrace Martin
- "Never Catch Me" (2014) – Flying Lotus, featuring Kendrick Lamar (vocals) & Thundercat (bass)

Assignment Two: Remix Analysis: Team Presentation

Task

Production teams will create an audio presentation (i.e., a podcast) or multimodal (video + audio) presentation that provides an analysis of a remixed audio text. This presentation should identify the texts that were "sampled, transformed and combined" and analyze how remix methods were used to create a new text; it should also examine the purpose and audience of the remix.

Group members must individually produce a short, written text that contextualizes and/or analyzes a specific "sample" in the remix.

For this assignment you can:

- Create a brief podcast-like recording in which you describe and analyze the text. Tip: for example, if you are analyzing a song, you can model your recording off of an NPR music review, as long as part of your review includes discussion of how the artist uses remix.

OR

- Create a digital visual/audio text using software tools (such as Keynote or iMovie).

Purpose

For many courses in college, as well as in most professional jobs, you will need to be able to work in teams to conduct analyses and present information clearly and creatively. For this project you will practice analyzing a text and presenting the results of that analysis in an aural or visual presentation.

Criteria for Success

This presentation should

- identify the texts that were sampled and combined in order to create the remix you are analyzing
- analyze how remix methods were used to create a transformed text
- examine the purpose of the remixed text; for example, did the text work to entertain, inform, or subvert norms?

1-Pager Criteria for Success

Each group member must also produce a written 1-pager (at least 250 words) about the remix. This written page can

- contextualize and/or analyze a specific "sample" or textual element used in the remix, OR
- discuss how remix techniques were used to create a new text, OR
- make an argument about the quality of the remix, OR
- describe how the remix challenges artistic or political norms.

Assignment Three: Analysis Essay

Purpose

The study of the humanities often involves producing written analyses of primary texts in a given area of study, using specific analytic frameworks or lenses, in order to make broader arguments about the cultural practices under investigation. In this case, you will be using the remix theories, big ideas, and keywords we've collaboratively compiled and developed to analyze a specific textual example of remix culture and make a claim about the importance of remix.

Skills

Throughout the academic and professional environment, you will need to be able to produce written analyses of many different kinds of texts and present your results in a way that engages your audience. In our network culture, you will often write in a digital environment, which requires that you incorporate multimedia elements into written products. For this project you will practice finding, analyzing, and synthesizing evidence and making a creative argument on the basis of that evidence.

Knowledge

This project will give you the opportunity to put what we've learned about remix terminology (keywords) and theories into practice within the context of a written "academic conversation."

Task

For this assignment you will sample, combine, and remix primary and scholarly sources to explore an example of remix culture. Your remixed research text should be produced using the analysis of textual examples of remix (known as primary sources) and the synthesis of writing about remix (aka, secondary sources). Your job is to investigate and produce a written analysis of a product that you believe exemplifies remix culture. The purpose of your essay is to explain why this product specifically, or remix culture generally, *matters*.

- First, you will choose a specific *primary* text—a song, video, image. You will then produce a written critical analysis of it, using remix theory as your analytic framework.

- To help you analyze your *primary* source you can reference (sample) as *secondary* sources any of the texts that we've read, viewed, or heard in this course, along with two to three additional texts you find through your own research.

NOTE: Students can work in **teams of two if the final product is digital** and includes embedded images and/or audio/video. *For examples of a model text see "Why Jazz Will Always Be Relevant" (Tate, 2016) and "Remixing Culture and Why the Art of the Mash Up Matters" (Murray, 2015).* (A brief report detailing the roles and work of both producers will also be required for this option.)

Criteria for Success

For this project you should:

- Provide an analysis of a specific remix text, or set of texts.
- Sample and remix primary and secondary sources to inform your analysis.
- Use the remix keywords and theories to establish an analytic lens or framework for your analysis.
- **Use your analysis of the remixed text to answer the question: Why does remix matter?**
- Begin with an introduction that contextualizes and introduces your purpose.
- Provide a central claim about the significance of remix in general, and/or about the text you've analyzed, specifically.
- Use logical organization and structure to paper.
- **Include at least two secondary sources from class readings and two to three appropriate outside sources.**
- Include proper documentation of all outside sources. Follow **MLA or APA citation guidelines for works cited page and in-text citations.**
- Incorporate peer and instructor feedback in the final version.
- Use effective grammar, spelling, punctuation, syntax, and other sentence level strategies.
- Include a logical conclusion that raises questions for further study on this topic.
- Write an essay that's at least five to seven pages long, double-spaced (not including works cited page).

If you work with partners, you must:

- Submit a final version in some kind of interactive digital format.
- Include images, video, and or sound.
- Incorporate elements of effective visual design.
- Submit a report detailing the primary roles of each team member, and the work you each completed.

Assignment Four: Audio/Video Remix

Work in teams to collaboratively produce a remix that includes a range of multimodal elements (e.g., sound, images, alphabetic text). Your remix should have some kind of purpose: to entertain, express, subvert, satirize, etc. Tip: Your remixed text can relate in some way to your team's Analysis of Remix.

A one to two-page "producers' statement" should accompany the final cut of each team's remix.

Producers' Statement and Presentation for Multimodal Remix

A 250–500-word "Producers' Statement" should accompany the final cut of each team's remix. This one- to two-page document should:

- Identify the major sources you sampled and remixed (be prepared to discuss and play excerpts from at least **two sources** (songs, movies, visuals, etc.)) that you sampled and remixed.
- Use Ferguson's copy/transform/combine framework to describe how you transformed and combined original texts to create a new remixed product.
- Explain the purpose of your remix, describing its central point and/or intended impact on its audience.

Presenting Your Remix

- Play excerpts of at least two sources that you sampled.
- Play your remix.
- Discuss your process and purpose.

Table 10.1. Remix forms, remix tools, and hardware

Remix Forms	Remix Tools	Hardware
Song	GarageBand	Laptop
Podcast	Fruity Loops	Smartphone
Video	Photoshop	Digital camera
Mixtape	Premiere Pro	Drum machine
Website	iMovie	Sampler
???	InDesign	Turntables
	???	???

Sample Student Projects

1. Sample Assignment One: Responding to Sound & Soundwriting (A Gateway Activity) by Anonymous. A response to "Never Catch Me" by Flying Lotus.[1]
2. Sample Assignment Three: Analysis Essay by Anonymous. A feminist analysis of a YouTube video that remixes Selena Gomez's "Me & My Girls" with scenes from movies.

Reflection

[Hip-hop beat fades into background.]

Justin Young: Hello, and welcome to "Sampling Sound, Text, and Praxis: Student and Teacher as Producer in a (Somewhat) Open-Source Course."[2] I'm Justin Young, Director of English Composition [*music fades out*] and the Writers' Center at Eastern Washington University. During this audio reflection, I'll give listeners a glimpse into my experience teaching a soundwriting course for first-year college students about and designed according to the concept of remix.

[Author-created hip-hop remix of John Coltrane's (1961) "My Favorite Things" fades into background.]

I'll talk about the cultural and pedagogical theories that inform my design and implementation of the class, as well as the specific assignment sequence that serves as the core of the curriculum for the course, how all of this relates to student engagement and integrative learning, as well as the challenges that arose in relation to my effort to promote open-source approaches, which ended up running counter to the culture of sampling that was fostered within the course itself. Finally, I'll be touching on samples of student work from the class, along with my own reflection on the learning experience I shared with my students while teaching the course.

So, you might guess that one of my favorite things is hip-hop. *[Music fades out.]* Ever since middle school, I've loved rap especially the kind with a lot of samples—*[hip-hop song "Plug Tunin' (last Chance to Comprehend)" by De La Soul fades into background]* my favorite album of eighth grade (and one of my favorites to this day) was De La Soul's (1989) *3 Feet High and Rising*, produced by the incomparable Prince Paul, which is universally recognized as a masterpiece of the art of sampling.

[Music plays without voiceover for 30 seconds then fades out.] (Of course, now, as Questlove pointed out, the only rappers that can afford to make hip-hop with

---

1. Two student examples (text-based) can be found on the book's companion website.

2. The audio version of Justin Young's reflection can be found on the book's companion website.

samples are Kanye and Jay-Z [Ketchum, 2016], but I digress, though we will have more on that later.)

[*"My Favorite Things" remix fades in.*]

So why am I talking about my favorite things? I want to get this started by briefly discussing how important and effective it is to help students make connections between their favorite things, the things that they love and care about, and whatever is going on in the classroom. Researchers like Melissa Peet, Director of Integrative Learning and Knowledge Management at the University of Michigan, point out that Bloom's taxonomy only focuses on the rational, cognitive components of learning, leaving out entirely any role that affect or emotion, or the body itself, might have in learning something new (Peet et al., 2010). Proponents of integrative learning therefore advocate embodied pedagogies that focus on encouraging students to tell stories and reflect, [*music fades out*] in order to help them make connections between their own interests and passions and the classroom. In fact, additionally, as Christy Price (2010) points out, a teacher's own passion for a subject can have a positive impact on student learning.

So I'm here to tell you that, based on my experience teaching this course, the framework of remix in particular, and soundwriting in general are particularly useful for encouraging and facilitating the kind of embodied, integrative learning I've just described. But before I go any further, I want to take a moment to define and contextualize the term "remix" and how it relates to the soundwriting course I'm discussing.

Let's start with the original meaning of remix, which is all about sound: [*"The Adventures of Grandmaster Flash on the Wheels of Steel" by Grandmaster Flash (1981) fades in.*] It's a type of music production that developed in a particular historical moment, namely in the Jamaican dance hall scene and then in the Bronx at the birth of hip-hop in the early 1970s as DJs like Kool Herc and Grandmaster Flash pioneered the techniques of turntablism (pun intended) using record players to isolate and extend breaks, sampling and remixing the music of others to create new jams and, of course, to keep the party moving.

Remix can also be used to denote a new era of creative production, applicable to many disciplines and industries, marked by a shift from what Lawrence Lessig (2008) calls [*music fades out*] "Read/Only culture" to the current "Read/Write culture" in which previously passive viewers now create original content by sampling and remixing and distributing that content freely online (p. 28). And, of course, the concept of remix is used in comp-rhet to understand and describe the processes of writing and multimodal composing in the digital age.

So why is this framework and topic of remix so useful in promoting the kind of integrative embodied learning I talked about earlier? To put it simply, at its most elemental level, encouraging students to remix, to create texts like a hip-hop producer would, gives them license to start the creative process with material they care about and build from there, creating new texts using pieces of things they already are invested in.

This seems like a good moment to shift gears and actually talk about the assignment sequence that I'm here to share. For each of these assignments, students are provided specific directions, requiring them to sample existing material in order to create a new text. In other words, students are encouraged to engage in the steps of the remix process, copy, transform, and combine, which Kirby Ferguson (2016) establishes in his video series *Everything Is a Remix*. Additionally, the assignments necessitate the use of this remix formula as a framework for the analysis of remixed texts.

The first assignment, a gateway activity that introduces students to the world of soundwriting, asks them to write about sound by responding to a playlist of songs produced via remix.

The next assignment, the Remix Analysis: Team Presentation, asks students to work in production teams to present in audio form, an analysis of some kind of primarily audio text.

The third project, The Analysis Essay, is a more traditional composition assignment, which frames research-based writing as a process of copying, transforming and combining.

For the final project, the Audio/Visual Remix, students work in teams in order to produce a primarily audio text by remixing other texts. All of these assignments enable the student producer to either write about or produce media based on the stuff they themselves care about.

I learned, however, that this fact, while a strength from the student engagement perspective, was a complicating factor in my effort to design and produce an open-source course. My original goal for the design of this course was that it would be entirely open source—that is, all of the materials used by and produced by students would be freely available and remixable. It quickly became clear that this aim was unrealistic; at least as far as student products were concerned. I was able to provide a course reading list and a music/video playlist out of material that students could access freely online. And I did begin designing the course with an open-source resource Copy This Syllabus (Russo, 2011) as a starting point for the course design, though the model I found was for a graduate course which needed to be adapted for first-year students. A list of readings, songs, and videos I used for the class can be found in the written portion of this chapter.

This commitment to open-source design and production couldn't be maintained, however, when students started producing their own remixes. For one thing, the culture of sampling which still permeates online DIY artistic production and which was fostered by the course itself was counter to an effort to ensure that everything students sampled and remixed came from something like Creative Commons. That is, my open-source ethic ran up against the realities of remix culture. This experience is consistent with how remix proponents like Lessig (2008) and Cory Doctorow (2014) describe the challenge of squaring the ways in which digital art can be and is produced with our antiquated and corporate-leaning copyright laws. Such scholars argue that current intellectual property law unnecessarily limits creative production. A point that's confirmed by the Questlove comment I mentioned earlier—when only Jay-Z and Kanye can afford to sell albums with samples, there's a problem.

Students did, however, produce remixed texts for my class out of copyrighted material. I would argue that this is fair use, since no one was looking to sell any of these products, and the only major audience for the creations was the class itself. It does pose a challenge for this chapter, though. Just to be safe, I will not be including as sample student texts any of the remixed texts my students created via sampling copyrighted texts. I will briefly describe a few, however.

Student 1 sampled and created a mash-up of "Heroin" by Badflower and "My Boy" by Billie Eilish. She had never done any music production before but managed to learn enough about how to use GarageBand (Apple's entry-level recording software) to combine two songs to create a single remixed song that was moving, as well as musically and thematically coherent.

Student 2 sampled and remixed (what he called) an "Old School" rap and beat by Biggie Smalls with "New Wave" (again, his term) raps and beats, including work by YG and Drake. His idea was to remix a Biggie rap from the song "Juicy" over a current New Wave beat and then transition to current artists like YG and Drake rapping over a beat from the original Biggie song. He wrote in his producer's statement that the remix "came out better than I expected." He continued, writing that "tons of people from the dorms" said that the remix "was really good and I should post it on YouTube," which made him feel like "I went from not knowing anything about how remix is used . . . to making a remix myself that people wanted me to publish."

Student 3 *[student remix described below fades in]* was a more experienced music producer, someone who had done a fair amount of hip-hop production and performance prior to the class. He created his own beats for two recent hip-hop songs, one from Future called "Covered in Money" and another by Young Thug, "NASA." His beats are in fact featured in this audio reflection, as I sampled and chopped parts of his remix that didn't include copyrighted vocals. *[student remix fades out]*

I should mention that for at least two of these students, this kind of audio production was a real stretch of their abilities. As I mentioned above, the student who mashed up the two songs "Heroin" and "My Boy" had never used any audio-production software and yet somehow, over the course of apparently five hours, learned enough about GarageBand to produce a seamless and affecting remix. Another student, as I noted earlier, was surprised by how good his final remix ended up and got peer feedback confirming his success.

For my part, I must note that producing this chapter was a learning experience for me, too. Like my students, in order to produce the very segment that you are listening to now, I had to push myself to try a new kind of composing and producing, learning to use audio software in ways that I never had before. While I've done a fair amount of music production, along with a couple of local public radio appearances, I'd never produced anything podcast-like, so to speak. Writing and recording in this way was challenging but enjoyable, and it gave me a much better sense of how writing for sound is a unique rhetorical experience. Based on this experience, my plan for the future version of this course is to require students to produce their own audio podcast reflections on the class. While the course sequence, specifically the Remix Analysis Team Presentation assignment, allows for and encourages students to produce spoken audio segments, this is one of two options for the assignment, and most students take the other, which is why there aren't any student samples for that particular assignment in the chapter. In the future, I want to ensure that students gain experience in producing a spoken audio segment, so they will not only write about and produce sound, they will write for sound.

And, finally, *["My Favorite Things" remix fades in]* while I haven't included the audio remixes produced by students using copyrighted material, I have included such a text that I produced. The music that began this program and that you're hearing now includes samples from John Coltrane's (1961) cover of "My Favorite Things." It's my attempt to create a trap version of what Maria sang for the Von Trapp children in *The Sound of Music*. Get it?

Which brings me back to what I believe is a real strength of this class. My experience suggests that the design of the course encouraged embodied, affective learning as students were able to write about and produce new versions of artistic and cultural texts that they wanted to engage with, because those texts mattered to them outside of the classroom. This remixed course enabled them to design and produce new pieces of written and audio texts out by sampling and remixing their own favorite things.

[Music fades out.]

References

Coltrane, J. (1961). My favorite things [Song]. On *My favorite things*. Atlantic.

Davis, A., Webb, S., Lackey, D. & DeVoss, D. N. (2010). Remix, play, and remediation: Undertheorized composing practices. In H. Urbanski (Ed.), *Writing and the digital generation: Essays on new media rhetoric* (pp. 186–197). McFarland.

De La Soul. (1989). *Three feet high and rising* [Album]. Tommy Boy Entertainment.

Doctorow, C. (2014). *Information doesn't want to be free: Laws for the internet age*. McSweeney's.

Dubisar, A. M., Lattimer, C., Mayfield, R., McGrew, M., Myers, J., Russell, B. & Thomas, J. (2017). Haul, parody, remix: Mobilizing feminist criticism with video. *Computers and Composition, 44*, 52–66. https://doi.org/10.1016/j.compcom.2017.03.002.

Edwards, D. W. (2016). Framing remix rhetorically: Toward a typology of transformative work. *Computers and Composition, 39*, 41–54. https://doi.org/10.1016/j.compcom.2015.11.007.

Ferguson, K. (2016, May 16). Everything is a remix remastered (2015 HD) [Video file]. *YouTube*. https://youtu.be/nJPERZDfyWc.

Grandmaster Flash. (1981). The adventures of Grandmaster Flash on the wheels of steel [Song]. On *The adventures of Grandmaster Flash on the wheels of steel*. Sugar Hill Records.

Hess, M. (2006). Was Foucault a plagiarist? Hip-hop sampling and academic citation. *Computers and Composition, 23*(3), 280–295. https://doi.org/10.1016/j.compcom.2006.05.004.

Ketchum, W., III. (2016). Questlove makes an appeal for musical, educational benefits of samples. *Okayplayer*. http://www.okayplayer.com/news/questlove-makes-an-appeal-for-musical-educational-benefits-of-samples.html.

Lessig, L. (2008). *Remix: Making art and commerce thrive in the hybrid economy*. Penguin.

Murray, B. (2015, March 22). Remixing culture and why the art of the mash-up matters. *TechCrunch*. https://techcrunch.com/2015/03/22/from-artistic-to-technological-mash-up/.

Peet, M. R., Walsh, K., Sober, R. & Rawak, C. S. (2010). Generative knowledge interviewing: A method for knowledge transfer and talent management at the University of Michigan. *International Journal of Educational Advancement, 10*(2), 71–85. https://doi.org/10.1057/ijea.2010.10.

Price, C. (2010). Why don't my students think I'm groovy?: The new "R"s for engaging millennial learners. In S. A. Meyers & J. R. Stowell (Eds.), *Essays from E-xcellence in teaching* (vol. 9, pp. 29–34). Society for the Teaching of Psychology. http://teachpsych.org/ebooks/eit2009/index.php.

Rife, M. C. & DeVoss, D. N. (2013). Teaching plagiarism: Remix as composing. In M. Donnelly, R. Ingalls, T. A. Morse, J. C. Post & A. M. Stockdell-Giesler (Eds.), *Critical conversations about plagiarism* (pp. 78–100). Parlor Press.

Russo, J. L. (2011). *Copy this class (The art of remix)*. [Syllabus]. Palo Alto, CA: Art Department, Stanford University. https://hcommons.org/deposits/objects/hc:31212/datastreams/CONTENT/content.

Tate, G. (2016, May 5). Why jazz will always be relevant. *The Fader*. http://www.thefader.com/2016/05/05/jazz-will-always-be-relevant.

Walker, J. R. & Cox, K. (2013). Remixing instruction in information literacy. In R. McClure & J. P. Purdy (Eds.), *The new digital scholar: Exploring and enriching the research and writing practices of nextgen students* (pp. 349–368). Information Today.

Williams, B. T. (2012). The world on your screen: New media, remix, and the politics of cross-cultural contact. In B. T. Williams & A. A. Zenger (Eds.), *New media literacies and participatory popular culture across borders* (pp. 28–43). Routledge.

Winkelmes, M.-A. (2013). Transparency in teaching: Faculty share data and improve students' learning. *Liberal Education, 99*(2), 48–55.

Chapter 11. Audio Engineering and Soundwriting in an Interdisciplinary Course

Doyuen Ko and Joel Overall
BELMONT UNIVERSITY

As a multidisciplinary field, sound studies should seek to find and teach the interdisciplinary aspects of sound. Fortunately, our institution, Belmont University, requires two interdisciplinary linked courses as a part of the general education curriculum, allowing us to bring our English and audio engineering perspectives to the same 25 students. We each teach a course—one titled Writing with Sound and another called Critical Listening for Audio Production—that attempts to bring these two disciplines together in a search for common technical and theoretical ground. Critical Listening provides the listening skills to evaluate objective components of audio quality such as timbre, spatial attributes, and technical attributes. Writing with Sound offers students the opportunity to apply this new technical knowledge by composing texts with sound within a rhetorical framework that examines sound's meaning.

In this chapter, we highlight a series of assignments that engages students in listening to and using sound within the technical framework of audio engineering terminology. The first assignment is a series of four listening journals. Using the language of analysis from the discipline of audio engineering to evaluate and compare songs and other audio artifacts, students examine how timbre, spatial quality, and technical quality of sound communicate meaning for the listener. Students are initially introduced to these terms through Jason Corey's (2016) textbook *Audio Production and Critical Listening: Technical Ear Training*. Since this is an assignment that is graded by both professors to offer collaborative feedback from two disciplines, the grading process also serves as an important collaborative space for faculty to provide feedback from each disciplinary perspective. Following the journal assignment, students compose an episode of a class podcast series in Writing with Sound that carefully considers rhetorical sound attributes when mixing their own composition. In addition to submitting the audio portion of this assignment, students also submit an audio track analysis of their own sound design choices by excerpting 5–10-second clips from the podcast episode to highlight approaches to sound and meaning as an audio engineer and a musician.

While some teachers and scholars in rhetoric and composition may not be able to replicate this partnership with a colleague in audio engineering, we advocate for the use of audio engineering terminology in the composition classroom to provide students with the vocabulary to talk about sound alongside linguistic

DOI: https://doi.org/10.37514/PRA-B.2022.1688.2.11

symbols. Similar to Katherine Fargo Ahern's (2013) use of terms from acoustics and musicology in her composition courses as described in her article "Tuning the Sonic Playing Field," audio engineering terms help "introduce students to uses of sound that do not necessarily draw on the spoken word, voice, or discourse" (p. 78). Thus, these terms help students move beyond the linguistic-centered composition classroom to more fully understand the value of sound as more than simply ornament. Additionally, knowledge of terms from audio engineering has an added benefit for students looking to pursue podcasting beyond the composition classroom by equipping them with a vocabulary to communicate with engineers or to effectively navigate the more complex features of audio-editing software.

In the following paragraphs, we highlight the terms involved in this listening analysis. Whether recording a symphony orchestra or creating podcasts on a laptop, our hearing must perform an accurate evaluation of the audio quality before starting the production process (Corey, 2016). According to Jan Berg and Francis Rumsey (2003), there are two main approaches to audio quality evaluation: The "objective" method analyzes physical parameters of the audio signal such as frequency, reverberation time, and total harmonic distortion, and the "subjective" method considers the perceived quality of sound that is expressed by human judgments.

The Critical Listening course is designed to improve students' ability in both objective and subjective audio quality evaluation. The curriculum is based on the "total audio quality" evaluation model proposed by Berg and Rumsey (2003), and its schematic is shown in Figure 11.1. The model suggests three principal components of total audio quality—timbral, spatial, and technical qualities—and the course introduces a systematic training program for the students to improve their auditory sensitivity in each category.

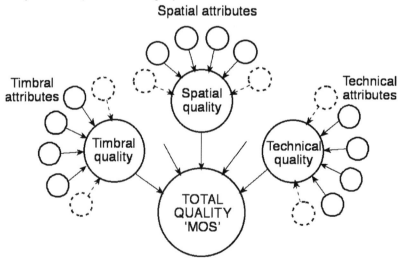

Figure 11.1. Relations between total audio quality and its subsets and attributes (diagram by Jan Berg and Francis Rumsey, 2003).

According to Corey (2016), timbral quality (also called tonal or spectral quality) refers to an audio signal's frequency content and the relative power of each frequency or frequency band across the audible human hearing range, from 20 to 20,000 Hz. The characteristics of a human voice and musical instruments are primarily determined by its "timbre," so the ability to hear the timbral difference in audio programs is crucial. Previous research by René Quesnel (2009) has verified that the listener's ability to discriminate timbral quality could be improved in a relatively short period by using a systematic training method. In our Critical Listening course, specific frequency matching tasks are designed to help students identify timbral differences between audio signals. The tasks are provided with interactive computer software developed by Jason Corey and David Benson (2018), and the practice data are stored in the database and visualized real-time with supported graphical user interfaces.

Francis Rumsey (2001) defined spatial quality as the three-dimensional nature of the sound sources and their environments. Since spatial audio quality listening is a perceptually complex process, breaking down the properties into discrete components and learning how to distinguish between these specific parameters are tasks (Neher, 2004). In our course, a simple snare drum sample is used to create different spatial impressions using a digital reverberation processor. To develop their own internal timing, students listen to and remember a set of different reverberation times (0.5, 1, 1.5, and 2 seconds) and pre-delay times (20, 60, 100, and 200 milliseconds).

Technical quality listening training is designed for students to improve their skills in detecting specific artifacts of the sound. Throughout the media production process, we encounter various technical issues such as noise and distortion. If we are not able to detect and fix them appropriately, the total audio quality can be degraded even if the program features excellent timbral and spatial characters. Students listen to a 30-second recording of a musical selection, immediately replaced by the same recording with a technical anomaly. The anomalies include stereo vs. mono, reversed left-right channel, inverted signal polarity, poor MP3 encoding, and various levels of distortion. After listening to the pairs of examples, students have to identify the technical anomaly.

Assignments

Listening Journals

Musicians, podcasters, and audio engineers often need to converse in writing, describing sound qualities in emails to each other or explaining their audio approach in grants. Using the sound discernment language/terms that we define throughout the course of the semester, please write about your listening experiences in response to the four following prompts. Describe the aural events you encounter, and your impressions of these events. Be sure to answer all questions completely. Apply topics covered in class to your listening evaluation.

Each two-page journal entry must include details such as song title, artist, album title, engineer, and producer. Specify the medium you were listening to it on (MP3, WAV, streaming service, etc.) and the headphones/speakers you used. The following songs by Fleetwood Mac, Steely Dan, Maria Schneider, Prince, and Fred Stride were intentionally chosen for their reference-quality sound and unique sonic characteristics that demonstrate each of the three audio quality attributes.

Listening Journal #1: Timbral quality evaluation

"Dreams," Fleetwood Mac vs. "Gaslighting Abbie," Steely Dan

Compare and contrast the two recordings with a focus on the timbral (spectral) qualities of the two recordings.

Listening Journal #2: Spatial quality evaluation

"Walking by Flashlight," Maria Schneider vs. "Purple Rain," Prince

Compare and contrast the two recordings, specifically focusing on the spatial qualities of the two recordings.

Listening Journal #3: Technical quality evaluation

"Something for Ernie," Fred Stride

CD quality WAV file (16bit, 44.1kHz, 40MB) vs. medium quality MP3 file (96kbps, 3MB)

Download the two files attached below. Compare and contrast the sound quality of the song in two different audio file formats. As we discussed in the class, specifically listen for the following aspects of the sound:

1. Clarity and sharpness of instruments
2. Reverberation, background noise and sustained note
3. Non-harmonic high-frequency sounds (cymbals and hi-hats)

Listening Journal #4: All things together

Choose and listen to a song from an album that won a Grammy award for Best Engineered Album, Non-Classical category. Describe the spectral, spatial, dynamic and technical aspects of the song in greater details (at least one long paragraph for each aspect).

The list of the albums: http://en.wikipedia.org/wiki/Grammy_Award_for_Best _Engineered_Album,_Non-Classical

Group Podcast + Audio Reflection

The major assignment for this course (Writing with Sound) is a class podcast series. As a class, we will decide the theme and content for the podcast, and in groups of two (or three), you will be responsible for producing an episode of the series between 10–15 minutes with a full transcript. The podcast should demonstrate the best practices of writing for the ear and audio production that we've been discussing all semester in Writing with Sound and Critical Listening for Audio Production. Your podcast episode should follow the best practices of narrative journalism that we've been learning about in Jessica Abel's (2015) *Out on the Wire*. In addition to submitting the podcast episode MP3 file, you should also turn in a Word document that includes a full transcript of your podcast episode.

Individually, you will include a 3–5-minute supplemental audio file that takes four different 5–10-second excerpts from your podcast episode to explain how you used audio engineering listening qualities like timbre, spatial, or technical qualities to make meaning with sound. Use this audio description to make an argument for how your group's podcast uses sound to reach an audience.

Requirements

- A 10–15-minute podcast episode submitted as an MP3
- A transcript of your group's podcast submitted as a Word document
- A 3–5-minute audio argument about your group's use of sound quality submitted as an MP3

Sample Student Projects

1. A Listening Journal sample by Rebecca Waldron in response to prompt #4.[1]
2. An excerpt from a sample group podcast, *Live Nashville*, Episode 8 by Jackson Badgley, Benjamin Dufresne, and Shannon Harper
3. A sample audio reflection by Benjamin Dufresne

Figure 11.2. Podcast art created by student Shannon Harper.

---

1. Three student examples (text files, audio files, and descriptive transcripts) can be found on the book's companion website.

Reflection

Joel Overall: My name is Joel Overall, and I am an English professor at Belmont University, teaching a course called Writing with Sound.[2]

Doyuen Ko: My name is Doyuen Ko. I'm an assistant professor at Belmont as well. I teach audio engineering technology, specifically for this course is called Critical Listening for Audio Production.

Joel: And, Doyuen, his course is actually part of the major for audio engineering.

Doyuen: Yes.

Joel: So one of the things we're doing is partnering our two courses together as a part of the gen ed requirement, a course called Learning Community Courses, and that means that two courses are partnered together, and there has to be a link between maybe one common assignment, and that's what we'd like to present to you today is the common assignment for both of our courses.

Just a quick insight into our institution: Belmont is in Nashville, Tennessee at the very top of music row, and we have about 8,000 students. Many of them major in music business, in audio engineering, in songwriting. Am I leaving anything out?

Doyuen: Entertainment industry study.

Joel: Yes, so there are quite a few music-related majors here that students take. So this seems to have been a very popular Learning Community Course for those students. Doyuen, I'll let you talk a little bit about the common assignment that we have.

Doyuen: For this Critical Listening class, I've been teaching this class more than four years. Normally, we spend a lot of time on listening practice, using those technical terms and technical quality evaluation tools. That is our normal Critical Listening class, but for this version of the class, which is Learning Community Courses, we introduced a new concept of evaluating the sound quality, which is using a listening journal. The listening journal is about writing about the sound quality while they are listening to the music samples.

Joel: Right, and the music samples are important because it allows students to make objective evaluations, using the technical language of audio engineering. But we're also asking them in these listening journals to make a subjective evaluation as well from a rhetorical perspective. For instance, many students might want to explain how a sound quality might make them feel, but the addition of a subjective analysis allows them to do that by adopting an audience perspective to explain the potential meanings of that sound or music. So, Doyuen, what kind of technical language do students use in this listening journal?

Doyuen: They have to write about the timbral quality of the sound, and spatial quality of the sound, and the technical quality of the sound. They learn about those objective evaluation strategies during the course. They can perform the objective

---

2. The audio version of Doyuen Ko and Joel Overall's reflection can be found on the book's companion website.

evaluation in different kinds of assignments, but now for this assignment, they have to write about it, using the proper descriptors, proper words, which was taught in the Critical Listening course, and Joel's Soundwriting course as well.

Joel: So, let's hear a few examples of a few of these sound qualities. The first one is timbre, and this is an example of optimizing timbral qualities in the voice.

Doyuen: Yes, so we have the first sample, has some timbral quality issues, which is a typical issue you can find in a recording done in a small space. So, let's hear it first.

[a 5-second clip with a man speaking the following words in a muffled voice]

    Man: The box was thrown beside the parked truck.

Joel: Wow, that was bad.

Doyuen: *[laughter]* Right, if I explain it in technical terms, there was a significant boost at around 1000 Hz. So when you have too much 1000 Hz energy in the audio, you get those kind of nasal, very canny sound quality in the voice. So in our Critical Listening class, our students have to train themselves to be able to hear those different timbral qualities, and specifically, they can distinguish those different frequencies to solve the problems. So after they recognize the problem at 1000 Hz, they can fix it, and this is the fixed version of the audio.

[a 5-second clip with a man speaking the following words in a much clearer voice]

    Man: The box was thrown beside the parked truck.

Joel: Wow, that was better.

Doyuen: Right, so it cleaned up those nasal qualities of the voice. The listeners may think it's not a huge deal, it's not a big difference, but you can hear the quality difference between before and after audio. The difference is that our students were able to hear the problem, and they were able to fix that. So at the end, you get better program in your podcast and other media program.

Joel: So here, we have two examples of different spatial qualities.

[a 7-second clip of a snare drum with .5 seconds of reverb, followed by a 7-second clip of a snare drum with 2 seconds of reverb]

Doyuen: What you just heard was two drum hits, two snare hits with a different reverb time. As you heard, there's a big difference in spatial quality. The first one only had about .5 second reverb time, and the second one had about 2 seconds of reverb time. It's very long and wet. For creating audio programs, sometimes you have to add those spatial effects to create some sort of spatial dimension in your recordings. So we use those kinds of digital processors to make it happen in the recording.

Joel: Can I ask a question?

Doyuen: Yeah.

Joel: So my question is "Why would a student who's creating a podcast need to pay attention to the spatial qualities of the voice or whatever sound effects they have?"

Doyuen: Right, there are different podcasts, of course, sometimes it can be just dry and very direct-sounding voice. But sometimes, such as for dramas and more dramatic stories, sometimes they want to add those special effect for effective deliveries. So, depending on the programs, if they know how to use those effect efficiently, their program could be much more interesting and could be much more effective.

Joel: So reverb is one way to actually either cut the confusion out. Let's say reverb is distracting the audience, they can learn to identify it and cut it out, or they could actually use it as a part of the story.

Doyuen: Yes.

Joel: As a part of creating the effect of what they are trying to say.

Doyuen: Yes, in fact for musicians, it's been the acoustics or reverberation is known as a part of the instrument. So, especially classical musicians, they are always actually playing with the room, right? Not just their instrument, but their instrument is playing with the room. So it is a part of the story, part of the program, and I believe it is the same thing for the voice and dramas and radios and podcasts.

Doyuen: So we have those examples, and students have to go over different samples. They have to memorize the quality of those samples, and we have a specific way to evaluate for each category in our assignments. So, that's what we do in Critical Listening class.

Joel: And this is something that we're both trying to assess and look at, and part of the purpose for assessment in this situation is to help me, a non-specialist in audio engineering, to learn to also listen with the students to understand some of those qualities that they should be listening for. So, as we grade these together, I'm looking forward to learning but also using this as a scaffolding assignment that goes into my assignment.

That assignment, then, is a Group Podcast and Audio Reflection. I am asking my students, the entire 25-student class, to come up with a theme for a podcast, and then they will split off into groups of two or three, since we're an odd number of students, in order to produce each in these smaller partnerships an episode of the podcast that ranges from 10–15 minutes. And this episode will also include a full transcript. In addition to this, students will individually be creating a 3–5-minute supplemental audio file that takes some 5–10-second excerpts from the podcast in order to do this same thing: to listen to what they've created, to talk about why perhaps they've left in a technical quality, something like reverb. But to do this maybe in more so a rhetorical way or an intentional way to affect the story that's happening that they're reporting on. We're using Jessica Abel's (2015) book *Out on the Wire*. As she and Ira Glass talk about in that book, they discuss the genre of podcasts known as narrative journalism, and this is something that

I think is very important to narrative journalism, and that is knowing how to use specific sound effects, how to manipulate the audio in certain ways, and rather than just say, "Okay, each of your groups needs to go out and find an audio engineering student at Belmont to help you," I'm asking them to engineer their own mix and to do it very intentionally as a part of the story.

In the end, some of the takeaways that we have for this assignment. I'm very thankful to Doyuen for allowing me to kind of piggyback on an assignment that's already well-oiled and something that the teachers in audio engineering do. But I think it's very important as sound studies scholars and also people who teach sound assignments or soundwriting assignments to find ways to become more interdisciplinary, to borrow from fields like audio engineering or some of the other fields that we're looking at that deal with sound studies in order to provide students with that interdisciplinary experience that is necessary. In particular, our group of students, most of them want to be songwriters or audio engineers or something involving creative work. This I think is a very important assignment for them that helps combine the fields for them to be dynamic producers, and creators, and soundwriters in their field.

Doyuen: What I learned from teaching this course for many years was that I can teach them to evaluate the sound quality objectively, but what I was feeling lacking is the subjective evaluation part, which is about talking about the sound quality, and express their feeling in writing and speaking. And I think this assignment, this combined assignment, will give them to think about those aspects, and then develop their skills to convey their feelings and opinions in terms of the writing. So I think it's an interesting combination of the disciplines.

References

Abel, J. (2015). *Out on the wire: The storytelling secrets of the new masters of radio.* Broadway Books.

Ahern, K. F. (2013). Tuning the sonic playing field: Teaching ways of knowing sound in first year writing. *Computers and Composition, 30*(2), 75–86. https://doi.org/10.1016/j.compcom.2013.03.001.

Berg, J. & Rumsey, F. (2003). Systematic evaluation of perceived spatial quality. In *Proceedings of the 24th International Conference on Multichannel Audio.* https://www.aes.org/e-lib/browse.cfm?elib=12272.

Corey, J. (2016). *Audio production and critical listening: Technical ear training* (2nd ed.). Taylor & Francis.

Corey, J. & Benson, D. (2016). Parametric equalization. *Technical Ear Trainer.* Focal Press. Retrieved September 15, 2020, from http://webtet.net/apcl/#/parametric.

Neher, T. (2004). *Towards a spatial ear trainer* [Unpublished doctoral dissertation]. University of Surrey.

Quesnel, R. (2009). *Timbral ear training.* VDM Verlag.

Rumsey, F. (2001). *Spatial audio.* Focal Press.

Chapter 12. The Resonance Is the Composer: Students Soundwriting Together

Trey Conner, Emma Hamilton, Amber Nicol, Chris Burton, Kathleen Olinger, Alyssa Harmon, and Ivan Jones
UNIVERSITY OF SOUTH FLORIDA ST. PETERSBURG

Figure 12.1. From The Medium Is the Massage *by Marshall McLuhan and Quentin Fiore (1967, p. 112).*

We chose this McLuhan/Fiore sample as an epigraph (of sorts) because amplifying soundwriting in our class (advanced composition) in turn amplified "a world of simultaneous relationships" in our scene of writing (a course wiki).[1] We grew accustomed to listening without earlids, with our whole being. There's a certain point in writing together where the interference patterns determine what we're hearing. We need these interference patterns of persuasion/invitation/celebration/dissipation, and we need to learn how to listen deeply to one another there. Soundwriting helped us create this space of writing and this sense of community.

In an advanced composition course for the University of South Florida St. Petersburg's (USFSP) Department of Verbal and Visual Arts, we (the professor and students enrolled in the class) formed a community both in person and online on

---

1. A gif of this image, created by the authors in GIMP, is available on the book's companion website.

DOI: https://doi.org/10.37514/PRA-B.2022.1688.2.12

a classroom wiki. Right away, we named our wiki space "emergeconvergefall2017" to assert our plan to balance emergent techniques of compositional practice with classical strategies for the invention, arrangement, and sharing of prose.

Our experiments and exercises proceeded on this course plan: We divided the semester into two phases (emergence and convergence) and created a portfolio for each phase. First, we took emergence as an Ur-metaphor for our own individual and collective compositional practices. For the second phase, we created "convergence portfolios" that directly combined our separate portfolios into new forms. The soundwriting assignments and examples in this chapter share some of those moments of compositional convergence.

Soundwriting, a central theme and practice of our semester, allowed the class to embrace some of the oldest approaches available to writers: listening, dialoguing, and engaging the practice of our own writing with our whole beings. The assignments and responses we share here both demonstrate and facilitate the power of emergence to bind a community of writers. These exercises are adaptable to allow students to experience compositional emergence (our first phase) through collaborative writing, where they learn that low-stakes, high-frequency writing on a common medium activates prior knowledge: When everyone brings together their own knowledge and background, the whole is greater than the sum of its parts. To us, soundwriting is the convergence of oral and written traditions and the collaborative practice of sonic and textual composition—creating a common space of exploration that transcends intellectual boundaries. We recognize that this definition is somewhat larger and more organic than the manipulation of recorded sound, as others in this collection use the term. Although a wiki is great for forging literal connections in hypertext, soundwriting opened up our collaborative process to a deeper sense of connection, and an experience of older, oral rhetorical traditions.

Throughout the early stages of the class, students were encouraged to post links to their most valued writing resources in the wiki and share them with the class. We completed a "communities of practice" exercise where students were encouraged to list places they often go and the characteristics of those places and the people found in them. Then, students were invited to comment on each other's reflections and informative writing about their own scenes of composition, their own communities of practice. The result was a growing group sense of the ways students were connected and the areas where they may have held differing opinions. The wiki facilitated the low-stakes space for this to happen, and the classroom environment brought it life.

As the class continued to engage in the prompts and exercises shared below, it became apparent that the emergence of ideas from the many exercises performed had facilitated a larger conversation and a more detailed map of our discourse community. Students were excited to engage and were committed to the conversations they were having. And as they completed these exercises, soundwriting was fundamental. Students embedded noise clips into their wiki posts. Students played guitars and instruments in class while other students read each other's assignments aloud. Students remixed each other's works, and one student even composed music to go along with the sensory writing projects posted by her classmates. Some students turned other students' poems into songs. Some students recorded the in-class discussions and made actual musical compositions by mixing in the voices of their classmates. There were no strict guidelines, but the overlying principle was this: Take what your classmates are doing and use it in your own new unique work.

Workshops and Exercises

On the first day of this advanced composition class, we shared prior knowledge through a prompt that invited each participant to write about their own communities of practice. This assignment set the stage for soundwriting in two important, related ways. First, it allowed the practicing musicians enrolled in the course to share in detail the compositional practices of their own music communities. Second, it put musical practice into a generalized space of compositional practice available to all the enrolled students. Through conversation and sharing, students—whether they identified as musicians or not—began to see how compositional practices threaded through different communities of practice.

The following workshops were introduced mid-semester, after the "emergence" segment of the semester, to encourage new collaborative dynamics for the upcoming "convergence" segment of the semester.

Exercise: Freesound!

The freesound! exercise takes its name from the collaborative database of un-composed sound elements at freesound.org. Although the script seems strict, in practice it functions best as an icebreaker on the terrain of soundwriting, and that's how we'll leverage the prompt in this community. This exercise helps you work on questions such as, "How much experience do the writers in your community or class have with soundwriting?" and "What are the different attitudes and dispositions towards noise and music in your scene of writing?" The exercise also asks us to consider relationships between how we respond to different sounds and our awareness of/responses to the different premises and conclusions we encounter in compositional practice.

Writing takes work, but writing together requires play. So, in this exercise, you'll listen to each other's freesound compositions (instructions below) and add layers of sounds in response. Actively responding to each other in sound focuses the class's collective attention on important steps in collaborative rhetorical processes and teaches us the art of identifying and reconsidering the premises we bring to our acts of reading and listening.

Step 1

Sequencing and layering sound can alter how you feel and where you focus your mind.

Navigate to Freesound.org, browse the sounds that are there, choose a few to combine, and download those audio files.

Then choose an audio editor in which you'll edit together the audio files you've downloaded to create a new sonic composition. There are plenty of online audio-editing sites cropping up these days; feel free to compose with any sound technology of your choosing. Audacity is a great free software option.

In your audio editor, edit the audio files you've downloaded from freesound. org to create a new audio file, layering the sound however you'd like. Create a wiki space for your composition and upload your new audio file along with links to the Freesound audio that you used. At this stage, you might want to write on our course wiki about your recording process and experience. Think like a composer (you are writing a "score"), or even a game developer (you are creating the rules of play); listen to the layers of sounds you've selected, and tell others (performers, listeners, and fellow composers and players) about them (by giving us directives, establishing rules, writing out liner notes, sharing associational thoughts, etc.). You may be compelled to place images, links, and previously composed text (prose or poetry) on this page as well.

Upload. Now, your peers can open the Freesound pages you selected and con-catenated, and in doing so, read your writing while they listen to your composition.

Step 2

Listen again to your classmates' compositions. At your wiki space, post links to the two you liked best. What effect does the music seem to induce in listeners? Are the compositions you selected musical or just plain noisy? Write a couple hundred words and post to your wiki.

Step 3

Perhaps the easiest way to make something new is to simply "mash" two things together and then carefully consider the new "mesh" that results.

Listen again to our Freesound compositions. Select two compositions that you think would sound good together. Now, create a mashup with your web browser by simply playing both scores at the same time.

What is the relationship between your intention (what you want it to sound like) and the outcome (what it sounds like)? How would you alter it to improve it? You could think in terms of "rhetorical effects," along the lines of the three appeals (logos, ethos, pathos), or any other effect that you might create with sounds, words, or images. Go further, add sounds, images, or words to your remix. Or subtract sounds, images, and words from the compositions you selected for remixing. Describe the effect of the composition before and after your additions and repurposing. What do your additions and/or subtractions do? Do they amplify the effects of the composition as you found it? Reverse them? Did your changes simplify or add complexity?

Exercise: Bring a Small Noisemaker

This exercise aims to help participants share personal writing in the context of a playful atmosphere. This time, we focused on using our objects to provide feed-back on our various drafts on the wiki by reading/singing peer drafts to collective improvisatory noisemaking. Responding to each other's wiki writing in sound opened up the text and the conversation to larger possibilities. An excerpt of this process can be heard in the sample student projects for this chapter.

Step 1

For this workshop, each of us will bring a noisemaker and/or a musical instrument to class. Also bring a pencil, pen, and paper.

We will move through the workshop in timed increments, according to a rhythm of timed writing (solo), group work (pairs and small groups), written dialogue, and council circle activities. Take notes throughout this activity (in preparation for Step 3 below).

- We will warm up with a timed writing exercise, during which you will describe your object for your classmates, in writing.
- We will then place the objects all together on one table. Then, each of you will select an object other than your own object. Then, we'll mix it up informally for a short duration, each of us with the common aim of finding out who brought the object we selected.

We will then get into pairs and small groups, and talk about what these objects mean and why we have brought them to our first meeting. Your primary purpose in these interactions is to prepare a short, written description or argument to be shared on our course wiki before our next face-to-face meeting. Your report will introduce the owner of the object and articulate that object's significance in a way that is informed by your interview session, your reading of your peers' wiki posts, and by your understanding of our course goals. You will experiment with and leverage an introductory progymnasmata exercise (fable, tale, chreia, or proverb) to develop your report. Crucially, your presentation will direct audience attention to the writing you produce in Steps 2 and 3 of this workshop, which can provide further details and offer readers opportunities for further exploration of what we can create meaning through dialogue and exchange.

Step 2

Engage in written dialogue with the aim of introducing the owner of the object—and the object itself—to the class via wiki. Complete this report before our next face-to-face meeting. Conduct research and cite sources that help you articulate the significance of the object in broader terms, asking yourself how this object could hold meaning for others.

You can pursue your conversations on the wiki or any other medium that facilitates timely response—just be sure to post conversations that take place in other media (which you can revise, enhance, and develop as you would any draft) to our course wiki (fodder for revision!). Begin posting this process to the wiki immediately—share early and often! Feel free to also experiment with video chat technology to record conversations for review and to spur further exploration of presentational techniques.

During our next class meeting, we will gather in a circle, so that each of you will have a chance to articulate the significance of a peer's object in a brief (60–90 seconds) presentation.

Step 3

As you reflect on your live workshop experiences and subsequent interactions in writing, you will need to do research to support your presentation of the interviews and conversations. Analyze the information from the sources that you found or encountered in this workshop: sources that you or a peer researched and deliberately referenced, that you discovered via a reference in a peer's writing, or that you feel the need to search out having discussed, and in preparation for your presentation (where you will introduce and illustrate the significance of a peer's small object). In your analysis, critically focus on the sources that you used in terms of audience, genre, modality, and rhetorical situation. How are these texts put together and who produces these texts? What is the exigence driving the production of these texts? What is at stake? For whom? What is the function/role of "genre" and "mode" in the rhetorical situations, narratives, arguments, and research programs you encounter? What shifts in tone, poetics, or persuasive technique did you notice as your object and the objects of others came in for renegotiation and interpretation? In your own report, which progymnasmata exercises did you work with, and what did this exercise do for your writing?

Exercise: Sensory Writing on the Harbor

This exercise can take many forms, and in this case, because soundwriting was beginning to be a regular routine in our scene of writing, music and soundwriting became an important part of the way our community responded to the prompt. As part of this exercise, we read Steph Ceraso (2014). Our understanding of soundwriting expanded when, during an outdoor sensory writing workshop, Chris opened his laptop and began to type directly to the wiki in live response to sounds and music made during the workshop. Chris's response, in turn, became subject to subsequent soundwriting responses and was revised into a song. In this way, students continued to build new compositions with the elements of their peers.

Instructions

Sensory writing exercises will help us discover how a writing practice can engage our whole being.

We'll start by going outside and writing together near the water. Bring paper and pencil. With two or three other students, choose different spots in approximately the same area/space, but be sure to create some amount of space; do not sit to write too close together. Then begin to take notes on what you see, hear, and smell there. Think of what you write as notes to yourself that will be used to write something else in the future, even though we haven't decided what that will be yet.

Bring your notes back to the wiki: Photograph or scan them and transcribe them. Approach the transcription as you would a revision session. Don't worry about spelling, correctness, or grammar; write in whatever way allows you to capture on paper what you observe, imagine, and feel during this timed exercise. Be certain to include thoughts and feelings about what you observe and the process of recording it, as well as recording some sense of what everything around you looks, sounds, and smells like. After we write together on the harbor, we will transcribe/upload our sensory writing to the wiki, where we will discuss and workshop further.

Further Experiences: Sample Texts Online

Our experiences always exceeded the boundaries described in these exercises; see our sample texts and their surrounding commentary on the companion website for more ways that our soundwriting emerged and converged in practice.

Sample Student Projects

The ambient penumbra of creativity, learning, and collaboration around the instances of direct soundwriting sample texts in this chapter are just as important to us as the texts themselves. For example, Chris+Amber+Ivan+Trey grouped together for sensory writing by the water, and the professor (Trey) was surprised when he arrived to see Amber and Ivan armed with guitars. Crucially, the ensuing soundwriting acquired amplified meaning in Chris's writing that happened alongside the acoustic guitars and singing and in the way this experience built on previous workshop experiences to further weave different types of soundwriting throughout different learning itineraries. Each soundwriting event manifested in and as part of a larger rhetorical ecology, and some soundwriting events changed the prompt that prompted them in the first place.

The sample student projects give glimpse to our process by sharing key sound-writing texts that we found ourselves reflecting on often as we assembled this chapter.

1. "Well This Is Different than What I Expected . . . ": Kathleen and Amber singing poetry written by Alex over music performed by the classroom collective. During the noisemaker workshop, we improvised feedback over read-alouds of each other's drafts. In doing so, students were able to provide auditory feedback to written works. Some students created songs that were inspired by their peers' works so that their peers could see what resonated with them and how the other students viewed their work. The experience is similar to standing up in front of a live audience, reading your piece aloud, and seeing how the reader reacts to which pieces. Through this other form of feedback, the author then has more insight on how to go back and revise their piece. As you listen to what follows, we especially want you to notice these things that you could adapt to your own classes: that the desire for such authentic feedback trumped self-consciousness; how the spirit of play provided a platform for students to experiment, emboldening one student—Kathleen—to reinterpret another

student's draft through song; and how the results were not expected, but perhaps impossible to achieve without that spirit of play.[2]

2. "Thymesis" by Alyssa Harman: This video, which began as a poem by Alyssa Harmon, became a soundwriting composition driven by Emma's guitar, and finally grew into a video that Alyssa created by mixing her words and Emma's music into a slideshow of photographs culled from her "convergence portfolio." At first, Alyssa's "Thymesis" sequence emerged gradually, over the course of many weeks. Then, after the freesound! and sensory writing workshops, Emma provided soundwriting feedback on Alyssa's poems with multitracked acoustic guitars. Alyssa then responded by creating a new narrative, selecting key passages from the poems, and arranging them with a sequence of images over Emma's guitars. As you listen to and watch this project, we especially want you to notice these things that you could adapt to your own classes: how multimodal composition created a new digital space of play; the way that collaboration allowed these students to venture outside of their comfort zones; and the new feedback that can be achieved for students when peers interpret texts sonically instead of through written prose.

3. "Chop-n-Whine" by Chris Burton (lyrics), Amber Nicol (guitar), and Ivan Jones (guitar): Whereas Amber Nicol (a practicing musician) and Ivan Jones (a practicing musician and DJ) embraced the nonsemantic and asignifying force unleashed in the freesound! and noisemaker workshops, Chris Burton was at first a bit perplexed by all this noise. Chris at one point challenged the turn to soundwriting, asking what all this noisemaking had to do with our recursive process of growing compositions by emergence. But his question was earnest—he was curious, not annoyed. This question was a watershed, a critical incident for the community. Trey shared Steph Ceraso's (2014) multimodal listening article with Chris, added this text to the freesound! sequence, and shifted the calendar so that we could do a sensory writing workshop for our next class session. Chris's sensory writing, which he composed directly to the wiki while listening to Amber, Ivan, and Trey sing and play guitars outside during the sensory writing workshop. This example shares an audio-recorded conversation between Amber, Trey, Ivan, and Christina, lyrics for "Chop-n-Whine" written by Chris, an audio file of chords written for Chris's song, and Chris's reflection on his experiences. Although he had no prior knowledge of or interest in DAWs, Chris, after working with Ivan during class, taught himself Audacity and reframed DAWs as a valuable and generalizable writing tool for his process. Following Paul Théberge (1997), we noticed the ways that compositional practices and procedures are built into the design of DAWs.

---

2. Four example student projects (audio or video files and descriptive transcripts with accompanying introductions) can be found on the book's companion website.

4. "Refrain" by Ivan Jones: In this song, Ivan stacked three guitar tracks, marked transitions with reverse-reverberated gongs (a trick we had discussed in the context of comparing analog and digital techniques for this trope), leveraged Ableton's sampling/soundswitching affordances to create percussion (handclaps, 808 bass-drops, high hats), a bassline, and a refrain built out of various utterances and exclamations he recorded during a workshop. As you listen, notice how even musically experienced students can benefit from simple soundwriting exercises, like this student who created a refrain with just seemingly throwaway phrases.

Reflection

Figure 12.2. Harmon, Hamilton, Burton, Olinger, Nicol, and Conner (not pictured) reflect together.

Trey Conner: I'm Trey Conner. I'm associate professor of writing studies at University of South Florida St. Petersburg.[3]

Chris Burton: I'm Chris Burton. I'm actually a student—a senior at USF St. Petersburg.

---

3. The audio version of Trey Conner, Emma Hamilton, Amber Nicol, Chris Burton, Kathleen Olinger, Alyssa Harmon, and Ivan Jones's reflection can be found on the book's companion website.

Alyssa Harmon: My name is Alyssa Harmon. I am a USFSP student, and I'm an English writing studies major.

Emma Hamilton: My name is Emma Hamilton, and I'm also a USFSP student and an English major with a concentration in writing studies.

Kathy Olinger: I'm Kathy Olinger, and I'm a USF English major with a concentration in writing.

Amber Nicol: I'm Amber Nicol, and I'm a USFSP English major as well.

Emma: In a broader sense, I thought the communities of practice exercise was really great for kind of defining and starting to think about our discourse communities that we're all members of and sort of like a cool first exercise to act as a precursor to the class that ended up being like a huge discourse community.

Amber: When I started going back through the wiki for our podcast today, I thought, this is really where it all started, because once we did the communities of practice assignment, we realized what we had in common with each other.

Alyssa: I liked starting the class off with discourse communities, and I've had Dr. Conner for a few classes, and we normally start with "bring a small object," which is where you bring a small object and then you interview someone else and then you write about it. But this one was almost, maybe better for a first class because it was interesting to see different interests for everyone within that discourse community—like we had music. . . .

Trey: I couldn't help but notice how many musicians were in our midst. *[laughs]*

Amber: People do seem to be drawn to music.

Alyssa: I think it's something that we can all connect to. I read somewhere it was saying that music is kind of like a universal language, like no matter what language you speak everyone can understand music and it makes them feel a certain way.

Amber: And the nature of just having the ability to be able to turn something like a sound pressure wave moving through air into what we experience as a person is amazing.

Trey: It is, and it's something that we don't want to render as something that's exclusive to experts. This community really surprised me, to tell you the truth, in the way that we all manifested as musicians, really, and just expanded, I think, our definition of musicianship through this idea of soundwriting. We took, we all are affected by the vibrations that you describe. We should all be able to participate that in our writing practice too in some way. And I love the way that we explored different ways that sound weaves its way into our writerly lives, yeah.

Amber: It made us comfortable to the point where, as writers, we were talking about very personal things with one another. We got to this level in Dr. Conner's class, and now we all know each other.

Alyssa: It was kind of nice to be able to come into this class for an hour and 15 minutes and just use music and writing as a way to forget everything else that was going around. Like during that semester, we had Hurricane Irma, and it was difficult to recover after that, so coming into this class and being able to focus on just this was a nice way to vent and get our feelings out and just ignore the rest of the world for a little while.

Kathy: I think getting together with everybody and just chilling, just chilling out—it is very therapeutic.

Emma: I think that I agree with you guys because, to me, it was the structure of the class or—not lack thereof, because I don't want to say that it was unstructured, but the sort of the jamming, freewheeling, evolving structure of the class was what really made me excited, even with a busy semester, to get home and work on the stuff for 4311. Because I felt that in soundwriting there are so many infinite possibilities that it's exciting to explore and kind of opens your mind rather than an assignment that has so many parameters and so many requirements that you have to consider when you're working on it.

Trey: Everything started to, like you say, and they started to emerge, and you didn't know what was gonna happen next, but you knew it was gonna be interesting. It gave us a space to speak from our heart, and to try to bring those complexities into the space, to me are sometimes more challenging than the elaborate headspace logos vertigo that we usually experience in the classroom. So, it just, yeah—the way that you took that turn and the way it sort of played out during the sensory writing on the seawall was amazing, too. That was a fun day. Everybody was within earshot, so it was one of those "we don't have earlids moments" that McCluhan (McLuhan & Fiore, 1967) talks about, right? In discussion of sound, modality. Everybody, whether they wanted to or not, got to hear Trey, Amber, and Ivan play guitar.

Chris: I remember thinking, you know, I can sit here and just write about what I'm hearing, what I'm listening, what I'm experiencing. And in the end, Ivan basically started looking at what I had written, and he was creating an actual song, playing the guitar and just reading everything I wrote in that little short poem, and it was fantastic.

Trey: You took that turn, and the way it sort of played out during the sensory writing on the seawall.

Amber: And that's what's so cool about the wiki, too. Earlier, Emma was talking about how she didn't wanna call it not organized, or something like that you said, and I thought, yeah, well, it's super organized the way nature is: Everything exists, and it works somehow.

Kathy: [As opposed to] "Here do this, do that at this point in time, at that point in time, and how many words all the time," and it's nice.

Chris: It felt very organic to me.

Amber: Yeah, natural and very open, which is great for inspiration and just connecting with one another. Because when you go around life and you're all closed up and you're stressed out all the time, you don't get to enjoy it at all, and you're probably not in your most inspirational moment.

Alyssa: I think it's also important as writers to have an open space and be able to share all of our works, because the way we get better is by reading other people's writing and helping each other with our writing, so having the wiki and the open space allows us to do just that and become better writers.

Emma: Yeah, yeah. I think the wiki is a real mirror of your teaching style too, Dr. Conner, that you said you went into a certain day thinking, "I am not thinking, 'I'm the professor of this class,' and I don't think any of your"—I mean I guess I can only speak for myself—but to me, your teaching style is so much more like a catalyst, and that's how the wiki is too; it just kind of is a catalyst, and there are little spots for you to jump off and explode. It's almost like soundwriting, like your teaching style kind of embodies all the benefits of the possibilities of soundwriting.

Amber: I feel like I learned more about life in that class than any class that is more of a textual-based, rigid, top-down approach. I really learned more how to be patient.

Emma: That's perfectly said—the top-down approach. Day one to day . . . whenever.

Chris: Exactly.

Kathy: I learned to expand my horizons more.

Trey: I guess I'd have to definitely defer all credit and attribution to my teachers when you say something like that. That's all I can say. I guess maybe what you all are—what a nice transition we just wrote too! I like the way that music and wiki were . . . we're weaving them. That's really beautiful what we're doing the past five minutes or so. But, I guess that's maybe what we're signifying with this handle of "the resonance is the composer." Maybe that's . . . because I would certainly—I mean, it's beautiful testimony, and I hope that's what's happening! *[laughs]* But it certainly is the resonance that's doing that. It's certainly something that's manifesting between us; it's this figure of rhythm, I think, is what I'm trying to invoke with the idea of resonance; it's manifesting between us somehow. I wish it could happen every day every way like that.

Amber: This really could help change the world for the better. This could be applied to our city or to a work environment.

Chris: I think one of the things I enjoyed most is when Emma added music to Alyssa's poem.

Amber: That was my favorite thing ever.

Chris: It was fantastic. I mean, the music you played to it went right along with the . . . I guess you could say the ambience of the poem itself.

Emma: It was fun; I was inspired by when Alex brought the metronome in, and I just thought that was so cool like to read his work along with the metronome, and that was really cool, because that's maybe not necessarily soundwriting, but applying sound to prose that was written without any type of apparent rhythm in mind and finding the rhythm, or maybe discovering the rhythm that maybe was subconscious was kind of a cool exercise that I would never do, you know, in any other class.

Alyssa: It was also helpful, as the author of the poem, when I head Emma's song it kind of showed to me how she perceived the poem and what undertones she interpreted, I guess, and it was interesting to go back to that poem and see which spots were the best, which spots maybe needed work, and how different people interpret it, which can help me as a writer.

Emma: It was cool to kind of create your own assignments in that way; it's interesting to see what everybody created, had created, by the end of the semester and how they all had a similar foundation, but they were all really different projects. And I think that's the difference between this sort of class and teaching style—soundwriting, wiki, whatever you wanna call it—and another class. It's the difference between logging on to meet a deadline for an assignment, and you're doing something because you have to. And it's frustrating when I experience that as a student because I don't have to be here, you know, I choose to be here, and it's a weird dissonance that I feel. Whereas, in this class it's like you get excited to log on and take what you're learning and mold it into what you want it to be, and you get so much more out of it than a typical, like you said, top-down class.

Alyssa: And you can tell people feel that way because people will still log on to old wikis and still post and everything.

[excited laughter and talking over each other]

References

Ceraso, S. (2014). (Re)educating the senses: Multimodal listening, bodily learning, and the composition of sonic experiences. *College English, 77*(2), 102–123.

McLuhan, M. & Fiore, Q. (1967). *The Medium is the massage: An inventory of effects.* Bantom Books.

Théberge, P. (1997). *Any sound you can imagine: Making music/consuming technology.* Wesleyan University Press.

Chapter 13. The Sound of Type: Multimodal Aesthetics

Helen J. Burgess and Travis Harrington
NORTH CAROLINA STATE UNIVERSITY

The mind is a grammar-making device and it is difficult to turn it off.
—*Susan Stewart, "Letter on Sound"*

This chapter discusses the role of multimodal work as synesthetic work—that is, the strange activity of apprehending one sense in terms of another, as when we "see sound" or "hear images." In this chapter we focus on an "accidental" sound project, in which a student author (Harrington) responded to a visually based assignment (set by Burgess) exploring typographic design and letterforms, culminating in a project based in sound. The resulting aural artifact, a three-track musical composition, lays bare some interesting potentials in typographic language; already strongly associated with the body in its terminology, type can clearly be thought of as having aural qualities too.

The study of typography relies on a double practice: learning to "look at" as well as "look through" letterforms to discern layers of meaning. This is partly an effect of the practice of multimodal reading, where the "modes" in this case are image and text—and in typography's instance, the transformation of image to text and vice versa. Despite this emphasis on the eye, though, type, in its traditional terminology, is beholden to a whole metaphorical language resting in nonvisual forms of materiality. Gunther Kress's (2000) observation that "human semiosis rests, first and foremost, on the facts of biology and physiology" (p. 184) is made abundantly clear in type's descriptive terminologies: Letterforms have a "face," "feet," "ears," and "shoulders." Kress's "modes of materiality" (2000, p. 190) are further evident in historically based technological terms such as "leading" (a reference to the space between each printed line on a page, achieved formerly by placing bars of lead in the gap) and "upper and lower case," referring to the placement of "cases" of type in the drawer of the printer's cabinet.

Given the multiple embodied modes in which type is embedded, it seems clear that any attempt to apprehend its effects fully should include the modality of sound. As an exercise in transliterating a letterform from one modality (in this case, graphical) to another (sound), multimodal composing, in the case of this exercise, embodies what Jentery Sayers (2015) and David Rieder (2017) called "transducing": the transformation of energy from one form to another, in this case from the movement of the eye along x and y axes to the movement of sound waveforms through the eardrum. And the result of the exercise is an opportunity to participate in what Steph Ceraso (2014) called "multimodal listening": to hear

DOI: https://doi.org/10.37514/PRA-B.2022.1688.2.13

the long and short, high and low, major and minor sounds of type and reconstruct their shapes and meanings in the mind's ear.

While Kress (2010) sometimes prefers the term "semiotic resource" to "grammar" (pp. 7–8), there is something specific to the structuring principles of grammar that makes the term useful: the idea that one can translate forms from one medium to another while retaining their analogical structure, in the same way metaphor does in literary and rhetorical writing. Susan Stewart's (1998) statement in the epigraph suggests that our minds are highly attuned to structural similarities. And indeed, when used as a way of expressing patterns, sound as a mode of alternative notation for what we see or do in the world can produce some interesting effects. We already see attempts to "visualize in sound" in other fields, notably mathematics: for example, Timo Bingmann's (2013) work on the "sound of sorting," in which he translated commonly used computer algorithms for sorting numbers into sound. As sorting operations are implemented by comparing items against each other, Bingmann's "audibilizations" use a simple structure: "The generated sound effects depend on the values being compared. Only comparisons yield sound output" ("Usage" section). These comparisons lead to short sounds in the range of 120–1212 Hz, what Bingmann referred to as "'the 8-bit game tune' feeling" ("Usage" section). Similarly, Herman Haverkort's (2018) "sound of Space-Filling Curves" creates "sonifications" of mathematical curves such that "the sound track plays the above sketch vertex by vertex, at a leisurely pace of 75 beats per minute, so it is quite possible to follow the curve every step of the way while listening" ("Background and Description" section).

*Figure 13.1. Travis Harrington's cassette package for his project
The Ampeg Tape: A Musical Approximation of Typeface.*

The original assignment (not included in this chapter) was presented by the instructor (Burgess) in the context of an upper-division class on rhetorical style. One of the particular focuses of the class was on multimodality as a form of rhetorical style (*elocutio*), tasking students over the semester to produce multiple assignments (both graded and ungraded) in the form of objects, interactive games, and image/text collages. Sound, though, was mostly left unexplored in favor of haptic and visual modalities. But in the case of this assignment, the student author (Harrington) took on aurality without prompting, isolating qualities of type and mapping them onto similar qualities of sound. The resulting sound-based piece required a fluency in two literacies: one in typography and one in aural composition. Packaged finally as a cassette tape with typographical paper inserts, the work suggests to us that perhaps aural composing can go beyond the usual podcasts or soundscape recordings to include purposeful acts of transductive, multiliterate work.

In this chapter we package together the following:

- Burgess's retooled version of the original assignment that attempts to more closely investigate the "sound of type," including assessment criteria and grading rubric;
- Harrington's audio reflection, in which he discusses his composition process, interleaving his observations with the music files produced for the assignment; and
- a reflection by Burgess on the process of reworking the specifications to encourage more student submissions in sound and other nonvisual modalities.

Assignment Prompt and Contract Sheet

Typographic Style Assignment, Revised for Multimodal Synaesthetics

Purpose

An exercise partly in research/writing and partly in typographic interpretation.

Step 1

Choose a document or object and analyze & evaluate the visual and typographical choices made by the designer. Write this analysis up in a paper, following the appropriate specifications for your choice of contracted grade.

Step 2

Find a way to re-present your analysis in a compelling way, utilizing one or more alternative modalities such as sound, movement, or taste.

Step 3

Include a 1-page process paper as a separate page at the end of your paper. Include some brief justifications for your reinterpretation of the essay. On the due date, bring your project to class and be prepared to discuss it.

Guidelines

Analysis means a thorough description and discussion of the choices made by the designer. *Evaluation* means making a thorough and critical judgment of the effectiveness of those choices. *Do both.*

In Step 2, think about the way type is constructed. Remember leading, kerning, and other ways type is spaced; the way shape and font styles elicit specific emotional responses; and the way placement and contrast of fonts and colors can speed up or slow down the eye. For example, consider the following possible mappings for sound:

- Serifs: "ornamentation";
- Letterspacing: a wider letterspacing takes longer to read. Think about the length of the sounds you can produce: long and slow, short and quick (map to length);
- Letterweight: the "boldness" of a word (map to volume);
- Font size: try mapping to sound frequency, e.g., a large font could map to a low, booming sound; a tiny font to a high, squeaky sound.

How can you leverage an alternative modality to show how type works? See the following examples for sound and movement:

- Dance your dissertation: https://www.sciencemag.org/news/2017/11/announcing-winner-year-s-dance-your-phd-contest
- Dance bubble sort: https://youtu.be/Iv3vgjM8Pv4
- The sound of sorting: https://panthema.net/2013/sound-of-sorting/
- Space-filling curves: https://web.archive.org/web/20180110113418/http://www.win.tue.nl/~hermanh/doku.php?id=sound_of_space-filling_curves

If the project is missing a required component in order to achieve the grade contracted for, it may be resubmitted with a voucher in the next class period. In addition to your contracted grade, I reserve the right to add a "plus" or "minus" to your assignment where appropriate.

Contract Sheet

☐ *I'm Contracting for an A.* I have included the following in my submission:

☐ An essay, minimum 1,500+ words, which:

☐ describes the document in detail

☐ analyzes how each element works (what it "does" to the viewer)

☐ evaluates how effective this strategy is

☐ quotes three or more external sources to support my points above

☐ includes a works cited page, formatted correctly in MLA, APA, or Chicago style

☐ A project reinterpreting the essay, which:

☐ makes use of an alternative non-visual modality (sound, smell, taste, touch, movement)

☐ includes an interactive component that requires the reader to engage in some way (play, open, assemble)

☐ incorporates citations/sources in a unique way

☐ A colophon, which:

☐ lists all fonts and other elements used, and says where they came from

☐ describes what choices I made in the project portion, and why

☐ *I'm Contracting for a B.* I have included the following in my submission:

☐ An essay, minimum 1,200 words, which:

☐ describes the document in detail

☐ analyzes how each element works (what it "does" to the viewer)

☐ evaluates how effective this strategy is

☐ quotes at least two external sources to support my points above

☐ includes a works cited page, formatted correctly in MLA, APA or Chicago style

☐ A project reinterpreting the essay, which:

☐ makes use of an alternative non-visual modality (sound, smell, taste, touch, movement)

☐ incorporates citations/sources

☐ A colophon, which:

☐ lists all fonts and other elements used, and says where they came from

☐ describes what choices I made in the project portion, and why

☐ *I'm Contracting for a C.* I have included the following in my submission:

☐ An essay, minimum 1,000 words, which:

☐ describes the document in detail

☐ analyzes how each element works (what it "does" to the viewer)

☐ evaluates how effective this strategy is

☐ A project reinterpreting the essay, which:

☐ makes use of an alternative non-visual modality (sound, smell, taste, touch, movement)

☐ A colophon, which:

☐ lists all fonts and other elements used, and says where they came from

☐ describes what choices I made in the project portion, and why

I understand that if I fulfill the minimum requirements in my category, I will achieve the grade I have contracted for. I understand that Dr. Burgess will be doing a word count, and that she reserves the right to add a "plus" or "minus" for excellent/sub-par work. I understand that if any component of the project is missing, the project will be returned to me ungraded for revision with a voucher.

Student Reflection: Seeing Differently

Travis Harrington: In his appearance in the 2007 documentary film *Helvetica*, typeface designer Jonathan Hoefler said, "There's really no way to describe the qualitative parts of typeface without resorting to things fully outside it" (Hustwit, 2007).[1] He used this statement to reinforce a phenomenon that he described in working with his design partner: That when endeavoring to create type design together, they'd often use descriptors unrelated to type as a means to effectively communicate their aesthetic vision.

This idea of what we could call "interdisciplinary description" is not exclusive to design contexts only; we as humans tend to use abstract associations often, as a way to create contextual understanding for these objects and ideas. These associations are rooted in composite sensory experiences; they are the reason expressive literature relies on metaphor, and the reason two things as literally different as the taste of hot dogs and the smell of chlorine could imply a collective visual image of a summer pool party. Our brains operate in synesthesia far more fluidly than we consider. And these are perceptions that create human context; wedged between these perceptions and the language used to communicate them is typography.

In this instance, my professor, Dr. Burgess, wanted our class to each individually choose an object and dissect the composition of its typography for an assignment. She wanted us to make evaluations as to what the typographic composition was attempting to communicate to its audience and how effectively it did so. And then after committing these evaluations to paper, she wanted us to create an object of our own that represented the components of our chosen object's typography and our positions on the effects it took. Because I play a lot of music in my free time, I ended up choosing my guitar amplifier. I figured that because its typography was relatively sparse and simple that it would be an easy effort to make evaluations about.

And it was fairly easy: I argued that the sparse bits of type weren't for a lack of creativity or some kind of visual carelessness; it was a conscious decision to ensure minimal distraction from the object's function and to create a subtle iconography between the type present and the yield of the amplifier's function, its sound. The argument was clear enough, but I had trouble when deciding how I would then synthesize it for the object portion of the assignment. It was clear Dr. Burgess operated within a visual context when creating the assignment, but with so much of my argument founded in aural qualities, I took my chances and decided that I would create a piece of music where each part represented each of the three different typefaces in the composition and what role they played.

[A rapid melodic sequence plays. It loops with persistent abandon, but never escalates past a vague calmness. The electronic, synthesized

---

1. The audio version of Travis Harrington's reflection can be found on the book's companion website.

tonal quality of each note emphasizes this feeling; each one lands with a softened attack, as if the source is emanating from just beneath the surface of water, and decays with a diminished ripple. The sequence continues under the narration that follows.]

This is what I started with, a synthesizer sequence to represent the amp's use of Helvetica typeface. Helvetica isn't the most immediately noticeable typeface in the amplifier's composition, but its role is the most foundational. It is the script that adorns all the functional components of the amp: the knobs, the switches, the input. So in the piece of music, I attempted to mirror this association and make Helvetica's part the representative starting point from where the rest of the piece could form.

Visually, Helvetica is a very neutral font. Its tight spacing and tall x-height give it a stern, but calm presence. And tonally, I tried to represent this in the synthesizer part: a tight, even rhythmic pattern, and a light, marimba-like timbre. I thought these sounds suited these visual components of Helvetica well.

[A second, more complex melody begins, played on a guitar, landing somewhat abrasively against the first. This melody, although still discernibly following a consistent pattern, is far more frenetic and angular. Notes dance between short jerks and thoughtful pauses as they ring out bright and piercing.]

This is the part that I wrote to represent the use of Eurostile Bold Extended No. 2 on the amplifier. Compositionally, this typeface is used only once to delineate the model name of the amp itself. It's placed directly under the power switch and light, giving a direct association to the amp's internal components. Because of this, I thought musically I would give this part the most complexity and character; if this typeface is dictating the nature of the amp's configuration, and the amp's configuration is what makes it functionality unique from other guitar amplifiers, then the part meant to represent it sonically should stand out as well. To further complement the typeface's visual attributes, Eurostile is a geometric typeface, and this particular weight is exceptionally heavy with wide spacing. I created an angular melody with more forceful strums and a staggered rhythmic pattern to represent this.

[The final melody is added to the previous two, which continue playing, its notes ring as tensely and bright as the second as its presence overwhelms the piece. The lumbering, warped guitar notes pulsate and stagger over themselves, and as the piece progresses, their attack becomes more and more careless.]

Finally, I added this part to represent the logotype of the amplifier's brand name Ampeg. The embossed badge bearing the amp's logo is the largest piece of type set in the whole composition and it adorns the grill cloth, which directly covers the amplifier's speaker. With this presence, and the most direct association with the actual sound emitted from the amplifier, I wanted to create a part for it that sounded literally like soundwaves reverberating and pulsing. I put it at the front of the mix, the most noticeable melody in the composition and used very hard strums, letting the notes ring out into each other along with my guitar's vibrato to shift the pitch of the notes back and forth. It seems that visually, the logotype perpetuates this notion as well: It is deeply italicized, with a stunted x-height, and a pseudo-ligature that runs entirely throughout. These guitar techniques create an intertwined, slanted sound.

Most of the evaluations in my attempt to represent these typefaces through music stemmed from the notion of "grand design" in the book *The Elements of Typographic Style* by Robert Bringhurst (2013). I tried to pay very close attention to how the relationships between the type and the functional components of the amp communicated a larger message, which inevitably will result in its audience engaging with sound. But granted, these notions of design do initially stem from a visual context, and in the confines of my research, I did not really consider aural qualities of these elements until creating my music piece. But I think that a lot of these cross-sensory perceptions are instinctual: Even though I had a prior understanding of how music works and generated a lot of these representational sounds on my own, a lot of these connections I made from the visual to the aural side of type weren't necessarily musical at all. Anyone with an ear and intuition for comparison could relate a typeface's visual composition to some sound that occurs in the world. I think the important part is to remember that these visual components are trying to drive its audience to feel a certain way about what it is displaying, and that if you break it down to the raw affect, you can trace it back toward similar feelings in different sensory contexts.

[Repeating music grows louder after the narration ends and plays on for a few more seconds until it ends on a single, lingering chord.]

Instructor Reflection: Retooling for Sound

Helen J. Burgess: One of the reasons I was so surprised and delighted by Travis's submission is that soundwriting is something I haven't really spent much time thinking about as a modality in my classroom.[2] Of course, I know it exists, and it's an active area of study, but I've never thought of myself as "trained in sound"—I have no musical experience or upbringing, for example. And, unless you count the burgeoning podcast playlist on my iPhone, I have no specific interest in the kinds of technologies that produce or define sounds or sound studies. So being confronted with such a submission forced me to think again about how I might

---

2. The audio version of Helen J. Burgess's reflection can be found on the book's companion website.

be shutting out a whole spectrum of creative possibilities by not foregrounding what those possibilities might be.

You might be asking why this assignment makes use of contract or specifications grading. I choose to use these kinds of grading strategies because of the anxieties that multimodal composing can bring up in students, who are often accustomed to simply writing a paper and getting a grade. This is a familiar literacy they've internalized over many years in high school and college. Being asked to compose in different (and sometimes multiple) media can bring up any number of anxieties about one's ability to perform in an unfamiliar mode. Even as an instructor, and you can hear, my own anxieties about expertise in unfamiliar modes shapes my understanding of the assignment. So the contract grading specifications are aimed at allowing for maximum "play," in the sense of the play one has within generic bounds.

I've provided here a retooled version of the assignment, revised along two axes. First, I provided stronger possible guidance and some examples in the prompt sheet, referring to not just sound but also dance (another modality I'm not fluent in). This work usually happens in class sessions, where we spend time discussing font styles in terms of their rhetorical and affective dimensions; but I was more careful to provide a set of correspondences or "mappings" that students could use to begin thinking about how one modality might map to another along specific dimensions. So, for example, I mapped boldness to volume, letterspacing to length, and size to frequency.

Second, I reworked the contract grading specifications to foreground the way we apprehend and engage with different modalities: using the concrete phrases "sound, smell, taste, touch, movement" and "play, open, assemble" in place of more abstract terms such as "reinterpret" and "engage."

There are some possible downfalls to providing more specific examples of mapping and modalities. I've come to see over the years that if I provide an example of a previous student's work, more of that type of work will subsequently appear (although it can be also beneficial and sometimes delicious, as in one semester where I showed a photo of a cake-related submission and received many food items in response). Why we should expect otherwise is something to consider—after all, cake, and mixtapes, and pasteboards all have their own well defined languages and genre bounds. Still, there is something exciting about introducing an assignment like this for the first time in a class—it can have unexpected outcomes and ask us to (re)consider what we're doing when we do it, both as students and instructors. Ultimately, I think, Travis's work suggests to me not only that students can have more agency, if given the opportunity, but also that instructors need to be aware of the choices that they're making: not just by forestalling certain kinds of action but by failing to recognize them as possible actions at all.

References

Bingmann, T. (2013). The sound of sorting—Visualization and "audibilization" of sorting algorithms. *Github*. https://github.com/bingmann/sound-of-sorting.

Bringhurst, R. (2013). *The elements of typographic style* (4th ed.). Hartley & Marks Publishers.

Ceraso, S. (2014). (Re)educating the senses: Multimodal listening, bodily learning, and the composition of sonic experiences. *College English, 77*(2), 102–123.

Haverkort, H. (2018). *The sound of space-filling curves: Examples.* https://web.archive.org/web/20180110113418/http://www.win.tue.nl/~hermanh/doku.php?id=sound_of_space-filling_curves.

Hustwit, G. (Director). (2007). *Helvetica: A documentary film* [Film]. Plexifilm.

Kress, G. (2000). Multimodality. In Bill Cope & Mary Kalantzis (Eds.), *Multiliteracies: Literacy learning and the design of social futures* (pp. 182–202). Routledge.

Kress, G. (2010). *Multimodality: A social semiotic approach to contemporary communication.* Routledge.

Rieder, D. (2017). *Suasive iterations: Rhetoric, writing, and physical computing.* Parlor Press.

Sayers, J. (2015, January 10). *Transduction literacies* [Conference session]. Modern Language Association Convention, Vancouver, BC, Canada.

Stewart, S. (1998). Letter on sound. In Charles Bernstein (Ed.), *Close listening: Poetry and the performed word* (pp. 29–52). Oxford University Press.

Part Three. Soundwriting with Primary Research

Chapter 14. From Cylinders to WordPress: Using Digital Sound Archives for Short-Form Radio Programs

Jason Luther
Rowan University

The Phono Project was inspired by an assignment I originally taught in a required, sophomore-level, research-writing course at Syracuse University back in 2012. That course focused on remix and copyright, and as such it opened with an expansive unit that framed digital writing and information as largely assembled, networked, ecological, and multimodal; needless to say, it was an ambitious course. Students used WordPress to blog about their reactions to watching Brett Gaylor's (2008) documentary *RiP!: A Remix Manifesto*; read Lawrence Lessig's (2008) *Remix: Making Art and Commerce Thrive in the Hybrid Economy*; and practiced working with sources using Joe Harris's (2006) *Rewriting: How To Do Things with Texts*. (Note: In an attempt to make up for this lack of context in my revised version of the course, instructors will notice that I front-load a basic definition of multimodality in the actual assignment.)

The second unit, and the one that inspired The Phono Project, was based on my class's partnership with a nationally syndicated radio program called *Sound Beat*, a short-form podcast that focuses on the history of recorded sound. *Sound Beat* is sponsored by the University—and Syracuse Libraries Special Collections, in particular—since its programming source comes directly from The Belfer Audio Laboratory and Archive, a building that houses over half a million sound recordings and related items. In each 90-second episode of *Sound Beat*, host Brett Barry narrates a story about one of the items found in the archive, focusing on anything from historical events and pastimes to unique achievements of individual performers.

The archive is also home to the Belfer Cylinders Digital Connection, a database that includes more than 1,600 digitized versions of the archive's 20,000 cylinder recordings. Such recordings are some of the most vulnerable phonographs in existence, since cylinders, invented by Thomas Edison in 1877, were not only primarily made from less durable materials (tinfoil in early cases) but also predated disc phonographs, which were easier to mass produce. As a result, recordings that have been carefully digitized by their laboratory's resident sound engineer are shared publicly on their website as high-quality MP3s. Students in my class, then, searched the Belfer Cylinders Digital Connection for potential recordings to be used in future *Sound Beat* episodes. They toured the space, looking at various devices for playing and recording sound and meeting with writer Jim O'Connor to get a sense of *Sound Beat*'s genre and tricks to his process and

DOI: https://doi.org/10.37514/PRA-B.2022.1688.2.14

working with subject-specialist librarians like Patrick Williams, who co-wrote a study guide for the partnership. (I interview Jim and Patrick in my reflection below.) Students then wrote multiple drafts of scripts, cutting them down and recording demos of their episodes in Audacity.

Such an exciting and tightly woven unit, however, poses a challenge. How might a project that relies on a world-class sound archive or an NPR-sponsored radio program export to institutions that have neither of those resources or contexts? How might such an idea be adapted for different institutions and unfamiliar curricular contexts? Although recordings from the Belfer Cylinders Digital Connection and episodes from *Sound Beat* are publicly available, I began to wonder what other archives and resources might be utilized and how I might approach revising this unit for myself and other teachers, who were working with students in these divergent, multiple contexts.

What follows, then, is an assignment that is meant to be taught in eight to ten class meetings and that replaces *Sound Beat* with a self-published podcast series I call The Phono Project (housed at phonoproject.com). The Phono Project opens up students to virtually any publicly archived recording that has been digitized, or one that students want to digitize themselves. However, the assignment has increasingly drawn from The Great 78 Project, a collection of 78s hosted and organized by the Internet Archive (https://great78.archive.org/). This has led to recent collaborations with stakeholders who have both digitized these 78s in nearby Philadelphia and advocated for their usage at the Internet Archive (Adams, 2021). I have used the assignment with students taking Rowan University's introductory course to the major (called Introduction to Writing Arts), which is a module-based course, cotaught with two other faculty who focus on different aspects of our major. Although the course enrolls 60 students, cohorts of 20 students rotate every eight class meetings so that faculty actually teach their curricula three times per semester. Because my module focuses on writing technologies and is taught in a lab equipped with 20 state-of-the-art iMacs, the assignment below is framed through a lens of multimodality, where students tinker with a variety of tools the lab offers, including Audacity. Students also blog using WordPress, which gives them some experience with the interface that they will ultimately use for their contribution to The Phono Project. Throughout the unit, students practice writing with and about sound by composing audio essays, describing popular podcasts, and reviewing contemporary songs that interest them, mimicking techniques from critics who write about singles (e.g., *Pitchfork's* track reviews).

While I was initially concerned about designing this assignment so that it would respond to local soundwriting exigencies for my students at Rowan, which is located in southern New Jersey, the shift to Rowan from Syracuse afforded a serendipitous moment. Rather than frame the unit around an on-campus archive, I considered The Phono Project as an opportunity for students to connect with New Jersey's unique contributions to the history of recorded sound. After all,

Edison's famous laboratory in North Jersey, which is now a national park, is considered the birthplace of the phonograph; and perhaps more significantly, it was in nearby Camden where the founders of the Victor Talking Machine Company, Eldridge R. Johnson and Emile Berliner, fused their patents to re-engineer Edison's cylinders to discs, thereby increasing fidelity and preparing the phonograph for mass consumption. Finally, many of the 78s hosted at the Internet Archive have been digitized locally in Philadelphia, at George Blood Audio LP, who have offered my students and me tours of their facilities (GeorgeBloodAudio, 2016).

In my reflection, I look back on my partnership with *Sound Beat*, interviewing Jim and Patrick, thinking about the choices I made in the revision, and making predictions about potential sticking points.

A final note on accessibility: While The Phono Project may present unique challenges for students who are D/deaf or hard-of-hearing, it also requires all students to approach sound textually and historically, researching the context of the recording and finding a narrative worth telling to public audiences. While some students may require accommodations via peer collaboration or voice actors, the project is, at its heart, multimodal, as the work requires all senses. This is, in part, reflected in the way that final projects are hosted on a website that includes transcripts of the audio.

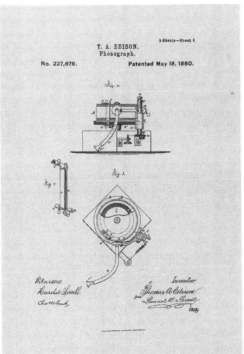

Figure 14.1. Thomas Edison's (1880) patent for the phonograph, whose media was originally cylinder based and not the flat vinyl discs we now see.

The Assignment

Introduction

In "'Convince Me!' Valuing Multimodal Literacies and Composing Public Service Announcements," Richard J. Selfe and Cynthia L. Selfe (2008) provide four compelling reasons why writing in the 21st century requires authors to go beyond composing sentences, paragraphs, and pages. Increasingly, as Selfe and Selfe argue, writers are multimodal (literally "many + modes"), drawing from a range of communicative resources—including sound and video—as they design, craft, and share compositions across various forms of media, both in person and through digital networks. This is especially true for writers who are offering up their work to public audiences, audiences who are also increasingly accessing information using these multiple modes; as Selfe and Selfe put it, "we learn about, act in, and understand the world using multiple channels of communication" (2008, p. 84).

One of those modes or channels is online radio. According to Edison Research (2020), 68% of all Americans listen to online radio at least once per month; that number jumps to 86% when accounting for 12–34-year-olds. In addition to streaming music services like Spotify, serialized radio programs like WBEZ's *Sound Opinions*, WXPN's *World Cafe*, KUTX's *This Song*, or Radiotopia's *Sound Exploder* let listeners choose how to play them—from their computer or on-the-go from a mobile device. Moreover, podcasts are reaching younger audiences. As Edison Research notes, almost half of Americans ages 12 to 34 say they've listened to one in the past month—a number that has nearly doubled since 2017.

And yet, the ubiquity of digital media has also led some consumers to turn to analog media, buying print books and vinyl records. According to the Recording Industry Association of America, sales of LP vinyl records have grown for 14 consecutive years, recently outpacing CDs for the first time since the 1980s (Brown, 2020).

Enter The Phono Project. In this four-week assignment, I'm asking you *to draw from multiple modes—text, sound, html—and several tools, to create a very short demonstration of soundwriting ("demo," in music industry parlance): a 90-second MP3 file that is a recording of you speaking over a sample of sound that was reproduced by a phonograph.* Your demo will then be published with the other 175 episodes on phonoproject.com.

A digitized phonograph recording is a digital recording of a vinyl record—as in, someone hooked up a record player to a computer and recorded the sounds using audio software. As you'll learn in this unit, phonograph recordings have existed in a variety of formats since the beginning of recorded sound more than 140 years ago—first as cylinders, then later as discs, which gradually changed size and slowed their rotation from 78 RPMs to 45 and finally, the most common, 33 1/3. You will engage this history, critically listen to recordings in the public domain through their digital archives, and experiment with the translation of sound through time and space to make new meaning.

This assignment will likely present you with two new challenges: First, you'll need to obtain a digitized phonograph recording that "speaks" to you and your audience. Although you'll only write about 125–150 words of copy for your script, you'll need to do quite a lot of research to make those words worthy of a public listener. Second, you'll need to learn how to use a free, open-access audio recording program, called Audacity, to record your voice and mix it successfully with the recording. This is essentially what 21st century multimodal composing is all about.

In the end you'll submit a Word file of your script and bibliography, an MP3 of your digital recording, and a 600-word doc file that reflects on the successes and challenges of this project.

Finding the Story: Researching Recordings

Once you have some experience writing about contemporary music, I'll introduce you to a digital archive of phonographs called *The Great 78 Project* where you can download tens of thousands of recordings. Hosted at archive. org (aka The Internet Archive), The Great 78 Project has 50,000 78s (3+-minute records that spin at 78 rpms) that were recorded mostly from 1898 to the 1950s. A variety of digital audio formats (MP3, FLACs, OGG, and more) can be downloaded directly from the site.

Since The Great 78 Project contains tens of thousands of digitized recordings, how do you go about finding one that "speaks" to you? In class we will talk about several ways you might both search and browse them, but mainly what you should keep in mind is that this process takes time. First, you'll want to spend some time browsing these archives, noticing how they use genre, topic, language, and dates to organize themselves. Of course, you can also search them, experimenting with certain keywords that reflect your own learning goals and interests. But most of all, you'll want to listen to them. What do they sound like? What do you notice? What instruments, lyrics, or voices, or noises jump out at you? What questions does this recording raise for you? Once you've narrowed your interests down to two or three recordings, it's time to do some research.

Whether it's a feature on NPR or a sound bite on *Sound Beat*, much of what you hear on public radio is a story—a narrative that audiences remember and appreciate. But in order to find a compelling story and tell it with the kind of efficiency this project requires, you need to know as much about it as possible. In class we'll talk about strategies for getting started and mapping the various ways you can approach the recording, whether in terms of the artist or speaker, the format or genre, the exigence or culture at the time, and so forth. For example, while the name "Vernon Dalhart" is barely recognizable to most people in 2020, he was a household name in 1926 with the recording of "The Wreck of the Old 97" and forged a lucrative path for the entire genre of country music. While this is interesting, it doesn't really tell a story, so you could keep pushing to find more out by reading about Dalhart, the music scenes he belonged to in the early 20th century, the history of country music, the lyrics and genre of

"The Wreck of the Old 97," and more until you get to a story that is interesting and works for the project.

Scripting and Soundwriting

As you research, you'll be taking notes and drafting your scripts. Since it's difficult to stick to 125 words in your first script, you'll instead work with a limit of 500 words, citing sources as you go. We'll workshop these in class and try to cut your draft down to a few shorter possibilities that are still faithful to the narrative you're trying to share with the world.

Meanwhile, you'll also begin to record your voice, reading drafts of your script and mixing it over your chosen recording using a free, open-source program called Audacity. We'll read about writing for sound and workshop some of these demos in class using SoundCloud, looking at aspects such as timing, volume, and sampling, and using effects like amplification, normalization, and fading in and out.

Reflection

Finally, you'll include a 600-word reflection wherein you introduce me to your project—why you chose your cylinder, the processes you went through during the selection, research, writing and revision phases of the project, noteworthy successes and challenges you faced, and what you learned.

Sample Student Projects

The first two samples are from my partnership with *Sound Beat* at Syracuse University in 2012.[1] Each sample was selected and lightly revised by both the student and lead writer, Jim O'Connor, and then read and recorded by the host of *Sound Beat*, voice-over professional Brett Barry. Like all *Sound Beat* programs, they are all hosted publicly on their website (and these two are reproduced on the book's companion website). The third sample was produced for *The Phono Project* and made by a student in my Introduction to Writing Arts course at Rowan University.

1. In "Der Graf von Luxemburg," theatre major Craig Kober discovered an interesting story about a German operetta and its author, Franz Lehar, who thought it would be a failure. (http://soundbeat.org/episode/der-graf-von-luxembourg/)
2. In "The Unknown Soldier," Dennis Bitetti wrote a script that spoke to his dedication as a former U.S. soldier. (http://soundbeat.org/episode/the-unknown-soldier)
3. In her program on Bing Crosby's "White Christmas," Paige DeMarco chose to focus on the recording technologies that made Bing Crosby's

---

1.   Three student examples (audio files and descriptive transcripts) can be found on the book's companion website.

song a holiday classic. (http://www.phonoproject.com/2018/10/04
/white-christmas-by-bing-crosby)

Reflection

*[Plays 30-second recording of Victrola being operated, which include
sounds of the lid opening, a disc being placed on the turntable, multiple
cranks of the machine, and the rotation of the turntable, which fades
into the background (a remix of Thaighaudio, 2016a, 2016b, 2016c).]*

Jason Luther: My name is Jason Luther, and I'm Assistant Professor of Writing
Arts at Rowan University in Glassboro, New Jersey.[2] Those sounds you hear are
from a digital recording of Victor's classic phonograph machine, the Victrola
VV-XI or VV-eleven. You can hear its mahogany lid being opened, the machine's
crank being yanked and spun, and its two-spring motor cantankerously animat-
ing the heavy, felt-lined turntable. The Victor Talking Machine Company made
nearly a million of the VV-elevens between 1910 and 1921 in Camden, New Jersey.
This particular invention helped birth and sustain a musical public eager to purchase and play 78 rpm discs of brief, acoustical recordings. All across America,
living rooms played the likes of proto-country artists like Vernon Dalhart . . .

*[Plays sample of Dalhart's (1926) guitar and vocal accompaniment on
"The Wreck of the Old 97" with lyrics that sing, "It's a mighty rough
road from Lynchburg to Danville in a line on a three-mile grade" which
fades quickly into background.]*

. . . classical pianists like Sergei Rachmaninoff . . .

*[Plays 5-second sample of piano solo (Rachmaninoff, 1920) which also
fades quickly.]*

. . . and early blues singers like Mamie Smith.

*[Plays sample of horns and vocals from "Crazy Blues" (Mamie Smith
& Her Jazz Hounds, 1920) with lyrics that sing: "I can't sleep at night, I
can't eat a bite, 'cause the man I love, he don't treat me right," which
fades quickly.]*

The digitization and historicizing of phonograph recordings is the essence
of my assignment, The Phono Project. As I mention in the introduction to this
chapter, the idea for The Phono Project began in 2012, when I was a graduate student at Syracuse University. It was there where I taught a required, research-writing course that partnered with a radio program called *Sound Beat*.

---

2.   The audio version of Jason Luther's reflection can be found on the book's companion website.

Sound Beat was, and still is, a 90-second show about the history of recorded sound. Its selections come from the Belfer Audio Archive, one of the largest audio archives in the world, which is housed within the special collections at Syracuse University Libraries.

While *Sound Beat* draws from an archive of over 400,000 recordings, students in my class had to pull from the digitized archive at Belfer, which housed Edison cylinder recordings in the public domain. Once they found a recording in that archive, my students researched the recording for a 90-second narrative, writing several scripts, the final of which they committed to a recording through Audacity. From these demo recordings, writer and producer Jim O'Connor selected five to revise and produce for the show, which then aired in over 350 markets, reaching millions of listeners in the US, Canada, and the Philippines. Here's one from one of my students, about the Jubilee Singers of Fisk University:

[Fisk Jubilee Singers singing the peppy chorus of "Peter on the Sea," which fades out.]

> **Brett Barry of Sound Beat**: You're listening to the Jubilee Singers of Fisk University sing "Peter on the Sea," from 1927, and you're on the *Sound Beat*.

["Peter on the Sea" fades in and back out.]

> Fisk University struggled financially from its very founding just six months after the end of the Civil War. On the verge of closure, the Singers began a series of fundraising tours in 1871. By appearing in many venues in the US and embarking on a visit to Europe where they sang for Queen Victoria, the Jubilee Singers broke color barriers and made an enormous impact on the world of music. Oh, and they saved the university. As a matter of fact, the Jubilee Singers continue to sing today.

["Peter on the Sea" fades in and back out.]

> In their words, "We stand on the shoulders of the original Jubilee Singers, continuing their legacy, as we sing Negro Spirituals." This episode was written in part by Syracuse University student Tesia Elder as part of the *Sound Beat* Class Partnership. For more on the Jubilee Singers past and present, check out Sound Beat dot org right now.

["Peter in the Sea" cuts out and Sound Beat *theme plays.]*

> *Sound Beat* is produced at the Belfer Audio Archive, Syracuse University Library. I'm Brett Barry. (Elder & O'Connor, 2018)

Jason: At the time of our partnership, my research-writing students and I were the first and only class working with *Sound Beat*. Six years later, the class partnership is going strong as *Sound Beat* works with students in music journalism and ethnomusicology classes. As I prepared to redesign this course for students at Rowan University in the spring of 2018, I wanted to reflect on the 2012 partnership by interviewing both Jim O'Connor and subject specialist librarian, Patrick Williams. Both Jim and Patrick helped build the original curriculum, and so we talked about key strategies and ongoing challenges with an assignment like The Phono Project, six years after.

One of the first challenges is deciding which recordings students can choose and where they come from. While I've provided several sites to use for The Phono Project,³ the partnership with *Sound Beat* was limited to its archive. That said, "limited" is a misnomer as the Belfer Archive has nearly half a million recordings. One of the first things I learned in talking with Jim is how he specifically limits students' choices when it comes to this process.

Jim O'Connor: The pool we have to choose from—the large pool—is obviously almost, you know, for our purposes limitless. In terms of the demands that we want to put on staff and the work that they're kind of doing there anyway, what we've taken is equal parts of cylinders, 78s, and vinyl. What I do basically now—and I can't remember if this is how we did it?—I select a larger pool. The typical class size will be 20 and so I'll give them 40 choices and try to make it kind of representative of a month of *Sound Beat* episodes. Where it's, you know, that spectrum-wide range of genres, and also formats.

Jason: Even with these imposed limitations to the archive, another challenge quickly emerges: how does a writer find a story worth telling in 90 seconds? A helpful place to start, Jim suggests, is the recording itself.

Jim: What I always, always say to everyone when they're writing these is to play that recording throughout, while you're writing. Because, you know, personally, I feel that music is so transformative that it automatically puts you right in that time and place when you're listening to that music. And when you hear certain, you know, when you hear the trill of violins or something that accentuates your point, you can really nod to that in your piece. Part of it is direction obviously as well, so you have to see yourself as the writer, the producer, and the voice artist. The most important thing for me has been putting headphones on and playing the song while I'm writing about it—you're locked in.

Jason: Once students are aurally familiar with a track and notice particular sounds or lyrics coming from the recording, they can begin to raise questions. That's when additional outside sources begin to play a role in the project. As

---

3. While I currently draw only from The Great 78 Project in order to simplify this assignment for students, I have used a range of other archives of 78s in previous iterations, including those stored on the Smithsonian's website, the National Jukebox from the Library of Congress, and the Belfer Cylinders Digital Collection at Syracuse University.

Patrick notes, those sources can be invaluable not only for understanding an artist's legacy or a song's resonance, but also for the larger cultural contexts that shape genres. Here he refers to Vernon Dalhart's "The Wreck of the Shenandoah," comparing the disaster-song genre of the 1920s to more contemporary diss tracks.

Patrick Williams: Getting some of that historical context is really difficult. The example I still almost without fail use in classes is Vernon Dalhart's "Wreck of the Shenandoah" because it's like the collision of this thing that we think of as strange, you know, this blimp crash, and if you start looking at his catalog and you start looking through the magazines of that era, you see that this is a type of song, one of many songs—whether the crash of a train or a blimp or whatever—and so looking at those historical resources that have lists of songs, or have reviews or something like that, can give students that context that helps them pick out what's interesting. And maybe it's not interesting that this is a song about a blimp crashing, but what's interesting is it's a song about one of many blimps crashing in our music and recorded sound. We know that there's a bunch of diss tracks are a thing for us, we understand that, but we don't see . . . like somebody coming in in 25 years picking out some particular diss track might not necessarily recognize that it's a part of this cultural currency that exists. And I think that if you just look at information around an artist or information around a particular track, you lose some of that and you're sort of forced to encounter it when you are in these historical periodicals.

Jason: As Patrick's comparison suggests, researching and historicizing genres of sound are helpful for writing a strong script; however, as Jim notes, your audience and the very format of *Sound Beat* and soundwriting are important considerations too.

Jim: The format is 90 seconds and you've got music in the background. It's radio, so it's not like you have a captive audience—people could be driving their car and a dog walks across the street, as we say in class all the time. You know, people need to be able to recoup, so complex points that you're making at the beginning of the episode to tie in at the end don't typically work. The episodes we write, some of them are autobiographical, so you have to come at it from that perspective. You wouldn't say in a *Sound Beat* episode, "Elvis Aaron Presley was born in Tupelo, Missouri." [Note: he surely meant to say *Mississippi*.] People will know that dude. When it comes to a performer like Elvis it's more about telling—not even a story, you know, you've got 150 words. It's more about telling a little chapter of the story.

Jason: Jim, Patrick, and I discussed other components of the assignment—how intellectual property structures the show's format, how students respond to their writing when they hear it on the radio for the first time, and writing for things like tone; however, it is the short form that is perhaps one of the assignment's best and most challenging aspects. I look forward to revisiting this again as I teach the assignment to a new group of students this spring at Rowan University.

[Rachmaninoff (1920) piano solo fades in and plays in background.]

Thanks for listening. Once again, I'm Jason Luther, and you've heard a reflection on The Phono Project, featuring an interview with Jim O'Connor and Patrick Williams, both of Syracuse University. I'd like to thank Jim and Patrick for speaking with me and encourage you to check out *Sound Beat* online at soundbeat.org, where you will find several great examples of short form podcasts, written by Jim, that you can use with your students. *[Rachmaninoff piano solo fades out]*

References

Adams, C. (2021, June 9). University professor leverages 78rpm record collection from the Internet Archive for student podcasts. *Internet Archive Blogs*. Retrieved March 15, 2022, from http://blog.archive.org/2021/06/09/university-professor-leverages-78rpm-record-collection-from-the-internet-archive-for-students/.

Dalhart, V. (1926, March 18). Wreck of the old 97 [Song]. Internet Archive. Retrieved January 19, 2018, from https://archive.org/details/78_wreck-of-the-old-97_vernon-dalhart_gbia0007165a/Wreck+of+The+Old+97.

Edison, T. A. (1880, May 18). *Drawing for a phonograph* [Image]. National Archives. https://catalog.archives.gov/id/595515.

Elder, T. & O'Connor, J. (2018, January 8). The Fisk University Jubilee Singers [Audio podcast episode]. On *Sound Beat*. http://soundbeat.org/episode/the-fisk-university-jubilee-singers .

Gaylor, B. (Director). (2008). *RiP!: A remix manifesto* [Film]. National Film Board of Canada. https://www.nfb.ca/film/rip_a_remix_manifesto/.

GeorgeBloodAudio. (2016, October 25). Mass 78rpm disc digitization [Video file]. *Internet Archive*. https://archive.org/details/mass78rpmdiscdigitization.

Mamie Smith & Her Jazz Hounds. (1920). Crazy blues [Song]. Internet Archive. Retrieved January 19, 2018, from https://archive.org/details/MamieSmithHerJazzHounds.

Rachmaninoff, S. (1920, November 3). Spinning song, Op. 67, No. 4 (Songs without words, No 34) [Song]. Internet Archive. Retrieved January 19, 2018, from. https://archive.org/details/SergeiRachmaninoffPiano.

Selfe, R. J. & Selfe, C. L. (2008). "Convince me!" Valuing multimodal literacies and composing public service announcements. *Theory into Practice, 47*(2), 83–92. https://doi.org/10.1080/00405840801992223.

Thaighaudio. (2016a, July 14). 071416 Victor Victrola open and close top lid.wav [Audio file]. *Freesound*. https://freesound.org/people/thaighaudio/sounds/350316/.

Thaighaudio. (2016b, July 14). 071416 Victor Victrola switch on and ramp up to speed.wav [Audio file]. *Freesound*. https://freesound.org/people/thaighaudio/sounds/350329/.

Thaighaudio. (2016c, July 14). 071416 Victor Victrola winding two speeds.wav [Audio file]. *Freesound*. https://freesound.org/people/thaighaudio/sounds/350320/.

Chapter 15. Toward a Feminist Sonic Pedagogy: Research as Listening

Brandee Easter
YORK UNIVERSITY

Meg M. Marquardt
MISSISSIPPI STATE UNIVERSITY

Feminist scholars have argued for the importance of listening in our research and teaching (Powell, 2002; Ratcliffe, 2005; Royster & Kirsch, 2012). Scholars of sound have likewise advocated for soundwriting as a way to push the boundaries of what students view as critical, generative, embodied, and complex compositions (Ceraso, 2014; Sterne, 2012; Stone, 2015). In this chapter, we develop a feminist sonic pedagogy that emphasizes listening, collaboration, embodiment, and positionality to rethink approaches to student research projects. In particular, we reflect on the opportunities that soundwriting offers for incorporating these feminist pedagogical principles.

Through a series of soundwriting compositions, this sequence of assignments frames research as a feminist act of listening. Sonic rhetoricians such as Mary E. Hocks and Michelle Comstock (2017) have discussed the importance of a listener-centric pedagogy, emphasizing "resonance" and sonic rhetorics as "fully embodied listening practices" (p. 137). We draw on these connections with feminist methodologies to approach teaching research as a collaborative act of listening and embodiment. Soundwriting encourages students to approach feminist listening practices from multiple angles, listening to research listening to others' work, and, ultimately, listening to their own reflections throughout the semester to develop a final episode rooted in collaboration and embodiment.

When designing an intermediate composition course, coauthor Brandee Easter knew she wanted to incorporate soundwriting. However, after the first iteration of the course, she realized that the audio essay assignments weren't quite working. She decided to rework this assignment into podcasting to better emphasize feminist pedagogical practices of listening, collaboration, and iteration. Students are taught to approach research as collaboration with texts, resources, and interviewees, upending the more traditional view of research as a colonizing act of taking and claiming. By asking them to create weekly podcasts, as students work through the different methods, they begin to subtly shift their research questions in response to how they "hear" the text—how they craft their podcasts for others to consume. Together, Easter and Marquardt have taught through four iterations of the course and have found the affordances of soundwriting for teaching research as a feminist act of listening.

DOI: https://doi.org/10.37514/PRA-B.2022.1688.2.15

Across eight weeks, students collaboratively attempt to answer a "mystery," taking up and reflecting on a different research method each week in a short podcast episode. The methods include traditional secondary research, observation, interviews, hypothesizing, and archival research. At the end, students reflect on the information they have gathered to produce a final full-length episode. This final episode asks them to both reflect on ways they have learned to listen and also produce a sonic text that invites others to engage in such listening.

This chapter includes the full sequence of assignments and a student example across the seven weeks of production and revision. In our audio reflection of the class, you can find more details in how we go about setting up class structure and some troubleshooting ideas. In the end, we've found that foregrounding listening to research and collaboration opens up space for all sorts of listening, especially to one another in the classroom space, and that collaborative podcasting in particular affords opportunities to promote accessibility through shared skills, experiences, and resources. We discuss how these practices have generated projects that embody feminist practices, helping students see how their projects fit into larger societal conversations.

This research has been approved by UW–Madison IRB, ID: 2017–1370.

Assignments and Sequence

This project is divided into three sequences:

- Sequence 1: Narrating Mystery
  - Episode 1: Narrative
- Sequence 2: Research Methods
  - Episode 2: Secondary Research
  - Episode 3: Interview
  - Episode 4: Observation/Testing
  - Episode 5: Archives
  - Episode 6: Deduction & Hypothesizing
- Sequence 3: Revision
  - Standalone Episode Revision

Sequence 1: Narrating Mystery

Episode 1: Narrative

Inspired by *Serial, Mystery Show*, and *RadioLab*, this sequence will build toward creating a pitch and demo episode for a podcast serially investigating a real-life mystery—anything you want to know but can't figure out from a simple Google search or asking an expert. This podcast will span six episodes and explore your mystery from a different research method each time, so make sure your mystery or question is interesting and complex enough to pursue all semester.

The audience for this pitch will be a board of producers at the student radio station, making your podcast audience the university community, especially students. In a short, 3–4-minute podcast episode, introduce a mystery through narrative. Your mystery should use description, narration, and sonic strategies to engage your listeners. Think of this assignment as an exploration into mysteries and audio composing. The writing and production skills and content you explore here are a foundation for the course's major projects.

Sequence 2: Ways of Knowing

In this sequence, we will collaborate to investigate our chosen mysteries through a series of podcast episodes. Each episode will ask you to take up and test a new research method and report on your findings, telling your investigation that week as a **compelling 3–7-minute audio story**. Although you may use more than one research method per week, the only requirement is that you test out that week's method. (For example, for episode 4, you must try observation; however, you may also conduct an interview or research online, etc.)

Each episode in this sequence has the following requirements:

- 3–7-minute audio narration of this week's investigation
- Tests traditional research methods to solve your mystery (though may include others)
- Discusses or uses at least one piece of evidence found through traditional research
- Reflects on the benefits, as well as limits, of that method
- Uses sonic strategies to tell a compelling account of your work
- Includes a short reflection on process/product/collaboration

Episode 2: "Traditional" Research & Asking Questions

This week, let's start where we usually start: those ways of knowing that I've bunched under the label "traditional research." By this, I mean the types of secondary research we've been taught is how we answer questions in school: libraries, books, articles, databases, and search engines. What kinds of evidence can you find? What kinds of questions does this research help you with?

Suggestions:

Consider the ways that you might take a relevant angle on your question if your mystery specifically isn't available. For example, how can you use secondary research to provide background and context for your question?

Remember that you don't have to necessarily come to answers here. Thinking critically about why you were not able to find answers using this method is as important, if not more so, than finding answers.

Episode 3: Interview

This week, we'll turn from secondary to primary research. Using interviews, what aspects of your mystery can you solve?

Suggestions:

You can interview more than one person.

Try to schedule your interview early. It can be difficult to work out schedules. If possible, an in-person interview gives you more opportunities to ask better questions.

Ask your interviewee's permission to record their answers upfront, letting them know what you'll be doing with their interview.

Plan for your interview by drafting questions but be prepared to go off script as well.

Remember that you don't have to necessarily come to answers here. Thinking critically about why you were not able to find answers using this method is as important, if not more so, than finding answers.

Episode 4: Observation/Testing

Observation as a way of knowing has been foundational to the rise of scientific thought. It is the foundation of any scientific lab. What can you see and verify with your own eyes? This week asks you to get out into the field to learn about your mystery. A good example for this assignment may be *Serial*, Episode 3, where Sarah Koenig (2014) goes out to Leakin Park herself. Testing may be another way to think of this assignment, depending on your question. What scenario can you watch that might help answer some aspect of your mystery?

For this assignment, choose a location and/or community to observe. Plan to spend at least 1 hour there. What do you notice? Hear, smell, see, sense? Who do you notice? What is it like to be an observer? What can you know from watching?

Suggestions:

Be aware of your own positionality. How are your own positions, beliefs, identities shaping what you notice? What are your biases coming in?

Take lots of notes.

How can you set the scene of your location for listeners? How can you help them feel like they are with you? How can you be descriptive with sound?

Episode 5: Archives

Archives are collections of materials, documents, oral histories, and other artifacts and objects that have been gathered and maintained by organizations, often historical or governmental.

Using the holdings of the university archives, find at least one artifact that interests you about your topic and learn as much as you can about it through any other research methods, including further archival research, secondary research, interview, etc.

We will meet at the archives for one class, and after an introduction, you will have the remainder of class to explore.

Suggestions:

How can you help your listeners see and understand your object?

Take pictures! You can't use them in your podcast, but once returned to the archive, you may have difficulty finding that exact item again.

It may be helpful to plan to record during class on Tuesday as you explore the archives, capturing your reactions and experience.

Consider also what isn't in an archive: What wasn't deemed important enough to save? What is missing?

Episode 6: Deduction & Hypothesizing

Hypothesizing and deduction are two crucial processes to finding knowledge. Hypothesizing involves generating theories based on what you have observed while deduction is ruling them out.

This week asks you to take stock of your investigation thus far. Knowing what you know now, what theories do you have for your answer? Which of these seem promising to explore (hypothesize)? Which do you think you can rule out (deduction)?

For this assignment, you do not need to venture a final answer. This is, after all, not your final episode. Additionally, the ultimate goal of this assignment is not only to get you closer to answering your mystery, but to also prepare you for the work you'll need to do for your full episode. Using any methods that seem appropriate to you, explore the range of possibilities your answer might take.

Suggestion:

It will help to keep nuancing your research question. In other words, if your research question hasn't evolved since the first episode, you are probably not making much progress. So, this is not only imagining answering your question in different ways, but you might also imagine asking your question in different ways.

Sequence 3: Revision

Standalone Episode Revision

In this sequence, we will build on the work and research completed so far to produce a full-length, standalone episode on your mystery. This is the culmination of all of your hard work this semester, and it asks you to bring together your research, listening, storytelling, and sonic strategies to tell an engaging account of your mystery and investigation.

This assignment is also, at heart, a revision, asking you to re-vision your mystery, research questions, and evidence into something new.

Requirements:

- 15–30-minute episode telling a compelling story of your mystery and investigation
- Uses multiple research methods to investigate possible answers
- Made up of no more than 50% of material recorded in your previous episodes

- Presents a substantially deepened and nuanced research question compared to your starting point
- Includes relevant in-process pieces to demonstrate your work this sequence
- Includes a reflection on the piece and process, noting anything you'd like your listener to know

Sample Student Projects

1. "Episode 1: The Pitch" by Abby. In this episode, Abby gives her first pitch for looking at the mystery of Robert Grunenwald, the man behind a UW–Madison urban legend.[4]
2. "Episode 2: Traditional Research" by Abby, Carly, and Emily. In Episode 2, Abby, Carly, and Emily tackle the first research method: traditional research. This research mostly yielded videos and current newspaper articles about Grunenwald.
3. "Episode 3: Interviews." In Episode 3, Abby, Carly, and Emily interview fellow students about their interactions with Grunenwald on campus.
4. "Episode 4: Observation/Testing." In Episode 4, Abby, Carly, and Emily try to retrace Grunenwald's steps in places where his urban legend is most commonly recurs: College Library.
5. "Episode 5: Archives." For their archival research method, Carly, Emily, and Abby discover that Grunenwald's story stretches across decades, and they begin to really wonder why the UW campus is so obsessed with the legend.
6. "Episode 6: Deduction and Hypothesizing." Students were not required to fully produce the episode this week, although we have included the script here.
7. "The Revision." In their final revision, Abby, Emily, and Carly create a podcast that is focused on members of the UW campus and why they are so concerned with retelling the legend of Grunenwald.

Reflection

Meg Marquardt: So, why did you switch to podcasts?[5]
Brandee Easter: It's weird, but there wasn't enough listening.

[Podington Bear's (2013) "Twinkletoes," quick tempo music with flutes and xylophones in minor key, plays.]

---

4. Seven student examples (audio files and descriptive transcripts) can be found on the book's companion website.

5. The audio version of Brandee Easter and Meg Marquardt's reflection can be found on the book's companion website.

Brandee: Hi, I'm Brandee Easter.

Meg: And I am Meg Marquardt. We're both Ph.D. candidates in the composition and rhetoric program at the University of Wisconsin–Madison.

Brandee: In this audio component of our praxis chapter, we're going to share the origins of the class and assignment structure.

Meg: We'll then walk through a student example from my fall 2017 course.

Brandee: And we'll talk about some questions we're still thinking about.

Meg: Brandee, why don't you start us off because you are the original class designer. But it looked a lot different the first time you taught it, right?

Brandee: Yeah, so English 201 felt like a bit of a daunting class to teach because the structure and content is so open. It fulfills a communications requirement, but what you do with that is pretty flexible. And so, although we've both taught courses with more standardized structures, this is the first time I've taught a class that felt truly my own.

Meg: And doing all that for the first time is hard!

Brandee: Yeah, hard but exciting. I really wanted to use this opportunity to think about anti-racist, anti-sexist pedagogy. I used a grading contract. I themed the course "Bad Writing," which focused on asking what our rules about writing are, why, and what the consequences are. And all of this was accomplished through collaborative audio essays exploring research on writing rules.

Meg: And everything you taught was brand new, right?

Brandee: This was the first time I went into my class with the goal of being actively and explicitly anti-racist and anti-sexist in my teaching. Though I loved how the content was working toward these goals, I wasn't making the best use of the structure and assignments.

Meg: Huh. What wasn't working with the assignments?

Brandee: Well, I noticed a couple of things. Revisions weren't happening. Once an audio draft was made, it was very unlikely to undergo major revisions. I also found that groups didn't have many opportunities to practice collaborating since they only made one audio essay altogether. And, ultimately, what was lost, somehow, seemed to be listening.

Meg: What do you mean?

Brandee: Well, I'm thinking of Krista Ratcliffe's (2005) rhetorical listening: deliberate listening that helps the whole class investigate and interrogate their own positionalities and the positionalities of their research.

Meg: Got it. So what did you change?

Brandee: Well, I changed the theme, but the major change was switching from audio essays to podcasts. I wanted to focus on collaboration and listening. And so podcasts, as serial and iterative projects, made the heart of the class about practicing research as a feminist act of listening, reflecting, and collaborating.

Meg: By the time you changed the course to podcasting, I already knew I would steal it when I started teaching my own 201 course.

Brandee: *[laughing]* Not stealing, Meg—collaborating!

Meg: The course has three sequences: the idea pitch, the collaborative research phase, and a final revision. In each, students are creating podcasts to try to solve a mystery, broadly defined as any question they can't answer by a Google search or asking an expert.

Brandee: Yeah, I brought this approach to the course from Caroline Levine's (2003) work on suspense and mystery fiction to present research as a mystery and research methods as ways of knowing.

Meg: So, how does this class start?

Brandee: Well, in the first sequence, we set up podcasts as a genre and understand how research is like solving a mystery. The capstone assignment is to make a short, 3–5-minute episode that introduces a mystery they want to explore in the next sequence.

Meg: Yeah, I call that first episode as a "trailer," meaning they should tell the story in a compelling way that draws listeners into the question.

Brandee: Then, in Sequence 2, which I think is really the heart of this course, we first spend a week teaching, forming, and building collaborative practices around the most compelling mysteries. Then, students, in groups of three or four, produce a weekly 5-minute podcast episode that examines their mystery from a different research method.

Meg: We start with traditional research (like Google or library searches), move to interviews, observation and testing, archival research, and then deduction and hypothesizing.

Brandee: Finally, Sequence 3 is a 15–20-minute revision of all of this hard work into a standalone audio essay, much like an episode of *RadioLab* or *Reply All*.

Meg: Because one of the most exciting things about this course, to us, is the iterative and serial nature of podcasting, we're going to focus on only one student example so that we can walk through the process of the class.

Brandee: So the example we are going to focus on is from your class in fall 2017. So, do you want to introduce it, Meg?

Meg: Sure! This is a podcast about Robert Grunenwald, a man at the heart of a UW–Madison urban legend.

Brandee: Ok, but I've never heard of Robert Grunenwald?

Meg: I hadn't either! Maybe because we weren't undergrads here. But on campus, he is known as Tunnel Bob.

[clip from The Badger Herald *(2015) video report]*

> **Student 1:** Um, to give you a little bit of an idea about the environment down here, it's extremely hot. Blisteringly hot. We've been walking for, I don't know, probably 30 minutes in tunnels going in mostly one direction. We went out under Engineering Hall. Tunnel Bob is, seems like a really good guy. He's waiting for us and kind of letting us do our own thing, explore the tunnels as we wanted to. We should keep going though.

Student 2: Can I ask why, why tunnels? What is it about tunnels that you like? Is it, is it, like, something about the underground?

Grunenwald: Not just tunnels. Steam tunnels are what I like. If it's just an ordinary tunnel, I don't care much for it.

Student 2: But why? Is it the steam? It's not the heat aspect, is it?

Grunenwald: More mystery on them.

Meg: That's students from one of the student newspapers, *The Badger Herald*, interviewing Grunenwald. It's rumored that he spends much of his time alone in the steam tunnels that run under the campus.

Brandee: Okay, so what is the mystery here? Like, what did your student want to find out?

Meg: So the student who started this had heard stories about him popping up in unexpected places and lingering late into the night in libraries, scaring hapless undergrads. He's described as spooky and abnormal, so I was nervous from the beginning.

Brandee: What were you concerned about?

Meg: I didn't want the podcast to end up further characterizing Grunenwald as an outsider or an other. As the student who pitched this mystery, Abby, notes in her first episode, she is already thinking about how the strangeness of the legend has led to some problematic characterizations of Grunenwald, characterizations that she wants to challenge. Here's Abby in her first episode:

> **Abby**: Tunnel Bob is a genuine person with genuine emotions, interests, and ambitions, but his attraction to these tunnels kind of distracts everyone from his humanity. *[background music begins]* His past might have a serious impact on why he does what he does in the present, but his life story is uncharted territory. That is the mystery I'm attempting to unravel in this podcast. Who is the genuine Tunnel Bob? And why does he spend so much time in the tunnels?

Brandee: So where did this project go next?

Meg: Carly and Emily joined Abby's group, and they first interviewed their peers about their experiences with Grunenwald, which were, to their surprise, overwhelmingly positive. They next tried observing, which was a research method they struggled with. Not only could they probably not observe Grunenwald, they also didn't *want* to observe him, knowing that he's not a participating research subject. Instead, they tried hanging out in the spaces Grunenwald is usually spotted to see how people act.

Brandee: Okay, I want to talk about the archive episode because in listening to them, this is where I felt a lot of interesting things happened.

Meg: That's where everything happened. We took a trip to the University Archives, where the archivist David Null pulled several yearbooks and newspapers that referenced Grunenwald. Watching them flip through the pages was a great moment because I could see in real-time as their research question pivoted.

[Music plays in the background of excerpt from podcast episode.]

> **Abby**: For generations, Tunnel Bob has been a name we like to associate with a creepy, underground system. We never stopped to think to ask how or why this came about.
>
> **Emily**: Overall, the archives really showed us that over time, Robert Grunenwald has morphed into a semi-fictitious character named Tunnel Bob. Students and community members like to have something to talk about. They don't care or know much about the steam tunnel system and its importance. But when they learn that a guy likes to spend time down there, it suddenly became so much more interesting.

Brandee: So in response to their findings, their question shifts.

Meg: Right. They stop asking questions about Grunenwald and started asking questions about themselves and the UW campus as a whole.

Brandee: This is also where your students stop using the name "Tunnel Bob," right?

Meg: Yeah, or if they do, it's in quotes because they're referencing other people calling him Tunnel Bob. They just start calling him "Robert."

Brandee: So where does this group end up?

Meg: By the final revision, they are fully focused on presenting a story that puts the wider UW campus under the microscope.

[Music plays in the background of excerpt from podcast episode.]

> **Abby**: After weeks of research that began with a desire to know more about an urban legend on our campus, our focus turned and made us wonder why we are so obsessed with him. We're now left asking ourselves what it says about us that we've spent decades continuing to talk about and be fascinated by him.

Meg: The Tunnel Bob project is an instructor's dream. It does everything I hoped for in terms of listening to research. They really let the research guide their questions week to week, allowing them to create a thoughtful and thought-provoking audio essay.

Brandee: Not all of your students picked mysteries that took on a question so explicitly about identity, right?

Meg: Right, but I was surprised at how the process of listening through research often brought students to these kinds of questions. For example, one project about a stolen flag from a house party ended up also reflecting on race and national identity.

Brandee: I'm also really interested in how the iterative nature of podcasting emphasized collaboration and listening *to each other*.

Meg: Me, too! I was actually surprised by how much of that sort of listening was going on I wasn't aware of. I think that was my biggest takeaway from teaching this semester.

Brandee: What do you mean, Meg?

Meg: For example, another group noted in their final reflections how they had two really dominant voices in the group. They all noted how the emphasis on listening helped them learn to navigate what could have been potentially a really tough semester of working together.

Brandee: And you had no idea they had that issue?

Meg: None at all! They worked through it on their own by being careful to allow everyone's ideas to be heard. And not knowing what was going on makes me think about how I can keep changing this course in the future to better emphasize listening and collaboration. What was your takeaway from teaching this course, Brandee?

Brandee: I think for me, this course helped me see how soundwriting can afford thinking about listening as an embodied, feminist practice.

Meg: And the iterative nature of podcasting emphasizes reflection and collaboration.

Brandee: Yeah, I love getting to see groups learn not only how to work with sound but how to better listen to each other. So, you're teaching this class again now, Meg. What are you thinking through?

Meg: So, I'm changing the order of research methods. They could go in any order, but I wanted to move archives earlier because of shifts like the one in this example about Grunenwald. I'm also doing a lot more grounding in the beginning, helping students think through storytelling and critical listening skills. There are always more pieces of the course to figure out, but I think we're getting closer!

[Quick tempo music with flutes and xylophones in minor key fades in.]

Brandee: We hope these resources are helpful to your next soundwriting project, and we'd love to hear about your experiences with it.

Meg: We'd also love to hear your student's stories, if they are willing to share. The projects produced in this assignment are always fascinating.

Brandee: Good luck with your soundwriting!

References

Badger Herald. (2015, April 13). Sneaking into UW's steam tunnels with Tunnel Bob [Video file]. *YouTube*. https://youtu.be/lYn9WVkiGkw.

Ceraso, S. (2014). (Re)educating the senses: Multimodal listening, bodily learning, and the composition of sonic experiences. *College English, 77*(2), 102–123.

Hocks, M. E. & Comstock, M. (2017). Composing for sound: Sonic rhetoric as resonance. *Computers and Composition, 43*, 135–146. https://doi.org/10.1016/j.compcom.2016.11.006.

Koenig, S. (Host). (2014, October 9). Leakin Park (Season 1, no. 3) [Audio podcast episode]. In *Serial.* https://serialpodcast.org/season-one/3/leakin-park.

Levine, C. (2003). *The serious pleasures of suspense: Victorian realism and narrative doubt.* University of Virginia Press.

Podington Bear. (2013). Twinkletoes [Song]. *Free Music Archive.* http://freemusicarchive.org/music/Podington_Bear/Background/Twinkletoes.

Powell, M. (2002). Rhetorics of survivance: How American Indians use writing. *College Composition and Communication, 53*(3), 396–434. https://doi.org/10.2307/1512132.

Ratcliffe, K. (2005). *Rhetorical listening: Identification, gender, whiteness.* Southern Illinois University Press.

Royster, J. J. & Kirsh, G. (2012). *Feminist rhetorical practices: New horizons for rhetoric, composition, and literacy studies.* Southern Illinois University Press.

Sterne, J. (Ed.). (2012). *The sound studies reader.* Routledge.

Stone, J. W. (2015). Listening to the sonic archive: Rhetoric, representation, and race in the Lomax prison recordings. *Enculturation: A Journal of Rhetoric, Writing, and Culture, 19.* http://enculturation.net/listening-to-the-sonic-archive.

Chapter 16. From Postcards to PSAs: Activist Soundwriting

Timothy R. Amidon

COLORADO STATE UNIVERSITY

This chapter discusses Postcards for Privacy (PfP), a transmedia activism project that included a soundwriting component undergraduate students at Colorado State University undertook as part of Writing Democracy in a Digital Age, a capstone course in fall 2017. This chapter includes materials related to two elements of this project: assignment directions for the public service announcements (PSAs) students produced for our campus radio station, KCSU 90.5, and an image of a postcard students designed to collect stories about community members' experiences with digital privacy and security.

In the course, students explored the nexus of democracy and digitally networked writing technologies while cultivating critical digital literacies necessary for safely and ethically entering civic conversations in a digital age (Beck, 2015; DeVoss & Porter, 2006; Hutchinson & Novotny, 2018; Selber, 2004; Vee, 2017; Vie, 2008). As the culminating assignment in the capstone, PfP built upon work that students had completed earlier in the semester. They had formed a local chapter of the Electronic Frontier Alliance (EFA at CSU), researched activism and digital rights, and engaged in multimodal composing to produce content and documents for the organization. For this particular project, students were asked to consider how discourse circulates on campus before producing activist soundwriting that sought to promote awareness about the effects of online privacy and security issues.

Pedagogically, two broad goals for the course were to provide students with opportunities to critically enact activism and to design and compose content that would support the aims their teams had established. For the culminating project for the course, I hoped "[to] encourage students to deploy multiple modalities in skillful ways—written, aural, visual—and [to] model a respect for and understanding of the various roles each modality can play in human expression, the formation of individual and group identity, and meaning making" (Selfe, 2009, p. 626). During the semester, the tragic events associated with Unite the Right Rally in Charlottesville, Virginia, had given rise to expansive discussions about the materiality of, and suasive force that surrounds, civic rhetorics. Students had remarked on the arresting *imagery* (white supremacists carrying torches; Nazi salutes; American and Confederate flags) and popular *hashtags* (#charlottesville; #thisisnotus; #altright; #antifa), but they also dwelled on the ways that *sound* (white supremacist chants; screams from counter-protesters; silence from government leaders) and *phrases* ("blood and soil"; "you will not replace us"; "many sides"; "no place for hate") echoed with a different kind of resonance—magnifying, aiding, abetting, or countering the acts of hate-speech and terrorism we had witnessed.

PfP grew directly from these conversations, as students had reflected on "the complex ways that a greater variety of senses, semiotic resources, and rhetorical positionings might be taken up together and brought together" as they turned toward creating their own content for activism (Shipka, 2006, p. 355). Turning toward the goals of raising awareness about how online privacy issues impact members of our campus, students developed informational pamphlets and fliers and organized teach-ins. Discussing potential options for a culminating assignment, I proposed adapting Frank Warren's (2005) PostSecret project into a multisensorial, transmedia activist project. Students, staff, faculty, administrators, and/or community members would anonymously submit stories about their experiences with online privacy and security via postcards that the English Department sponsored. Thereafter, students could practice soundwriting by transforming the words and images we would receive via anonymous postcard submissions into embodied oral performances and digital PSAs.

Figure 16.1. The Postcards for Privacy postcard.

By centering sound, students were invited to consider how "sensations of sound attune us, through attention to our human communities and connections and a renewed access to the non-human environment and agents that surround us" (Hocks, 2018, p. 96). For example, students took stock of both the physical and digital environments that comprise campus, analyzing the existing sound- and media-scape, and based strategic decisions—such as selecting The Stump, a high-profile location on the center mall at CSU as a place to publicly read the postcards—that enabled them to amplify and boost the circulatory potential of their message. By carefully adapting and recomposing the handwritten stories, and by weighing decisions about how the media, modalities, and locations where they could reach audiences across campus in order to raise awareness about online privacy issues, students leveraged "the power of language fluidity [that] lies not within bounded words and symbols systems but within the rhetorical expertise of the communicators negotiating meaning across contexts" (Gonzales, 2018, p. 18, citing Canagarajah).

Upon receiving the submissions, we headed out to the Stump where students who had volunteered took turns reading aloud the stories that community members had shared. Again, students had selected this location to read the postcards for its prominence in the center of campus, as this aural and visual performance had the potential to scaffold more expansive conversations with individuals passing by. For the hour that students held the Stump, a sizable crowd stopped to listen and converse with the student activists. In turn, other students answered questions from the crowd, shared facts about digital privacy issues they memorized, engaged in dialogue with passersby about these issues, and handed out pamphlets. The written words on postcards had been reorganized into a living moment. By translating textual submissions into an embodied, voiced, emplaced, dialogic event, students were able to construct a moment when their activist work could perceptibly circulate and resonate across and beyond the physical soundscape of CSU. Their next objective was to extend the reach of their work by recomposing those submissions into PSAs.

Students returned to class eager to design their PSAs. As we debriefed on the successes and limitations of the embodied performance, students began to realize that the PSA genre would provide another opportunity for recomposing and resounding how those stories might mean. Designing the PSAs for the campus radio station, which has a considerable listener base, for instance, extended a distinct exigence and seriousness to their work. To increase their familiarity with the genre, students broke up into teams and critiqued other PSAs. Then, they turned toward the work of composing scripts, offering peer feedback, and revising the scripts to ensure they conformed to the constraints KCSU had outlined for PSAs (e.g., each PSA had to be 30 seconds or shorter and clearly identify who was sponsoring the message). Thereafter, they turned toward production, locating and/ or creating sound assets, editing and weaving soundtracks, and polishing and submitting radio-ready PSAs.

In sum, by integrating a soundwriting component within the Postcards for Privacy project, students were asked to "prepar[e] themselves to become effective and literate citizens of the 21st century" (Selfe & Selfe, 2008, p. 84). They coordinated, translated, and composed meaning across and through textual, visual, aural, and oral modalities by vocally embodying and emplacing those stories in a physical location and then recomposing those stories as PSAs that utilized a different set of semiotic resources and held a distinct set of circulatory potentials. In doing so, students designed activist and civic rhetoric, while considering particularly how various modalities, delivered via embodied, broadcast, and digital media, may resonate across particular audiences and locations.

Assignment and Sequencing

As noted above, the PSA soundwriting assignment was a component of the PfP transmedia activist project. By this time in the semester, students had designed and produced logos, recruitment information, event flyers, and presentations. As a soundwriting assignment, the PSAs assignment challenged students to expand their activist repertoire by cultivating skills such as identifying and accessing existing sound assets, recording voiceovers using cellphones and high end microphones, navigating the copyright and ownership issues when selecting copyrighted content, editing, considering the ethical and affective impacts of various sonic compositions for audiences, and blending and layering tracks using software such as Audacity or Adobe Audition. The content below was included on the assignment prompt that students were given for this component of the project. The background section provides topical framing on online privacy and security issues relevant to the project, so educators interested in assigning PSAs as a soundwriting activity would likely want to revise this particular section when adapting this assignment to address topics appropriate in their classes.

The Assignment Prompt

Background on Online Privacy and Security

Citizens across the world make use of online platforms for work, leisure, and civic participation. Yet internet users must navigate an increasingly complex set of privacy and security issues when interacting within digitally networked platforms. According to Lee Rainie (2016) of the Pew Research Center, "91% of [American] adults agree or strongly agree that consumers have lost control of how personal information is collected and used by companies." Rainie also found that nearly half of the survey respondents were uncertain how personal data and information is used by these platforms. Indeed, Zeynep Tufecki (2017) observes that platforms, as "corporate entities," devote little effort toward protecting individual privacy and security in comparison to the resources they invest to protect and police intellectual property in these spaces (p. 146).

Aim

Your aim is to develop a public service announcement (PSA) that will air on KCSU that offers students, staff, faculty, administrators, and members of the broader regional community information about an online privacy issue that can adversely impact their life or the lives of those they care about. More specifically, you will work as a team to identify one story or topic raised within the PfP submissions and develop a PSA that might raise awareness about how that critical digital literacy issue affects our local community.

Design Criteria

Groups will develop a script and produce a 25–30-second audio PSA about online security and privacy for KSCU. KCSU (2017) notes that the PSAs it airs are "designed for CSU or Northern Colorado listeners with the objective of raising awareness and/or changing public attitudes or behaviors toward a social issue." Additional design requirements include the following:

- 2–5 seconds should be reserved for a message that identifies EFA at CSU as the sponsor of the PSA and briefly describes the aim of our group (e.g., "This PSA is brought to you by Electronic Frontier Alliance at CSU, a student group that . . .").
- The PSA should incorporate content from at least one of the Postcards for Privacy submissions that we received.
- Your production should include one sound effect, two or more voices, and/ or make use of music.
- All secondary content elements must be in the public domain or available for use under a Creative Commons attribution license. (By selecting content licensed under a CC BY 3.0 License, you can adapt and freely utilize content in this project, as long as you are sure to give attribution to artists who originally create the content).

Genre Exemplars

PSAs are a common genre that organizations use to raise awareness about issues of public concern. Consider the rhetorical situation that impacts the design of these examples, and note how the designers have carefully incorporated voice, music, silence, and sound effects to create an appropriate tone and communicate information:

- Cuyahoga County Prosecutor's Office, *Let's Face It*, https://youtu.be/ erhpSMkqGSY
- NYC Mayor's Office, *Pre-K for All NYC*, https://youtu.be/WBoFbFgg_Ls
- American Association of People with Disabilities, *I Am Not Going to Be Bullied*, https://youtu.be/VbFmoI9WXrg

Locating Media Assets

There are many sites where you can locate sound assets that are in the public domain or available for use under open source or creative commons licenses. Here are websites where you might begin your search for secondary or supplementary sounds that can enrich the voice work you will perform in your PSA:

- Creative Commons: creativecommons.org/use-remix/
- Freesound: freesound.org
- Jamendo: jamendo.com
- American Folklife Center: http://www.loc.gov/folklife/onlinecollections .html
- Zapsplat: zapsplat.com
- Wikipedia Public Domain Resources: https://en.wikipedia.org/wik i/Wikipedia:Public_domain_resources

Tutorials for Editing Audio with Audacity or Adobe Audition

- Instructables, *Basic Recording and Editing with Audacity*: http://www .instructables.com/id/Basic-recording-and-editing-with-Audacity/
- Kyle Stedman, *Audacity Basics: Recording, Editing, Mixing*: https://youtu .be/8ClwSNm362E
- David Taylor, *Complete Tutorial Guide to Audacity for Beginners*: https:// youtu.be/aCisC3sHneM
- Adobe Audition Tutorials, *Record, Edit, and Mix Audio for Video, Podcasts, and Effects*: https://helpx.adobe.com/audition/tutorials.html

Sample Student-Designed PSAs

1. "Webcams" by Jenn, Kristy, Jaton, and Emma: In this example, Jenn, Kristy, Jaton, and Emma adapted a specific Postcards for Privacy submission, which had described how a member of the CSU community had their webcam turned on by an outside computer. One element of authorized webcam hacking that the authors of the submission had emphasized was how relatively easy this is for hackers to do.[1]

2. "Photos" by Anastasia, Elizabeth, Natalie, and Zihan: In this example, Anastasia, Elizabeth, Natalie, and Zihan developed a PSA that involved one member of the production team reading verbatim from one of the Postcards for Privacy submissions. Their PSA demonstrates how the unexpected resharing of intimate images by downstream audiences might lead to harmful outcomes.

3. "Cyberstalking" by Tim, Danny, and Kara: One of the most prevalent themes across the Postcard for Privacy submissions was how cyberstalking adversely impacts and has directly affected students, especially those students with female and gender-nonconforming identities, at CSU.

---

1. Four student examples (audio files and transcripts) can be found on the book's companion website.

In this example, Tim, Danny, and Kara demonstrated how text messaging can quickly lead to a form of threatening, unwanted harassment.

4. "Words Are Weapons" by Lara, Hannah, and Laura: Another prevalent theme that appeared across the Postcard for Privacy submissions was the issue of cyberbullying. Drawing from a range of submissions, Lara, Hannah, and Laura demonstrated how digital environments can amplify hateful and hurtful words.

Reflection

[A brisk and fast-paced music track, Podington Bear's (2018) "Frog in Tuxes," fades in. Peppy xylophone notes speak back to one another, then fade into the background at 00:15 as voiceover begins.]

Timothy R. Amidon: Hey! I'm Tim Amidon, an associate professor of English at Colorado State University.[2] Today, I'm going to talk to you a little bit about a soundwriting assignment called Postcards for Privacy. This is an assignment that English students completed as part of Writing Democracy in a Digital Age, a capstone course I taught in 2017. In this audio reflection, I briefly contextualize this assignment within the larger trajectory of the course. I discuss how students undertook the work of transforming and recirculating stories they had received as text-based submissions as embodied and digital sonic recompositions. I close reflecting on some of the goals I sought students to pursue within the soundwriting components of this assignment. I also discuss aspects of the assignment that other educators might consider if they too are thinking about integrating soundwriting in their courses.

[Music fades out.]

Welcome to CSU, y'all! Our campus is located in Fort Collins, *[ambient sound of a city: engines from vehicles; horns; a skateboard resonates, as it strikes the concrete from an ollie; distant voices of people conversing]* a mid-sized city located in foothills of the Rocky Mountains in northern Colorado. Like other universities, CSU can be a clamorous place. Student organizations line up on the walkway to the Lory Student Center entrance to wage a daily battle of decibels, attempting to drown out the jams pumping from neighboring booths *[fast-paced EDM build-up enters and volume increases and quickly decreases]*; evangelists, activists, artists, and politicians line the center mall upon campus *[sounds of skateboard trucks increases as a skateboarder nears microphone and skates away; voices of people conversing in background increases]*, competing for the attention of any passersby brave enough to make eye contact; BNSF engineers blare their locomotive's horn *[train horn booms and sounds of train cars passing on a rail can be faintly heard]*,

---

2. The audio version of Timothy R. Amidon's reflection can be found on the book's companion website.

interrupting all campus activities until their cars safely travel the railway that divides campus east and campus west.

[Happy-sounding, upbeat music track, Podington Bear's (2007) "Budsbursting," fades in. Volume fades as track becomes background for voiceover.]

Listener, if you're like me, right now you're probably thinking: What do all those random details and sounds have to do with Postcards for Privacy? What exactly was this assignment and how did the assignment fit into your course? What were your pedagogical goals, Tim? And, perhaps, most importantly what did students learn about soundwriting from this assignment? Well, those are good questions. Let's get to that.

I'll begin by sketching out how Postcards for Privacy fit into the course. When I initially conceived of using postcards in the class, I thought of it as a way to scaffold a critical digital literacy project where students could practice multimodal and transmedia composing for activism. It ended up aligning well with the topical focus and learning outcomes for course, as I had organized the capstone using a collaborative, project-based learning approach. While I had the idea to utilize postcards, via Frank Warren's (2005) PostSecret project, as a way to collect stories, it was through discussion and brainstorming with students that we truly developed the Postcards for Privacy project and assignment sequence. Early in the semester, I had tasked students with helping create documents and a brand for a student organization that would champion digital rights issues like net neutrality or internet surveillance on campus. Students dedicated a good part of the semester to researching digital rights issues and building infrastructure to support that organization. As students completed the work of filing paperwork, establishing operating procedures, recruiting members, and developing a brand for the organization, they turned toward a group project that involved planning and hosting an educational event about one of the digital rights issues their groups had focused on: cyberviolence, fair use, accessibility, fake news, and surveillance.

This is where sound and Postcards for Privacy came in. As the groups worked on their events, many students thought it would be beneficial if we organized and sponsored an event collectively. Doing so would help raise awareness about the student organization they had formed, a local chapter of the Electronic Frontier Alliance. I shared Frank Warren's PostSecret project and pitched the idea of using postcards to anonymously collect stories about digital rights issues because it would involve a participatory element that would invite students, faculty, staff, and administrators at CSU to share their own stories and experiences with digital rights. Within our planning discussions, we narrowed our focus to privacy because it was a topic that students in our class had a strong opinion about. It was an issue that impacts students, faculty, and citizens. Students also understood that online privacy is an issue that has real material impacts for our community.

From a pedagogical perspective, I was also interested in pushing students to branch out in terms of the genres, modes, and media they had been using up to this point in the semester. They had composed a range of alphabetic, graphic, visual texts, and they had also planned presentations, but they hadn't performed any soundwriting up to this point. As mentioned in the introduction, members of our class had observed that sound plays a powerful role while examining civic, protest, and activist rhetorics, including the white supremacist terrorism that had unfolded that semester in Charlottesville, Virginia. Consequently, one of my aims in this project was to challenge students to directly consider how their activist message might resonate within the existing physical and digital spaces that comprise campus. I asked: How could their message reverberate within and across the soundscapes that make up campus? How might they carefully take up the rhetorical work of translating textual submissions received on postcards into activist performances and discourse that would circulate in these public spaces. What genres might be the most effective as a vehicle for amplifying the material impacts that digital privacy issues have within our community?

Collaboratively, we designed a postcard, including a prompt that asked members to share their stories. The language clarified that we planned to disseminate the stories to the wider campus community by giving voice to the stories on the Stump, a prominent public location outside of the student union. And we noted that we would develop PSAs incorporating those stories to air on our campus radio station, KCSU. Put differently, as students considered how to realize their activist aims, they had to take stock of existing sound- and mediascapes, consider the affordances of various performances, and develop strategies about how to raise the volume on these online privacy issues. They had to identify moments (when) and locations (where) their voices and transmedia projects might resonate across campus, and they had to pick genres that would be manageable in terms of the time, effort, and expertise.

[A fast-paced, fun, and snappy bassy music track, Podington Bear's (2017b) "Smooth Actor," fades in and then fades down to background music as voiceover begins.]

On the day we were scheduled to read the submissions, I gathered the sealed box, and we opened it in class discovering that there were about 30 in all. We read and discussed the submissions, identified volunteers to read the stories, and walked out to the Stump. Two students from the class had volunteered to do the reading, and they took turns climbing up and sharing each of the submissions we had received. As the students read and performed those stories, members from campus stopped to ask about the project and members of the class engaged them by sharing facts they had learned and memorized or inviting them to join the EFA at CSU. While this might not seem like soundwriting, following Crystal VanKooten (2016) I want to argue that we "invent meanings, find juxtapositions, and make personal, bodily associations with what [we] see and hear" (chora section). That is, activist rhetoric that unfolds through embodied, oral perfor-mance is soundwriting, precisely because it is purposefully curated and carefully orchestrated as a sonic and extra-discursive modality within a situated rhetorical performance. Students had carefully planned this event, investing considerable effort in the work of how giving voice to these stores might promote their larger rhetorical aims: promoting the importance of digital rights and recruiting mem-bers of the community to join EFA at CSU, as you'll recall.

The emphasis on soundwriting in the PfP project continued the following week when we returned to the class. I provided students with the assignment sheet for the PSA that you'll find in this chapter. Thereafter, I shared a couple of exemplars and asked students to identify and share PSAs that they had also found effective. We critiqued the examples as a group, identifying features of those exemplars that they might seek to emulate within their own scripts. Next, each group identified postcards that they could use to focus their PSA around a central topical issue before brainstorming how the stories could be transformed into scripts for an educational PSA. Many groups approached the task in a wholly collaborative fashion, but a number of them wrote individual scripts and then later combined the best elements to form a master script. (I thought that was a wicked smart approach.)

[Background music crossfades as a transition to Podington Bear's (2017a) "Lightfeet," a moderately paced music track with synth-y piano keys placed gently over a funky backbeat. Then the music fades as the voiceover begins.]

After that, groups paired up and provided one another feedback. We also engaged in a round of group share and feedback at the class level. Again, the class had been working together for a couple of months at this point, so they were really effective as collaborators and were able to offer each other high quality feedback and had become accustomed to sharing and incorporating peer ideas within their work. I asked students to finish revising their scripts before turning toward the task of identifying and downloading sound effects or music that they might want to incorporate before our next class. The assignment sheet provided information on some starting locations where students could find assets, but a couple students who were experienced soundwriters knew about other locations where they could locate sound files. In fact, a number of the students worked for KCSU, so they had suggested PSAs as a genre when we were considering options because they had broadcast PSAs produced and sponsored by other student orga-nizations while working at the radio station.

The following class, we began with a brief overview of fair use. I reiterated the design parameters set out by the radio station, and I demonstrated how to record audio tracks using a high-quality microphone. Thereafter, I set up a computer and microphone in my office and allowed groups who wanted to record voiceovers to use my office as a sound booth, just as I am right now. The building where our class was located is a pretty high-traffic classroom area, so we decided that the best place to capture high quality recordings would be in the office spaces on the third floor. While groups took turns recording in my office, I worked with teams who were editing, mixing, and weaving soundtracks for their PSAs. One pedagogical strategy that proved to be really beneficial at this step was identifying the more experienced soundwriters in the class and inviting them to serve as peer-helpers and resources for groups that were less experienced and/or confident. They were able to teach peers how to successfully carry out technical tasks using sound-editing software, such as creating multiple tracks, cutting a longer clip, filtering out unwanted sounds, and organizing sounds on a timeline. So that's kind of the gist of the Postcards for Privacy project, including the activist performance and PSA soundwriting assignments. I want to spend the next few minutes just reflecting on the lessons we learned and offering insights into aspects of the project you might do differently if you choose to use PSAs or postcards.

> [Music crossfades to the more contemplative tone of Podington
> Bear's (2015) "Floating in Space," a gentle slowly paced instrumental
> of a lightly keyed organ notes resonating. Music then fades to the
> background as the voiceover begins.]

So one of the coolest parts of this project was that students were super into this. We had a lot of fun over the semester, but going out to the center mall to read the submissions aloud as well as developing a PSA that was going to air on a real radio station motivated students to work incredibly hard on these assignments. Initially, a number of students had voiced uncertainty about the public nature of the project, but by the time we did this, they were really quite confident about the knowledge they had developed, and they had also come to understand that they were empowered to participate in public-facing events in ways that aligned with their own comfort levels.

Another pleasant surprise was that I didn't have to spend a great deal of time preparing students to do the technical work. Now, I've done similar assignments in the past, and usually I need to spend a couple of weeks with students practicing with sound-editing software. The level of technical proficiency, especially with a couple of students, was unparalleled in my experience. Partially, this was likely due to the fact this was a capstone and a number of the students in the class had taken another class I teach where we had practiced soundwriting before. Because of the high level of functional literacy that students possessed working with these tools, we were able to more readily focus our work on the rhetorical dimensions of these soundwriting assignments. For instance, during our class debrief, after listening to all the PSAs, we reflected on what we had learned and talked through the ethical and rhetorical challenges of designing these PSAs. One of the real generative conversations that unfolded surrounded the use of trigger warnings. A couple of students noted that the examples felt like they could be triggering and they were concerned about that. Conversely, there were also students who acknowledged that, yeah, PSAs definitely can be triggering but that trigger warnings are not something that PSAs tend to employ. They commonly utilize surprise and shock. We spent about 20 minutes discussing the various choices about using or not using a trigger warning in a PSA. And, we reached out to KCSU to see if they had guidance. As a class, I don't know that we came to a firm conclusion, but we realized that trigger warnings are definitely a thing that could and should be considered when designing PSAs.

You ask, what would you do differently? Well, I have a couple of pieces of advice here. One is I would spend more time on fair use. I am totally a copyright geek, and I enjoy spending time in class talking about it. But we just didn't have that kind of time this semester to dedicate to the issue. To avoid any complications, I required students to use copyleft/public domain resources. But, I'll admit, I didn't check on them, so when they submitted their sources, I discovered that there were submissions that potentially included assets that may not have been public domain or copyleft. Now for the purpose of this chapter, I'm going to claim that each of the PSAs shared here does fall into a fair use category, especially with respect to the purpose and character of these uses because this is a critical educational text and the goal of the PSA as an assignment was to raise awareness of digital media literacy in soundwriting. Still, there were definitely opportunities to explore fair use composing with more breadth than we did. If it had been a class that was centrally focused on digital composing, I would have been certain to dedicate more time to the topic.

An additional thing I would consider differently would have been adding more reflection within the project. Writing studies scholars have long understood that the metacognitive work associated with reflection is a powerful and generative tool for learning. We integrated a reflection during our class debrief, but one of the things I thought could have been really cool, especially as another soundwriting assignment, would have been to have every individual in the group audio record reflections on the contributions they made and the lessons they took away from participating in the PfP and the PSA projects. As the instructor for the course, I was able to gain a general sense of what students learned, but those individual reflections would be really valuable for gathering more specificity about aspects of these assignments that they had struggled with. It also would have been cool to take those reflections and then to remix then into another sound project. I think that might have been able to engender even deeper engagement and reflection than we had in the class-wide debrief we had carried out.

A final thing that I have to share is that after when we sent the PSAs out, we discovered that there was an ally and advocate at the local radio station. They were pretty amped about these PSAs coming from a group of students. So one takeaway is that if you have a campus or local radio station you might partner with, there's a chance they would be really excited to work with you. Through this assignment, I discovered a colleague on campus that possesses a great deal of expertise about soundwriting, and they are interested in working with students in the future.

Finally, we focused on privacy, but there really are a host of issues that could connect to a range of English, composition and rhetoric, or professional writing classes, so I would say go for it. Find a topic that seems to resonate with students, and do something that's real, and you'll get students excited and they'll do really cool work. Thanks for listening, I hope you enjoyed Postcards for Privacy and that you give it a try!

Hey, thanks for listening again! I just wanted to take a quick minute to say thank you to some of the folx that made the sounds freely available for us to utilize in this project, so I'm just going to list some of those here. So all of the music you heard in the background on the audio reflection comes from Podington Bear. The specific songs you heard were "Frogs in Tuxes," "Budsbursting," "Smooth Actor," "Lightfeet," and "Floating in Space." They're excellent! Thank you, Podington Bear! Additionally, the ambient sounds came from Freesound. org. Specifically, you heard "Ambience: Urban City Campus" by CBJ_Student (2020). You also heard "Urban Lullabies: Boston Common" by Inkhorn (2019), "EDM Sounds: EDM Buildup 4," by theartguild (2020), and "Train Horn" by L83 (2018). Thank you to those contributors on Freesound! Have a great day.

[Music slowly fades out and ends.]

References

Beck, E. N. (2015). The invisible digital identity: Assemblages in digital networks. *Computers and Composition, 35*(1), 125–140. https://doi.org/10.1016/j.compcom .2015.01.005.

CBJ_Student. (2020, November 17). City campus [Audio file]. *Freesound.* freesound .org/people/CBJ_Student/sounds/545182.

DeVoss, D. N. & Porter, J. E. (2006). Why Napster matters to writing: Filesharing as a new ethic of digital delivery. *Computers and Composition, 23*(2), 178–210. https://doi.org/10.1016/j.compcom.2006.02.001.

Gonzales, L. (2018). *Sites of translation: What multilinguals can teach us about digital writing and rhetoric.* University of Michigan Press. https://doi.org/10.3998/mpub .9952377.

Hocks, M. E. (2018). Sonic ecologies as a path for activism. In J. Alexander & J. Rhodes (Eds.), *The Routledge handbook of digital writing and rhetoric* (pp. 95–103). Routledge.

Hutchinson, L. & Novotny, M. (2018). Teaching a critical digital literacy of wearables: A feminist surveillance as care pedagogy. *Computers and Composition, 50*(1), 105–120. https://doi.org/10.1016/j.compcom.2018.07.006.

Inkhorn. (2019, May 25). Boston Common [Audio file]. *Freesound.* https://freesound .org/people/inkhorn/sounds/472744/.

KCSU. (2017). Underwriting KCSU FM. *KCSU FM.* http://kcsufm.com/under writing/.

L83. (2018, December 28). Train horn [Audio file]. *Freesound.* https://freesound.org /people/L83/sounds/455157/.

Podington Bear. (2007). Budsbursting [Song]. On *Said lion to bear* (Disk 3). https://freemusicarchive.org/music/Podington_Bear/Said_Lion_To_Lamb_Box_Set_Disc_3.

Podington Bear. (2015). Floating in space [Song]. On *Daydream*. https://freemusicarchive.org/music/Podington_Bear/Daydream.

Podington Bear. (2017a). Lightfeet [Song]. On *Uplifting*. https://freemusicarchive.org/music/Podington_Bear/Uplifting.

Podington Bear. (2017b). Smooth actor [Song]. On *Soul*. https://freemusicarchive.org/music/Podington_Bear/Soul.

Podington Bear. (2018). Frogs in tuxes [Song]. On *Meet Podington Bear* (Disc 1). https://freemusicarchive.org/music/Podington_Bear/Meet_Podington_Bear_Box_Set_Disc_1.

Rainie, L. (2016, September 21). The state of privacy in a post-Snowden America. *Pew Research Center*. http://www.pewresearch.org/fact-tank/2016/09/21/the-state-of-privacy-in-america/.

Selber, S. A. (2004). *Multiliteracies for a digital age*. Southern Illinois University Press.

Selfe, C. L. (2009). The movement of air, the breath of meaning: Aurality and multimodal composing. *College Composition and Communication, 60*(4), 616–663.

Selfe, R. J. & Selfe, C. L. (2008). "Convince me!" Valuing multimodal literacies and composing public service announcements. *Theory into Practice, 47*(2), 83–92.

Shipka, J. (2006). Sound engineering. Toward a theory of multimodal soundness. *Computers and Composition, 23*(3), 355–373. https://doi.org/10.1016/j.compcom.2006.05.003.

theartguild. (2020, September 2). EDM build-up 4 [Audio file]. *Freesound*. https://freesound.org/people/theartguild/sounds/533732/.

Tufekci, Z. (2017). *Twitter and tear gas: The power and fragility of networked protest*. Yale University Press.

VanKooten, C. (2016). Singer, writer: A choric explanation of sound and writing. *Kairos: A Journal of Rhetoric, Technology, and Pedagogy, 21*(1). http://kairos.technorhetoric.net/21.1/inventio/vankooten/index.html.

Vee, A. (2017). *Coding literacy: How computer programming is changing writing*. MIT Press.

Vie, S. (2008). Digital Divide 2.0: "Generation M" and online social networking sites in the composition classroom. *Computers and Composition, 25*(1), 9–23. https://doi.org/10.1016/j.compcom.2007.09.004.

Warren, F. (2005). *PostSecret: Extraordinary confessions from ordinary lives*. Regan Books.

Chapter 17. Research Remix: Soundwriting Studies of the English Language

Jennifer J. Buckner

GARDNER-WEBB UNIVERSITY

With Benjamin Flournoy, Katie Furr, Sarah Johnson,
Katie Lewis, Angela Meade, Hannah Ray, Garrett Simpson,
Kate Vriesema, and Ally Ward

Every English major has had that moment at a social gathering when a new friend asks the innocent question, "What's your major?" They respond, "English." And the now quieter person mumbles something like, "Ugh, I'm no good at grammar." Grammar historically gets a bad rap, understandably so; yet those who love linguistics revel in its complex structures. Those who study grammar understand it to be more than a punitive tool used by iconic red-ink-bearing teachers to bring down students who use dangling modifiers. Many universities still require classes to help majors study the more nuanced grammar of the English language.

Our department's response is ENGL 363: Structure of the English Language, a course with student learning outcomes that address the rhetorical purposes of grammatical structures and usage-related issues such as dialect and diversity. This course is taught on a two-year rotation in our department at Gardner-Webb University, a private liberal arts university in western North Carolina.

Many students who take this course are education majors required to take the class, planning to teach English (e.g., middle grades, high school, teaching English as a second language). Others who enroll are writing majors, looking for an in-depth study of language to improve their own sensitivity to choices in their writing. And there is usually at least one student who takes the class just because of their natural love of linguistics. When I agreed to teach our Structure of the English Language class, I knew that I wanted assignments that balanced this examination of language structures and their situated use to meet students' varied goals in taking the course.

At a micro-level, we geeked out, identifying word classes and functions, diagramming and illustrating syntax. At a macro-level, students researched English language use through field observations, textual artifact analysis, and interviews in a discourse community. A discourse ethnography, a classic language study genre, seemed an appropriate way to invite students to do field research studying English in communities of their choice.

DOI: https://doi.org/10.37514/PRA-B.2022.1688.2.17

223

Though a couple of undergraduate programs on our campus use empirical research in classes, almost all the students in my class—majoring in education, English, and world languages—had never conducted human research. So, honestly, I was pretty nervous about the learning curve of teaching undergraduate students about qualitative research, considering our time limitations for course content and the IRB process.

While I knew a discourse ethnography would help them learn, I felt that a traditional, written version would limit their ability to connect with the people speaking the words. I also wanted this project to reflect the embodied nature of language use; in other words, I wanted them to listen to these voices speaking words to study affective aspects of English. When they rehear voices in the process of remixing an audio essay, their perception of language shifts from parts of speech to bodies, whose voices echo dialects, tone, and dynamics. Also, I was concerned that their reproducing a written essay from their research would result in an ethos of distant disinterest in their object of study, typical of undergraduate research papers. So I wanted to teach them a classic form but for them to remix it in a strange way.

That's when I heard *audio essay*: more to essay (i.e., verb: to attempt or try, to test) than essay (i.e., noun: a short piece of writing on a subject).

This assignment would be a mutt genre in the way it would blend traditional ethnographic methodology with multimodal media and genres. Even though I had no models, I felt that inviting students to create an audio discourse ethnography would empower them to actively engage with their participants and research. I hoped that making the process strange would hypermediate their process, synthesizing data and analysis in a final mash-up of voices. Technically, remixing audio from participant interviews and soundscape clips with their observations would help them synthesize data in an embodied way, implicating multiple acts of language use in a layered 3–4-minute essay.

Once I decided on the assignment, I realized that I was going to have to think carefully about how to scaffold this assignment to walk students through a research process. I planned a series of workshops, beginning in the second week of classes to work on research design and begin our university's IRB process. In the weeks that followed, I staged workshops to help students with research methods (interviews, transcription), data analysis, audio editing, and peer review.[1]

Discourse Ethnography Portfolio Assignment

Students choose a discourse community to study during the course, engaging in an ethnographic study of its use of the English language. As part of this study,

---

1. Jennifer J. Buckner's guide for IRB workshops, a guide for workshops on interviews, recording, transcripts, and textual artifact analysis, and a guide for a "Writing for the Ear" workshop are available on the book's companion website.

they use several qualitative methods of research including gathering two textual artifacts created by the community, interviewing two members of the community, and conducting two field observations of language use in the community. Students compile their findings into 3–5-minute audio essays that highlight some unique aspect of that community's use of English language. Finally, all pieces of the research project are submitted as a research portfolio during final exam week.

Discourse Ethnography Portfolio

Rationale: The study of the English language should include a study of language as situated in rich, diverse contexts. In order to learn more about the structure of the English language, you are invited to conduct a semester-long study of its use within a discourse community of your choice.

The Basic Assignment: You will choose a discourse community to study this semester, engaging in an ethnographic study of its use of the English language. As part of this study, you will use several qualitative methods of research including gathering textual artifacts created by the community, interviewing two members of the community, and observing language use in the community and writing field notes. Finally, you will compile your findings into a 3–5-minute audio essay that highlights some unique aspect of that community's use of English language.

Table 17.1. Student Learning Outcomes Met with this Assignment

Assignment Portion	Student Outcomes Met
Textual analysis (textual artifacts, interviews)	• describe the structure of English sentences • identify principles of modification and coordination in English sentences • identify words and word classes in English
Audio essay (data drawn from observations and interviews)	• explain issues connected to the many varieties of English (dialects, usage, etc.) • analyze the evolving communication and use of language and grammatical structures for different purposes, to different audiences, and in different contexts, including multimodal communication

Portfolio Components

For this project, you will submit artifacts that reflect your research process, including data you collect, your analysis of that data, reflections/memos/notes about what you're learning throughout the process, and your final audio essay. This portfolio will include a range of media that will be hyperlinked within the body of textual documents you submit to Blackboard.

Proposal: Submit a proposal outlining which discourse community you wish to study and your rationale (see schedule, participation grade).

CITI Certification/IRB Application: In order to conduct research with human subjects as you will in studying a discourse community, you will need to complete an IRB application for "expedited" research. As part of this application, you will be asked to complete a CITI certification for Social and Behavioral Research. We will walk through this process together in class, getting you started. Then I will let you know the deadline for completing your certification and submitting your IRB application for review.

Observation: Choose at least **two** different settings in which to observe this community. Take notes about the activity within the community, especially related to their language use and the group dynamics. Submit notes with an informal reflection about what you are noticing early in the project to get feedback from prof (see schedule, participation grade). Also, include a copy in your final project portfolio.

Textual Analysis: Collect at least **two** different textual artifacts that represent genres of writing produced by this discourse community. Texts will likely be multimodal in nature, including a range of visual, aural, gestural, spatial, and linguistic features, presenting you with a challenge of questioning how other modes function with language in these texts. Annotate these artifacts, describing the structure of sentences and identifying grammatical structures present in the text. Submit these annotations with your final project portfolio, including a brief reflection (one page) that highlights features you find interesting/unique to this community's use of English.

Interviews: Choose two members of the community to interview, investigating the community's discourse features. Develop interview questions that will ask participants to think about their situated use of English with others within this discourse community. Acquire permission from two members of the discourse community to participate in your research. Audio record and transcribe those interviews. Submit your transcriptions with your final project portfolio with a brief memo about what interesting/insightful things you learned from your interviews.

- What are some of the shared goals of the community?

- What mechanisms/tools does the community use for communication? What are the purposes of each of these means of communication?

- What kinds of genres/texts does this community produce?

- What are some of its specialized language (lexis)? And what purpose does it serve?

- Describe the group dynamics (e.g., experts, newcomers) and how they impact language use and acquisition in the community.

Consent Forms: Include scans/photos of consent forms for those participants who helped with your project, including interviews and/or audio essay participation.

Audio Essay: Synthesizing all that you've learned about this community's language use, create a 3–5-minute audio essay that highlights some language-use feature(s) that you feel is/are important to this community. Present your findings in an engaging NPR-style audio essay that layers a range of voices, capturing the spirit as well as the insight of your findings in a way that invites language aficionados to celebrate nuances of this community's language use. Create a transcript for your audio essay. Share your audio essay with the class.

Table 17.2. Grading Rubric

Criteria	A	B	C	D	F
Data Collection	Portfolio reflects robust evidence of data collection including observation field notes, interview transcripts, and memos.	Strong evidence	Evident, though some gaps	Partial	Missing
Textual Analysis	Analysis of two textual artifacts from discourse community describes the structure of English sentences; identifies principles of modification and coordination in English sentences; identifies words and word classes in English; and reflects on aspects of English language as evidenced in these texts.	Strong evidence	Evident, though some gaps	Partial	Missing
Audio Essay	Audio essay celebrates some aspect of English language use unique to this discourse community in a 3–5-minute audio project, using evidence drawn from research project to present findings to an interested audience in an engaging manner.	Strong evidence	Evident, though some gaps	Partial	Missing

Touchpoints (Hear: You are not alone.)

Ethical Research Workshops: Two class meetings designed to introduce you to empirical research and issues of ethics. In addition to these workshops, a body of resources are provided in Blackboard to guide you through the process while you work between classes.

- Rationale: In the first workshop, we will talk briefly about why conducting research with human subjects requires Institutional Review Board approval and review that process, registering you for CITI Certification. Following that workshop, you should complete Social and Behavioral Research Certification, uploading your certificate to Blackboard.

- IRB Applications: In the second workshop, we will review the IRB application and work on composing your own applications, given your targeted discourse community, including required portions (e.g., application, interview questions, consent form, debriefing form). You will submit a draft of your IRB application for feedback. Finally, you will polish your IRB application and bring a printed copy to class for handwritten signatures.

Methods Workshops: Workshops designed to help you work on research methods.

- Observations and Field Notes: We will explore observation and field notes methods, focused on capturing language use.
- Interview Protocols: We will examine interviewing methods including setting up the interview, designing open questions, handling awkward moments, and recording methods/options.
- Transcribing Interviews: We will explore basic transcription methods for interviews, introducing you to optional open-source tools for transcription.
- Textual Artifacts: We will practice annotating English structures in a range of textual artifacts and genres.

Soundwriting Workshops: Workshops designed to introduce you to composing with sound, including software introductions, genre discussions, and peer feedback.

- Audio Genre Studies: Throughout the semester, we will use audio pieces related to topics we are discussing in class as a discussion starter. Listen to form and content of these podcasts, preparing to discuss ideas raised as well as thinking like a soundwriter (i.e., how did they do that?). For example, you will find links to the World in Words in the navigational menu of the class; click and listen. As we approach the latter portion of the semester, we will start thinking about a range of short, audio projects in terms of genre to help frame your response.
- Audacity Workshops: We will use open-source software called Audacity, which you will download to your personal computer. These workshops will teach you how to import sounds, manipulate tracks, and edit sounds.
- Peer Feedback Workshops: In these workshops, you will be asked to bring samples of your soundwriting project for peer feedback.

Sample Student Projects

1. Benjamin Flourney's Discourse Ethnography on Campus Resident Life. Flournoy examines the balance between professionalism and personalization of a campus residence life program.[2]

---

2. Nine student examples (audio files and descriptive transcripts) can be found on the book's companion website.

2. Katie Furr's Discourse Ethnography on the University Wrestling Team. Furr celebrates the unique discourse of a college wrestling team, focusing on ways language helps to build a community of brothers.

3. Sarah Johnson's Discourse Ethnography on Intrinsic Bible Study. Johnson examines how language helps a group of Christians delve deeper into intrinsic Biblical study.

4. Katie Lewis's Discourse Ethnography on Be Your Own Beautiful Cancer Support Group. Lewis visits a Be Your Own Beautiful cancer support group to learn how language works to help cancer victims reshape their notions of beauty.

5. Angela Meade's Discourse Ethnography on Theater Discourse. Meade goes behind the scenes to learn about the activities and terminologies used by a theater community.

6. Hannah Ray's Discourse Ethnography on Professional Newsroom. Ray discovers how clarity can be both essential and ubiquitous in a professional newsroom.

7. Garrett Simpson's Discourse Ethnography on the University Swim Team. Simpson considers how a college swim team uses a specialized discourse to meet its athletic and team building goals.

8. Kate Vriesema's Discourse Ethnography on Wattpad as a Discourse Community. Vriesema enters the world of an online creative writing community to think about how language serves as a medium through which strangers become writing group partners.

9. Ally Ward's Discourse Ethnography on the International Equestrian Center. Ward considers how language functions to establish a community at a dynamic, international equestrian center.

Reflection

[Sounds of dog tags jingling; dog panting; someone says, "Go get it" . . . "Good boy. good boy. Go get it!".]

Jennifer Buckner: When it comes to dogs, I have always been attracted to mutts.[3]

[Underlying beat begins.]

The scrappier, the better. They have great genetics, benefitting from the best qualities of each parent. Our mutts have had healthier, longer lives than the pure breeds we've raised. And many times, I've stood in the vet's office, you know looking at that breed poster on the wall, and I'm trying to find which nose or which body type looks most like my dog. And some of my favorite pets have just defied

---

3. The audio version of Jennifer J. Buckner and her students' reflection can be found on the book's companion website.

this visual mash-up. They don't look like any breeds on the poster. So I can't have any preconceived ideas about their behavior or appearance, their history, or how friendly they might be. It's just me and Ivan getting to know each other.

I've been thinking lately that mutts aren't limited to animal classes. In 20 years of teaching English, first in high schools and now at a university, I've come to see that pedagogy has its own mutts. We combine the best of different approaches to create somethin' scrappy, somethin' better. And when we do this, we're often pulling genetics from some trusted lineage, and we introduce these new genetics to help the pedagogy evolve.

[sounds of a class discussion in the background, with laughing and lively chatter]

I introduced a mutt genre—what I called the audio discourse ethnography—to a Structure of the English Language class in fall semester of 2017. So these students would spend a semester studying a discourse community of their choice, and then they would compile the data from portfolios of material, and that included textual artifacts from the community, field observations and soundscape recordings, and audio interviews. And they compiled all of this data into a 3–5-minute audio essay, rather than writing a term paper.

I knew it wouldn't be an easy sell to this group, especially because they were upperclassmen, undergrads, and very comfortable in their ability to write, at least in the traditional sense. But, at first, it seemed like they loved the idea of remixing their research into audio. But when we got into the nitty gritty of, like, really creating the audio essay, we all found ourselves kind of metaphorically staring at that *[laughs]* poster in the vet's office and trying to find this assignment on it. So the aural equivalent of "what does my dog look like?"—I guess—was "what does an audio essay sound like?" Or, in this class, we were trying to understand the grammar of audio discourse ethnography.

> **Computer Voice Reading**: Noun: a word (other than a pronoun) used to identify any of a class of people, places, or things.

Garrett Simpson: One thing that I, uh, thought about yesterday was that you, um, kind of realize doing this, doing soundwriting versus actually writing an essay, the rhetorical effects of things that aren't words, so you know the effect of fading out a sound versus things cutting together and background music. And that sort of thing. Like, there's so much effect that nonverbal sounds have.

Sarah Johnson: Well, like listening to their tone rather than just reading. Something, like, there was like this of list of things, and one of them that if I just read it, it would have seemed really important to me. But listening to it, I could see how, like, she just mentioned it and kind of moved on, brushed it aside, and actually these other points were more important to her.

Hannah Ray: Yeah, it forced—it forced me to take them at their word. Because if they didn't expound on it. And even a few times I would say, "Could you tell me more about that?" and they didn't, then I couldn't force it to be something important if it wasn't. And I think with writing we supplement the material that we've received with our thoughts a lot more. And even though, obviously, all of us did that with this, we could only make it work so much as the sound bites that we had. So, we, I think, were a lot more truthful in this, in a weird way.

Jennifer: In this discussion, I realized that they were exploring the affordances of this genre we had created, and they were also talking about their identities as scholars. What was interesting was that working with sound had created an intimacy with the data that translated into what I thought was more investment in the project itself. And I started to realize that an audio discourse ethnography shifted their role as scholars in a powerful way.

Angela Meade: *[laughs]* Like, um, find my own voice and know how to influence the sound to be what I wanted it to be. . . .

Garrett: I felt like I had a right to be saying what I was saying, like I actually had some sort of authority.

Hannah: Listening to the audio over and over and over again to make those tedious sound changes. Without even realizing it, I processed what they told me a lot more thoroughly than if I had just written down and tried to turn that into a paper. Because I listened to two 30-minute interviews and a 45-minute staff meeting endlessly to find clips when people said "clarity." Because I knew that that was there, but I had to process all the other stuff, which led me to a lot of other conclusions that I included in my essay that I wouldn't have if I would have just heard it and said "clarity" and then just gone and copied and pasted sentences with "clarity." Because you can do Control-F on a document, and you can't do it on an audio essay.

[group laughing]

> **Computer Voice Reading**: Adverb: a word belonging to one of the major form classes, typically serving as a modifier of a verb, an adjective, another adverb, expressing some relation of manner or quality, place, time, degree, number, cause, opposition, affirmation, or denial.

[Student in background says, "I can make friends elsewhere, you know what I'm saying!".]

Jennifer: *[laughs]* I don't think I have ever laughed that much during a final exam. If that wasn't evidence that the project was a success. . . . They were enthusiastic—I mean, perhaps a little sleep deprived, it was exam week—but enthusiastic and invested. Invested in their projects in a way that I don't often see, especially in a Structure of the English Language class.

Angela: Fun, I'm loving it so much more because if I had to sit down and write a paper about this, I would have put it off. But like I put off other projects to do this one because I enjoyed it more. *[laughs]*

Hannah: For me, this project completely made the class worthwhile, in that I didn't come for the grammar. I thought I did, and then I got here and the grammar was like *chhh chhh chhh*—insert in the transcript "mimics slapping." *[laughs and others laugh too]* Um, but like, grammar suddenly didn't matter to me, and that was something that was really hard to care about knowing where all these, like, adverbial clauses and bleh, bleh, bleh, um, and so I was really burned out on the semester, and then when I started working on this, it started to matter again.

Sarah: The structure of the class itself helped, like going through all of the, like, grammar in the beginning and then going into the application part. Um. In most classes it's like, "Yeah, there's application to this, and, in the end, we're going to come back to just this formal information," and that's pushed on you. But I feel like in this class the application was more important.

Jennifer: It was interesting when I learned that they weren't all on board from the start, though. Our English majors, well, they're typically introverted. I wonder, if most English majors aren't introverted? And, so, I was asking them to go interview people and record their voices. And when you have to record your own voice in an audio essay, there's not a lot of places for you to hide.

What was that like, being a researcher in the field?

Kate Vriesema: It was terrifying. I'm not going to lie. *[others laugh]* When you first pitched this project to us, I was like, No, no way . . .

[laughter from whole group]

Hannah *[as Kate talks]*: I'm dropping this class.
Kate: . . . I'm probably going to drop this class just to avoid this project.
Angela: WP [withdraw pass]!
Hannah: There were some stressful conversations about it.

[sound of fire truck driving by]

Angela: Pauses. For fire truck.
Ben: Yeah, just passing down the road . . . as normal.
Kate: Just the normal daily fire truck.
Jennifer: You did a hard thing too, going into a cold community.
Ally Ward: Oh my God, it was so scary. *[laughs]* I was just super nervous because I kind of was just like by myself over there, and I didn't like it. It was really scary.

[Beat begins.]

Jennifer: So, they really had to step out, from behind written letters and paragraphs into a newsroom, an international equestrian center, a Bible study group, a pool house, a cancer support meeting, a wrestling room, a theater, and even an online creative writing community of strangers.

I'm still getting to know this mutt genre that is audio discourse ethnography, or audiography, or soundwriting.

[Return to sounds of Jennifer playing with dog, tags jingling, and dog running by.]

I am fond of it though. And I've decided: It will have a home in my next Structure of the English Language class.

[In background, Jennifer says, "good boy," "sit," "that's a good boy," "you ready?", "go get it," dog running away, "that's a good boy." Beat fades.]

Note

References include texts referenced in Jennifer J. Buckner's materials hosted on the book's companion website. Buckner's reflection used sounds from Apple's GarageBand.

References

Branick, S. (2011). Coaches can read, too: An ethnographic study of a football coaching discourse community. In E. Wardle & D. Downs (Eds.), *Writing about writing: A college reader* (pp. 557–573). Bedford/St. Martin's.

Gee, J. P. (2004). *Situated language and learning: A critique of traditional schooling.* Routledge.

Gee, J. P. (2014). *How to do discourse analysis: A toolkit.* Routledge.

Grech, D. (n.d.). *Writing for the ear.* Poynter. https://www.poynter.org/shop/self-directed-course/writing-for-the-ear/.

Jacob, S. A. & Furgerson, S. P. (2012). Writing interview protocols and conducting interviews: Tips for students new to the field of qualitative research. *The Qualitative Report, 17*(42), 1–10. https://doi.org/10.46743/2160-3715/2012.1718 .

Phillips, B. (2011, April 13). 5 ways to write for the ear, not the eye. *The Throughline Blog.* https://www.throughlinegroup.com/2011/04/13/5-ways-to-write-for-the-ear-not-for-the-eye/.

Swales, J. (1990). *Genre analysis: English in academic and research settings.* Cambridge University Press.

Chapter 18. If These Walls Had Ears: Applying Sound Rhetorics Through Audio Tours

Lance Cummings, Hannah Lane Kendrick,
and Devon Peterson
University of North Carolina Wilmington

This chapter presents a reoccurring applied learning project, Virtual Tours and The House Museum, where students create virtual tours for local house museums in a core professional writing class, ENG 314 Digital Composing. The University of North Carolina Wilmington (UNCW) lies only a few miles from a historical riverfront, a site for many historical buildings and house museums from the 18th and 19th centuries. This chapter will describe how students use theories from rhetoric and digital composition to produce digital content for these community stakeholders. Though most students' final projects produced a video tour for a museum house, the class takes over half the semester to practice analyzing digital texts related to museums, while playing around with different modes, including sound. This chapter will specifically focus on an assignment that asks students to "remediate" client texts and/or previous projects into an audio tour that focuses on a specific audience mentioned in our client introduction.

Funded by UNCW's Quality Enhancement Program, Experience Transformative Education through Applied Learning (ETEAL), I was required to incorporate and implement "high-impact" practices as described by The National Society for Experiential Education (NSEE, 2013) and The Association of American Colleges & Universities (AAC&U) (Kuh & O'Donnell, 2013). The purpose of deploying these best practices in applied learning is to help students better "integrate theories, ideas, and skills they have learned in new contexts, thereby extending them" ("What Is Applied," n.d., para. 1). From a rhetoric and writing perspective, applied learning's focus on student inquiry and reflection ties closely to the goals of activity theory that place the responsibility of determining the goals of a project on the students (Shipka, 2006). For example, the first four principles provided by NSEE require students to set their intention, prepare and plan, and then reflect on their experience, giving students ownership of the project (National Society for Experiential Education, 2013).

In the case of applied learning, a specific client is consistently consulted, lending what NSEE called *authenticity*—a real world context that provides meaningful reference points for the project, primarily the stakeholders and audiences involved (National Society for Experiential Education, 2013). Working with sound, though, emphasizes the embodied aspects of this "real world context." In "Composing for

DOI: https://doi.org/10.37514/PRA-B.2022.1688.2.18

Sound: Sonic Rhetoric as Resonance," Mary E. Hocks and Michelle Comstock (2017) laid out the importance of "fully embodied listening practices" to help students produce more complex multimodal projects. This includes listening to the environment, not just considering how the human voice sounds. In a project like this, the historical environment and space are equally important. Students are required to visit the house museum multiple times, listening and observing the space around them, inspiring many of them to "listen" historically through the archives to learn more about these contexts. A video or written tour can also drive students to explore these embodied experiences, but focusing on sound helps them think more deeply about how to invoke these experiences in different kinds of audiences. After being constrained by a sound-only project, students can take what they learned and use sound to enhance a more multimodal project, like a video tour.

Accessibility has always impacted the range and quality of these sound projects. In some ways, this assignment assumes that the class is taught in a lab or a laptop classroom with access to sound-editing software. With support from the UNCW administration, we remodeled one of our computer labs into a laptop classroom, where students sit in "pods" with personal laptops around a larger monitor that can be used to display their work. Because this assumes that students own a decent laptop with access to the appropriate software, we acquired funds to provide backup computers that students can use when needed. The UNC system has also negotiated a deal with Adobe that gives all students access to Adobe's Creative Cloud Suite, allowing them to practice using Adobe Audition (one industry standard for sound editing).

That said, "high fidelity" is not necessarily my primary outcome for these projects. I want students to connect sound production to rhetoric, while also reflecting on their digital composing process. This does not require a high-quality project, though we all strive to produce something useful for our client. Having students work in well-chosen groups allows them to pool their resources, skills, and talents to eventually produce something that our client might find useful (and that students can put in their professional portfolio).

Assignments and Sequencing

In order to allow the students to explore this real-world context and become experts of museum rhetorics, the entire semester focuses on examining different kinds of digital texts produced by different museums from all over the country and abroad. For example, one of my favorite digital texts is a tour of the Louvre on YouTube by VisitParisRegion (2010, see https://www.youtube.com/visitparis-region), which embodies the viewer in several different ways by providing first-person views of different kinds of people enjoying a variety of experiences at the museum. Students also play around with different modes before embarking on the final project. This includes an analysis of a museum text, a photo essay, and a sound remediation. The following assignment prompts lay out this scaffolding:

Figure 18.1. Photo collage of Latimer House. Hannah Lane Kendrick.

1. Virtual Tours and The Latimer House
2. Analysis of Multimodal Text
3. Photo Essay
4. Audio Remediation
5. Intention Essay
6. Proposal
7. Critical Reflection

The audio remediation is a key component to this process. Constraining students to work with sound alone helps them think about ways they can invoke a more embodied experience without depending on visuals or video. This is also where students often see the potential for different audiences, such as children, nonprofits, garden fans, and more. They then take what they learn in this project and usually expand on it in their final project, which is usually a video tour.

For this context, I include only the first and fourth assignments, giving readers the initial context as presented to students and the soundwriting aspect in the audio remediation.

Virtual Tours and the Latimer House (Assignment 1 of 7)

All writing is recursive . . . digital composing is no different. Good digital composers go back and forth between theory and practice. In other words, they compose and experiment, but also think about how they compose and experiment. The heuristics and theories we've engaged in thus far are useful tools for thinking about digital composition. Now that we've explored those ideas, we will begin to move towards composing a multimodal text for a specific client. In this case, we will be composing a short introduction video/tour for the Latimer House, using the expertise we've developed thus far.

Applied Learning Project Overview

We will be spending much of the rest of the semester exploring the different modes of digital composition and how they might apply to this specific context and help produce a good text for our client. Each week will look specifically at a mode and experiment with different means of production. This exploration will culminate in a 2–3-minute promotional multimodal text for our client. Though our client expects videos, you may, in consultation with me, consider other emerging genres.

Even though our project has the following distinct stages, it is important to remember that these are intertwined throughout the process and certain aspects will be foregrounded at specific times. In other words, we will be researching non-profits like the Latimer House at the beginning of the project, but it may be important to continue that research in later stages of the process.

Phase I – Intention Essay (50 points)

An intention reflection is where you consider your expectations for this project. After doing some research on nonprofits and the Latimer House, you will write a 300–600-word essay that reflects on how the knowledge you've attained thus far will help you with this applied learning project and what kinds of impact this project may have on our community and on your own personal educational experience.

Phase II – Application Essay (50 points)

After exploring the different modes, you will reflect on how you applied specific theories in rhetoric and digital composition, as well as how these might be further applied in your final project for the Latimer House. You will further reflect on the kind of impact these kinds of application may have on our community and on your own personal educational experience.

Phase III – Drafting (150 points)

Once we've prepared ourselves sufficiently for this project, you will compose your multimodal text for the Latimer House collaboratively with three to four of your peers. You will receive points for each stage of the composing process and for interacting with our client.

- Proposal (25 points)
- Draft (25 Points)
- Client Visit (50 points)
- Final Draft (100 points)

Phase IV – Critical Reflection (50 points)

After revising and discussing our projects, each of you will individually write a 600–800-word critical reflection on the project and what you've learned. We will also gather input from our client.

Audio Remediation Assignment Prompt (Assignment 4 of 7)

Understanding aural elements of digital composition and how they work rhetorically is critical to the creation of effective texts in today's web-driven world. The goal of this project is to explore the nuances of audio and video, familiarize yourself with editing apps, and experiment with different ways of deploying these elements of multimodal rhetoric. We will also be thinking about how established texts can be "remediated" or transformed by changing modes and media.

Assignment

Review the different assets that we've collected from our museum client, including tour scripts, videos, websites, etc. Thinking of a specific purpose, focus, and/or audience, develop a 30-60-second audio "tour" that remediates one of these assets by describing or telling a story about a specific aspect, room, or object from the Latimer House. Your goal is to make an argument or reveal a specific perspective of the house using only audio. This will involve writing a script and producing your clip in Audio Audition. You should also use at least one soundtrack (sound effects, music, etc.). You will then write a short reflection describing your remediation and how you applied aural aspects of rhetoric. Be sure to reference specific course material. You want this to be detailed and concise. Good versions are usually 300–500 words.

Criteria

A full rubric will be added to the assignment in Blackboard.

Table 18.1. Rubric for Audio Remediation Assignment

Category	Criteria
Remediation	Remediation shows an in-depth exploration of specific rhetorical, design, and Adobe skills. Makes significant and meaningful changes to original audio.
Reflection	Reflection states a clear thesis that describes learning or achievements of this project. For example, how did you use the affordances of this mode of meaning rhetorically? References specific details from the composing process, class, or the remediation itself.
Course Material	Clearly applies course material to remediation. Makes use of specific ideas and principles from recent and previous readings. All material is cited.

Sample Student Projects

Though we've done our best to track down the sound assets and cite them for these sample projects, we found this process very difficult. Before this project, we go over fair use, copyright, and Creative Commons. All of these projects make use of sound files found via the Creative Commons search at https:// search.creativecommons.org, which led us to many assets (if not all) found at Freesound (freesound.org). Since this project was for experimentation purposes only, students did not keep track of these files or provide citations. That said, I recommend incorporating this element in future iterations, so that students can practice this important element of digital composing.

Most of these samples focused on remediating a video tour created by the office manager of the Latimer House, Travis Gilbert. This video summarized several of the tour's speaking points for a general audience. During client visits, students looked for ways to rework some of these ideas for different audiences and purposes. The audio remediations tended to focus on transforming this text.

1. "Entrance to Latimer" by Hannah Lane Kendrick: Hannah uses the audio tour to introduce a scavenger hunt around the house based on Travis's original video.[1]
2. "Creepy Latimer" by Devon Peterson: Devon created this creepy introduction to Latimer in order to play with the power of sound to change our perceptions of a place like Latimer. This was inspired by the Latimer family's upcoming Halloween event.
3. "Character Tour" by Mike Egan, Devon Peterson, Sharryse Piggot, and Devin Wensevic: This audio tour puts the listener in the presence of one of the main characters of the house: Zebulon Latimer.
4. "Restoring the Slave Quarters" by Shannon Bradburn, Hannah Lane

---

1.   Four student examples (audio or video files and descriptive transcripts) can be found on the book's companion website.

Kendrick, Kendall C. Rogers, and Tyler L. Young: This is one of the final projects given to our client. Students visited the house museum several times to do archival research and talk with our client. The end product was a video showing the importance of preserving slave history at the Latimer.

Reflection

Devon Peterson: It can be tricky to understand the rhetoric of sound and how it's applied during the composition process.[2] We are constantly surrounded by noise, even when it is the sound of silence.

[pause]

Effective audio is often felt, not heard . . . like a sudden, loud crash makes you jump.

[loud crashing sound (bone666138, 2013)]

Or birds chirping signal safety and reassurance.

[birds chirping pleasantly (InspectorJ, 2016)]

Lance Cummings: I am Lance Cummings, Assistant Professor of English at University of North Carolina Wilmington, and that was one of my professional writing students, Devon Peterson, describing her experience working with sound in our digital composing class where we focus on an applied learning project that asks students to create a virtual tour of one of the many house museums in Wilmington, North Carolina—in this case, the Latimer House. You may notice Devon's focus on what Hocks and Comstock (2017) call "embodied listening" or "rhetorical engagement with sound" (pp. 136–137) that includes more than just voice. In other words, extending our listening practices beyond the spoken word will create what they call "increasingly complex and sonically rich multimodal projects" (Hocks & Comstock, 2017, p. 137). Applied learning, where students work with a client to produce real-world texts, supports the goals of embodied listening by lending authenticity to the experience and allowing students to craft rhetorically meaningful projects that use sound in complex ways. In this case, authenticity is the embodied experience of working with a specific location and with specific stakeholders, allowing students to develop a strong sense of how sound can affect audiences and their perceptions of space and time.

Imagine the last time you visited an interesting and unfamiliar place, like a museum, historical home, or just a new and fascinating location. You must remember looking around, taking it all in—that is what I remember seeing my

---

2. The audio version of Lance Cummings, Hannah Lane Kendrick, and Devon Peterson's reflection can be found on the book's companion website.

students do during our client visits to the house museums. It might be easy to ignore the sounds in these places with so many visually interesting things to see, but having students focus only on sound for one project allows them to practice this embodied listening.

Devon Peterson: Show, don't tell. How many times have you heard that? In our audio tour, our group wanted to vividly recreate the drawing room for someone completely absent from the house. This forced us to change how we address the audience. If it was one person listening in, where would they be in the house? Who were they and what would they care about? Looking at the house from different lenses and perspectives made us think about the different historical "characters" or figures that had lived there. We decided to focus on the drawing room from the perspective of the once owner, Zebulon Latimer—played by Michael Egan.

> **Michael Egan**: [*quote from Sample 3 on the companion website; classical violins play in the background*] Welcome to my home! Come in. Come in. Please, let's retire to the drawing room.

Devon: Not only was Michael the only masculine voice, the tone of his script was written haughty and more conversational, distinguished from the rest of our more feminine voices.

Lance: Funny that Devon uses the phrase "show, don't tell" for a completely audio project, right? Being in a space like the Latimer House helped students see that there are multiple ways of seeing the different objects in the house, requiring them to think about how to make that happen in audio . . . in this case, by bringing in different voices. Probably what fascinated me the most, as a scholar who loves archives, is how this drove students to explore local archives at the museum and in the UNCW Library, which was not required at all for this project. Most groups made extra trips to explore the different stories and how those might be transformed into rhetorically complex projects.

Hannah Lane Kendrick: Digging through the archives at UNCW was a very impactful part of the researching process for the video. We had gathered a lot of important site documents and records, but it was all from the house. We were told by another worker at the Latimer House that the archives held extra information that the house did not have. Zebulon Latimer, the homeowner, kept many documents. He started a church in Wilmington and most of the contents in the archives were from the church. We did not know what to expect when we went to the archives, but I believe they held around 13 different boxes of information. It was so interesting! . . . and a bit overwhelming to thumb through pages of historical documents, old church papers and programs, and confirmations. When we gathered information at the Latimer House, one particular slave had some letter writings and documentation. Her name was Hannah, and my group and I focused the majority of the video on her and her story. At the archives, we found Hannah's confirmation date from 1860 and this further solidified that she existed at the Latimer House and attended the church. The archives help us to verify the information and we were able to more effectively listen to the stories from a historical perspective.

Lance: Sound became a way to connect the audience to people they discovered in the archives. Hannah Kendrick's group wanted to highlight the lives of enslaved people—something that doesn't always come through in house museum tours.

Hannah: Our group noticed how often the stories of enslaved people were missing from the many narratives told in local house museums. My group and I decided to tell their story, focusing on how we could bring an emotional experience to our listeners. Sound made this possible for us and helped to establish a mood of deep caring compassion by giving voice to a particular slave's writings.

> **Kendall Rogers:** *[quote from Sample 4 on the companion website; somber music plays]* My dearest mistress. I was pleased to learn from your letter of August 24, that you and your family are all well. I hope that you have all spent a pleasant summer and are benefited from the trip. I'm sorry and hope that you do not think I was not glad to hear from you, as it has been so long since I've received your letters. Mary has been quite sick and I was not very strong and the weather so warm, then moving in a few months.

Hannah: We hoped the music would give a sense of togetherness, while also emphasizing key textual moments like the listing of slave names.

> **Tyler Young:** *[quote from Sample 4 on the companion website; somber music plays]* Listed here are just some of the many enslaved peoples of color who contributed to the Latimer household in some shape or form. Their names and legacies are also preserved by Wilmington's Lower Cape Fear Historical Society. However, there is one that we are privileged to know more about than the others. And her name was Hannah.

Hannah: With emotions at a heightened level by the end of the video, we were able to emphasize why our audience should care one last time.

> **Tyler:** *[quote from Sample 4 on the companion website; optimistic guitar music plays]* The Lower Cape Fear Historical Society is a nonprofit corporation. Money raised through memberships, donations, and events fund educational programs and the maintenance of the archives and the Latimer House. Your addition to the Society for your generous donation would be a vital investment into the past and a crucial step in the sowing of the seeds for the future.

Lance: Students quickly discover that making these connections with sound is easier said than done.

Devon: The layers of sound need to be cohesive, so we experimented with different background music before we discovered that perfect sound . . . which can be difficult when working with fair use music. Anything that ran on too short of a loop can become distracting and eventually annoying.

["Pop Goes the Weasel" played on a music box (cgrote, 2012)]

House music didn't fit our frame . . .

[house dance music clip with thumping bass (frankum, 2017)]

. . . but classical music was perfect.

[relaxing piano music (orangefreesounds, 2016)]

Hannah: I did not realize going into this project that there were so many elements to sound. From pitch, to tone, to evoking mood to the listeners, it all comes together to form an effective multimodal project. But working with sound just in simple ways changed the way I looked at this project. I can say with full confidence that our video would not have had the same effect had it not had sound elements. Working with Travis, our client, made our experience seem more real. Interacting with Travis, visiting the Latimer House, asking questions, collecting research, and gaining insights and ideas helped us better understand how sound should work with our projects.

Lance: In other words, participating in an applied learning experience helped students rhetorically listen to their audiences and stakeholders in embodied ways, whether with clients, audiences, or even historical figures from the past.

As a part of the applied learning experience at UNCW, students are required to do several reflections throughout the course. I try to emphasize how reflection connects theory and practice, especially in multimodal composing. To become an effective multimodal composer, one must play around with the different tools, modes, and genres. Reflecting is what helps us figure out what is working and what is not. Even though we are working with real stakeholders, there needs to be a safe place to play—that's why I do these mini-projects that allow students to play around with just one mode—like sound.

Devon: So much of this was a matter of trial and error. It was hard to find what would work until we found what didn't and learned why. By the deadline, even after all the editing and reframing and rerecording, our final product fell short of our aspirations. It is too long and clunky. The transitions between narrators are indelicate. In other words, it does not sound professional. Which is fine, this is an amateur audio tour. One created by students who, in working with a real client, were able to begin again a cycle of learning that is an ongoing rotation of theory and experiment.

Lance: Working within an applied learning experience helped students delve into the rhetorical complexity involved with professional writing projects, while also allowing them to play around with their understanding of that complexity by interacting with our client, researching archives, and exploring different kinds of sounds for their projects. Applied learning brings an authenticity to soundwriting that extends beyond just the classroom.

Remember that space you visited at the beginning of this audio? Think about what sounds you might have missed . . . what perspectives . . . or even what stories. If those walls had ears, what would they know? This could be the start of your next sound project.

References

Arola, K. L., Sheppard, J. & Ball, C. E. (2014). *Writer/designer: A guide to making multimodal projects.* Bedford/St. Martin's.

bone666138. (2013, September 8). Crash [Audio file]. *Freesound.* https://freesound .org/people/bone666138/sounds/198876/.

cgrote. (2012, April 11). Pop goes the weasel music box.WAV [Audio file]. *Freesound.* https://freesound.org/people/cgrote/sounds/151320/.

frankum. (2017, January 30). Red - hard lead techno house [Audio file]. *Freesound.* https://freesound.org/people/frankum/sounds/378665/.

Hocks, M. E. & Comstock, M. (2017). Composing for sound: Sonic rhetoric as resonance. *Computers and Composition, 43*, 135–146. https://doi.org/10.1016/j.comp com.2016.11.006.

InspectorJ. (2016, March 10). Bird whistling, A.wav [Audio file]. *Freesound.* https:// freesound.org/people/InspectorJ/sounds/339326/.

Kuh, G. D. & O'Donnell, K. (2013). *Ensuring quality & taking high impact practices to scale.* The Association of American Colleges & Universities.

National Society for Experiential Education. (2013). *Eight principles of good practice for all experiential learning activities.* http://www.nsee.org/8-principles.

orangefreesounds. (2016, March 18). Piano melody [Audio file]. *Freesound.* https:// freesound.org/people/orangefreesounds/sounds/340075/.

Shipka, J. (2006). Sound engineering: Toward a theory of multimodal soundness. *Computers and Composition, 23*(6), 355–373. https://doi.org/10.1016/j.compcom .2006.05.003.

VisitParisRegion. (2010, November 30). Visit the Louvre Museum [Video file]. *You-Tube.* https://youtu.be/xJxH-QuJeXo.

What is applied learning? (n.d.). UNCW.edu. https://web.archive.org/web/2017082 5070209/https://uncw.edu/eteal/overview/appliedlearning.html.

Chapter 19. Engaging and Amplifying Community Voices: An Interview Assignment Sequence

L. Jill Lamberton
WABASH COLLEGE

This chapter presents a community-based interview unit that I teach in a sophomore-level soundwriting course—a course that focuses almost exclusively on audio—at Wabash College in Crawfordsville, Montgomery County, Indiana. The assignment is called Humans of Montgomery County (HOMC), and it is modeled on Brandon Stanton's immensely successful *Humans of New York* website (Stanton, n.d.) and book projects (2013, 2015).

The course is called Audio Rhetoric and Creative Writing, and it is cross-listed by our English and rhetoric (formerly, speech communication) departments. Throughout this chapter I refer to the course as simply "Audio Rhetoric."

I had tried an interview assignment in the previous iterations of the course, but I felt the students' products fell somewhat flat. In those versions, students interviewed family members or favorite professors and coaches, and the soundwriting was not frequently framed for a larger audience. Many of these interviews had a twinge of stories we'd heard before, even if they were meaningful to the students who conducted the interview. My soundwriters sometimes failed to imagine an audience outside the college community, or they were too close to the interviewee to be able to edit ruthlessly enough to produce a concise story. In the final analysis, these early interviews were not surprising or compelling enough to be successful.

The idea for HOMC came from a Wabash staff member, Steve Charles, Editor of the *Wabash Magazine*. Steve had followed my soundwriting course from the beginning and had featured some of the student work on our college website (Paige, 2015) and profiled one audio essay in his blog and in the alumni magazine (Charles, 2014a, 2014b). He stopped by my office one day to ask whether we might get students to do an audio version of what Humans of New York does in image and text.

I was drawn to Steve's idea for Humans of Montgomery County for many reasons, but I'll focus on two. I liked the idea of facilitating for students a positive, genuine, face-to-face conversation with a local community member. Our students have many misconceptions about the town where they attend college and its residents. Could the interview project help correct assumptions and dispel some myths about local residents whom students sometimes derisively call "townies"? Second, I liked the idea of producing a dedicated website for the

DOI: https://doi.org/10.37514/PRA-B.2022.1688.2.19

community about the community. This seemed a way to give back to, rather than simply use, the community for our own educational purposes. Perhaps this project could be something like sustainable storytelling and soundwriting.

Access and Accessibility

As with any course and assignment-sequence design, it is crucial to think about inclusion and Universal Design for Learning (UDL). The challenges and opportunities surrounding accessibility are present in two ways in this assignment sequence.

First is the question of which students can access the technology needed to complete the assignment. There were three ways I provided students access to recording equipment in the course:

- Our Educational Technology Center has a soundbooth where we record the campus podcast and other audio tracks, and I worked with the supervisors of the space to ensure students could reserve time in this booth to record interviews.
- I was also able to apply for a small grant from our Center for Innovation, Business, and Entrepreneurship to purchase Zoom recorders and external microphones for students to record community members. Students checked out these Zoom recorders from me when they wanted them for an assignment.
- My institution's Educational Technology Center has a program where instructors can apply to have an iPad for each student in the course for the length of the semester. Each time I've taught the course, I have been able to issue students iPads to use as recording and listening devices. I use the free application Voice Record Pro as the supported recording software for the class.

I suggest instructors outline two or three ways students can complete the assignment requirements using campus-owned equipment in your syllabus. I've made sure that students have access to the computer lab in the Educational Technology Center (where student workers can assist with software questions) for editing their assignments. The iPads that students use throughout the course and the Macs in the computer lab have GarageBand pre-installed, but my students and I prefer the open-access software Audacity. While most students have some way to record voices on their smartphones and have access to a personal computer for audio editing, I think it is crucial that instructors not assume equal access to recording and editing technology and account for it in some way.

Second is the question of whether audio interviews assume all participants and audience members can hear, and therefore exclude Deaf and hard-of-hearing students. Whether or not you have Deaf or hard-of-hearing students in the class, I think all soundwriting courses should include readings and discussion of how audio reaches and fails to reach certain audiences. I suggest two close-captioned videos for the syllabus.

Early in this course, students watch *Touch the Sound: A Sound Journey with Evelyn Glennie* (Riedelscheimer, 2004), a film about the music-making and musical collaborations of a percussionist who is Deaf. In discussing the film, students note how sound is a bodily experience, rather than simply "an ear thing." Another powerful text for discussing how educational spaces, and the hearing community more broadly, excludes deaf and hard of hearing learners is Brenda Jo Brueggeman's literacy narrative on YouTube, *Why I Mind* (InfoStories, 2011). With these viewing assignments, I show how soundwriting can include the work of writers and artists who hear differently than the majority population. These videos are especially useful for amplifying the abilities of Deaf and hard-of-hearing artists and writers, as well as for introducing the necessity of transcription for making soundwriting inclusive. Other ways instructors might expand this assignment to include Deaf or hard-of-hearing students and interview subjects include the following:

- Allowing students to videotape the interview so that interviewees and subjects can communicate in American Sign Language
- Requiring transcripts of all audio interviews. I have not consistently done so in the past; I will confess that it was something I too easily overlooked when I did not have students in the course who needed hearing accommodations. But I recognize this is also an excuse, and transcripts are something I will require in future iterations of the assignment. Even when students may not be Deaf or hard-of-hearing themselves, the audience members for completed audio interviews may find an audio-only text inaccessible. Creating and requiring transcripts is an excellent opportunity to teach students about the importance of reaching many audiences with their work.

Exploring professional transcription services. They are quite affordable for short interview assignments. For instance, Rev.com charges about $1.00/minute. You might be able to get a small grant from your institution or the community to transcribe interviews, especially when an assignment builds bridges between campus and community, such as this one does. If you do outsource the transcripting, students MUST edit the transcript to make sure it matches the audio; a transcription service saves time, but it is not perfect.

The Soundwriting Assignment and Its Place in the Course

This community-based interview assignment takes up nearly half the semester-long course—though there are certainly ways to condense that timeline. The interview is the second of three major soundwriting assignments in the semester: The first is a single-voiced, unlayered audio essay; the second is the HOMC interview; and the third assignment is a layered creative production of the student's design.

For this assignment, students met with a community member not directly affiliated with the college who had volunteered for an audio interview. Students took the interviewee's photograph, recorded an interview, and then later edited the interview into a 2–3-minute story. The photographs and soundwriting clips were posted on a dedicated *Humans of Montgomery County* website, sometimes after further editing. I would like to do more with the website; I don't feel it got the visibility I was hoping for. In the future, I would like to work with a local library or museum to do a Humans of Montgomery County installation.

Assignment Sequence, Annotated

1. Readings, Listening Assignments, and Reflection to Observe Interview Skills and Frame the Assignment

Below is the main assignment prompt I give students, which gives a brief overview of all 12 of the steps you'll find below.

Humans of Montgomery County Interview Assignment

Audio Rhetoric and Creative Writing

Note: The final draft of this assignment contains an audio component, a photograph, and an alphabetic reflective letter.

Your Assignment

You will work in pairs with a classmate to interview and photograph a resident of Montgomery County who is not closely affiliated with Wabash College. The purpose of the assignment is to have a genuine conversation with someone who has chosen to make their home in Montgomery County and to publish that conversation for all who have access to our collaboratively created Humans of Montgomery County website. Your goal is to edit the interview into a 2–3-minute clip—to produce a "sound paragraph" that tells a story and captures something compelling—human—about your interview subject.

We will spend several weeks in this course preparing for this assignment via readings, listening assignments, practice interviews, and editing/production exercises. But as we break down the Humans of Montgomery County [HOMC] assignment into discrete tasks, let's keep in mind the overarching community-based goals for this assignment.

Three Community-based Goals for this Assignment

1. By meeting people in the local community and recording their stories, you will get to know and understand Crawfordsville and Montgomery County as a community in its own right, not simply as the location of Wabash College.

2. Your interview subjects will get to know a Wabash student one-on-one, in a respectful and intellectually interesting relationship, and their stories will be honored by students and the College through inclusion on the HOMC website.

3. The HOMC website will be a visual and auditory representation of the symbiotic nature of Wabash and Montgomery County.

Due Dates for This Assignment

[I allot approximately one month for full assignment cycle.]

[Begin date] Practice Interview with a Wabash "stranger" is due. Three to 5 minutes.

[Next class] Receive name and contact info for interviewee. Meet with class partner and agree on times you are both available for interviews.

[Before next class] Contact your interviewee and arrange a time and place to meet. Give the interviewee options for meeting place (quiet public space, soundbooth on campus, interviewee's home) and honor their choice.

[Next class] Submit seven to ten interview questions for your interview and two-paragraph rationale for your questions/approach to the interview. Include both discovery (What was it like?) and reflective (What do you think it means?) questions.

[Five days later] Interviews must be recorded and photographs taken by this date. Post full-length interview to Canvas.

[Over the next week] Meet with either Steve Charles, Rich Paige, or Dr. Lamberton for a "production conference" to discuss your raw interview and approach to the edited version.

[One week later] Edited interview (rough draft). Aim for 2–3 minutes. Email your two best photographs to Steve Charles and Dr. Lamberton. **BRING HEADPHONES TO CLASS FOR PEER FEEDBACK.**

[One week later] Final draft of edited interview and Reflective Letter due. **BRING HEADPHONES TO CLASS FOR LISTENING PARTY.**

[Next class] Rough draft of thank-you note due in class. Revise notes and copy to College notecards in class.

Bring interviewee's address if you have it, or let Dr. Lamberton know if you don't. Dr. Lamberton will supply stamps and mail cards.

While I was working out these details, and assembling a list of 15–16 interviewees, I gave students assignments that focused on listening to and reflecting on various audio interview techniques.

Texts I use for these scaffolding assignments vary from year to year, but some of my favorites include a selection from the StoryCorps.org website, Terry Gross's (2011) interview with David Carr, Marc Maron's (2015b) interview with Barack Obama, and Maron's (2015a) interview with Terry Gross. Alex Blumberg's (2014) CreativeLive workshop, titled *Power Your Podcast with Storytelling*, has two helpful episodes, "The Art of the Interview" and "The Power of the Right Question." Finally, the graphic essay *Radio: An Illustrated Guide*, by Jessica Abel and Ira Glass (1999), is helpful for many phases of the interview assignment, from preparing to interviewing to editing. We focus particular attention on Abel and Glass's point about the *visual nature* of audio storytelling and how an interview must help their listeners see the story or scene by asking the right question (1999, pp. 13–14). I follow each of these listening, viewing, or reading assignments with in-class discussion of how interviews work, and I often ask students to post a two-paragraph reflection on Canvas before the class period that focuses their attention on the choices that interviewers make.

Note: The difference between these listening assignment interviews—all long form interviews—and what we eventually asked the students to produce is largely one of length. We asked for 2–3 minutes of produced soundwriting, and in order to honor and foreground the story, most students edited out their own voices. We did, however, fudge the 3-minute limit when we felt we could not do justice to the story without a longer clip. Our rule of thumb was, if it was over 3 minutes, it had to be very good, very tight.

2. Storytelling Website Exploration and Low-stakes Alphabetic Reflection

We also asked students to spend a day exploring the *Humans of New York* website and to post a reflection on an entry (photo + paragraph-length quotation) that they found particularly compelling. One of our explicit instructions was that students should aim for the soundwriting version of a compelling paragraph, a brief narrative moment.

In the second and successive years, we also assigned students to listen to interviews on the Humans of Montgomery County website, so that their peers' soundwriting also became model texts.

3. In-class Session(s) with College Public Relations Team: Interviewing and Photographing, Answering Questions and Troubleshooting

Richard Paige and Steve Charles from our institution's Public Relations office came in as guest experts, and after some lessons and practice with photographing human subjects, Rich plugged his headphones into a Zoom recorder and asked for a student volunteer to be interviewed in front of the class. Rich told the class that he often mentions his own proclivity to make mistakes as a way of making the interviewee more comfortable, and he also suggested keeping the headphones off of one ear so that you look less shielded from the interviewee.

Students were asked to listen for when Rich and the volunteer got to "a story," or at the very least to identify the most interesting thing the volunteer said in the 3–4-minute demonstration. The mock interview helped students see the importance of asking follow up questions. Part of the reason this worked as a demonstration, I think, is that the instructor of record did not conduct the interview; it was conducted by a guest speaker who interviewed people for a living. Though we never asked deeply personal questions, I worry the power dynamic might be uncomfortable if the instructor were interviewing the student. Even if you do not have co-teachers from public relations, you might consider asking a local journalist or other expert to come in for a one-day class session to model interviewing skills.

4. On-campus Audio Interview with a Student They Don't Know

Following Rich's in-class interview, we asked students to find someone on campus (in the gym, in the cafeteria, on the campus mall) and ask if they could interview them for a class assignment. Audio Rhetoric students were instructed to follow Rich's in-class interviewing example, asking questions and then follow-up questions for 5 minutes or so until they thought they had something interesting. Assigning students in the class to interview one another as an in-class assignment, and pairing them with someone they don't know, may be a simpler way to practice interviewing and could avoid concerns about obtaining permission forms for recording strangers.

This assignment helps students work out jitters and test equipment before the higher-stakes interview with the community member and also gives them a chance to reflect on what they think went well and not well about the interview. We spent some of the next class session sharing interview experiences and exchanging strategies and insights. For the on campus "stranger" interview, I simply gave credit for completion.

5. Receive Interview Subjects and Contact Information. Work with Project Partner to Come Up with Initial Interview Questions.

One question Steve, Rich, and I debated the first time we taught this assignment was how much to tell our students about their interview subject before they met.[1] Should we give students a lead on the story, or allow them to discover it for themselves? The first year, we allowed students to draw the name of an interviewee out of a hat, and we decided not to tell them much about their interview subject; we especially didn't want to over-direct the story we wanted them to "get." Then we waited. Would the nursing home resident whose parents had died in a murder-suicide when she was 19 years old and about to depart for college share her story? Would the single mother who had temporarily lost custody of her child due to drug addiction but was now a social worker and rehab leader at her local church talk about her journey of recovery?

In both cases, the answer was "yes." But in subsequent years we decided to do less random pairing of students and interview subjects, and to give the students a few sentences of background about the interviewee that hinted at a story or point of entry for conversation. For example:

---

1.   See this book's companion website for a detailed checklist to help ensure students are prepared for their interviews.

> Has lived in Montgomery County since 1990. Graduate of Southmont High School. Project Manager on a crew that builds grain elevators all over the Midwest for a local company, so he is on the road all year except for the winter. He hires a crew of largely Spanish-speaking migrant workers. Has a teenage daughter and is an Army veteran who was in the 82nd Airborne at Fort Bragg, NC, so he jumped out of planes frequently. Loves video games. Helps care for an adult brother with a disability.

Or:

> Historian for Bethel African Methodist Episcopal Church with a deep knowledge of the church's connection to the underground railroad. Her husband was a Wabash alumnus, and her mother made "soul food dinners" for Wabash students who were brothers of the Malcolm X Institute.

I prefer the less random pairings, where students whose interests or backgrounds align in some way with their interview subject's. For example, a theater major at the college might pair with a woman who has been a leader in local community theater, or a student from a rural town and working-class background might pair with a community member who builds grain storage elevators for a living. Because students are not journalism majors and this is often their first interview assignment, I found some engineering for interests made for more excitement on students' parts going into the interview. Yet because human beings are complex, there were still plenty of surprises and differences among interviewees and students. In any case, other instructors may have very good reasons for taking a less directive approach.

A couple of times, students who had community ties asked if they could choose their own subject. One student had a fraternity brother from town whose father was a paramedic and had many stories of opioid interventions. Another student had worked for a moving service in town and thought his co-worker, a young single father, had a fascinating story. Still another wanted to interview the owner of his favorite Mexican restaurant. In these cases, we were happy to accommodate the students' own suggestions for interview subjects—as long as we talked with them about their interviewee first. I tried to make sure these interview subjects received the same initial explanatory email from me. In all cases, students had to get a signed informed consent letter whether I had successfully contacted the subject or not.

6. Set Up Interview Time and Conduct Interview in Pairs. Take Photograph. Take Informed Consent Letter, Get Required Signatures, and Return Signature Page to Instructor.

It was important to me that students worked in pairs for several reasons. The first is the increased safety and comfort of both students and interviewees. Second, each student had the chance to be a photographer and an interviewer—but didn't have to be both at once. Third, students had a second set of ears during the interview and found their project partner was a resource as they made tough editing decisions or reflected on the meaning of the community-based interaction.[2]

I urged students to let the community member choose the meeting place, among a set of options where there was likely not to be a lot of background noise: in the interviewee's home (or assisted-living unit); on our college campus in the sound booth; or at another neutral space, such as the interviewee's church or the public library. One reason it seemed important to let interviewees select the space is that we wanted them to feel at ease.

My students were also incredibly receptive to etiquette suggestions and tips when it came to meeting their subject for the first time. I did not assume that they would know things like "Be sure to position yourself near the entrance to the public library so your interviewee will have no trouble finding you upon arrival."

7. Upload the Full, Uncut Interview. Upload the Best Two Photographs.

It is important to have the uncut interviews in case you decide the final draft needs further editing before publication and in case the community member later asks for a copy of the interview.

We asked students to submit two photographs. In a few cases, the photographs had to be reshot, but most were suitable—especially the second year after a little more in-class instruction in photography skills.

8. Prepare an Interview Log and Create Storyboard for Interview.

Students resist doing this in great detail, but it is a reverse outlining exercise that allows them to see what they have and see patterns, especially if the interviewee circled back to stories throughout the interview. Abel and Glass's (1999) *Radio: An Illustrated Guide* provides a helpful model and rationale for how to do this (pp. 15–16). In subsequent years, student models may be even more helpful for prompting students to generate the most useful interview logs so they can draft the story.

9. In-class Peer Feedback on Rough Drafts

I give students the following form to guide their peer review in class:

Peer Feedback Form for Rough Draft of Edited HOMC Interview

Student Who Conducted the Interview:

---

2. See this book's companion website for a sample letter and form to give interview subjects. Your institution's IRB may have specific suggestions or requirements.

Reviewer's Name:

After listening to your peer's audio rough draft, answer the following questions. Try to explain your own thinking with specific examples or justifications.

1. What's your favorite part of this interview? Explain.

2. Is it clear what/whom the interviewer and interviewee are referring to all the way through? If not, what specific additions or explanations you would recommend and why?

3. Are there any cuts that don't make sense and maybe something becomes confusing? Explain your questions or responses as a listener.

4. Do you have suggestions about where the narrative can be cut? Explain your thinking.

5. Do you have any suggested revisions for the **sound quality** of this recording? Explain.

These can be done outside of class, but I always do them in class for about an hour and then end with a discussion. Students set up listening stations with hard copies of the peer feedback handout next to their interview draft. The class members and I circulate and listen to the drafts, filling out a feedback form for each story we listen to. I ask students to complete five to six during the hour and direct them a bit to keep them circulating rather than congregating at their friends' story stations so that I can ensure that all students receive about the same amount of peer feedback.

For the last 15 minutes of class, we gather as a group for reflection and discussion. Some of my favorite questions during this wrap-up are the following: 1) What did you hear that you can learn from? 2) What was one of the best things you heard and why? 3) What suggestions do you have for the class collectively about how to revise? 4) What questions do you have for your classmates and me about your next revision steps?

10. Revision Conferences

If you can find the time to meet with students individually to discuss their first drafts and their storyboards (even better—if you have time to listen to the full audio interviews beforehand), I think this revision/editing conference can go a long way toward ensuring the quality of the final edit and minimizing the amount of post-semester editing you may feel you need to do before publishing the story on the website. At a minimum, I do provide students one to two paragraphs of written feedback on their rough drafts.

11. Final Edit and Reflective Letter

Students reflect on their final draft by writing a reflective letter with the following guidelines:

Reflective Letter Assignment on Final Draft Interview, Humans of Montgomery County

After you've completed your final draft of the Humans of Montgomery County Interview, I would like you to write a letter (addressed to me) in which you reflect on what you've learned through the different phases of the assignment.

Remember that one goal of this course is that you increasingly think about *soundwriting as a process* (in all its glory and frustration), rather than hold onto the belief that everything you write as "finished" the moment a deadline arrives. So think of the Reflective Letter as an opportunity to consider and comment on what has happened in this creative process and what it adds to your critical thinking about audio rhetoric.

In your Reflective Letter, you should address the following:

- In one to two sentences, state the main idea of your final interview. What story does it tell?
- Describe the *composing* and editing process used to revise your audio project.
- Discuss what you see as the strengths of the final version in terms of content (ideas, explanations, editing decisions) and style (sound elements, organization, voice, clarity, etc.).
- Which of the response/feedback activities were most useful in writing and revising the recording? If you had more time (or inclination), what would you add to or change in this project?
- What have you discovered about soundwriting, the craft of interviewing, and perhaps even about yourself more generally through this project?
- What questions remain for you as you submit this recording? These might be specific questions for your interviewee, for me, or they may be more general questions about the process of soundwriting.

As a final word of explanation and caution, let me say that the Reflective Letter need not and should not be an "advertisement" for your project. I am looking for your evolving ability to think about soundwriting and the task of inviting others to share their stories, that is, how and why it works—or doesn't!—in certain situations.

I look forward to reading your Reflective Letter and your revision of the audio assignment! As always, please let me know if you have questions about this assignment. I'll be happy to help as much as I can.

I make the final draft due about a week after the first draft, but if you can afford the time for individual revision conferences, I think it makes sense to give students more time to revise (so that they can meet with you and then have time to process and implement your ideas and theirs).

The reflective letters serve two main purposes. First, they encourage students to reflect the soundwriting process as a way of solidifying what they've learned. Second, the letters allow me to gauge the students' individual responses to the Humans of Montgomery County Project, their comfort and their recommendations for whether to continue the project—and why.

12. Thank-you Note

I find these notes are an important element of increasing good will among students and community members, and I also happen to think my students get a bonus life-skills lesson in how to write a meaningful note of thanks.[3] I devote part of a class session to revising drafts of the thank-you notes as a way to signify its importance to the project. Saying thank you is not an afterthought; instead, it is an extension of the goodwill built into the project.

I use department funds to purchase stamps for the notes and mail them myself, to ensure each community member receives one. One community member told me he called and left a voicemail for the college president about the quality of our students upon receiving the note.

Sample Student Projects

In the initial iterations of this project, we did not require transcriptions of the audio interviews.[4] This was a mistake, something I simply failed to think about, and upon reflection, we missed a valuable opportunity to engage students in conversation about the importance of universal design. In future iterations of the project, I will require transcriptions.

1. "Don't Be the One That's the Life Sucker" by Austin Myers
2. "Struck by Lightning" by Brent Poling
3. "Growing Up with a Handicapped Sibling, Kids Can be Cruel" by Zachary Kintz
4. "The People Like It Here. It's Real Mexican Food" by Noah Levi
5. "We Had Some Really Great Nurses and Some Really Bad Ones" by Dylan Seikel

Reflection

Jaleel Grandberry: This has been one of my favorite classroom projects here at Wabash. I really enjoyed the process of going out into the surrounding community and meeting new people.[5] In my letter to my interviewee, I talked about how, as students of Wabash, we can often separate ourselves from Crawfordsville and Montgomery County. I feel projects like this are really beneficial in getting students to break out of the box and have the opportunity to meet great people of

---

3. See this book's companion website for a template assignment to guide students in drafting thank-you notes.

4. Five student examples (audio files and descriptive transcripts) can be found on the book's companion website.

5. The audio version of L. Jill Lamberton's reflection can be found on the book's companion website.

the community. From experiences like this, not only do we build connections, but we better understand our surrounding community. We see how we can continue to help impacting the community, or how the community impacts us.

Jill Lamberton: That's my student, Jaleel. The assignment he's referring to is an interview with a local community member whom he'd never met before. My name is Jill Lamberton. I teach in the English Department at Wabash College in Crawfordsville, Indiana. Crawfordsville is in Montgomery County, and for the past couple of years, my audio rhetoric students have been conducting audio interviews with community members who are not formally affiliated with the college. Once our students have recorded these conversations—and many of them run between 30 and 90 minutes—I ask the students to create a log of the interview and to edit it into one story, something like an audio paragraph. I tell them to aim for 2 to 3 minutes, though students frequently end up with final drafts that run as long as 4 or 5 minutes in order to honor the story.

Eventually, we post the story and a photograph of the interviewee on a dedicated website we call *Humans of Montgomery County*. It's a project we've modeled on Brandon Stanton's enormously successful *Humans of New York*. So, I've had two collaborators in teaching this unit. They're talented journalists from our college's public relations team.

Rich Paige: My name is Richard Paige. I am the Associate Director of Communications and Marketing at Wabash College.

Steve Charles: I'm Steve Charles. I'm the editor of *Wabash Magazine*.

Rich: How long have you been helping people tell their stories?

Steve: *[laughs]* Um, let me see. First time was probably recording my grandparents when I was in high school. I was 14, so that would be about 48 years. How about you, Rich?

Rich: You've got me beat by a couple of decades there. I've only been doing this full-time for about 25 years now.

Jill: I asked them to help for two reasons. First, they tell stories for a living. As members of the PR department, their stories are designed to keep the college community connected to itself. I thought I could learn something from them, and second, I knew my students would respond well to having interview experts as guest lecturers.

Frankly, I was hoping I might get a class session or two out of Rich and Steve, but I asked if they'd be co-teachers for the whole unit, and they said yes. Having the right collaborators infused this assignment with all kinds of life, even if it also came with a bit of attitude.

Rich: *[jokingly]* It's hard to be serious when everybody else in the room is not!

Steve: *[laughter]* That was a good one. *[sarcastically]* That's for you, Jill!

Rich: *[sarcastically, as if impersonating Jill's response]* Screw you guys! *[laughs]*

Jill: We had two major learning outcomes for the community interview assignment, and I'll tell you what they are, even though I realize they may sound crazy-ambitious. First, we wanted to teach our students to be better listeners.

Steve: A stereotype of guys in this age group is that they talk a lot but don't listen, and so what we wanted to do was teach them to listen.

Jill: Second, we wanted to see if we could improve the town-gown relationships by getting people to sit down together and tell stories.

Steve: This town-gown thing here is pretty interesting and sometimes strained, and it seemed like stories is a real good way to break through barriers. A way for people to realize that we had much more in common.

Rich: That was what was interesting about it to me. We were going to try to arm the students with the skills necessary to collect these things and then send them out into the community and do it.

Jill: It might be useful to know a bit more about our context. So, Wabash College is one of three remaining all-male colleges in the United States. The other two are Hampden-Sydney in Virginia and Morehouse in Atlanta, in case you're wondering. Our student body is small, under 1,000, and though my students come from all over the US and from around the world, about 75% of them are Hoosiers. Those of us who work at Wabash know it's a place where young men defy cultural stereotypes about college-aged men way more often than they confirm them. It's a fascinating place to teach, but that's a topic for a different audio essay.

So, about the town: Crawfordsville is a town of about 16,000 in the corn and soybean fields of west-central Indiana. The young people who grow up here, and those who attend college here, have a tendency to see their futures shining most brightly somewhere else. Yet, there are many who choose to stay in Crawfordsville, and those of us who live here know scores of local residents who are thoughtful, educated, big-hearted, human beings. We wanted our students to see more of that.

In the alphabetic part of this chapter, I outline all the scaffolding steps we took and share several assignment handouts, so I won't repeat myself here. Instead, what I want to emphasize right now is how impressed I was, even touched, by how much the students *wanted* to do a good job with these interviews.

Steve: Yeah. The level of buy-in . . . I mean, right from the beginning. I think that was one of my hesitations. I mean, for anybody who Jill is trying to talk about this program, where you think the students might not really want to do it, *they wanted to do it*.

Jill: The students worked really hard, perhaps especially after they had met with the community member and felt a responsibility to tell their story well. But they worked hard beforehand too. Here's one of my students, Zach.

Zach Kintz: I was super-nervous for the whole thing in the beginning. As for preparing for the interview, I did a lot of work in the recording booth. I received help from a senior who helped me understand the equipment. I spent at least three hours getting comfortable in the booth before my interview. The day of the interview, I got into the recording booth about an hour and 30 minutes before my interview to set everything up and to test the sound levels.

Jill: Zach interviewed a community member named Cory Thrush who talked about his older brother, Rob, who has an intellectual disability. Cory explained that, at 50, Rob's mind is more like that of a 12-year-old.

Cory Thrush: One of the tough things about growing up with a handicapped sibling: Kids can be very cruel. I spent a lot of my younger years growing up with Rob getting into fights defending him, and getting my butt kicked by older kids. It shaped me from the sense that I have zero patience for people that make fun of handicapped, disabled, special-needs people. I'm a pretty calm guy, pretty laid-back. Situations that involve stuff like that, I, I, there's no place for it. I tend to look at people like that, that there's something missing in you. If you can make fun of somebody like that, or be cruel to somebody like that, you're missing a human part that I don't know how to give you or how to teach you.

Zach: As for the interview itself, I thought it went very well. I'm not sure if it was my connection with him about handicapped siblings, or just the context itself. The conversation between Cory and I was deep and meaningful. Honestly, the interview highlighted one of the best moments of my short time here at Wabash. After I had my interview recorded, I knew exactly what story I wanted to pursue. The story of his brother, and how it shaped him as a person really needed to be told.

Jill: If the first part of this project was about developing interviewing skills and making a human connection, the soundwriting portion came in the editing and production phase. After the students had completed their final drafts, I asked them to write a reflective letter in which they articulate their soundwriting process and what they think they learned from the unit. The reflective letters tend to highlight one of the reasons I'm a born-again soundwriting teacher. Here's the thing: After 20 years of teaching traditional college writing classes where I urge students to put voice in their writing and, especially, trying to get them to grasp the power of deep revision, I'm amazed at how my audio rhetoric students get editing. I mean, listen to the kinds of things they say about the time and the care they put into their final drafts. First, here's Jaleel.

Jaleel: I believe I ultimately captured the story. However, the process of doing so was very tedious. Audio editing is a great tool, but through this project I learned the many challenges of it. I see how time consuming it actually is as you work toward that perfect cut and capturing the best sound. Spending hours in GarageBand cutting and dragging different clips to try and create the best narrative was a very patient part of this project. Luckily, throughout the process, we had the help of our peers, as well as Dr. Lamberton and Mr. Charles. This was really beneficial as we could get another ear on our project. In times where we may have just thought it sounded good enough because we were tired of editing, the extra ear was able to provide unbiased advice, helping the overall quality of the projects.

Jill: And here's Zach:

Zach: The final audio clip has about 20 different splits in it. The hardest part of it all was getting the audio to flow like natural talking. Sometimes, in between two splits, there wasn't a long-enough pause, and it sounded choppy, so what I found, was finding his natural pauses in different parts of the interview and just squeezing it in between the clips. At one split, the pause wasn't enough, so I had to search the whole audio clip to find an "and," "um," or a "but," to have it sound natural.

Jill: I mean—thoughtful, if painful, editing choices; collaboration and tapping into a writing community; remaining faithful to the story even when you're tired of it and feel like quitting. . . . *It's all there.*

But I'll be honest and say that after we received the students' final drafts, Steve and I did find ourselves doing more editing before we were ready to post them on the website, especially in the first year of teaching the unit.

Steve: What particular challenges or pitfalls do we need to consider when doing this? Time! How much time it took on the back end. The first year, Jill and I both doing a lot of editing after the students.

Rich: The work on the back end is going to take more time than you expect in any given year. More so in the first year than any.

Steve: The second year, either it was just the guys had more familiarity with their program, the editing was stronger.

Jill: One of my comp-rhet mentors once told me, "I always have to teach something once before I know how to teach it." That was certainly true of this assignment. Part of the reason I think students' essays were closer to publication quality in the second year is that we were better able to articulate what we were looking for and what made a good Humans of Montgomery County audio clip. Students in the second year could also listen to the previous year's examples as guidelines.

But, again, even in the first year, our students' engagement with the project, and the community members' reports of the interviews, made us feel good about the work.

Rich: As far as the students go, I mean that, the ability to listen was immense in our students. To see those guys go through that process and really tune in to what was there, was impressive.

Jill: We feel pretty satisfied that, for the 30 or so people who participated in this project each year, we were able to complicate their impressions of each other. For Zach, who took the course as a first-year student while he was still finding his way at the college, the project had personal benefits:

Zach: Overall, I loved this project. The idea of extracting stories from people excites me. I'm a very quiet person, but, on an intimate level, I love to talk. The experience of this project has made me a better talker, listener, and audio editor. I'm quite sad to have this project behind me now because I would love to do another one.

Jill: Steve and Rich said they felt reinvigorated in their day jobs after spending time in the classroom and listening to the students' productions. Perhaps most gratifying, we were all reminded of the ways that storytelling and careful listening are still the building blocks of community.

Rich: I don't know how to properly quantify it, as to who got more out of this? To see the guys do so well and to engage in the project and sort of in the way that we envisioned was really rewarding.

Steve: Yeah. And as a storyteller, to watch them embrace it . . .

Rich: *[in agreement]* Oh!

Steve: . . . and watch them realize how rewarding this is and how cool this is, I found I really believed this stuff! Like, I really believe stories are really important.

Rich: What do you think the project did for the community members?

Steve: Well I *know*. I mean, I talked to several of them. It changed their perception of our students. A lot of the kind of stereotypes of what, certainly a male college student, is, fell for several of these people. Even people who kind of knew the college were surprised at their ability to sit there and listen. The idea that these guys came and listened and they were polite. You could tell that they wanted to hear the stories, so for that community member, it changed that perception. Also, it did what we hoped, which was it honored them. They felt honored. They felt like they mattered, because they *do*.

Acknowledgments

Funding for audio recording equipment for the Humans of Montgomery County project was generously provided by a Lilly-Endowment Mini Grant through the Center for Business Innovation and Entrepreneurship at Wabash College, with additional funds from the Wabash College Rhetoric Department.

References

Abel, J. & Glass, I. (1999). *Radio: An illustrated guide*. WBEZ Radio.

Blumberg, A. (2014). Power your podcast with storytelling. *CreativeLive*. https://www.creativelive.com/class/power-your-podcast-storytelling-alex-blumberg.

Charles, S. (2014a, September 7). Students tell their stories. *Wabash Magazine*. https://blog.wabash.edu/magazine/2014/09/07/students-tell-their-stories/.

Charles, S. (2014b). Telling their own stories. *Wabash Magazine*, Spring, 68–69. https://issuu.com/wabash_college/docs/___wm_spring_3 .

Gross, T. (Host). (2011, October 27). David Carr: The news diet of a media omnivore [Audio podcast episode]. On *Fresh Air*. https://www.npr.org/programs/fresh-air/2011/10/27/141754757/.

InfoStories. (2011, February 17). Why I mind with Brenda Jo Brueggeman with subtitles [Video file]. *YouTube*. https://youtu.be/RoNR6EWT7D4 .

Maron, M. (2015a, May 23). Marc Maron interviews Terry Gross, Letterman's producer [Audio podcast episode]. In *Fresh Air Weekend*. https://www.npr.org/programs/fresh-air/2015/05/23/408462278/fresh-air-for-may-23-2015 .

Maron, M. (2015b, June 22). President Barack Obama (No. 613) [Audio podcast episode]. In *WTF with Marc Maron*. http://www.wtfpod.com/podcast/episodes/episode_613_-_president_barack_obama .

Paige, R. (Host). (2015, May 15). Audio rhetoric (No. 53) [Audio podcast episode]. In *Wabash on My Mind*. http://wabashcollege.libsyn.com/episode-53-audio-rhetoric.

Riedelscheimer, T. (Director). (2004). *Touch the sound: A sound journey with Evelyn Glennie* [Film]. New Video Group.

Stanton, B. (n.d.). *Humans of New York*. Retrieved January 31, 2018, from http://www.humansofnewyork.com .

Stanton, B. (2013). *Humans of New York*. St. Martin's Press.

Stanton, B. (2015). *Humans of New York: Stories*. St. Martin's Press.

Wabash College. *(2015). Humans of Montgomery County*. https://blog.wabash.edu /humans/.

Chapter 20. The Sound(s) of Sustainable Stewardship: Composing Audio Essays with the JHFE

Janice W. Fernheimer
UNIVERSITY OF KENTUCKY

Featuring Madison Cissell, Hannah Thompson,
Hannah Newberry, and Laura Will

Since 2013, I have worked with Doug Boyd, Director of the Louie B. Nunn Center for Oral History at the University of Kentucky (UK hereafter) and Sarah Dorpinghaus, UK Director of Digital Services, to develop pedagogical strategies for introducing undergraduates to oral histories, primary archival research, and the production of audio essays composed to share such primary materials with broader, public audiences. Early collaborations detailed in our 2015 *Oral History Review* essay "Indexing as Engaging Oral History Research: Using OHMS to 'Compose History' in the Writing Classroom" (Boyd et al., 2015) showcased the value of teaching students to create digital indexes for oral histories using the cutting-edge, open-source platform designed by the Nunn Center, OHMS (the oral history metadata synchronizer). Since 2015, our team has expanded to include Dr. Beth L. Goldstein and to further develop this pedagogical model for undergraduate research engagement alongside our design and establishment of the Jewish Heritage Fund for Excellence (JHFE) Jewish Kentucky Oral History Project. Although the JHFE-funded project was initially imagined to collect, archive, and index 55 oral histories of Jewish Kentuckians over three years, we've now collected 120+ oral histories representing the diversity, depth, and complexities of Kentucky Jewish experiences across the Commonwealth, and the project continues to grow.

To enable this tremendous growth, our team built "sustainable stewardship" into the project's design. Described more fully in our 2018 *Oral History Review* article, "Sustainable Stewardship: A Collaborative Model for Engaged Oral History Pedagogy, Community Partnership, and Archival Growth" (Fernheimer et al., 2018), sustainable stewardship engages undergraduates in "original knowledge production while simultaneously fostering archival access and growth" while also providing a method "to connect the classroom, community, and the archive in enduring, mutually beneficial, and transformative ways" (p. 321). With sustainable stewardship guiding our pedagogy, students are involved at every step of the oral history process, from making extant interviews more searchable and accessible by creating digital indexes using OHMS, to conducting their own

DOI: https://doi.org/10.37514/PRA-B.2022.1688.2.20

original oral histories with Jewish community members, to contextualizing those interviews with further research to create compelling audio essays to introduce a broader public to the interviews and the issues they raise. At each step, students became attuned to the power and importance of critical listening—to make content more accessible, to generate strong interviews, and to create engaging audiocasts which contextualize the oral histories for broader public audiences. The sustainable element hinges on students' work with us to both index extant interviews and conduct their own original oral histories which then become part of the collection (to be indexed by another set of students at a later date). We found that the indexing work attunes their ears and sensibilities to the sounds of successful interviewing, thus enabling them to conduct better original oral histories themselves. The research they perform both to conduct and contextualize these interviews also prepares them to produce the "sounds of sustainable stewardship," evoked in this chapter's title: a 10–15-minute collaboratively authored, *This American Life*-style, audio essay final project. Student work from this project was presented at the Southern Jewish Historical Society in Cincinnati on November 5, 2017, the Kentucky Jewish Historical Symposium at the University of Kentucky on April 12–13, 2018, and the Kentucky Jewish History Symposium 2 in April 2019. By learning to compose with the "sounds of sustainability," students engaged with oral histories in a variety of ways, becoming increasingly aware of their own active participation in the creation and processing of public, living history. By approaching first-year writing in this way, with attuned focus on listening through sustained immersive work with oral histories from a specific local community students might not otherwise encounter, our team aimed to increase their critical listening and awareness of the way writing shapes history, who has access to it, and how those historical narratives in turn shape other types of collective identities. We also aimed to facilitate ethical interactions with the local Jewish community, thus allowing students to learn by listening, interacting, and collaborating with their peers and local community members.

What follows here is a brief explanation of the assignment sequence, introduction to select assignment prompts, and, on the book's companion website, some sample student work produced for the final audio essay. The overall course design, syllabus, and daily schedule for this honors, first-year writing course Writing Jewish Kentucky can be found at http://wrd112.fernheimer.org. The assignment sequence was designed to provide students with an introduction to the various ways composition and rhetorical selection work across several genres and media, including oral history, print-based rhetorical analyses, public oral presentation, oral history interview protocols and interviews, public audio essays, and print-based, individually authored, self-reflective essays. First, students worked with a peer to engage in important listening exercises to authenticate a professionally produced written transcript and create an index for an oral history interview. Next, students used the collaborative indexes they created to aid them in individually authoring a rhetorical analysis of the identity work that oral histories perform.

In-Class Collaborative Invention Interlude

After students completed draft indexes and rhetorical analyses, I introduced Projects 3 and 4. The whole class engaged in a "speed-teaming" activity for collaborative rhetorical invention, where they shared themes, issues, and/or questions that arose and determined research questions and queries they might pursue in larger teams. After speed-teaming, students formed larger teams (of at least four students) to complete Projects 3 and 4, with the idea that the original oral history they conduct would further develop the research questions (or context) guiding their final audio essay.

Project 3: Original Oral History Interview and Collaborative Annotated Bibliography

In these projects, students work in teams of two or three to select an interviewee, schedule a time, create an interview protocol based on the JHFE project template but tailored to their interviewee, and conduct an original oral history interview, which elicits and records an abbreviated life-history style "primary document" from the interviewee that then becomes part of the JHFE collection housed at the Nunn Center. They also work in larger teams of four to six students to generate an annotated bibliography to research issues they are interested in presenting in their final, team-authored audio essay. Then they individually reflect on the process of working with each other and a community member to conduct an original oral history and further research.

Project 4: Final Audio Essay

In this final project, students work in larger teams (of four to six) to create a 10–15-minute *This American Life*-style audio essay that combines and contextualizes at least four oral histories the students engaged with over the course of the semester; they then reflect individually on the composing and collaboration processes for creating this final project. Additionally, they give a final team presentation to the class to share their composing insights from this project with a broader audience. This team presentation forms the basis for more public presentations when students are selected to participate in national conferences.

The sustainable stewardship model mutually benefits students, the Nunn Center, and the local Jewish community through its facilitation of engaged interactions based around the shared responsibilities of listening, storytelling, collaborative composition, and public history preservation and access. Although this chapter focuses specifically on the way this method was used in partnership with the local Lexington Jewish community and the University of Kentucky, the sustainable stewardship model for introducing oral history and composition into the classroom could be used in any classroom where the instructor has strong community ties to facilitate student-community member interactions. Teaching writing through critical listening, summary metadata authoring, and the creation of public oral histories enables students to interact with community members one-on-one and to recognize that their own writing has real impact on historical preservation and access. Whether through listening to and indexing already recorded interviews or conducting their own, students encounter the voices of others within and outside the class confines. This opportunity to engage others ethically (especially community members they might not otherwise encounter) asks them to listen carefully and is one they often describe as transformative. Hearing the actual voice of another and then later working in an interview to elicit another's stories changed how these students thought about research, history, writing, and the role of listening and representation in each. Focusing on how metadata tells stories about stories and how interviewing relies on listening to elicit compelling narratives teaches students about the way voices and listening matter. Such critical listening and careful attention to the intimacy of voice helps students find their own on issues of historical representation and local public histories while also allowing them to contribute to the historical record beyond the classroom confines. They emerge from class with well-honed composition skills in summary, information literacy, and local history along with familiarity with new communities fostered by the intimate interactions working with voice facilitates. Such interactions highlight human connection and emotion and bring public history into the lived, experienced, high impact pedagogy of undergraduate research.

Assignments

Here I provide the explanation for the final project(s) overview and separate, detailed assignment prompts for Project 3, Project 3B, Project 4A (the Draft Script), and the Final Reflection. Note: As the instructor of record and as a member of this community, I reached out to individuals before the class began to make sure they were both willing to be interviewed and able to work within the tight time constraints of the semester rhythm. I also provided a list of these individuals that included their names and topics I thought they might be able to address, so that students could select an individual based on their own research interests.

Final Project(s) 3 and 4 Overview: Going Public with Oral History

Final Group Audio Essay Assignment due in Week 15 (Projects 3 and 4)

This project is worth 55% of your total grade for the course broken up in these ways:

Project 3: Oral History Interview Collection: 20%

- Interview/questions: 10%
- Collaboration: 5%
- Reflection of three to four pages: 5%

Collaborative Oral-History Based Final Project (either audio essay or short video documentary): 30%

- Team Contract/Plan: 5%
- Project 3B: Annotated Bibliography/Research: 5%
- Project 4A: Draft Script 5%
- Project 4B: Rough Cut 10%
- Final Reflection: 5%

Final Team Oral Presentation: 5%

Overview

Working in teams of four to five, you will produce a 10–15-minute *This American Life-* or *Radiolab*-style audio essay. Initially, you will work as a group to discuss the interviews you worked on during the semester, decide on some themes/ideas/issues that they touch upon and that you will research further together, decide on a target audience (or audiences) for your podcast, strategize how to frame them in a cohesive way, and create a schedule and series of task assignments for group members. In order to produce this collaborative work, you will work together on several smaller steps.

First, you will further divide into smaller groups within your whole team. Each smaller group of two to three will work together to create questions and conduct an original oral history interview, write an annotated bibliography, and write individual reflective essays on this process. Once each smaller team has completed annotated bibliographies, you will work as a larger team to create the collaborative final audio essay project.

At two points in the project, you will turn in reflective essays—after conducting the oral history interview/drafting the annotated bibliography essay and at the end of the project. These essays will reflect on the process of transforming audio interview into narrative audio story, researching historical context, working with a partner or two to conduct an oral history interview, and working with others to make these stories truly publicly accessible. There are separate prompts for these reflective essays.

The Rationale

We've been working with these oral history materials all semester, and though they are fascinating in and of themselves, they will reach a much broader audience if you can interpret them to tell a story. Now that you've both indexed and rhetorically analyzed them, your job in this assignment is to work with your team to create a compelling audio or video narrative that features them. Your team will work to deepen a public audience's understanding of the interviews by carefully combining them both with other interviews and with the narrative segues and historical context that will make them into a cohesive story. Though they appear to you "out of context," your job is to work with your team to enable a broader audience to make sense of them by putting them in context. This is no easy feat, so I've broken it into several smaller, more manageable chunks, as indicated by the list of assignments above and the "nitty gritty" below.

The important skills you're working to develop in this project are research, collaboration, and synthesis for a specific, public audience.

The Nitty Gritty

Your first step will be to think about the things that make your interview interesting and think about the larger stories it helps to tell. To help you identify team members, you will have a chance to "showcase" your interview and listen to your colleagues in some "speed-teaming" style mixers. Once you form teams of four to six, together your group will create a work plan to help you complete the necessary research and composing for your final project. Your next step will be to research and write your team-authored annotated bibliography based on the oral histories you indexed and the original oral history interview you conducted, placing them in a broader context that reflects the theme or idea that your group has chosen to explore in the podcast. (You'll find more specific instructions for completing these smaller group assignments under Project 3: Original Oral History Interview and Project 3B: Annotated Bibliography). Once you've completed your original oral history interview and your annotated bibliographies, you will work with your larger group to create a cohesive radio show episode. To complete this task successfully, your group will write a title for your podcast, a short introduction to your show, short transitions between the pieces in the show, and a conclusion to your show. You will be allowed some class time for the planning, but you should use this time to create a schedule of deadlines for these parts of the assignment and divide up the labor evenly between group members.

You will download Audacity (it's free!) onto your computer and use it to record and edit your audio essays. The podcasts will incorporate sound bites from the interview as well as other sound effects that add depth, dimension, affect, or comic relief to your stories.

(Credit to Emilee Egbert for coining the term "speed-teaming.")

Tips for Getting Started (Invention!)

Since you're likely pretty familiar (and in fact a resident expert!) on the interview assigned to you, you may already know how you want to approach this project and which aspects of historical context you wish to research. I suggest that you read through and complete the Project Speed-Team handout and that you read through and think about the questions raised by the Turning Interview into Story Handout. We will formally complete this exercise later in the semester, once you've done some research, but you may find it helpful in shaping the way you approach your research. Since you all have listened to more than one interview from the Nunn Center's Jewish collections, feel free to choose which one you want to focus on for these final projects.

Your interview will be assigned from following list:

- Ethnicity in Lexington (Multi-Culturality) Oral History Project
- Lexington Jewish Community Oral History Project
- JHFE Jewish Kentucky Oral History Collection

Research

Since a large part of this assignment depends on the strength of the contextualizing research you complete, you might begin to investigate the following resources put together by Sarah Dorpinghaus in Special Collections: https://tinyurl.com/SCRCJewish

Project 3: Original Oral History Interview and Interviewing Reflection[1]

Overview: Working in small teams of two or three you will work together to do two types of original research. First you will identify a community member to interview, contact him or her, and schedule a time to conduct the interview. Then you will create an original interview protocol based on the template I provide and tailored to meet the needs of your group and the experiences of your interviewee. Second, you will follow the directions for creating an annotated bibliography to further research the questions your larger team is investigating to better contextualize the interviews you indexed and you conducted.

The Basics

Pair Portion: In order to produce this collaborative work, each small group of two to three students will do three important things.

1. Conduct an original Oral History Interview that will become part of the JHFE Jewish Kentucky Collection.
2. Research and write an annotated bibliography of no less than six to eight contextual, scholarly resources to help you develop knowledge and shape your perspectives on the research topic questions. (Each person is responsible for a minimum of two sources.)
3. Write an individual reflection essay about the process of collaborating with your peers on the interview/research/writing of this portion of the project.

First, you will identify some issues that you wish to explore/include in your collaborative piece, then you will identify an appropriate interviewee from the provided list, and next you'll conduct an oral history to deepen the context. You will work together to both create the interview questions and schedule/conduct the interview.

The Rationale

You've been working with oral history interviews all semester, and I hope by now you've realized how valuable they are for complicating the historical record. Now it is your chance to conduct an original oral history interview that will become part of the JHFE Jewish Kentucky Oral History Collection. This assignment serves two important functions:

---

1.   The Interview Protocol that Janice W. Fernheimer provides to students can be found on the book's companion website.

1. It helps you conduct necessary outside research to contextualize and deepen our understanding of the oral histories you've been working with all semester, thus enriching the narrative you'll tell in the final audio essay.

2. It helps build and sustain the collection itself by furthering the scope of material included within.

For this small-group interviewing assignment, the goal of the assignment is to help you learn more about primary and secondary research, to create and conduct an original oral history interview, develop the ability to synthesize and analyze resources in order to better contextualize interviews, and eventually create a compelling, contextualized narrative for a public audience.

The Nitty Gritty

Resources/Potential Interviewees

The Nunn Center recording studio is available to you as are several professional-quality audio recorders. To schedule a time to use the professional recording studio, email Kopana Terry and Doug Boyd in the Nunn Center with your scheduling requests. In addition to allowing for professional quality audio, the Nunn Center staff will work with you to ensure that the recording devices are set up and used properly. The interview you collect must be accompanied by a signed Nunn Center release form (downloadable from our Canvas site under files), so it can be added to the Jewish Kentucky Oral History Collection, thus building and expanding the repository. (You will not be tasked with indexing it, but future students will, so it will become searchable and accessible.)

A list is available on our Canvas site of local community leaders and participants have already agreed to make themselves available for an oral history for the purposes of this class and the larger JHFE Jewish Kentucky Oral History Project. You are not limited to selecting from this list, but I did want to provide you with contacts who are already amenable to participating in the project. If you have other ideas of potential interviewees, please discuss them with me and we'll determine if it is feasible to complete the interviews in the timeframe you need.

Possible themes to flesh out with the interviewees:

- Jewish community life in Lexington
- Experiences as a rabbi in a mid-size, Southern town
- Contemporary perspectives on Jewish student life at UK (Hillel, Jewish fraternity/sorority life)
- Women's leadership roles
- Generational issues within the Jewish community: attitudes toward Israel, Holocaust memory/education, others?

Other possible lines of inquiry:

- Hadassah and Lexington Jewish women's national prominence in this organization
- Jewish summer camp in Kentucky
- B'nai B'rith Organization

Scheduling

It is best for your team to find several times that work for your group first, then reach out to Kopana Terry at the Nunn Center to reserve these slots in the studio. After you have a tentative hold on the studio times, reach out to your interviewee to see what (if any) of the slots work for them. Use the template below to contact them by email. Note: you want to reach out as soon as you can, as scheduling is often a challenge for all parties involved.

Template for Contacting Potential Interviewee:

Dear Mr./ Ms./ Dr. /Professor /Rabbi_____:

Hello, we are A and B, students in Dr. Fernheimer's WRD 112: Writing Jewish Kentucky course this semester. We've been listening to and learning from interviews in the Lexington Jewish Community and Jewish Heritage Fund for Excellence Jewish Kentucky Collections all semester, and as part of our final project, we hope to conduct an oral history with you that will become part of the JHFE Jewish Kentucky Collection. Our group is interested in contextualizing X issue, learning more about Y, hoping to learn more about Q. . . . [tailor to your needs!]

We would like to schedule a morning or afternoon with you to conduct what we hope will be a 1.5–2.5-hour interview to take place in the Nunn Center for Oral History's professional studio on the UK campus. Which of the following windows is most convenient for you? [You should find some slots that work for both students and the Nunn Center's availability and offer a minimum of three windows for the interviewee to choose from.] If none of these times work with your schedule, please provide some windows that do.

Sincerely,

Student A and Student B

*Note: You can offer the interviewee a free parking space on campus if you coordinate with Marie Daley in the Nunn Center and/or with me, as I have an arrangement with the Boone Center. It is important that if your interviewee parks on campus, one representative from your team should meet him/her in the parking lot and escort them to the recording studio, as they are not likely to be familiar with how to navigate campus.

Once you've scheduled the interview, you want to begin working on the protocol right away.

How to Get Started

You may have noticed that all interviews for the JHFE Jewish Kentucky Oral History Collection incorporated some similar questions. I'll provide you with the general protocol template we used for developing the first section of questions based on Jewish life and community. Usually, the second part of the interview was focused more on the person's unique professional or communal contributions. You will be responsible for working with your peers and creating a complete protocol (selecting and reformulating appropriate questions for Parts 1 and 2), which is due in class on October X. You will receive feedback and revise the questions (if necessary) before you conduct the interview. In our experience, such interview protocols are revised at least two to three times before Dr. Goldstein and I sign off on them. Of course, if you end up scheduling your actual interview earlier than that, you'll want to make sure you get your protocol approved by Dr. Jan before the interview takes place.

Project 3B: Annotated Bibliography

In order to be well prepared to draft your transcript for the final audiocast, you'll need to conduct some research to help you better understand the context (historical, cultural, etc.) of the research question your group hopes to answer with your project.

Each large team will turn in one big annotated bibliography as a Google Doc that is shared with me.

Each person is responsible for authoring two annotations of 250–500 words each. The annotations should include a full MLA citation for the source (and a link or PDF attachment posted to the appropriate forum on Canvas), a summary of the scholarly argument made in the source, a description of the way the information or argument helps to advance your project, and one to two sentences about how you hope to use/cite the material in your project. Alternatively, if after reading it, you feel it is no longer relevant to your project, please explain why.

Groups of four will provide no fewer than eight annotated sources. Groups of five will provide no fewer than 10 annotated sources, and groups of six will provide no fewer than 12 annotated sources. You are welcome to include additional annotations as two per team member is the minimum.

Project 4A: Final Audio Essay Script

For this assignment, you want to create a full-length working script for the audio essay you will record. For a 10–15-minute audio essay, you will need approximately five to seven written pages. (Most people read one typewritten page of about 250 words every 2 minutes.)

Before you begin drafting, you'll want to answer the following questions as part of your group *invention*:

Topic:

Research Question:

Way that your proposed audiocast or short documentary answers the research question:

What is your rhetorical purpose in making the audio essay? Do you hope to inform a specific audience about a particular issue or little-known fact about Kentucky Jewish communities? Do you hope to raise awareness of a specific Kentucky Jewish custom or practice? Something else? Specify.

Who is your audience? What can you presume they might reasonably know or understand about what you hope to communicate? What will you have to teach/explain? What is the best arrangement/organization of the material to ensure listenability and audience engagement?

Remember, in order to make life easier for yourselves when it comes time to actually record the audio essay, you want to have the most well articulated script you can. You want to make notes about what types of sounds you want to include, what kinds of voice emphasis you hope to have, what pacing/tempo you want to use for both, and what other audio effects you plan to include—music, sound effects? Which ones?

You have the added requirement that your audio essay needs to include clips from some of the interviews you indexed or conducted (clips from a minimum of four to five separate interviews), and they need to be appropriately introduced and framed to show how they fit into the larger story your group is telling. You also want to draw from the research you conducted for the annotated bibliography and include it as well. It is likely you will need to do additional research once you have a more clearly defined idea of your audio essay and how you want to frame it.

Remember all the things you noted when we listened to audio essays/podcasts in class and keep them in mind as you plan:

- Voice emphasis matters—both the way it emphasizes (is it monotone, does it get louder, softer, something else?) and how fast someone speaks (i.e., tempo).

- The tempo, pacing at which someone speaks and information is included

- The use of silence or audio space to create emphasis

- The length and introduction of audio clips

- Conversations were more engaging than one person talking.

Final Reflection Assignment

This final reflective essay asks you to reflect back on the various assignments you've completed (and are in the process of completing) this semester and connect what you're learning in class to what you are learning in other courses and to what you will need to do for your future, both in academe and beyond. In this final reflective essay, you are invited to discuss the following:

- What you have learned from the experience of working with your team to create a collaborative radio show addressing a specific audience for a specific purpose.

- What you have learned about audience and rhetorical situation from moving across different genre/media conventions (rhetorical analysis, indexing, radio audio podcast/audio essay, oral presentations, oral history, interview, research).

- What you have learned about the rhetorical affordances of one media/genre over another. How has this impacted the way you think about writing, presenting, rhetorical situation, and audience?
- You may also use this essay as an opportunity to reflect on what you have learned about your writing process, presentation skills/anxieties, and collaboration strengths/weaknesses.
- You are invited to think about the way engaging with the course material has helped you learn about academic research, Jewish culture/history/ practice in KY, the US, globally, and perhaps why it is important for non-Jewish audiences to learn about this culture/history/practice and different cultural ideas and practices more generally.

The essay should be four to five pages long, double-spaced in 12-point font. You will submit it both electronically and in hard copy.

Sample Student Projects

1. Untitled by Team Hillel (Lizzie, Mary, Bilal, Cameron, Madison, and Laura). In this audio essay, six students explore the organization Hillel International.[2]
2. "The F-Word" by Team Feminism (Emma, Emilee, Ashton, Veronica, and Lindsay). This audio essay explores the role modern conservative Jewish women in Kentucky play in the larger context women's liberation movements.

Reflection

Janice Fernheimer: Let's see, is everything moving?[3] It looks like we're a go. *[laughs]* Okay. The Sounds of Sustainable Stewardship: Indexing and Composing Audio Essays with the Jewish Heritage Fund for Excellence, Jewish Kentucky Oral History Repository, and Undergraduate Researchers. Hello! My name is Janice W. Fernheimer, and I am Associate Professor of Writing, Rhetoric, and Digital Studies and the Zantker Charitable Foundation Professor and Director of Jewish Studies at the University of Kentucky in Lexington. I'm here with University of Kentucky undergraduates Madison Cissell, Hannah Thompson, Hannah Newberry, and Laura Will, who were students in two different sections of Writing Jewish Kentucky, a special section of WRD 112. This course is a special section of an honors version of first-year writing that I've been developing and implementing

---

2. Two student examples (audio files and descriptive transcripts) can be found on the book's companion website.

3. The audio version of Janice W. Fernheimer's reflection can be found on the book's companion website.

with the support of the broader Jewish Heritage Fund for Excellence Jewish Kentucky research team, which includes Dr. Beth Goldstein, my co-researcher, Dr. Doug Boyd, Director of the Louie B. Nunn Center for Oral History, and Sarah Dorpinghaus, University of Kentucky Digital Archivist. In this audio reflection, we hope to illuminate the ways our broader research team's model for sustainable stewardship for collection growth and accessibility engages undergraduates from across the disciplines as researchers and public authors attuned to what we call the "sounds" of sustainable stewardship.

Madison Cissell: So, Dr. Jan, before we go any further, can you explain what sustainable stewardship is and how our class, WRD 112, helped your research team develop this concept?

Jan: Sure, thanks, Madison! Sustainable stewardship is a concept Dr. Goldstein, Dr. Boyd, Sarah Dorpinghaus, and I coined for the work we did to innovate a new approach to both oral history collection design and an accompanying pedagogy that enables student researchers to participate in every step of oral history collection from creation to curation. It's a pedagogical practice we developed to engage undergraduates in original knowledge production while simultaneously fostering archival access and growth. It builds on some of the theory that Charlotte Nunes (2017) articulates in her essay "'Connecting to the Ideologies that Surround Us': Oral History Stewardship as an Entry Point to Critical Theory in the Undergraduate Classroom," where she advocates for postcustodial stewardship as an approach that "represents a significant break from the tradition of archival custody . . . [that] connotes an ongoing collaborative relationship in which a repository manages but does not own a community's archives" (p. 351). In her article she argues that "Oral history stewardship, then, is an effective conduit to theoretically engaged pedagogy" (2017, p. 355). And we agree! While the collection we've built is not postcustodial in the way that she defines it, because we work directly with the Louie B. Nunn Center, we are building on the stewardship model she introduces with its emphasis on "ongoing collaborative relationship" (2017, p. 355).

Hannah Newberry: Okay, so how does "sustainable stewardship" work?

Jan: Excellent question, Hannah! By indexing an extant interview, and thus making it more searchable and accessible and then later conducting an original oral history interview that becomes part of the collection to be indexed by future students, this model produces a sustainable model for both collection growth and increased access. Students participate in making interviews, [rather] indexing interviews that might otherwise not become digitally searchable and available to a public while also conducting an interview to get indexed by a future group of students.

Hannah Thompson: So, how did this shape out in our assignments, Dr. Jan?

Jan: Well, the assignment structure, as you all well know, included the following: First, students were asked to use the Nunn Center's open-source platform OHMS (the Oral History Metadata Synchronizer) to create a searchable, digital index for an extant oral history conducted by someone else. In our case these were interviews that were already part of the Jewish Heritage Fund for Excellence Jewish Kentucky Collection. Then students authored a rhetorical analysis of the identity work that the oral history helps to perform. Next students worked in small teams to conduct an original oral history interview that became part of the Jewish Heritage Fund for Excellence Jewish Kentucky Collection. I'm gonna call that JHFE from now on. This interview is one that gets indexed by future students, and then with a larger small team, students work to create a final audio essay that put the oral histories in context and created a narrative addressed to a public audience. The lynchpin for sustainable stewardship thus hinges on the way that students both learn to listen critically to an interview in order to create a usable digital index, which includes things like keywords, segment synopses, contextualizing hyperlinks and GPS coordinates, and then, through this more engaged listening learn to become better interviewers themselves when it's their turn. At least that's our hope.

So, tell me, from your perspective as students in two different versions of the course, from both spring and fall 2017, how did this play out? How did this sustainable stewardship model of indexing/followed by interviewing/followed by audio-essay authoring help you become better attuned to "sound" and its place in the composition process across media?

Madison: Hi, I'm Madison Cissell, first-year political science major and Jewish studies minor here at UK. I think that when we are taught about storytelling or rhetoric in public education, the oral and digital component of these elements is often left out. Our class introduced these elements right off the bat, however, and they continuously expanded off of each other as the semester progressed. When working with indexing, students are often still on the "audience" side in a sense that they're listening to media and producing work that complements the interview. By listening to our interviewees, we can feel their emotion and recount their stories more accurately. Once we got into conducting our own interviews and producing a team podcast, I felt more like a facilitator of the new research. It was a great feeling to be incorporated into the digital storytelling aspect and vocally representing my findings and ideas. My excitement came from hearing these people share their stories and the memories pertaining to life in the modern Jewish community. I enjoyed hearing how reminiscent or excited the interviewees were to share details they recollected, no matter how important the memory was to the research itself. Seeing how passionate they became about a story was what made it worth it. I felt a duty to relay this passion to others because of the unique situation we had. I feel like not many college students, or Kentuckians in general, have much knowledge on Jewish Kentuckians and their impact. So, being able to relay the sounds and details I was picking up was very exciting. I loved being able to share their memories with those interested in listening.

Hannah Newberry: Thanks, Madison! It was really exciting to relay the sounds of our interviewees. Hi, I'm Hannah Newberry, and I'm a second-year biology student at the University of Kentucky. From the beginning, you had a blank slate that you had to think about in terms of composition and how things went together in a nearly two-hour long, sometimes jumbled and rambling interview. I probably listened to my entire two-and-a-half [hour] interview five times in the span of a few weeks. When listening to someone talk about their life like that, in an unprepared and slightly less professional environment than giving a speech or writing an autobiography, you can hear in their voices the emotions behind their stories. You can hear the excitement behind them recounting a memory of their wedding, and the fear and apprehension of recollecting an event where they were called a racial slur or faced discrimination. These emotional elements often do not translate in more prepared speeches and in books. Being able to use these more emotional fragments in the audio essay made it more powerful and allowed their stories to be told more effectively than if the quotes were pulled from a script.

Hannah Thompson: Wow! Thanks, Hannah! I think the emotional elements of interviews are also very important. Hi, I'm Hannah Thompson, and I'm a second-year biology student at the University of Kentucky. If you would've asked me a year ago what came to my mind when I heard the word media, I would've said videography, which combines images with sounds. This form of media is the one I had the most experience with previously. We're introduced to movies, documentaries, and the news at a very young age. However, this experience of indexing followed by interviewing gave me a different perspective of media. I no longer think of movies or documentaries, but I think of storytelling. With indexing, you categorize the interview into different parts and each part has its own purpose in the bigger story. I think of it like the chapters of a book. Each chapter has its own meaning, described by experience the character has. When I began to think of questions to ask my interviewee, I remembered how the interview I indexed flowed naturally and shared an interesting story. I strived to do that with my own interview. The interviewee's answer to a question may lead to another question that wasn't planned and that was okay because it was her story to share. The model of first indexing and then interviewing made the interview process much easier and more natural. I learned that "sound" was more than just noises, but also included the voice of the interview and the stories that were shared. We all have a voice to share, but sometimes people don't use them, and as a result, their experiences, knowledge, and wisdom are lost. It's extremely important to share your voice with others. I indexed the interview of Madeline Abramson (2016), a woman who was raised Catholic and had a unique experience converting and integrating into the Jewish community. She used her voice to explore her identity, faith, and family throughout the interview, telling a story of self-growth and acceptance. Her emotional expression described to listeners that it was difficult at times, however, the support of her family and community made the transition much easier. While listening to her voice, I realized she seemed truly happy and proud to be part of a community that welcomed her with open arms and made her feel comfortable. She used her voice in a way that elicits emotion and as a result, others could relate to her feelings.

Laura Will: Wow, thanks, Hannah! It's so fascinating to hear about your experience in the WRD 112 class. I'm Laura Will, and I'm a first-year accounting and finance major at the University of Kentucky. I actually had a similar experience coming into the fall 2017 section of this WRD 112 class. I was completely oblivious to the whole concept of "sound" within the composition process across media. On top of that, I knew nothing about indexing, conducting oral history interviews, or creating an audio essay. Reflecting on the class now, I am so proud of my work and my group's work, having completed an index for an interview that recounted a person's life and contribution to the Jewish history of Kentucky, in addition to conducting our own interview that will be permanently available to the public. This process taught me so much about the value of oral history and the necessity to preserve it. Just listening to stories from interviewees and how they built their lives is so amazing, and to think that if it hadn't been for this process of recording, cataloguing, and indexing them, we would never know! This course made me more aware and appreciative of all the work that goes into documenting histories and preserving them, and I am so glad that I had this experience.

Jan: Thanks Laura, Hannah, Hannah, Madison. I'm really glad to hear about how you connected with the emotions and the sounds of the interviews that you were working with, and I'm wondering if you can talk to us a little more now about how your experience in composing in these different ways increased your awareness of sound and voice and helped you maybe even reimagine or redefine how you thought about research, or yourself as a student and a researcher, or even maybe, as Laura just started to suggest, your understanding of how history works?

Madison: Well, I've always enjoyed my history courses in the past, and I've also had a passion for Jewish history, so getting involved with the historical aspect of oral interviews added more interest to the class. And like Laura stated above, you know, the whole concept of sound within the course was kind of oblivious and new to me, so something I learned when indexing was just how important these elements in the interviews themselves were. I had a great deal of responsibility to the—to index the interviews to the best of my ability because I realized how important it was to share these stories with the Jewish community and members outside of the Jewish Community too. I found that indexing and interviewing are both great methods to share these stories. With indexing, you're providing great . . . you're providing information that can lead to more discoveries. Dr. Fernheimer told us early on that researchers could be using our indexes to look . . . for researchers to look at their specific interests, so attention to detail was imperative. You wanted to make sure that if you could provide a connection, that it was there. In the interviewing process, it's almost like you're creating the information itself. You get to decide what is asked, discussed, elaborated, and disregarded, which is really cool! By having the power to direct conversation, you also want to make sure to bring out and emphasize the most important parts of the story being told.

Hannah Newberry: Thank you for sharing, Madison. I agree with you that it was very new to me as it was to y'all—elaborating and making information out of the interviews. As a biology major, if you had asked me two years ago what I thought research was, I probably would have said something about working in a lab trying to cure cancer or digging at an archaeological site in Egypt or Mexico. I never imagined this type of work with oral histories and conducting interviews. This work is so exciting to me because I am working with living history. History is dynamic, and we are capturing the history from the recent past or the present. We are taking snapshots of a person's life as it is at the time of the interview and collecting their thoughts and stories and memories. This isn't some dusty history lesson. This is real-life people talking about their experiences, and you are hearing it first-hand. This is so important because oftentimes history is "cleaned up," and you lose the voices of people, especially those in the minority, like the Kentucky Jews we focused on. They are in the religious minority of the state and living in the geographical minority for people of the Jewish faith. Their histories and stories would have likely been lost if not for these efforts. I had always heard the old adage "History is written by the victors." But I had never considered it in this manner before. Historians often focused on the majority, and we lost the history of so many others. From hearing the real voices of Kentucky Jews, we hear an alternate history that differs from so many others but is also similar to the experiences of other Kentuckians. Without them, we could not accurately analyze the real history of the state. From the recollections of a Jewish Kentucky sharecropper who remembers his mother fixing traditional Jewish food for other sharecropper families, to stories of menorahs being placed in windows facing away from Christian pastors in order to not offend them, these are the voices that come through when oral histories are made.

Hannah Thompson: Like Hannah explained, when I think of research, I also think of bench research in the lab due to my experiences, and as a result I think of research in a scientific perspective. However, through this class I learned that research in the humanities and history is also extremely important. We might not be following the scientific method the same exact way, but we followed our own method of understanding the history, adding a first-person voice that could provide their own perspective of the historical events, and relating real-life experiences with historical importance. I believe it's incredibly important to connect something that's written about in textbooks to the voices and stories of the people that experienced those events unfold in front of them. For example, Rachel Adler (1973), a Jewish studies scholar and woman of Jewish faith, elaborated on the stereotypical responsibilities of Jewish women of the 17th through 20th centuries and once said, "It was to cry down our doubts that rabbis developed their prepackaged orations on the nobility of motherhood; the glory of childbirth; and modesty, the crown of Jewish womanhood" (p. 77). Adler bucked these expectations and explained how the Halacha, Jewish law, must be interpreted differently so that women can participate in Jewish traditions typically reserved for men. Fast forward to the 21st century, and women are able to become rabbis. I had the pleasure of interviewing Rabbi Cohen (2017), the first female rabbi of Lexington's conservative synagogue Ohavay Zion. She reflected on her work as a rabbi and specifically a female rabbi. Rabbi Cohen's perspective shined a light on the progress Judaism has made to accept women in leadership roles. Perspectives like hers are important to understand our history. It is clear that interdisciplinary research is necessary to advance our knowledge of the past and future.

Laura: Thanks, Hannah! I completely agree. One of the first assignments we had in this class was to read an article about the pros and cons of oral history and its credibility in regards to research. This really stuck with me throughout the semester as I indexed an interview and conducted one of my own. It wasn't until my group and I had to develop a research question to base our own audio essay off of that I was able to experience for myself what this article summarized. As my group explored written documents, including journals, newspapers, pamphlets, and articles, in addition to searching through previously conducted interviews, I began to realize that I actually valued the oral histories more. They were so personal and so genuine, from the way they phrased specific events to the emotion behind their words that I could feel as if I was there, in that moment. These oral histories gave me a completely new perspective on research and "history," because I know that I would not have felt as connected or invested in the stories and evidence for my research, even if I was reading the same interview in a transcript. I am so used to searching through books and online sites for evidence, but this was different. This was listening to someone's life stories, and I loved it!

Jan: What Laura is pointing to is some of the intimacy that comes with working with oral history. Working not just with a person's words, but with the sounds of their voice, the spaces in between those sounds, the cracklings, the laughter, the uuhhhs and the aaahhhs, of spoken utterance—students and I got a sense for what it means to hear the sounds of history composed one person's story at a time. As Hannah and Hannah point out, history is a research method that expanded how they conceived of research and knowledge, and as Madison chimed in, working with such oral histories enabled her and other students to feel responsible to both the interviewees and to the stories they told. This type of responsible research, which allows students even in their very first year to contribute to the growing body of knowledge, engages us in part because of its sounds. Investigating the specifics of which sounds and which voices are included helped us to better understand and prompt more questions about the relative inclusivity or representational nature of history. Who *is* part of the record? Whose voices get counted? Why or why not? Who gets to decide?

The work of sustainable stewardship we're engaged in—making those voices that are already part of the record more searchable and accessible for others, and making sure that we are not just indexing those interviews and increasing access, but also adding additional voices to the record, and ensuring the growth of the collection, increasing inclusivity and access simultaneously through our acts of public authoring—these too are the sounds of sustainable stewardship. At times harmonious, at times cacophonous, at times something still in process, the sounds of sustainable stewardship are multi-faceted. They allow more voices to become part of the symphonic, historical record, and in so doing, they allow more authors to become part of the process of making them part of the record and making that record so much more available. These are exciting moments in connecting first-year writers with public writing that does work inside and well beyond the writing classroom, and through the work of sustainable stewardship continues to resound beyond the constraints of any one particular semester. We are very grateful to the Jewish Heritage Fund for Excellence, which helped to fund the project, and to the Nunn Center for allowing us to use their studio, and of course to all of the amazing students, some of whom you got to hear from today: Hannah, Hannah, Laura, and Madison, who participated in helping us develop this model. Thank you!

References

Adler, R. (1973). The Jew who wasn't there: Halacha and the Jewish woman. *Response: A Contemporary Jewish Review, 7*(2), 77–82. https://jwa.org/media/jew-who-wasnt-there-halacha-and-jewish-woman.

Abramson, M. (2016, September 14). Interview by C. Ely [Audio file]. Jewish Kentucky Oral History Project, Louie B. Nunn Center for Oral History, University of Kentucky Libraries. https://kentuckyoralhistory.org/catalog/xt7f7m041n26.

Boyd, D. A., Fernheimer, J. W. & Dixon, R. (2015). Indexing as engaging oral history research: Using OHMS to "compose history" in the writing classroom. *The Oral History Review, 42*(2), 352–367. https://doi.org/10.1093/ohr/ohv053.

Cohen, Rabbi S. L. (2017, March 31). Interview by H. Thompson, T. Patel & D. Morris [Audio file]. Jewish Kentucky Oral History Project, Louie B. Nunn Center for Oral History, University of Kentucky Libraries. https://kentuckyoralhistory.org/catalog/xt780g3h147g.

Fernheimer, J. W., Boyd, D. A., Goldstein, B. L. & Dorpinghaus, S. (2018). Sustainable stewardship: A collaborative model for engaged oral history pedagogy, community partnership, and archival growth. *The Oral History Review, 45*(2), 321–341. https://doi.org/10.1093/ohr/ohy052.

Nunes, C. (2017). "Connecting to the ideologies that surround us": Oral history stewardship as an entry point to critical theory in the undergraduate classroom. *The Oral History Review, 44*(2), 348–362. https://doi.org/10.1093/ohr/ohx042.

Chapter 21. Producing Community Audio Tours

Mariana Grohowski

INDEPENDENT SCHOLAR

Like community-based researchers Eli Goldblatt (2007) and Ellen Cushman (1996), I uphold a pedagogy that includes "access, critique, reflection, and connection" with one's community, to foster critical thinking through community engagement (Goldblatt, 2007, p. 151). As Goldblatt identified, students (and their professors) may not be natives of the communities in which their colleges reside and can, therefore, as Cushman (1996) warned, "risk reproducing the hegemonic barriers separating the university from the community" (p. 24). However, when students record and produce audio narrations about important sites in their area, they gain awareness of how a community and its location serve as a powerful literacy sponsor. In turn, a sense of connection with and ownership to their locale may result or be strengthened. This community-based, collaborative (e.g., entire class) project, An Audible Tour of [your community's or region's name], relies on students' willingness to immerse themselves—and their future listeners—in their community.

This project is inspired by Erin R. Anderson's (2017) article on "Oral History, Digital Storytelling and Project-Based Pedagogy" (the article's subtitle), which outlined three scaffolded projects, one that had students soundwrite about sites in their community using the mobile app VoiceMap (http://voicemap.me). Essentially, Anderson's students, all military veterans at the University of Massachusetts Boston, created "a mobile audio storytelling walk of war memorials" (2017, p. 85). This assignment inspired me because of what it asked students to write sound *about*: distinct sites in their community that are shared with a genuine audience. Similar to Anderson's assignment is one introduced by Olin Bjork and John Pedro Schwartz (2009) that they dubbed an activity in "sound-seeing," in which "students created unofficial audio guides for [a museum] as a free podcast" (p. 233). According to the authors, "The activity is called sound-seeing because the listener . . . 'sees' the event or place as it is described in 'sound' by the podcaster. The term privileges the podcaster's experience over that of the podcaster, whose activity may be dubbed as 'sight-sounding'" (2009, p. 232). Unlike Anderson (2017), Bjork and Schwartz (2009) were less interested in audio composing than they were in the affordances of mobile composing. In fact, their work challenged the audio tour's effectiveness for the listener, but praised it for what it teaches the student about writing.

In this chapter, I share a full explanation of a "sound-seeing" or "mobile audio tour" project: a series of 17 exercises that build on one other from the start to the completion of the project, and on the companion website, sample projects to guide both teachers and students to capture the sounds and sites of the communities in which they and their universities reside. I envision this project fitting into a course on new media, writing for the web, multimodality, technical writing, or community literacy.

Project Description

Below is the formal assignment prompt for the Audible Tour of [our community's or region's name], which was designed to be shared directly with students. The text introduces the project, establishes project goals and expectations, and provides information on essential technologies and best practices for producing audio.

Project Overview

The goal of this project is to collaborate in soundwriting and audio production to create a narrated tour of our community using the mobile app VoiceMap. This project requires complete participation to plan, scout locations, research, script (or story-tell), record audio, edit audio, transcribe audio, and finally, upload and organize our audio into a logical, cohesive audio tour to VoiceMap.

Our soundwriting project is a series of short, episodic, narrated audio files that coalesce into a step-by-step tour. This audio tour will be unlike a podcast—which can be a linear, multitrack audio file (think highly produced) and typically has a single theme or topic—or an ambient soundscape, which captures the sounds of a given environment in a single audio file. Your audio file will share directions to and information about a specific site in our community. Each clip should be mindful of the genre of mobile, audio composing—namely, clips will consider length (think short) and possess an informative tone.

Goals and Outcomes

Your audio should strive to capture the richness of sound. This means: 1) practicing and refining your speaking voice (think diction and volume); 2) efficient use of ambient noise; 3) careful editing to ensure clarity and efficiency—that is, it must account for listeners' needs and the genre and mode in which they are listening (e.g., mobile app, phone); and 4) produced in a manner that indicates your awareness of high quality, short-form audio.

It bears repeating: *Audience awareness is key*, as you are composing for actual listeners who are reliant upon you for accurate directions and factual information.

Your text must take on a balanced tone of being informative, interpretive, and engaging.

You'll need a title—as this is required for the VoiceMap platform. Ideally, your title is also the name of your location. It can include a relevant and/or quirky adjective if you desire.

You must include a transcript of your audio. According to VoiceMap's suggestions, your script should be a maximum of 450 words: "We've found from experience that listeners start to drift off and lose attention past this point." Additionally, your script must include directions from your location to the next. Since the listener is only using your voice to get from one location to the next, you must work closely with the classmates whose locations proceed and follow your own to ensure that you include accurate directions in your script and that our potential listeners experience a complete and cohesive tour. Lastly, your script should be written in the present tense and in the second-person point of view.

If you are using "found" sound materials (from the public domain; with a Creative Commons license), you must attribute appropriate authorship.

Your audio text must include a short summary description of the text's meaning, form, and materials (this is where you attribute authorship, if needed).

Equipment

- A set of headphones, preferably a pair that covers your ears or has a microphone (such as the ones that came with older versions of iPhones).
- Your phone for audio recording. Be sure to prep your phone through the following steps:
  a. Turn your phone to "do not disturb" or "airplane" mode to eliminate notifications, texts, or calls.
  b. Find a quiet room or space with minimal ambient noises. This may require some scouting and/or scheduling. Test rooms out prior to hitting record. Conversely, hit record while sitting in the space to test for noises your ear can't pick up.
  c. Plug in a pair of headphones (preferably ones that include a microphone) to your phone. Hearing what your listeners hear, and hearing yourself is helpful. What's more, using a microphone helps reduce ambient noises.
  d. Practice. Listen back. The likelihood of one perfect take is slim.

This assignment was adapted from "The Audio Assignment," authored by The Digital Media and Composition Institute (DMAC), Department of English, The Ohio State University (2018), which is licensed with a Creative Commons BY-NC-SA license and adapted here with permission. Additionally, this assignment was adapted with permission from Erin R. Anderson's assignment Collaborative Medal of Honor Storytelling Project as shared in her article "Voicing the Veterans Experience" (2017, p. 109).

Audible Tour Contribution Assessment Rubric

I've created a basic rubric to guide students to meet the project's requirements. Essentially, this rubric is the language from the "goals and outcomes" portion of the formal assignment sheet. I believe that multiple forms of representation of the same information can help students with differing learning preferences to successfully meet project requirements.

Table 21.1. Project requirements

Required Component	Complete	Incomplete	Suggestions
Audio is an MP3 file.			
Audio is of high quality. No ambient noise.			
Narration is informative, descriptive, and engaging.			
Speaker's voice is clear and well paced and uses an effective volume.			
Speaker uses the present tense.			
The text is of an appropriate length.			
The text includes a title (preferably the site's name or location).			
The text contains a 450-word written transcript of the audio file.			
The project contains a short summary description, written in third person, which includes the text's meaning, form (e.g., audio), and materials (attributes authorship if author used found sounds).			
At a minimum, the text shares the name of the location, describes its features, and provides relevant information about the site, and one "fun fact."			
Acknowledgement of the sequence of the route is addressed at the beginning and at the end, including explicit directions from one's location to the proceeding spot.			

Laying the Foundation for the Audible Tour of [Your Community] Project

Step 1: Gaining Momentum (option 1)

This is an invention exercise that relies on discussion and could proceed or follow the introduction of the assignment.

As a class, or in small groups, identify as many places in your community that

1. make the community unique,
2. may be historically significant, or
3. should be protected.

Consider a variety of places—properties unique to a community and worthy of preservation. Create a working list of places that can be accessed and edited by students asynchronously, such as a course website or course/learning management system.

Gaining Momentum (option 2)

Because it is possible that this step could stump students who lack familiarity with their college town, an alternative option is to have students conduct online research to gather information. Working either individually or in small groups, have students select and study a specific site. Students should be prepared to share their findings with the class.

If online research is a desired component of this step, a suggested resource is The National Park System's National Register of Historic Places Database (https://www.nps.gov/subjects/nationalregister/database-research.htm). Students can choose to search for historic places by state by choosing the link to an interactive map.

Of course, students may also try their hand at pertinent Google searches for things like "top state landmarks" or "The most Instagrammed places by state" (DiBlasio, 2016).

Step 2: Site Selection

Each student should select a place from the full list of places identified by the class. Prior to selection, the proximity of sites to one another should be considered. It may be a good idea to plot all the locations on a community map (which will be necessary for Step 4). VoiceMap asks for the user to designate the tour's mode of transportation (bike, car, public transport, walking). Based on the distance from one site to another, the class may decide to eliminate sites beyond a certain radius or make a driving tour.

Step 3: Analysis of VoiceMap Audio Tours

Before creating their own audio tour, students should experience an audio tour published on the VoiceMap app. This activity requires students to access their Android or iOS smartphone. The activity could be conducted in small groups or individually.

To begin, students will need to use their phones to download the VoiceMap app on Apple's App Store or Google Play. Once the app is downloaded, students will be asked to create a new account. This process is slightly time consuming, but eventually all of the students should have the app downloaded to their phone in order to complete (submit) their contribution to the class's audio tour.

Upon entry into the app, students are prompted to explore locations to find free audio tours. Yes, that's right. At the time of publication, there were 30 free tours (only one of which was in the United States). Listening through the app is very user-friendly, as is navigating through the tour through the app's features.

As they listen, a series of prompts could be projected on a screen in the front of the classroom or written on a whiteboard. The prompts should ask students to critique the audio tour's rhetorical features (purpose, context, audience, content, clarity, organization, and its use of ethos, pathos, and logos). Students should take notes and be prepared to share them with their analyses with class.

Step 4: Location Plotting and Route Planning on VoiceMap

Once locations have been chosen and a route has been planned, the next step is to create and plot the class's tour on the VoiceMap platform. VoiceMap (2016) has created the step-by-step video tutorial "Getting Started with your First Route" to explain the entire process.

As the video explains: "Location markers need to be placed exactly on the route line and wherever directions must be provided. Each location marker has its own URL"; therefore, the names of your location markers should be something that is searchable and relevant to the tour (such as the name of your location) (VoiceMap, 2016).

Once a location has been plotted and named, choose "save location" so students can edit their work. By clicking "Save and Submit" you can't make any changes until an assigned VoiceMap editor approves the submission.

Step 5: Exploring Sites

Now that sites have been selected, students are ready to complete the Observation Worksheet below for their location and (if possible) visit the location to become familiar with it. If visiting the place is a requirement, ensure that students get a picture of themselves at the location. Online research will help students complete the worksheet.

This worksheet was modified from the National Parks Service's Teaching with Historic Places materials. Essentially, this is a low-stakes, preliminary opportunity to gather research on students' chosen site. Completing it will help them with planning their audio composition. See a sample completed worksheet on the companion website.

Observation Worksheet

1. What is the name and location of the site?
2. When was it built or created?
3. What, if anything, do you already know about this place?
4. Have you visited this site previously? If so, how often and/or when (approximate date)?
5. What does this place mean to you?

6. Considering the visually observable features of your site, how would you describe it in general terms? Such as size, shape, appearance, setting, condition, and other characteristics?

7. What kind of clues can you find about its age or evolution over time? Where can or did you find this information (observation of site, online research)? List sources.

8. How is it being used today? Do you think the current use is different from the original use? How can you tell?

9. What hypotheses can you make about what people, events, or ways of life this place might have been associated with historically, based on what you can see?

10. What kinds of information would you need to confirm or deny your hypotheses?

11. If the place is vacant, can you think of any way it might be adapted for a new use?

12. If it has been restored, who restored it and why?

13. If it is open to the public as a historic site, what do visitors learn about why it is important? What should they know?

14. If your site is a preserved site, how has the place benefited the community? How has preservation contributed to economic growth in the community (i.e., by providing jobs, enabling businesses to stay downtown, creating homes for new companies, encouraging tourism, contributing to community pride, etc.)?

15. How do you think the community would be affected if it were destroyed or substantially altered? What might replace it? How might the character and appearance of the community or neighborhood change? How might the destruction of these places affect the appearance of the community? What stories about the history of the community and its residents would be lost?

Step 6: Full Immersion and Audio Practice, Take 1

Pulling from their responses in Step 5, students should now synthesize what they've learned into a brief audio response for you to review (covering the who, what, when, where, why, and how of their site), accompanied by a written description of what will be heard in the audio, along with a script and links to any sources consulted. This will give them practice recording and practice accompanying audio with textual writing. Hear a sample audio response on the companion website.

Step 7: Soundwriting on Location: Audio Practice, Take 2

Students are ready to compose a transcript for their site-specific audible tour contribution and record a draft. Their contribution should follow the guidelines established on the assignment sheet and rubric. Most importantly, this audio must include directions from their location to the next plot on the class's established route. Hear a sample of this step on the companion website.

Step 8: Peer Review

The following style of peer review (or "studio review") was introduced to me by Dr. Kristine L. Blair and by the facilitators at the Digital Media and Composition Institute at The Ohio State University. It is best conducted in a computer lab so that students can make their audio files readily available. Conversely, if a computer lab is not available, advise students to bring their emerging audio text on a listening device. All students should bring their own headphones.

Prior to engaging in peer review, students will need some direction on how to provide relevant feedback. The following direction set should be given to each student to help them successfully navigate this preparation-heavy activity.

Peer Review Directions

1. Prepare your space.
   a. Power on your listening device and set it up in a way that is easy for a partner to access.
   b. Open a Word document or sticky note on your computer or leave a handwritten note for your classmate, including any necessary directions for listening and/or a specific aspect of your draft you'd like to receive feedback on. Additionally, if your draft needs an explanation (such as how to interact with it or an excuse for its current state), be sure to leave that note in a place all viewers will see.
   c. Leave a means for classmates to leave you feedback (open document, sticky notes, paper).
   d. Also leave a copy of the assignment rubric handy for reference.
2. When you are finished setting up, come up to the front of the class or to an open workspace.
3. Read your classmate's note and then listen to their audio. Leave some feedback on this draft.
   a. Refer to the assignment rubric; does this draft include all the required elements?
   b. Try to craft your feedback through the method of "describe, evaluate, and suggest."[1]
4. After you've completed your review, move to another space and repeat the same steps.

---

1. "Describe–Evaluate–Suggest" is a model for peer feedback suggested by Eli Review (2014) that encourages students to first describe what their peer is doing, evaluate it according to criteria, and then make a suggestion for revision.

5. Continue moving from space to space, providing feedback, until time has been called or until you have reviewed at least five classmates' work.

6. Once time has been called, return to your original workspace. Read the feedback left by your classmates. Save this information, as you will need to respond to the feedback in a revision plan (see next step).

Step 9: Revision Plan

As a student of Dr. Kristine L. Blair, I completed a "revision plan" after every first draft. Revision plans helped me, and more importantly, they help students; they take peer review more seriously because they must rely on their classmates' feedback to complete this assignment. The revision plan also affords students the opportunity to work through the feedback we provide.

A revision plan is like a grocery list. Students create an outline of the steps they need to take to revise their work.

Revision Plan Directions

Upon receipt of peer and instructor comments on your first draft, write a revision plan before you begin working on your second/final draft. Revision plans take the following form:

In either a bulleted list or paragraph form, explain and synthesize the recommendations you received for revising/finalizing your work. Explain which suggestions you will implement and how you will go about making the suggested revisions. You can indicate the feedback you will not use or did not find helpful, or you can ignore it all together.

Be sure to include any questions or concerns you may have with the revision process.

Step 10: Soundwriting on Location: Finalized Audio Attempt 1

Based on their findings and revision plan from the report brief, students should now be ready to revise the transcript and audio for their site-specific audible tour contribution.

Step 11: Transcript Submission to VoiceMap

The process for submitting transcripts and audio to VoiceMap is recursive and reliant on an external partner (a VoiceMap editor). Provide students with the following directions.

The first step of your submission process is to log into the class's VoiceMap tour. Click on the locations tab (top of page), choose your specific location, and click the open window icon (next to the trash can on bottom right corner). A new window opens that allows you to edit. Here, you can modify your title. (See the goals and outcomes portion of the assignment sheet for advice on titles). Next, copy/paste your written transcript into VoiceMap. When you're finished, click "save and submit." This will notify our assigned VoiceMap editor that we're ready for their approval. This process can take 48 hours or more.

Step 12: Addressing Editor Feedback

Provide students with instructions on how to revise based on editor feedback, perhaps with language like the following.

Once you submit your location contribution, our assigned editor will review and in time, make any necessary changes or provide feedback for you to complete. Since I am the primary point of contact for our tour, I will forward the editor's message to your personal email. Once you receive the email, log back into the site, make your edits, and once again "save and submit" for re-approval. If required, this step may need to be repeated until the editor is satisfied.

Once the editor approves the route and scripts, access to upload your audio will be granted.

Step 13: Saving and Uploading Audio

Students may need detailed instructions on uploading their audio to VoiceMap. Your audio composition must be saved as an MP3 file. Please name your file location_order#.mp3.

Next, log back into the class's VoiceMap tour. Click on the locations tab (top of page), choose your specific location, and click the open window icon (next to the trash can on bottom right corner). A new window opens that allows you to edit. Upload your MP3 file.

Step 14: Reverberating on Your Audio Contribution

Below are the directions for the last component of the Audio Tour project—a self-reflection.

Reverberating* On Your Audio Contribution

* The word reverberate (verb) means to vibrate in sound and is synonymous with reflection. Synonyms of reverberate are echo and react.

Your last step is to compose a self-assessment to evaluate your contribution to the collective effort. This is your opportunity to catalogue and justify the grade you think you deserve. It will also allow you to reflect on the strengths and weaknesses of the project. Develop your case by providing specific details (evidence) and reflect upon your roles. Please submit this assessment by creating a brief audio reflection that critiques your participation in the audible tour and identifies how this project connects to the course's learning outcomes and key themes.

Sample Projects

1.   In an example of the worksheet for Step 5, a student collected information on her chosen site, "Veterans Memorial Park."

2. The second sample contains required components from Step 6's guidelines: an audio description, written transcript, and the student's audio composition.

3. The example for Step 7, an audio composition, is the student's first attempt to direct listeners from the previous location to her site, Veterans Memorial Park. The text ends with a preview to the next student voice and route.[2]

Reflection

Mariana Grohowski: Hi, listeners.[3] This is Mariana Grohowski speaking. In this audio reflection, I weigh the affordances and constraints of the Audible Tour of [Your Community or Region] project—a project that brings together elements of community literacy, mobile or "wireless" composing, and of course, soundwriting. Specifically, the assignment utilizes the mobile app VoiceMap and asks students to plan and execute a narrated audio tour of unique places in their community. While VoiceMap can be accessed through a web browser, it was designed to be used through a smartphone app. Composing sound for and through an app creates new instructional challenges for teachers and composing challenges for students. Scholars Cynthia Selfe, Stephanie Owen Fleischer, Susan Wright, Sylvia Church, and Elizabeth Powell have created helpful resources for preventing and solving potential challenges of working with sound. Their respective chapters in Selfe's (2007) collection *Multimodal Composition: Resources for Teachers* provide invaluable suggestions for "troubleshooting in the face of failure" (Church & Powell, 2007, pp. 134–141) and advice for instructing "students to compose with . . . sound [by comparing how we] teach students to compose with words" (Selfe et al., 2007, p. 18). Even though these suggestions were not designed for mobile composing, they were designed for audio assignments that ask students to compose sound on location.

It is precisely the notion of soundwriting on and about location that excites me about the audio tour project. Bjork and Schwartz (2009) excitingly sell Writing in the Wild or composing audio on location as "relocating writing and publication in the place of the object [which] embraces process-as-product genres . . . so that students will see the world of tamed and untamed writing spaces" (p. 235). Sounds enticing.

But unlike "sound maps" or "soundscapes," which record the sounds of nature (see Yellowstone National Park's Audio Postcards [National Park Service, n.d.]), people (see Sounds of Singapore [Neo, 2017]), and events (see The Religious Soundmap Project [American Religious Sounds Project, 2018]), this assignment

---

2. Three examples (a worksheet, audio files and descriptive transcripts) can be found on the book's companion website.

3. The audio version of Mariana Grohowski's reflection can be found on the book's companion website.

asks students to become informed about places in the community beyond university grounds—locations that some students would never visit.

I liken this assignment to a community literacy project, with the community off campus serving as the literacy sponsor—a sponsor that teaches students that meaning and communication is shared through various symbol systems. That literacy is collaborative and can inspire civic engagement and cross-cultural communication.

Unlike "traditional" community literacy projects, this assignment does not exactly have students working with a community partner (person/persons from the community). Like community literacy projects, the audio tour assignment when used through the voicemap.me mobile app, does have a sort of community partner in the editor assigned to your class's route. Yes, an actual human being is assigned to you once you establish a route. The editor is responsible for ensuring that your locations have been plotted correctly and that your written transcripts satisfy their requirements. Correspondence with my VoiceMap editor ensures me that they approve submissions in 48 hours or less. But at the time of this recording, I have waited 72 hours without any feedback on my routes. I share this information because having worked with community partners, I know the impatience and frustration students (and their teachers) can experience when having to wait for response from the community partner in order to complete their work. This can be especially concerning when students are pressed to meet a deadline. Which means that teachers of community literacy projects have to allow some permeability or flextime when it comes to deadlines.

As a newer professor, I have had to relocate for work. I share that with my out-of-state students and the students who may live in a state but commute from a town multiple hours away. In the past, I've wanted to implement community-based projects in my writing classes, but these projects can sometimes take months, even years to establish because they rely on becoming informed about one's new community and gaining trust from people within the community. While trying to make those connections, I've experimented with community literacy projects in which—to use the terminology of Thomas Deans (2000)—students "write about" their community and later share with their (global) community. This was not a soundwriting project, and it did not ask students to write about the places that made their community unique; instead, it asked students to investigate the people that made their community unique. Finding ways to help our students compose about community for community inspires in students a sense of agency and connectedness to their surroundings (Deans, 2000). This can be especially important when students are from out-of-town and living on their own for the first time. For me personally, it has helped combat my feelings of being an outsider and made me feel a bit more familiar with my new community. That said, I've not assigned this project and I have not had students use the VoiceMap app and website. But I have used it in writing this chapter. And here's what I've discovered.

I didn't experiment with creating the tour's route through the app. Instead, I used the website, which caused me a lot of frustration. Plotting the locations was tedious because the site uses GPS technology. Exact locations must be specified and making changes is a finicky, time-consuming process. Per the directions from voicemap.me, plotting your route should take a total of one hour. Once the route is mapped, locations are established with names (that you create), and then "saved" (not submitted). I suggest the teacher plot the route. I also suggest the teacher create an account that the entire class can login to. Why? Because the teacher will want students to be able to login on their own to upload their audio compositions and written transcripts.

For the community literacy project I mentioned earlier, I created a Gmail account specifically for class use and creation of social media accounts. I gave all students the username and password so that they could login in order to contribute their work. I did not experience any problems in doing this, as neither the Gmail account nor the social media accounts were personal to me. Giving all students access and asking them to contribute their work directly to the site gives students the message that you believe they will behave professionally. With their names on the account (something like "Students of Writing 101 at College X"), they assume a sense of ownership over the project when they know that their work is published online and immediately available to a global audience. At least this was my experience in asking students at two different colleges.

The editors at voicemap.me suggest having one point of contact for the tour. This probably should be the teacher but have the username of, again, Students of Writing 101 at College X. This is what Erin Anderson and her students did for their voicemap.me tour of South Boston.

So once the route is plotted, the next step is not about composing audio. Nope, soundwriting takes a backseat when using voicemap.me. The first step is the submission of transcripts. The editor must approve the transcript before granting access to uploading sound files. Yes, this may be cause for concern.

Before we get too concerned, I have yet another constraint to inform you about.

Voicemap.me offers tour creators to charge a fee to users. While any user has to "purchase" a route, some purchases are free, but others cost money and allow the creator to make a profit from sales of their tour. I have yet to explore the fine print on voicemap.me's terms of use pertaining to how big a cut they take from each sale. I've made my tour free, as did Erin Anderson and her students at University of Massachusetts Boston. But I can see the justification for a class charging a fee for their tour, with the intention of raising money for a community organization that maintains a park, monument, or historical center. Of course, the teacher would bear the ethical responsibility of collecting and donating these funds as they trickle in over time.

Overall, I'm left wondering if another platform would be better for emphasizing the audio production portion of the assignment. If the goal is for learning about the rich affordances of audio composition, then do the constraints of the voicemap.me platform help or hinder student learning? Or does having students soundwrite through the constraints of the voicemap.me app help teach students more about "authentic" soundwriting? It surely teaches them about addressing audience expectations by honoring genre conventions. Additionally, and perhaps most importantly, this soundwriting project still honors the recursive process of soundwriting—the planning, recording, listening, editing, re-recording, etc.

References

Anderson, E. R. (2017). Voicing the veteran experience: Oral history, digital storytelling and project-based pedagogy. *Journal of Veterans Studies, 2*(1), 85–112. https://journal-veterans-studies.org/articles/abstract/10.21061/jvs.v2i1.31/.

Bjork, O. & Schwartz, J. P. (2009). Writing in the wild: A paradigm for mobile composition. In A. C. Kimme Hea (Ed.), *Going wireless: A critical exploration of wireless and mobile technologies for composition teachers and researchers* (pp. 223–238). Hampton Press.

Church, S. & Powell, E. (2007). When things go wrong. In C. L. Selfe (Ed.), *Multimodal composition: Resources for teachers* (pp. 133–152). Hampton Press.

Cushman, E. (1996). The rhetorician as an agent of social change. *College Composition and Communication, 47*(1), 7–28.

Deans, T. (2000). *Writing partnerships: Service learning in composition.* National Council of Teachers of English.

DiBlasio, N. (2016, December 1). What's the most Instagrammed place in every state? *USA Today.* https://www.usatoday.com/story/tech/2016/12/01/whats-most -instagrammed-place-every-state/94701900/.

The Digital Media and Composition Institute. (2018). *The audio assignment* [DOCX file]. https://drive.google.com/file/d/1bDvKzILP3OAJuWTmC-SoykbqLtY5e4rJ/view.

Eli Review. (2014, December 19). Describe–evaluate–suggest: Giving helpful feedback, with Bill Hart-Davidson [Video file]. *YouTube.* https://youtu.be/KzdBRR QhYv4.

Goldbatt, E. (2007). *Because we live here: Sponsoring literacy beyond the college curriculum.* Hampton Press.

National Park Service. (n.d.). *Audio postcards.* National Park Service. https://www .nps.gov/yell/learn/photosmultimedia/sonics.htm.

Neo, D. (2017). *Sounds of Singapore.* https://soundsofsingaporeblog.wordpress.com/.

Ohio State University's Center for the Study of Religion. (2014–2022). *American religious sounds project.* http://religioussounds.osu.edu/blog.

Selfe, C. L. (Ed.). (2007). *Multimodal composition: Resources for teachers.* Hampton Press.

Selfe, C. L., Fleischer, S. O. & Wright, S. (2007). Words, audio, and video: Composing and the processes of production. In C. L. Selfe (Ed.), *Multimodal composition: Resources for teachers* (pp. 13–28). Hampton Press.

Staff of Heritage Education Services. (n.d.). A lesson plan from the National Park Service for middle and high school levels. *National Park Service.* https://www .nps.gov/subjects/teachingwithhistoricplaces/upload/TwHP_HISTORY_NHPA -50th-lesson-plan.pdf.

VoiceMap. (2016, May 20). Getting started with your first route [Video file]. *YouTube.* https://youtu.be/HTlX1MhmM_I.

Part Four. Writing with Stories

Chapter 22. Place-Based Podcasting: From Orality to Electracy in Norfolk, Virginia

Daniel P. Richards
OLD DOMINION UNIVERSITY

Introduction: Preface (to Plato)

Near the end of Plato's (1995) *Phaedrus*, there is an exchange between the two interlocutors—Socrates and Phaedrus—on the topic of writing. In this exchange, Socrates tells a story about the Egyptian god, Theuth, who, upon discovering writing, brings forth his art to Thamus, the king of Egypt, touting writing as something that, "once learned, will make Egyptians wiser and will improve their memory . . . a potion for memory and for wisdom" (§ 274e).[1] Thamus, skeptical, assesses writing to have the opposite effect, and indeed responds by stating confidently that writing

> will introduce forgetfulness into the soul of those who learn it: they will not practice using their memory because they will put their trust in writing, which is external and depends on signs that belong to others, instead of trying to remember from the inside, completely on their own. You have not discovered a potion for remembering, but for reminding; you provide your students with the appearance of wisdom, not with its reality. (Plato, 1995, § 275a)

It could be said that this fictional but damning assessment of the effects of writing reflect Plato's epistemology broadly: that the act of writing moves individuals away from the interpersonal ("soul to soul") dialogue that he found to be so foundational to philosophy and the work of the dialectician (Plato, 1995, § 276e), and that written text itself is but a shadow or imagistic representation of knowledge, unable to defend itself—ultimately impotent in the scene of dialogue. The title of this introduction is in fact a playful homage to the monograph of the same name by Eric Havelock (1963), which offered a reframing of the evolution of the Greek mind through investigating just why Plato felt "so committed to the passionate warfare upon the poetic experience" (p. 15) and, I might add, the

---

1. See Jacques Derrida's (1981) "Plato's Pharmacy," which delves deeper into writing as pharmakon—a remedy and a poison. Jasper P. Neel's (1988) *Plato, Derrida, and Writing* is a productive follow-up as well.

DOI: https://doi.org/10.37514/PRA-B.2022.1688.2.22

written word. Plato was concerned with the effects that the written word would have on our collective and individual memories. Since writing is itself a technology, Plato by way of ancient manuscripts gives us, then, one of the earliest visions of *technofear*.

Figure 22.1. Syllabus header image for Writing in Digital Spaces course. Photo credit: Raphael (1509), from Wikimedia Commons.

Classroom Framing

Situating the fear of new forms of writing as a consistent trope as ancient as Plato provided the necessary framing for students to conceptually understand the social reactions to newer, in our case, digital forms of writing. This is the framing—or, perhaps, argument—I brought to the process of designing a split fourth-year/master's course titled Writing in Digital Spaces. The course, according to our catalog, seeks to offer "composition practice in critical contemporary digital environments," and, as such, "students should expect to participate in, develop, and engage in critical discussions about a range of digital spaces, including websites, wikis, blogs, and various interactive media" (Old Dominion, n.d.). While this language oozes web 2.0-ness, I saw this course as an opportunity for students to produce new, aural/oral types of media through theoretical lenses that connect their compositions to larger popular debates about digital writing, namely the evidence-based and supposed technofear-driven effects digital writing practices have on memory (Wright, 2005), attention (Lanham, 2007), cultural identity (Schicke, 2011), and cognition (Carr, 2010). I wanted students to engage in deep synthesis between the media they consume and produce and the theories underlying them, as I've humorously symbolized in Figure 22.1 above.

To connect Plato more directly to digital writing, I turned to two main sources: Walter Ong and Gregory Ulmer. Ong's (1982) *Orality and Literacy: The Technologizing of the Word* dealt specifically with Plato's treatment of text and positioned this treatment within the largely tectonic cultural shifts from orality to literacy, from the spoken word to the written. Ong's convincing contention that writing restructures consciousness provides a firm foundation upon which to then speculate about what comes after literacy, providing a safe space within which to grapple with Ulmer's (2009) notion of *electracy*, which is, in his own estimation, the third and subsequent "apparatus" in the line of orality and literacy—where, respectively, the practice is not religion or science but entertainment, and the institution is not the church or school but the internet. Students in this class were thus asked to ruminate on how digital technologies offer our world an opportunity to productively re-sequence the seemingly dissonant mode of orality with and through a fuller embrace of digital writing technologies.[2] This re-sequencing, the course argued, happens (potentially) through production. It happens through podcasting.

In consulting existing work on classroom-based podcasting (Bowie, 2012a, 2012b), I was then left with the question: About what do the students podcast? Insistent that projects stay local and inspired by the work of Jenny Edbauer (2005) in her challenging of stale visions of rhetorical situations, I decided that students would compose podcasts investigating an object, theme, idea, history, person, building, or other element relating to the city of Norfolk. As such, the podcasts would be episodic. Collectively, the podcasts students created would constitute a public standalone series titled *Of Norfolk*, aimed at addressing and overturning the reductive conceptualizations and descriptions of the city as merely a military town, or an unsafe place to live, by way of telling stories about interesting or under-appreciated aspects of Norfolk culture. The objectives of the assignment, which blended high-level theoretical thinking with praxis-based production work, were as follows:

- Have students conceive of podcasts as a storytelling mode that productively challenges the historical splits between orality and literacy, technology and memory.
- Have students get their hands dirty with production tools like Audacity to connect the practical decisions they make in editing to the conceptual ideas underlying digital storytelling.
- Have students harness the power of digital storytelling to enact a sense of agency in having a say about the perceptions and histories of our local communities.

Overall, students would realize that the popularity and production of podcasts are connected in meaningful but complicated ways to ancient allegiances to

---

2. This contrasts, I think, productively with others who have used Plato as a theoretical touchstone for projects in podcasting, namely Lydia French and Emily Bloom's (2011) brilliant praxis-based work on auralacy as a theoretical space within which to think through connections between Plato, Ong, epistemology, podcasts, and writing.

orality, and perhaps represent a return, or re-visioning, of orality for our digitally mediated culture.

One important note about the podcasts I have listed below for required reading: If I had a deaf student in my class, and I assigned them to listen to my assigned podcast episodes, they would run into the problem of not having access to transcripts to all episodes. *This American Life*, for example, despite its popularity and place on public radio, insists that their work needs to be "heard" and thus does not provide any transcripts of their episodes. I might suggest for teachers that this might be a good opportunity for students to explore the different type of transcription software out there that transcribe audio files into text, or it might be a good opportunity as well as talk about whether or not these podcasts should even be included as "required" readings. I did not have any deaf students in the class, but if I had, this would present a serious problem.

Assignment and Sequencing

Assignment: Place-Based Podcast

Overview

Students will in groups of two or three create a podcast episode that investigates an object, theme, idea, history, person, building, or other element relating to Norfolk, with the specific intent of enlightening, challenging, or affirming the public perceptions of the city. Paying close attention to the narrative structures and elements outlined in Jack Hart's (2012) *Storycraft*, as well as our collective analyses of a variety of podcasts in class, students will craft a purely audio, placed-based nonfiction podcast that fits within the theme of the podcast series we are creating, *Of Norfolk*. You are encouraged to see the podcasts (or even, audio essays) as episodic, not in the sequential sense but in the thematic sense, connected in their concern to enlighten, challenge, or explore an underappreciated aspect of Norfolk culture. Students will use Audacity for audio editing and will be responsible for conducting whatever type of research is required to compose an engaging, informative narrative about an aspect or object of Norfolk culture. This research might be anything from ethnographic to observational to interview to archival.

Assessment

The criteria for assessment for this podcast assignment are divided into two separate but not entirely distinct sections: technical production and quality of storytelling. In terms of technical production, podcasts will need to include the following:

- musical overlays (open source music to facilitate introductions or transitions);
- multiple distinct voices (including each group member and a member of the public, if possible);

- three audio effects, used appropriately (these will vary, but might include insertions of white noise, echo effects, or noise reduction);
- non-original, non-musical recordings (these will vary, but might include innocuous background noises, such as traffic, birds chirping, etc.); and
- high-quality narration (all voices should be clear and crisp and of high quality).

Podcasts will be assessed not only by their technical quality but also for the effectiveness and rhetorical quality of the script—that is, the ability of the students to engage an audience and put forth a compelling story in a digital storytelling format. In terms of storytelling, podcasts will need to attend to the following:

- a type of story structure, as outlined by Hart's *Storycraft*;
- a question or hook to frame the episode;
- a cogent identification and explanation of a specific theme, object, or idea;
- interesting and engaging sources of research relevant for your specific topic; and
- an appropriate conclusion that presses the audience to consider further the topic of your choice and its overall importance.

As you will see, these categories are not always distinct, such as when an appropriate musical overlay facilitates an engaging hook, but for the purposes of assessment the podcasts will be divided as such.

Texts

To complete this assignment, you'll need access to the following texts:

- Dennis Baron's (1999) "From Pencils to Pixels: The Stages of Literacy Technology"
- Jenny Edbauer's (2005) "Unframing Models of Public Distribution: From Rhetorical Situation to Rhetorical Ecologies"
- Jack Hart's (2012) *Storycraft*
- Richard A. Lanham's (2007) *The Economics of Attention: Style and Substance in the Age of Information*
- Walter J. Ong's (1982) *Orality and Literacy: The Technologizing of the Word*
- Plato's (1995) *Phaedrus*
- Gregory Ulmer's (2009) "Introduction: Electracy"

Podcasts

To complete this assignment, you'll need access to the following podcasts:

- "Blame Game." *Revisionist History* with Malcolm Gladwell (2016). Season 1, Episode 8.
- "Freud's Couch." *99% Invisible* with Roman Mars (2015a). Episode 169.
- "Harper High School: Part One." *This American Life* with Ira Glass (2013). Episode 487.

- "Nazi Summer Camp." *RadioLab* with Jad Abumrad (2015).
- "No Place Like Home." *This American Life* with Ira Glass (2014). Episode 520.
- "Penn Station Sucks." *99% Invisible* with Roman Mars (2015c). Episode 147.
- "The Gruen Effect." *99% Invisible* with Roman Mars (2015b). Episode 163.
- "Wild Ones Live." *99% Invisible* with Roman Mars (2013). Episode 91.

Students: You may notice that not all podcasts have transcripts available. Why do you think this is? What can be done about it? Let's discuss this in class together.

Weekly Schedule

Table 22.1. Weekly Schedule: Overview

Week and Topic	Readings	Due
1. Writing with/as/is Technology	Baron (1999)	Responses to Baron
2. What Is with the Honey-Tongues?	Plato (1995), *Phaedrus*	Analysis of passage
3. How Did We Tell Stories?	Ong (1982), Chapters 1, 2, 6	Responses to Ong
4. How Do We Tell Stories?	Ong (1982), Chapter 4	Critical listening exercise
5. It's an EmerAgency—What Now?	Ulmer (2009)	Responses to Ulmer
6. Is Norfolk Weird?	Edbauer (2005); Hart (2012), Chapters 6, 9	Topic worksheet
7. How to Get Our Stories Straight?	Hart (2012), Chapters 1–4	Narrative structure
8. How Do We Keep Your Attention?	Lanham (2007), Chapter 1	5-minute clip
9. Did We Keep Your Attention?	Lanham (2007), Chapter 2; Hart (2012), Chapters 11–13	Peer review
10. What's Next for Text?	Lanham (2007), Chapters 3–5	Podcast draft

Weekly Schedule: Sample Specification

Week 1. Writing with/as/is Technology

Before even beginning podcasting, you'll first need to consider the relationship between technology and writing. This week, you will be reading an essay from Dennis Baron, titled "From Pencils to Pixels: The Stages of Literacy Technology" (1999) and then answer the following questions in your notebook:

- Baron states that writing itself is a technology. What does he mean by this?

- How do writing technologies become "naturalized"?
- Why was Henry David Thoreau's distaste for the telegraph ironic in Baron's view?
- How does "accessibility" play into the development of writing technologies?
- Why should humanists (those in the arts and letters) embrace digital writing technologies?

Baron's reading will help provide a framework for next week's class, which will unpack Plato's *Phaedrus*, a foundational dialogue that contains several important passages on the nature of writing, memory, and mind. Plato's dialogues can be challenging, so for the sake of focus pay attention to the social context within which the dialogue was written, historically speaking; how rhetoric and philosophy are compared and contrasted; and how Plato uses dialogic structure to develop his arguments.

Week 2. What is with the Honey-Tongues?

Read Plato's (1995) *Phaedrus* and analyze passages in groups. Consider how Plato's insistence on orality anticipates Baron's work.

Week 3. How Did We Tell Stories?

Read Chapters 1, 2, and 6 of Walter J. Ong's (1982) *Orality and Literacy* and relate Ong's ideas about narrative structure to this video by Ira Glass (creator and narrator for *This American Life*) on storytelling (Neo, 2013).

Week 4. How Do We Tell Stories?

Listen to the two assigned podcasts, read chapter 4 of Ong, and think about the connections between Ong's question of how we rediscover the "tenaciousness of orality" (p. 115) and the thoughts of *RadioLab* creator and co-host Jad Abumrad (as communicated in this video on why he thinks radio will never die: PBS NewsHour, 2016).

Week 5. It's an EmerAgency—What Now?

Read Gregory Ulmer's (2009) "Introduction: Electracy" and consider the larger social trend of podcasts. During class students will find a song online, upload it to Audacity, and cut and add in an effect of their choice.

Week 6. Is Norfolk Weird?

Watch the video *Norfolk Reinvented* (Lanpher, 2016) and highlight any connections you see between this presentation and Jenny Edbauer's (2005) article, "Unframing Models of Public Distribution." Then, listen to the two podcasts that will help in thinking more about the connections between objects, materiality, and place.

Week 7. How to Get Our Stories Straight?

Read Chapters 1 through 4 of Hart's (2012) *Storycraft*, thinking about the narrative structure of your own podcast. Students will visualize in draft form on construction paper potential story structures for their podcast episode.

Week 8. How Do We Keep Your Attention?

Read Chapter 1 of Lanham's (2007) book *The Economics of Attention* and draw connections with Ulmer's notions of electracy. Students will then create sample clips of their podcast after reviewing *The Way You Sound Affects Your Mood* (Lund University, 2016) and the National Co-Ordinating Center for Public Engagement (2014) work on *Podcasting*.

Week 9. Did We Keep Your Attention?

Read Chapter 2 of Lanham and Chapters 11 and 12 of Hart and then listen to the podcast episode "The Living Room" (Abumrad & Krulwich, 2015). As you listen to the podcast, consider what you found to be different about it from the rest we've listened to thus far.

Week 10. What's Next for Text?

Read Chapters 3 and 5 of Lanham and draw out a matrix for style/substance modeled after Lanham's work (p. 158, Figure 5.1). Consider: How does style and substance play out in podcasts? And how can this matrix guide the review of your peers' work?

Sample Student Podcast Episodes

1. In "The Glass Age," Danielle Thornhill and Star LaBranche explore the understated arts culture in Norfolk, with specific attention to the Perry Glass Studio (https://chrysler.org/glass/) in the Chrysler Museum of Art. Does the nature of glass mimic the nature of Norfolk? Listen to find out.[3]

2. In the playfully-titled podcast episode, "Ceremonial Norfolk: The Amazing Mace," Kimberly Goode and Matthew Pawlowski focus in on one specific object that connects the city of Norfolk, the Commonwealth of Virginia, and the king of England, and symbolizes the complicated power relationships between all three: the Norfolk Mace (https://chrysler.emu seum.com/objects/29714/the-norfolk-mace). While many city maces exist, the Norfolk Mace is the only one to still reside in the city to which it was originally commissioned. This, as Kimberly and Matthew found out, is not by coincidence.

These sample podcast episodes (along with the others on the channel, available at https://soundcloud.com/dan-richards-10/sets/of-norfolk) aimed to contribute to a class series, titled *Of Norfolk*, in which each podcast delved into some aspect or object of the city culture. Each podcast, to varying extents, followed the guidelines of the assignment described above.

---

3. Two student examples (audio files and descriptive transcripts) can be found on the book's companion website.

Reflection

[Opening music is hip, electronic instrumental music by Lee Rosevere (2017), a song titled "Ennui" from his album The Big Loop.*]*

Daniel P. Richards: Plato, podcasts, and place: These are a few of my favorite things.[4] As a professor with a Ph.D. in rhetoric and composition, the first usually generates polite nods, but my sympathies and fascination for Plato and his rhetorical facilities and epistemological sensibilities remain despite his relentless castigation of my field. (He loves us, but he'll never admit it.) As a man who is a part of many fan communities and who loves stories and stays updated on politics, the second is rather inevitable. This love does not generate polite nods but usually generative conversations at social gatherings about the specific podcast series and episodes that are *absolute must listens*. This remains constant across all three places I've lived: Windsor, Ontario, Canada (where I was born, raised, and got a master's degree), Tampa, Florida (where I did my Ph.D.), and now Norfolk, Virginia—where I am now, working as an assistant professor at Old Dominion University. Which takes me to my third love listed: place. Having lived, as many in my profession have, in multiple, entirely distinct places, I am fascinated at how municipalities create—or have created for them—specific identities. To borrow from Jenny Edbauer's (2005) thinking on rhetoric and place, how do we trace a given city's *affective ecologies*? How do city identities get created? And who gets to create them? And by which media or modalities do we learn about them? Perhaps this fascination stems from my experience being raised in Windsor, which many refer to as the armpit of Canada (not so affectionately), but I like to think of as the Twilight Zone of North America, where Canadians use Fahrenheit to measure temperature and where you cross over into the United States by heading North.

But that is neither here nor there.

What is here—here being Norfolk

[Radio scratch, person saying "downtown Nor-foke," radio scratch, person saying "This is Naw-fuk" Virginia, radio scratch, person saying "Nor-fik," radio scratch.]

—whoa . . . sorry. Um, did you hear that too? Was that just me? Seems every time I utter the word Norfolk

[Radio scratch, "person saying "Today I am in Norfolk, Virginia."]

[act disheveled] the other ways the city gets pronounced circulate in my mind. It is weird—not Austin weird, and definitely not Portland weird—but weird to live in a town where you might walk from your house to get a cup of coffee on the way to the university and hear your neighbor, the barista, and your students all

---

4. The audio version of Daniel P. Richards's reflection can be found on the book's companion website.

pronounce the city in which we all live differently. And everyone is like kind of cool about it (although, the moment you utter the city name you "out" yourself as one who hails from one part of town, another part of town, or another part of town, or as an outsider who tried to get it close, or an outsider who just doesn't care and who opts for phonetic consistency).

Anyways *[clears throat]*, let's try that again.

What *is* here is the course I taught a few semesters back titled Writing in Digital Spaces. While I don't often get to teach a course that integrates three of my favorite things (I can't imagine a class, for example, that resides at the intersection of hockey, turn-of-the-century post-hardcore music, and whiskey—but maybe that's for a project at a later date), this class did, as students read Plato's (1995) *Phaedrus*, thought about place, and then podcasted about it. The course, naturally, had intentional design; it was not just a slapdash potpourri of my interests. While the practical production stream of the class focused on podcasts (more on that later), web writing, and Twitter, the theoretical framework was built around Walter Ong's (1982) book *Orality and Literacy: The Technologizing of the Word*, which provides a rather persuasive analytical account of how cultures that have transitioned from oral to literate modalities experience a transformation of consciousness as a result.

Literacy, the very technologizing of the "word," Ong argues, produces patterns of thought that become normalized and naturalized—these patterns of thought are distinct from those of oral cultures, with particular distinction noticed in the way we tell stories. So, when students were creating podcasts of the city, of an object, histories, person, or building within the city limits of Norfolk, they were thinking about the storytelling structures that help create a particular municipal *mythos*; they were synthesizing orality with what Gregory Ulmer (2009) coins the third apparatus: orality the first, literacy and the second, and electracy the third. Electracy is an apparatus where the practice is not religion or science but entertainment, and the institution is not the church or school but the internet. In drawing connections between Plato's reservations in the *Phaedrus* about written text and its potentially erosive effects on memory, Ong's in-depth analysis of the distinction between oral and literate cultures, and Ulmer's speculative space generated by the vision of electracy, students were thus asked to ruminate on how digital technologies offer our world—and our cities—an opportunity to productively re-sequence the seemingly dissonant mode of orality with and through a fuller embrace of digital writing technologies. This, the course argued, happens (potentially) through production. It happens through podcasting. The popularity and production of podcasts, students would hopefully realize, are connected in meaningful but complicated ways to ancient allegiances to orality, and perhaps represent a return, or re-visioning, of orality for our digitally mediated culture.

The podcasts students generated were impressive. Topics varied. One group sought to explain why the city symbol is a mermaid despite the dearth of beaches. Another explored a historical cemetery embedded within the city, divided by a literal wall between the races of the dead. Another explored the glass studio extension of our local art museum. And another went in-depth on how and why people of the city pronounce its name differently. People were called. Linguists were consulted. Research was done. The ideas, the scripts, the attention to story structure—all were impressive. Especially given when asked on the first day of class who listened to podcasts: Two hesitant hands were raised.

As I sit here, in soundproof audio recording booth in our campus's technology and distance education building, I can't help but think that my biggest regret with the podcast series we produced and made available for public consumption on SoundCloud—search, if you wish, for the series *Of Norfolk*—is the lack of attention I paid to production. The class was quite immersed in theory, quite immersed in analyzing podcast story structures, and articulating carefully how students might structure their own, and why, but that attention to things such as high-quality microphones, recording spaces, ambient noises, and enunciation kind of took a back seat.

[in bad quality, with outdoor ambient noise] In 15 weeks it was challenging to attend to both storytelling and production quality—not that they are as divided as we might think—given how your listening experience has plummeted a little right now because I am using my iPhone, outside, in Norfolk.

Students certainly learned to appreciate the amount of time required to produce even a 15-minute podcast, which is good, and they learned about rhetorical theory and generated great discussion about orality, literacy, and electracy—also good, and not easy.

But with podcasts even I was surprised at how absolutely crucial sound quality is to the success of a podcast. Seems simple, right? Seems like I should have thought about that before, maybe? But when you have seven groups of two going around the city, as they were encouraged to do, equipment becomes an issue. Access becomes an issue. The very nature of the place-based podcasts took them out of the classroom, out of the quiet, and left them susceptible to technological considerations we didn't explicitly cover. Background noise. The proximity of microphones. We covered the use of Audacity, yes, as you can see in the write-up, but the actual on-site quality of recordings was lacking—as you yourself can attest if you choose to listen.

And when I reflect on this project, and that semester, I oscillate between two positions: on one hand, not *really* caring about the production quality of the podcasts because the key learning objectives were met and students engaged quite impressively with the readings, concepts, and projects as a whole. They bought in. And then on the other hand, *really* caring, since the very idea of the podcast project was to make a series for public consumption that might help reframe or challenge existing perceptions of the city. While production quality was not a major criterion for assessment in my evaluation of the podcasts, when they cross over into more public spheres—such as sharing the playlist on Facebook or Twitter or sending it to the people and places included in the episodes—there was a tinge of hesitancy. What might people think of the project, of our school, of our program, if little attention was paid to the production of the podcasts? Other questions I asked myself: Should I even have ever done this project in the first place, knowing our department didn't have the means necessary for all students to produce high-quality, in terms of production, work? Should I have just spent the entire semester on the podcast project, letting go of the others to afford more time to figure out the technology? How important is the production quality in terms of public perception? How much of my teaching should be spent in Audacity, in researching technology? What role or restrictive capacity does the type of technology we have access to have in our teaching? In our decision to design projects and courses?

I cannot give you answers to these questions, but they sure make darn good discussion questions for the next time I teach this course and project.

[Outgoing song is hip, electronic instrumental music by Lee Rosevere (2007), a song titled "Ennui" from his album The Big Loop.*]*

References

Abumrad, J. (Host). (2015, May 22). Nazi summer camp [Audio podcast episode]. In *RadioLab*. WNYC Studios. https://www.wnycstudios.org/podcasts/radiolab/articles/nazi-summer-camp.

Abumrad, J. & Krulwich, R. (Hosts). (2015, April 9). The living room [Audio podcast episode]. In *RadioLab*. WNYC Studies. https://www.wnycstudios.org/podcasts/radiolab/articles/living-room.

Baron, D. (1999). From pencils to pixels: The stages of literacy technologies. In G. E. Hawisher & C. L. Selfe (Eds.), *Passions, pedagogies, and 21st century literacies* (pp. 15–33). Utah State University Press. https://digitalcommons.usu.edu/usupress_pubs/119/.

Bowie, J. L. (2012a). Podcasting in a writing class? Considering the possibilities. *Kairos: A Journal of Rhetoric, Technology, and Pedagogy, 16*(2). http://technorhetoric.net/16.2/praxis/bowie/index.html.

Bowie, J. L. (2012b). Rhetorical roots and media future: How podcasting fits into the computers and writing classroom. *Kairos: A Journal of Rhetoric, Technology, and Pedagogy, 16*(2). http://technorhetoric.net/16.2/topoi/bowie/index.html.

Carr, N. (2010, May 24). The web shatters focus, rewires the brain. *WIRED*. https://www.wired.com/2010/05/ff-nicholas-carr/.

Derrida, J. (1981). Plato's pharmacy. In *Dissemination* (B. Johnson, Trans.; pp. 61–171). University of Chicago Press.

Edbauer, J. (2005). Unframing models of public distribution: From rhetorical situation to rhetorical ecologies. *Rhetoric Society Quarterly, 35*(4), 5–24. https://doi.org/10.1080/02773940509391320.

French, L. & Bloom, E. (2011). Auralacy: From Plato to podcasting and back again. *Currents in Electronic Literacy, 14*. https://currents.dwrl.utexas.edu/2011/auralacyfromplatotopodcasting.html.

Gladwell, M. (Host). (2016, August 3). Blame game [Audio podcast episode] (Season 1, episode 8). On *Revisionist history*. Pushkin. https://www.pushkin.fm/episode/blame-game/.

Glass, I. (Host). (2013, February 15). Harper's High School: Part one [Audio podcast episode] (Episode 487). On *This American life*. WBEZ Chicago. https://www.thisamericanlife.org/487/harper-high-school-part-one.

Glass, I. (Host). (2014, March 14). No place like home [Audio podcast episode] (Episode 520). On *This American life*. WBEZ Chicago. https://www.thisamericanlife.org/520/no-place-like-home.

Hart, J. (2012). *Storycraft: The complete guide to writing creative nonfiction*. University of Chicago Press.

Havelock, E. A. (1963). *Preface to Plato*. Harvard University Press.

Lanham, R. A. (2007). *The economics of attention: Style and substance in the age of information*. University of Chicago Press.

Lanpher, K. (2016). Norfolk reinvented [Video file]. *Vimeo*. https://vimeo.com/147333423.

Lund University. (2016, January 11). *The way you sound affects your mood* [Press release]. https://www.eurekalert.org/pub_releases/2016-01/lu-twyo11116.php.

Mars, R. (Host). (2013, October 14). Wild ones live [Audio podcast episode] (Episode 91). On *99% invisible*. https://99percentinvisible.org/episode/wild-ones-live/.

Mars, R. (Host). (2015a, June 16). Freud's couch [Audio podcast episode] (Episode 169). On *99% invisible*. https://99percentinvisible.org/episode/freuds-couch/.

Mars, R. (Host). (2015b, May 5). The Gruen effect [Audio podcast episode] (Episode 147). On *99% invisible*. https://99percentinvisible.org/episode/the-gruen-effect/.

Mars, R. (Host). (2015c, January 6). Penn Station sucks [Audio podcast episode] (Episode 147). On *99% invisible*. https://99percentinvisible.org/episode/penn-station-sucks/.

National Co-Ordinating Center for Public Engagement. (2014). Podcasting. https://web.archive.org/web/20160408171553/https://www.publicengagement.ac.uk/do-it/techniquesapproaches/podcasting.

Neel, J. (1988). *Plato, Derrida, and writing*. Southern Illinois University Press.

Neo, A. M. (2013, January 9). Ira Glass on storytelling, part 1 of 4 [Video file]. *YouTube*. https://youtu.be/f6ezU57J8YI.

Old Dominion University. (n.d.). English courses. http://catalog.odu.edu/courses/engl/.

Ong, W. J. (1982). *Orality and literacy: The technologizing of the word*. Routledge.

PBS NewsHour. (2016, January 28). "I love radio precisely because it is empty of the things that you are awash in, my impoverished friends" [Video file]. *Facebook*. https://www.facebook.com/watch/?v=10153906056058675.

Plato. (1995). *Phaedrus* (A. Nehamas & P. Woodruff, Trans.). Hackett Publishing.

Raphael. (1509). Plato; from *The School of Athens* [Painting, detail]. Fresco, Stanza della Segnatura, Palazzi Pontifici, Vatican. https://en.m.wikipedia.org/wiki/File:Plato-raphael.jpg.

Rosevere, L. (2017). Ennui [Song]. On *The big loop*. Happy Puppy Records. https://leerosevere.bandcamp.com/album/the-big-loop-fml-original-podcast-score.

Schicke, J. (2011). An autoethnography of sound: Local music culture in Colorado. *Currents in Electronic Literacy, 14.* https://currents.dwrl.utexas.edu/2011/anauthethnographyofsound.html.

Ulmer, G. (2009). Introduction: Electracy. In *networked.* https://www.scribd.com/document/239621382/Gregory-Ulmer-Introduction-to-Electracy.

Wright, E. A. (2005). Rhetorical spaces in memorial places: The cemetery as a rhetorical memory place/space. *Rhetoric Society Quarterly, 35*(4), 51–81. https://doi.org/10.1080/02773940509391322.

Chapter 23. YA On the Air: A Scaffolded Podcast Assignment on YA Literature

Jasmine Lee
CALIFORNIA STATE UNIVERSITY, SAN BERNARDINO

Jennifer Geraci
UNIVERSITY OF CALIFORNIA, IRVINE

In this chapter, we describe and reflect on a soundwriting project titled YA On-the-Air, which we assigned to students enrolled in a large, general education lecture course about Young Adult (YA) Fiction. Students worked through the process of writing and recording episodes of podcasts about YA in two contexts connected to the large lecture class: Jennifer's discussion sections, and an optional, four-credit "attached" writing course that Jasmine facilitated. Thanks to this unique setup, we can offer you here a variety of materials and reflections about a shared assignment in two very different learning scenes. Students working with Jennifer engaged with the course material in four class meetings a week (three days of lecture plus one 50-minute discussion section), where they focused primarily on developing the content of the podcast episodes about the required YA novels. Students in Jasmine's section engaged with the course material five times a week (three times during the lecture and twice in 80-minute writing class meetings); the writing class meetings emphasized rhetorical decision making and strategies for composing.

YA On-the-Air asked students to work in small groups to develop an episode of a podcast series about YA novels. Students in Jasmine's course were invited to conceptualize a podcast series and create one episode from the series; they could imagine the larger trajectory of their podcast and decide if they wanted to produce a first episode, middle episode, or final episode for their series. Students in Jennifer's class were asked to imagine their episode as part of a defined podcast series, one that used YA fiction as an access point for young listeners into larger social and political issues. Students developed context knowledge for their podcasts in the large lecture course, where they learned about the history of YA fiction, read a selection of YA novels, and discussed the themes and goals of YA.

In both of our classes, we relied on our training as teachers of rhetoric and writing to help us guide students through this project. For example, we introduced the medium of podcasts by inviting students to listen to a range of podcast genres (e.g., book review podcasts; "talk show"/roundtable podcasts; narrative podcasts; interview podcasts; etc.) and discuss the conventions, audiences, and purposes of those examples. Students then selected a genre for their own episodes based on their groups' rhetorical goals. Many of our scaffolding activities focus on helping students articulate those goals: They ask students to think about how they are positioning themselves in relation to their audiences through their episodes, what they want to achieve in speaking to these audiences, and how, through their content and concept but also specifically through sound, they can effectively reach their audiences.

We were very excited with the outcomes of the assignment. We found that the podcast medium not only encouraged thoughtful, critical, and collaborative engagement with YA, but also, more importantly, helped students achieve a deeper understanding of rhetoric. Composing with sound was a key part of those results: Students, in being given the opportunity to add their voices, literally, to conversations about YA and social issues that mattered to them, developed a different sense of themselves as rhetors. They explored ethos as an embodied concept and expressed a more robust sense of ownership and authorship of their compositions. Students engaged differently with matters of rhetorical decision-making than we had seen with more traditional composing assignments in our courses. That is to say, the aural dimensions of soundwriting made questions of, for example, how tone or pace affect audiences more present to students. We were excited to see that students engaged differently with revision as they composed with sound. Many groups approached revision radically after receiving feedback on their episodes. They rewrote scripts and re-recorded and re-edited audio in order to change the mood of their episodes, to make themselves and/or the content of their episodes more approachable and interesting for their audiences, and to try to find ways to keep their audiences' attention. When we introduced the soundwriting project to students, we learned that many of them had not listened to podcasts before; rather than hindering their work, however, the newness of the medium created exciting possibilities for students as they thought about how (and why, and under what circumstances) the podcast as a medium "worked" and what it could help them accomplish as rhetors.

The implementation of the shared assignment across these two different contexts produced some variation in how we introduced this soundwriting project and how we guided our students through it. Because of our students' general unfamiliarity with podcasts, the curricular complexities of this shared assignment, and the limited time we had with students in our courses (our institution runs on a quarter system), we designed this assignment with significant scaffolding. Our hope is that the materials in this chapter will assure you that while incorporating soundwriting into a curriculum can seem daunting, students can have meaningful learning experiences composing with sound in spite of time constraints and while still meeting diverse course objectives. This archive represents all the scaffolding activities we assigned between our classes. In other words, both sets of students engaged with different combinations of these activities. The preparatory assignments we share with you here are designed to help students develop an "ear" for podcasts, strategies for soundwriting, and a shared vocabulary related to rhetorical production. These activities create opportunities for students to workshop ideas, explore the rhetorical affordances of audio, and reflect regularly on both their textual products and their compositional processes. The project as a whole, and its scaffolded parts, can be completed with the tools students already have; our students recorded on their phones or laptops, and all students used audio-editing software that came with their computers or Audacity, a free, open-source editing program. (Many free tutorials and guides are available online for users new to Audacity, a bonus for both students and teachers who are new to audio editing!)

Assignments and Sequence

The Podcast Episode Prompt

For the Podcast Episode Project, you will work collaboratively in groups of four to 1) create a podcast episode (10–15 minutes in length) in which you discuss or review a work of young adult fiction, 2) draft a memo in which you explain why you chose to work on this particular episode, 3) create an introduction to your podcast for high school listeners, and 4) create a transcript of your episode.

Your podcast episode will address a specific audience and purpose. In addition, it will address the class theme (or respond to one of the class texts). While you must create a podcast episode, there are many types of podcasts. Your group will need to select an appropriate type of podcast for this project and make appropriate rhetorical choices for this situation. In other words, your podcast episode will operate within a clear rhetorical framework—with a clear context, genre, purpose and audience—that addresses the class theme (or responds to one of the class texts).

Additionally, with your consent, your episode might be made available to students in our local high schools interested in hearing your views about YA.

This assignment will have a few moving parts: Once you've been assigned a team, you'll develop an episode proposal, compose an episode storyboard and script, participate in peer review of your script, record your episode, and then write an introductory memo to local high school teachers introducing your episode and explaining why the episode might be meaningful to their students. Details are forthcoming about each step.

The Listening Reports Activity Prompt

Below you will find a list of podcast series. Each link will take you to the podcast homepage; from there, you can locate an archive of past episodes.

Listen to two episodes from two different podcasts (one episode from each) and write a brief report on them using the questions below. Coordinate with your team so that you choose different podcasts and episodes. Share your reports with your teammates.

Report Questions
- What is the podcast series about, and how is it structured (episodically, serially)? Where does this episode fit into the series?

- What is the purpose of the series and episode? Does the episode "fit in" to the series?
- Who is the intended audience for the series/episode? How do you know?
- Who is the podcast's rhetor? How does the rhetor's position influence his or her connection with the audience?
- Describe the structure and setup of the episode. How many speakers were there? Were they all hosts or were some invited guests? What did they discuss, and how did they interact with each other?
- Outline the episode: What happened first, second, third, etc.?
- What sound effects or music was included, and to what effect?

Podcast Series

- *Hey YA!*: a podcast from BookRiot (https://bookriot.com/listen/shows/thepodcast/)
- *BookHype*: news, reviews, recommendations, and banter from Hypable.com (https://www.hypable.com/podcasts/book-hype/)
- *The Split*: YA book reviews (http://thesplitbookreviews.com/category/podcast-episodes/)
- *88 Cups of Tea*: YA interviews, reader questions, craft Q&A (http://88cupsoftea.com/)
- *Mugglecast*: a Harry Potter franchise fandom podcast (http://mugglecast.com/)
- *Clear Eyes, Full Shelves*: reading and reading-related discussion (http://cleareyesfullshelves.com/thepodcast/)
- *The Dead Authors Podcast*: imagined conversations with dead authors (http://thedeadauthorspodcast.libsyn.com/)
- *Adventures in YA*: YA-related discussions + interviews (http://www.adventuresinya.com/)
- *Candlewick Press Presents*: from children's publisher Candlewick Press, an inside the industry look (http://www.candlewickpodcast.com/)
- *This Creative Life with Sara Zarr*: a YA author interviews other YA authors (http://thiscreativelife.libsyn.com/)
- *Says Who?*: a political podcast co-hosted by YA author Maureen Johnson (http://www.sayswhopodcast.com/)

The Pitch Activity Prompt

A "pitch" is a very brief (and engaging) account of what you have to offer to someone who might be interested in your idea. The quintessential pitch is the elevator pitch: Imagine that you've stepped onto an elevator with a person of influence who you want to sell on an idea or who you want a job from. You only have 30–60 seconds to make an impression and give the person all the relevant details about your proposal. You must "hook" them before the elevator doors open.

The genre of the pitch can also help us sift through and combine our various ideas into a cohesive one. In this exercise, we'll use the pitch to help us plan out our podcasts.

Refer to the podcast pitch proposal guide from WNYC (n.d.). Then, with your team, prepare a pitch for your own podcast. Share your pitch.

The Proposals Prompt

In your groups, compose a 500-word proposal discussing your plans for the Podcast Episode Project.

Your proposal should refer to the following:

1. **Content, Message, Purpose**
   a. Which text are you focusing on?
   b. Which topic would you like to discuss in your podcast episode, and how does this topic relate to our discussion of YA fiction? Why would this topic be important to your audience?
   c. What is the purpose of the podcast episode? How do you expect your audience to respond to it?
   d. Which cultural, social, or political conversations does your podcast join? How will you contribute to these conversations? Why is it important for you to jump in?

2. **Audience**
   What specific audience do you want to address in your podcast? (Don't simply say YAs. This is too broad.) Why do you want to speak to them? What's your relationship to them? Do some research on your intended audience: What do you think they want to know more about? Why do you think they care about these things? Which rhetorical choices are you going to make that will be particularly appealing to them?

3. **Podcast Composer**
   How will you present yourself as the podcast composer? If applicable, what persona will you adopt? (Are you private individuals, or are you the representatives of a public broadcasting agency?) Think about how this choice could influence the structure of your podcast.

4. **Structure**
   a. Which podcast sub-genre (solo; interview; roundtable; co-hosted; audio magazine; etc.) will your podcast belong to? Why is this format a good choice to reach your intended audience? How does it relate to your imagined position as podcast composer?
   b. What is the overall theme of the proposed podcast? How will the episode you produce fit into this theme?

    c. What is the position of the episode you are going to produce in relation to the podcast as a whole? Is it the first episode? Consider what may have happened before and/or what will come after this particular episode.

The Audio Inventory Prompt

Start collecting audio samples. You may need to go into the world to record ambient noise or sound effects. You may also need to search the internet for royalty-free music and sounds. You and your group will collect more audio samples than you will end up using, but having a good bank of sounds will be useful at this stage.

You might think of your audio sample inventory as a sort of sound "vision" board. As you curate sounds, you can begin to clarify your podcast's tone, style, and overall vibe.

Collect your sounds on your team page. Give each sample a distinctive and identifying filename. You need at least two sound samples per person.

Storyboard Prompt[1]

This prompt is delivered in a PowerPoint presentation and explains the concept of a storyboard, reasons to storyboard, and some suggestions for storyboarding.

The Script Prompt

Draft a script that sketches your episode's conversation. The purpose here is to build on your proposal ideas by adding more concrete information; think about what, exactly, you will talk about; consider how (and why) you will incorporate sound (musical breaks, sound effects, etc.); and explore how you will conclude the episode. Please also include timestamps for each segment or topic.

The Production Journals Prompts

Note: Students respond to the following prompts in their journals throughout the project in response to scaffolding and peer review activities.

Entry #1

Once you have received your teammates' podcast episode reports, read them! Then, using this information, write a paragraph wherein you begin to think about the kind of podcast episode you might want to make. You might discuss its structure/setup, topic/theme, music/effects, audience, rhetor, or purpose.

Entry #2

In your production journal, transcribe your team's episode pitch. Then, in at least 250 words, write about how your pitch came to be, what ideas you and

---

1.   See the book's companion website for a PowerPoint file that we used to teach storyboarding.

your teammates had to leave behind and why, and how you're feeling about the pitch and the podcast episode at this point.

Entry #3

After you have collected your sound samples, make an entry in your production journal wherein you describe what you were looking for on your sound search; what you collected; where you collected your samples; why you collected what you did; how you might use these effects; and what else you might need to collect. Write too about the overall sound "vision" you're imagining for your podcast episode, and how this tone/style/vibe relates to the rhetorical situation (purpose, audience, genre) of your podcast. (This entry should be at least 250 words.)

Entry #4

Today, your team received feedback on your episode proposal. In at least 250 words, reflect on that feedback and your team's responses to it. In your entry, you might consider these questions:

- What did you feel like the strengths and weaknesses were of your proposal? Were these in line with the feedback you received?
- How, specifically, does your group plan to revise the proposal over the next few days?

Entry #5

One of your tasks this week is to craft a storyboard for your podcast episode. As you and your group work on your storyboard, reflect on the experience. These questions might guide your entry:

- What did you and your team have to figure out and discuss as you were planning your storyboard?
- Were there any disagreements, debates, or competing visions about the podcast that were uncovered during this process? What were they, and how did you resolve them? Why did you ultimately end up with the solution that you did?
- What did storyboarding help you learn or understand better about your podcast episode?
- Did storyboarding prompt you to revise your podcast proposal in any way?
- What resources/scripting work do you need to do next to prepare you for production?

As always, your entry should be at least 250 words.

Entry #6

What has surprised you about drafting, recording, and editing your podcast episode? Be as specific as possible, and record both your successes and challenges.

Entry #7

Consider the feedback you received from your peer reviewers. Come up with a revision strategy with your team, and report about it here. What will you prioritize as you revise, and why? What specific changes will you make, and what effect do you hope they'll have on your final product?

Entry #8

Imagine an episode that would follow your episode in your podcast series. What might it be? How does the episode you made serve as the "set up" for this next episode? Why might your audience value it?

The Transcript Prompt

An important consideration when composing—in new media or more traditional media forms—is accessibility. For a range of reasons, your audience may appreciate a transcript of your podcast episode.

Additionally, producing a transcript of your podcast episode can give you a different perspective on your audio composition.

As your final task related to the podcast episode, produce a transcript (complete with timestamps). If you feel so inclined, reflect on the process of transcribing, and what you learned from it, in your production journal.

Sample Student Projects

1. "Food for Thought" by Alejandra Santana, Oriana Gonzalez, Amy Vong, and Jailyn Fierro. Using Angie Thomas's 2017 novel *The Hate U Give*, "Food for Thought" explores how the main character, a Black teenager named Starr, grapples with the death of her friend at the hands of a White police officer. "Food for Thought," through discussions of Starr's sense of double consciousness, close reading, relevant music, and honest, hardline opinions about police brutality, aims to teach listeners—high school juniors and seniors—about the perils of police brutality and soft racism.[2]

2. *Healing Through Narratives* by Alexis Garcia, Anika Flores, and Gabriela Martinez, Episode 1: "Voice of the Dead." This episode of *Healing Through Narratives* explores the relevance of counter-storytelling in historically underrepresented folks using David Levithan's *Two Boys Kissing*. The episode features The Recollectors, a storytelling community consisting of families and children, who are now adults, whose relatives died as a result of the AIDS crisis during the 1980s and 1990s.

Reflection

[intro music: Dee Yan Key (2018), "That Ain't Chopin"]

---

2.   Two student examples (audio or video files and descriptive transcripts) can be found on the book's companion website.

Jasmine Lee: Hello, and welcome![3] Thanks for tuning in. Before we jump into a discussion of our soundwriting assignment, we want to take a second to introduce ourselves.

My name is Jasmine Lee, and I'm an assistant professor of English at the California State University, San Bernardino. My primary research interests include rhetorical education, affect, and cultural critique. Through my work, I often find myself coming back to popular culture, and YA (or young adult fiction) and youth culture in particular. You may have noted that my list does not include sound studies or soundwriting. The fact is that the assignment that we're sharing with you today was actually my first foray into soundwriting, as a scholar and as a teacher. The same is true for my coauthor, whom you'll meet in just a second.

Though we are soundwriting rookies, we are excited to share this pedagogical practice with you because we're excited about what sound added to our experiences teaching rhetorical production and composing strategies to our students. Before we get too far into that though, meet Jennifer!

Jennifer Geraci: And I'm Jennifer Geraci, a Ph.D. student and teaching assistant [now a lecturer at University of California, Irvine]. My primary research is in Latino literature and life writing, and I teach composition courses focusing on rhetoric and research writing. Although my primary research is not in sound, I found that our experiences with students on this podcast episode project align very well with many of the objectives of rhetoric and research writing classes that I teach.

Over the next 10 minutes, we'll tell you about the contexts for this podcasting assignment, how we helped students to prepare and produce their episodes, and what worked well for us, and what we might try differently the next time we teach this class.

We should talk a bit about what our podcast assignment involved and the contexts in which we taught it. I say contexts—plural—because we taught this assignment in very different kinds of classes.

Jasmine: Yes, good point! The soundwriting assignment that we're sharing with you here comes from courses that Jennifer and I taught together at the University of California, Irvine, where we were graduate student colleagues. The curricular details about this assignment are a bit complex, but, in short, it might suffice to say that Jennifer and I taught two different kinds of classes attached to a large lecture course on YA fiction. Jennifer's classes functioned as discussion sections for the large lecture, and my class functioned as a separate, four-unit writing and rhetoric course. Because of this setup, Jennifer and I had different amounts of time with our students, a different number of students, and different learning objectives in our classes. We nonetheless shared this assignment, which we designed and developed with the professor teaching

---

3. The audio version of Jasmine Lee and Jennifer Geraci's reflection can be found on the book's companion website.

the large lecture course and two other TAs who taught their own sections of the attached writing courses. We wanted to share our experience in this collection because, despite the very different contexts that we taught our project in, our students in both cases really shined. We think that their successes speak to the flexibility, adaptability, and the great potential of soundwriting projects across a variety of courses.

When we began designing our classes, I think we had some reservations about soundwriting. Podcasting was an intimidating new medium for us, and we worried that we might not have the time or the technological know-how to guide students through the project, or that we (and our students) might get overwhelmed by the media production aspects and lose sight of our course goals. But we're happy to report that those anxieties proved unfounded.

Jennifer: You're also getting a sense of our students' work right now. We've borrowed some of their successful strategies in our own podcast introduction recording and used them here in our own reflection. This introductory structure, the music you heard at the top of our reflection, and the organization of our reflection intro sections into sections, and the sound effect transition are all features of our students' podcasts.

Jasmine: That's a great point, Jennifer. I guess we should say a little more about this specific soundwriting project, right?

Okay, so our soundwriting assignment, YA On-The-Air, asked students to work in groups to collaboratively produce one episode of a podcast series. In my course, students could imagine their own podcast series and produce one episode from that series. Most students chose to address young readers as their audience, but the rhetorical purposes of their podcast series and episodes differed widely.

Jennifer: In the class I taught, students created one episode, but the objectives behind creating that episode was to inform a student population—a high school student population in our area. So they were very conscious of some of the course requirements for this particular district of high school students, and they also had a visit from some of the teachers of those high school students.

Jasmine: Right. The authenticity of this podcast production assignment, I think, really helped students cultivate a deeper understanding of rhetorical decision making. But I don't think it was just the framework of the task that mattered in the project. Sound opened up a new dimension to the way that we, and our students, thought about and talked about rhetorical work and composing. I for one really enjoyed watching my students work with a more embodied understanding of authorship. In the writing courses I've taught that did not involve sound, I had sort of given up over the years in talking about "voice"; voice felt kind of like a jargon, teacher-writing-oriented word. And I knew if I wanted to talk about voice, I actually meant that I wanted to talk about something, about where style and ethos and perspective and how you engage with and relate to an audience all met, but just saying "voice" didn't always help me communicate that to my students. In this soundwriting project, though, there was something more direct and literal about talking to students about voice. Jennifer, what stood out to you about soundwriting with students?

Jennifer: Students working with sound are more attuned to the minute complexities of, literally, their every word or pause, and through recording and audio playback, they are able to see more clearly how each decision they make communicates meaning to their auditors. To me, asking students to produce episodes, and to really think of them as publishable, "real" sound projects, aligns with the objectives of process-based writing instruction: students had to envision their audience, come up with a project idea and the language, sound, and structure to execute it, and they revised their episodes based on group and instructor feedback.

One of the most beneficial takeaways of this sound project with students was that it gave them an opportunity to slow down and think differently about their projects. Like I said before, they're thinking about their language and pause, sound effects and music (if they're using any), and it's also helping them to think about the tone of their voices, the moods that they are creating through their episode, how they're going to introduce and talk about the complex terms that we went over in the lecture course, and which literary texts they are going to talk about and how they are going to be able to relay their analysis to an audience.

Jasmine: Yes, yes to all of that. So something that Jennifer and I have talked a lot about when we've been putting this chapter together is how interesting we find it that sound, or more specifically, introducing soundwriting into our classes, did important work in both of our very different learning contexts. What we found most valuable about soundwriting was different for each of us; soundwriting helped students engage with concepts more deeply in each of our classes, but what those concepts were weren't necessarily always the same.

So I know that I will definitely incorporate soundwriting again in a different class, at my new institution, in part because of how exciting and, I think, productive soundwriting and composing with sound was in this course. In our chapter, you'll find a whole host of scaffolding activities that we used between our two courses in setting up this project. So, if you are thinking about doing your own podcast episode project in a class that you teach, please feel free to take from this archive, change activities, mix them up, leave out what doesn't work for you. And we'd love to hear if you use or any adapt of these materials, and what happens with them.

Jennifer: Well, we're about out of time for this reflection, and we want to thank you all for taking interest in our soundwriting project. We hope our experiences are useful to you as you design and implement your own podcast episode units in your classes. Happy Soundwriting!

Jasmine: Happy Soundwriting! Bye bye!

[Outro music: Dee Yan Key, "That Ain't Chopin," continues to end.]

Jasmine: Jennifer and I would like to thank Jonathan Alexander, the professor who initiated and taught the large lecture course at the center of this project, for his excitement about new media composing and for inviting us to be a part of this innovative course. The podcast episode project would not have been what it was without the smart work of our teaching colleagues, Fran Tsufim and Taylor McCabe. We are grateful for the opportunity to share this work and for the generous feedback we received from the editors of this collection. Lastly, I would like to express my gratitude to the Faculty Center for Excellence and the Institute for Child Development and Family Relations at CSUSB for providing some of the research support that enabled me to work on this chapter.

References

WNYC Studies. (n.d.). *Pitch a podcast to WNYC studios*. https://wnycstudios. zendesk.com/hc/en-us/articles/115014369227-pitch-a-podcast-to-WNYC-Studios.

Yan-Key, D. (2018). That ain't Chopin [Song]. On *Frédéric would cry*. https://www. freemusicarchive.org/music/Dee_Yan-Key/Frdric_would_cry/That_aint_Chopin.

Chapter 24. Let's Get Technical: Scaffolding Form, Content, and Assessment of Audio Projects

Jennifer Ware and Ashley Hall
INDEPENDENT SCHOLARS

We focus on a soundscape project and the feeders used to scaffold the creative and technical skills students need to complete the larger projects. We use the term feeder for smaller assignments that are carefully sequenced to build upon one another. Each one feeds into the next and creates a trajectory to success for students. In designing these feeders, we deliberately balance rhetorical skills, research methods, and technical proficiency.

This format leverages scaffolded feeders, peer feedback, drafting, and revision processes to explore composing strategies that include technical specificity and assessment of the technical aspects. As students progress from one feeder to the next, they must transfer rhetorical knowledge and technical skill to complete each subsequent assignment. By scaffolding technical precision—and its assessment—in the feeders, both students and instructors are able to identify areas where more practice is necessary and devote attention accordingly. After completing a series of feeders, students are prepared to compose a variety of more technically and rhetorically sophisticated projects.

We outline a science fiction soundscape radio drama project—a collection of sounds woven together to help a listener perceive and experience an environment—which includes a variety of fictionalized elements that work to tell a story through a combination of characters, description and sounds.

The Numbers Station Soundscape

This assignment was redesigned after being inspired by the Rhetoric Society of America 2017 Summer Institute seminar on Digital Rhetoric: Behind and Beyond the Screen. At the institute, Casey Boyle, Jim Brown, and Steph Ceraso asked participants to transduce the space of the Herman B. Wells Library on Indiana University's campus and use an augmentation app to publish the resulting soundscapes (see also Boyle et al., 2018).

Students are challenged to produce a science fiction radio drama that reimagines and transduces a real numbers station. The short-wave radio station, of which there are many, broadcasts a mix of sounds, ones that appear to be coded, secret messages. We begin the project by reading about the mysterious numbers station described in a BBC article (Gorvett, 2017). Next, we listen to and discuss an audio

DOI: https://doi.org/10.37514/PRA-B.2022.1688.2.24

capture of a strange sound (Stemwulf, 2016) being broadcast constantly from a numbers station. The clip, which is 6 minutes and 25 seconds long, contains an unexplained disruption to the broadcast. The students take up this disruption as a point of departure for their soundscape. They brainstorm story ideas, imagining what happened at the station that caused the sound inexplicably to stop and then resume, again inexplicably. Since the station and its broadcast are a mystery, there are no "right" or "wrong" answers as to what occurred. This gives students the ability to be creative while refining audio storytelling concepts and technical skills.

We present the feeders below, not as assignment prompts that we would give to students, but in a descriptive fashion for instructors to see how the smaller assignments are structured to scaffold skills and concepts leading up to the larger project.

Feeders—Working with Loops: Creative Exploration

In the first feeder, students work in teams and are given a limited number of loops. First, they are asked to create a 30-second sound file using only the loops provided with the prompt. Their objective is to work with the loops and arrange them on the timeline to produce 30 seconds of sound that is different from what any other team produces. On a technical level, this feeder helps students practice audio-composing skills and gain comfort working in the audio-editing interface. On a conceptual level, this feeder introduces students to the idea of flexibility within a framework. The limitation of having only certain loops to select from is a rhetorical constraint. Creativity is required to imagine ways of working with those loops to create new sonic possibilities—cutting, fading, layering, and arranging the loops in different ways. Through this work, students engage with the following:

- Technical skills:
  - Creating and using tracks
  - Understanding of loops and how to work with them
    - Add them to tracks
    - Make cuts
    - Fade or transition between loops
    - Layer/arrange loops on different tracks to create new sounds
    - Save work and export in multiple file formats
- Concepts:
  - Creativity and exploration
  - What's there in the interface? And what are rhetorical affordances students can identify as they start composing?
  - What are the creative possibilities? Especially when everyone starts with the same set of materials?

Next, students are asked to create another 30-second sound file. Once again students are given rhetorical constraints; they are permitted to use only the loops provided with the prompt. This time, however, their objective is to work with the loops and arrange them on the timeline to produce 30 seconds of sound that is as identical as possible to what every other team produces. On a technical level this feeder requires students to apply the basic audio-composing and editing skills and provide them more practice. On a conceptual level, this feeder introduces students to the idea that, in a team setting or work environment, it is sometimes necessary to translate one person's vision or concept into practice through composing and editing. This helps prepare students for more advanced group projects where each person might have a different role on a team production and for future workplace settings where a client or supervisor might ask for a project to be completed and provide some resources and direction but it is up to the individual or team to implement that vision with technical proficiency. Through this work, students engage with the following:

- Technical skills: Same as Feeder 1
- Concepts:
  - Understanding audience needs and expectations by translating someone else's vision or concept for an audio piece into a 30-second MP3 file
  - Using knowledge of the interface and editing tools to compose proficiently produce the desired outcome for stakeholders

In the third step of the scaffolding process, students begin working with voice. In this step of the assignment sequence, the script is a rhetorical constraint with which the students must contend. Each team is given the same few lines from a script to read and record using a USB microphone connected to the audio-editing interface and out in the field using either a recording app on a phone or a handheld recorder. Students are prompted to revisit the idea of flexibility within a framework, as introduced in the first feeder, to explore how aspects of the human voice can be a rhetorical resource in audio storytelling. Students read and record the lines of the script multiple times, exploring how changes in vocal variety, pacing, volume, and tone or inflection can be used to convey meaning in audio storytelling. Students then combine their voice recording with audio loops before exporting their MP3 file and turning it in. Through this work, students engage with the following:

- Technical skills:
  - Working with a microphone
  - Audio recording in the editing software interface
  - Audio recording in the field using cell phone recording apps or handheld mics
  - Importing audio files from a phone or an SDHC card
- Concepts:
  - The alphabetic content of a script is only one part of how meaning is made in audio storytelling.

- ○ Particular qualities of the human voice also play an important role in audio storytelling:
  - Vocal variety
  - Pacing
  - Volume
  - Tone or inflection

By the time students have worked through these feeders, they are familiar with basic audio composing and editing concepts ready to compose their science fiction soundscape described as the Numbers Station assignment.

Assignment

Project: The Numbers Station Soundscape

Orson Wells rocked the nation when he brought science fiction to the air waves with his famous 1938 radio drama *War of the Worlds*. In 2015, an eight-episode science fiction podcast called *The Message* created another stir, telling the story of a mysterious sound seemingly transmitted from outer space and recorded by the U.S. military (Sriram, 2015). Inspired by these creative and powerful science fiction audio stories, you will create your own 3–5-minute science fiction soundscape. Your job is to reimagine the setting of "MDZhB" shortwave radio station (Gorvett, 2017).

You will develop and pitch a concept of your piece to the class. Your pitch must explain how you plan to include the mysterious buzzer sound being broadcast from the MDZhB station, including the unexplained silence in the sound clip.

Once your pitch is approved, you will outline, design, produce, record, and mix this project. You may work independently or as part of a team for this assignment. To complete this project successfully, you will need to search for Creative Commons or public domain loops and sound effects, record scripted audio and natural sound, then mix, fade, and equalize your audio seamlessly together. This piece is meant to be creative and should have a narrative story arc.

Guidelines

Each audio piece must be 3–5 minutes in length and include:

- Balanced levels for each track/element and the overall piece
- Fade ins and outs used to create smooth transitions
- Field recordings
- Foley or sound effects

All components must be licensed through Creative Commons, be from public domain sources, or be original creations.

Also required:

- Notes from your pitch to the class
- Written script

- Transcript with timecodes (A transcript includes not only the words from the written script but also descriptions that make the music, foley, and other sounds accessible to members of the audience using the transcript.)
- You must turn in a detailed, spreadsheet list of each sound you've used, the place where it came from, the link to that place, permission to use (if you had to email the artist, send the permission email as well).
- Final audio file must be submitted as MP3
- A well-organized .band file (or other appropriate file format if you are using Audacity or another program) inside a folder that also contains all the raw files used to create the work.

The Rubric

All of the feeders use the rubric below, which in this example provides equal weight to each feeder element. For the larger audio projects, this same rubric can be modified with point values adjusted as needed to facilitate grading of the more complex assignments.

Table 24.1. Grading Rubric

Script—Written description of location	No vivid descriptions, lack of description	Some level of vivid description, good draft	Shows and tells the story through rich, vivid descriptions	Listeners can easily visualize the story, pairs with breaks for nat sound without literal duplication
Field recordings	Distortion present or no recordings included.	Mic too far or too close to the object being recorded. Few recordings included.	Field recordings add to the story through cohesive flow, clear recordings.	Nat pop breaks are introduced in the piece to complement the narration.
Narration recording	Substantial problems with clarity or reading of lines; story arc is disorganized or difficult to follow.	Additional takes needed in some areas; slight distortion on clips; reconsider recording location.	Pacing, inflection and vocal variety are well utilized for the genre. Recording location minimizes background noise.	Pacing and vocal variety drive the piece, few-to-no fumbles or word jumbles in the piece. Crisp clear audio recorded with little-to-no unintentional reverb or background noise.

Table 24.1—continued

	Does not meet expectations 0	Shows promise but needs significant revision 3	Demonstrates Competency 4	Outstanding Work 5
Editing	Majority of sound levels are blown out or too low, few to no fades present. Choppy sounds	Some sounds are too loud or too soft, few fades, needs refinement.	Master sound levels are in acceptable ranges; fades and timing are used to polish the piece and move us through sounds and tracks.	Superbly balanced levels. No breaks in the flow of the piece. Sounds are seamlessly woven together throughout.

Sample Student Projects

1. "The Sound Is My Medicine": A sound engineer at a popular radio station is asked by his general manager to visit his residence after work to fix some custom technology. The engineer finds thousands of dollars of equipment, stolen, and repurposed for a higher calling.[1]
2. "The Calming Method": When two scientists, Thaddeus and Anne, are unable to conceive a child, they'll go to any means to create one. But what consequences await them when they create a monster?

Reflection

Jen Ware: This is Jen Ware and Ashley Hall.[2] We're going to dive in and talk about feeders for a little bit here and some of the additional learning processes that kind of undergird those feeders.

Ashley Hall: So, the feeders include peer feedback, drafting, and revision times.

Jen: Some of these are built into the class periods so that we can focus on composing and the technical aspects together. As students progress from one feeder to the next, they must transfer the rhetorical knowledge and technical skills to complete each subsequent feeder, so they're building upon those experiences in those smaller scale assignments.

---

1. Two student examples (audio files and descriptive transcripts) can be found on the book's companion website.
2. The audio version of Jen Ware and Ashley Hall's reflection can be found on the book's companion website.

Ashley: And, by scaffolding technical precision—and its assessment—in the feeders, everybody's on the same page and we can focus our attention strategically on what students need more practice with.

Jen: So let's talk about the assignment for a little bit. It was inspired by an RSA Summer Institute, Digital Rhetoric: Behind and Beyond the Screen. And there, Steph Ceraso, Jim Brown, and Casey Boyle had us do an assignment on location where we were asked to transduce the space of the Herman Wells Library on the campus of Indiana University.

Ashley: And then we used the Geotourist app to publish our soundscapes. I thought that was really interesting, and it pushed me as a participant in the workshop beyond what I had done with soundscape composing either on my own or in terms of designing assignments. So I was inspired by that and wanted to keep working with that idea. And I came across this article in the BBC about this mysterious numbers station (Gorvett, 2017), and I thought okay, that'll be an interesting project for the students.

Jen: So the assignment asked students to transduce this space of this mysterious numbers station. And this station just broadcasts this incessant droning sound. So that's the catalyst for the assignment, and the students have to create a narrative around that drone sound stopping and then restarting.

Ashley: And to get the students there, to the point where they can actually write a narrative, put together and make choices about the sounds that are going to be arranged in their soundscape and then edit it all together, we go through these feeder assignments.

Jen: And they haven't done a series of assignments like this before.

Ashley: Right. So for a lot of students, especially the English students—and this is usually a cross-listed class that has both English students and communication students in it, uh, and that's a nice dynamic. But for the English students in particular, they have very little exposure to composing with technology, composing sound, composing visually. But they might have more experience doing creative writing.

Jen: And the communication students generally know the concepts of composing media for different platforms, but they're kind of out of their comfort zone when it comes to the creative writing aspect, something that's not more of a formal type of reporting media at this point.

This is one of the reasons why I enjoy teaching this class, because of the different experiences that the majors have and bring into the course. It allows everyone to bring in their strengths and learn something new at the same time. And that structure of feeders works well here, I think.

Ashley: So, the feeders help everyone really get on the same page and also ramp up their technical knowledge along with their conceptual knowledge. We start out with a feeder where the students are given 10 or so loops, and really their job is just to explore and be creative and find out what the possibilities are.

Jen: And the loops don't have to be in the software even. Sometimes we provide them with sets of Creative Commons materials and audio loops. Depending upon the audio-editing software that's available, this is another way to provide the creative experience.

Ashley: And while they're doing that and they're trying to come up with something different, they're learning the basic interface, they're learning how to put loops on the timeline, they're learning how to duplicate loops, cut loops, and make fades. This prepares them for the second feeder, which is really a technical challenge where everyone is asked to produce the same outcome. So they have to go find key loops, arrange the loops in a particular way that are defined, and they have to draw from what they've learned in their first feeder and apply it in their second feeder.

Jen: I think this certainly helps in terms of drafting a project, outlining the transcript, and then using that dialogue and the sounds listing to really follow that as they move into production. And help them see what's working well or make adjustments.

Ashley: From that point, they're ready to take on more challenges, and the environment can become less controlled. So now they're ready to do things like record a human voice. And sometimes that takes the form of a script that they write and then record, sometimes it's going out and doing an interview. But they've ramped up, and they're ready to take on those challenges, and they're able to be strategic in how they're going to use that audio in conjunction with the loops and the sound effects that they're going to be working with when they come back.

Jen: And I think what we're talking about here a little bit is the creativity within the constraints of the assignment and that being a really big part of this. The creative fiction aspect opens up another way to listen to and understand the ways that sounds can set a scene and create a mood.

Thank you everybody for hanging out with us and hearing a bit about our experiences with the feeders in this project. I'm Jen Ware.

Ashley: And I'm Ashley Hall.

References

Boyle, C., Brown, J. J., Jr. & Ceraso, S. (2018). The digital: Rhetoric behind and beyond the screen. *Rhetoric Society Quarterly, 48*(3), 251–259. https://doi.org/10.1080/02773945.2018.1454187.

Gorvett, Z. (2017, August 2). The ghostly radio station that no one claims to run. *BBC.* https://www.bbc.com/future/article/20170801-the-ghostly-radio-station-that-no-one-claims-to-run.

Sriram, A. (Host and Actor). (2015). *The message* [Audio podcast]. Panoply. https://podcasts.apple.com/us/podcast/lifeafter-the-message/id1045990056?mt=2.

SteamWulf. (2016, July 27). UVB–76 –The buzzer breakdown – 25 July 2016 [Video file]. *YouTube.* https://youtu.be/Wcv_cGLjxCY.

Chapter 25. Speech, Invention, and Reflection: The Composing Process of Soundwriting

Tanya K. Rodrigue
SALEM STATE UNIVERSITY

The assignment described in this chapter was designed for the final project in a graduate-level course on composing with sound, yet the assignment is indeed appropriate for an undergraduate writing course in digital or soundwriting or a graduate course in digital writing. The assignment has four components: a project proposal, audio and/or alphabetic process notes, an audio project in a genre and rhetorical context of the student's choice, and a reflection essay. The bare-boned audio project assignment prompt—compose an audio project in any genre for any purpose and audience—is intentional in its loose structure and meant to provide students with an opportunity to create a project that is meaningful to them. Yet students may indeed feel overwhelmed by the many options available to them, so I encourage instructors to give students the choice to engage with this open-ended prompt or a more specific and structured prompt.

While students should complete all four components of this assignment, they are assessed only on the process notes (75%) and reflection essay (25%). The process notes rubric draws primarily on the *Framework for Success in Postsecondary Writing*'s identification of habits of mind known to be important for learning (Council of Writing Program Administrators et al., 2011). The reflection essay rubric is made up of two categories related to students' understanding of sonic rhetorical strategies and what the audio composing experience taught them about themselves as writers.

Prior to this final assignment, instructors need to do a fair amount of scaffolding, teaching students both content and technical skills. Students must be introduced to and learn about the following:

- rhetoric and genre
- the aural mode and its affordances and constraints
- the rhetorical function of sound and sonic rhetorical strategies (such voice, sound effects, music, and silence)
- strategies for active listening
- strategies for analyzing sonic rhetoric and genre
- the multitude of existing genres of audio stories, situated in authentic rhetorical contexts
- the elements of audio storytelling such as writing for the "ear," scripting, narration, and delivery
- possible ways to approach the audio composing process

- audio-editing software (such as Audacity) and how to use it

Instructors should use in-class time to lead students in the analysis of audio stories, asking them to think carefully about the genre characteristics and the employment of sonic rhetorical strategies and their effectiveness. Students should also engage in several low-stakes activities that will help them build their technical skills in audio editing as well as their knowledge about how to write for the "ear."

Assignment Rationale

There are five general goals of the assignment, as indicated on the assignment guidelines:

- to deepen understanding of rhetoric and the rhetorical function of sound
- to practice composing and revising in the aural mode with attention to aspects of audio storytelling
- to bring awareness to the value of play and experimentation in composing
- to strengthen metacognitive awareness and reflection practices during the composing process
- to practice and strengthen the abilities needed for deep, effective learning

While the four components of the assignment generally work toward helping students achieve the above goals, the assignment primarily emphasizes the audio composing process, as reflected in the assessment criteria. I designed the assignment in this way mainly because of my own learning experience from composing an audio documentary as well as my interest in the use of speech in the invention stage of the composing process.

The exigence for this assignment primarily emerged from reflections on the course in light of what I learned from composing my first longform audio project in 2017 on the Women's Marches (Rodrigue, 2017). My audio composing experience shifted my thinking about the purposes and goals in a graduate course and my responsibilities as a rhetoric teacher working with students who are studying to be high school English teachers or who are already teachers of record. From my own experience, I recognized that the real learning of rhetoric, sonic rhetoric, audio storytelling, and the learning of learning something completely new (in a foreign genre and foreign modality) was in the process, not the product. I determined the best way for students to recognize and identify this learning was to consciously activate the habits of mind associated with effective learning while composing their audio projects and to capture this learning either in alphabetic or aural process notes. I define process notes as brief, informal documentations and/or reflections—on paper or in an audio recording—about one's writing experiences at various intervals during the composing process. I encouraged students to try audio process notes because of my interest in the possible affordances of speech in the invention stage. In *Vernacular Eloquence*, Peter Elbow (2012) claimed that unplanned, informal speech is a haven for productive meaning making. Thus, the audio process notes, I determined, had strong potential to play a significant role in helping students achieve course learning goals, strengthen their capabilities to learn as well as their aptitudes, as the Framework for Success in Postsecondary Writing states, in writing and thinking.

The Assignment and Rubrics
The Assignment

The major project for this class is the construction of an audio story in a genre of your choice for any purpose or audience. There are several components of the project:

1. Plan: You will compose a detailed plan as to how you will execute your story. The plan should be at least two double-spaced pages. You will work on this plan and revise it during the week we meet.

2. Process notes and/or audio recordings: While composing your project, you will reflect on your process along the way (I recommend after, or even during, each work session) either in written form or in audio form (I strongly encourage you to try the audio form). You are required to have at least five entries, yet you can certainly have more if you'd like. Written entries should be three to six pages and audio entries should be 5–10 minutes. I will provide you with examples of what these process notes might look/sound like.

3. Audio project: You will produce an audio story that is appropriate in length and nature to its genre. The story will have a distinct purpose and target audience.

4. Reflection essay: You will compose a written reflection after you finish the final version of your audio project that should be at least five double-spaced pages. The reflection should be a thorough exploration and analysis of the decisions you made with regard to sonic rhetorical strategies and your rhetorical situation. You can look to my previous students' reflections in the *Kairos* article (Rodrigue et al., 2016) for examples. It also asks you to reflect on what this experience has taught you about yourself as a writer.

You must meet the minimum requirements of all four components, yet you will primarily be assessed on your process notes/recordings (75%) and your reflection essay (25%). Please create a Google Drive folder specifically for the final project and clearly identify each component of the project.

The purpose of this project is five-fold:

1. To deepen your understanding of rhetoric and the rhetorical function of sound
2. To practice composing and revising in the aural mode with attention to aspects of audio storytelling
3. To bring awareness to the value of play and experimentation in composing
4. To strengthen metacognitive awareness and reflection practices during the composing processes
5. To practice and strengthen the abilities needed for deep, effective learning

Table 25.1. Rubric for Process Notes/Recordings

	A range The composer demonstrates this ability in a sophisticated and thoughtful manner consistently across their process notes.	B range The composer demonstrates this ability in an effective manner across all or most of the process notes.	C range The composer demonstrates this ability in a proficient way with room for growth in most or some of the process notes.
Creativity and Innovation: The ability to use a range of approaches for generating and expressing ideas			
Metacognition and Reflection: The ability to think about one's thinking, and to reflect on the impact of rhetorical decisions and their effects			
Persistence: The ability to sustain/maintain interest in and attention to the project. The composer stays on task and works through problems or issues without giving up			
Problem-posing and Problem-solving: The ability to pose challenging questions and/or recognize a problem or issue and making a plan for how to approach solving it			
Play, Experimentation, and Flexibility: The ability and willingness to try out different ways to address a problem or achieve a rhetorical goal; and/or take risks in an effort to determine what strategy/method is most effective			
Rhetorical Knowledge: The ability to consider purpose, genre, audience, sonic rhetorical strategies, and context when making decisions			

Table 25.2. Rubric for Audio Reflection

	A range	B range	C range
Sonic Rhetorical Strategies (sound interaction, voice, music, sound effects, silence) and the Rhetorical Situation	Composer thoughtfully and in detail explains and describes at least five ways they used sound to achieve their desired effect with regard to purpose, genre and audience. The composer draws substantially on class readings and/or experiences to explain these strategies in a sophisticated way.	Composer sufficiently describes at least five ways they used sound to achieve their desired effect with regard to purpose and audience. The composer draws on some class readings and/or experiences to explain these strategies in an effective way.	Composer describes at least five ways they used sound to achieve their desired effect with regard to purpose and audience. The composer makes only minimal or superficial reference to class readings and/or experiences to explain these strategies.
Your Identity as a Writer	Composer thoughtfully and in detail explains and describes what this experience has taught them about who they are as a writer/composer in general.	Composer sufficiently describes what this experience has taught them about who they are as a writer/composer in general.	Composer briefly touches on what this experience has taught them about who they are as a writer.

Sample Student Projects

Carolynn, a graduate student from my summer 2017 Composing with Sound class, composed the alphabetic and audio process notes, the alphabetic reflection essay, and the audio project shared on the book's companion website.

1. Audio process note #1 (out of 9)[1]
2. Audio process note #7 (out of 9)
3. Alphabetic process note #5 (out of 9)
4. Alphabetic process note #8 (out of 9)
5. "Documenting the Mundane: Reflections on Documenting and (re)Creating Aurally," an alphabetic reflection essay
6. Documenting the Mundane, Carolynn's final audio project

---

1. Six student examples (audio files and descriptive transcripts) can be found on the book's companion website.

Reflection

[a loud horn sound]

Tanya Rodrigue *[Recording informally in a car. The sound quality is poor with lots of background static noise.]*: Bubba, I'm gonna record myself, so I'm just going to talk into this phone, okay?[2]

Tanya *[as narrator]*: That's me. It was sometime in March in 2017. And I apparently felt compelled to let my three-year-old know that I was about to start talking to myself.

> *[Car recording continues, poor audio quality, and lots of static continues in the background. Some words are audible, but most of the sound is muffled and words are unable to be deciphered. Sound plays under the following narration for a couple of sentences before fading out.]*

Tanya *[as narrator]*: Again. It was becoming a habit. At that time, I was work-ing on my very first long-form audio project. It was a documentary; it was similar to the kind of long-form audio projects I assign students in courses that either focus on soundwriting or include a soundwriting unit. The documentary was about the women's marches . . .

> *[Protest song fades in for a few seconds before fading out. The chant is: "We Want a Leader, Not a Creepy Tweeter."]*

. . . that took place the day after 45 was sworn in. At the time, I was really busy at work and at home, and the car trips back and forth to my kid's daycare, or to the grocery store . . .

> *[Car recording fades in. No words can be deciphered, but the faint sound of a voice and static is heard.]*

. . . became a time when I could dwell and flip over my ideas about this documen-tary. Initially, I just did it in my head. But then I decided to start recording, and I used the recordings as a way to work through some of the struggles I was having. And then.

Tanya *[car recording]*: So I got accepted to the Cs regional conference, and what I proposed was to talk about how my experience composing audio—an audio documentary—shaped my pedagogical practices in the teaching of writing with sound. So I thought, what better way than to record snippets as I work on, um, composing this thing.

Tanya *[narrator]*: And so that's what I did. I documented and reflected on my process in writing and in audio recordings, but mostly in audio recordings. And this was intentional. I already knew from my car recordings that talk was

---

2. The audio version of Tanya K. Rodrigue's reflection can be found on the book's companion website.

rich for invention. I had also recently witnessed talk as a productive invention tool, while facilitating student think-alouds for a research project I was doing on digital reading practices. Time and time again, I heard students use talk to draw connections, to make meaning, and to comprehend what they were reading. None of that awesome cognitive work made it to their writing, but that's a different story. So anyway, I observed the value of talk and Peter Elbow (2012) confirmed my observations in research. In *Vernacular Eloquence*, he argues that speaking is easier than writing and "the kind of language that we blurt" (2012, p. 5) is incredibly rich for meaning making. So knowing all that, I wrote or recorded a dozen process notes, before or during or after my work sessions. Some process notes were similar in nature to my car recordings—me just riffing on ideas or working through a struggle—while others focused on where I was in what I was doing at that moment in the composing process.

> **Tanya** *[process note recording]*: I got back some feedback from several people. One is a radio producer. I got feedback back from him, and I was completely overwhelmed. Um, I finished reading this and I thought to myself, wow, I have no idea what I'm doing.

Tanya *[narrator]*: After analyzing both the written and spoken notes, I learned that this is where I was doing my learning. I was learning how to write with unfamiliar rhetorical tools in a foreign genre—initially, I couldn't even figure out the genre—and in a mode I was uncomfortable in.

> **Tanya** *[process note recording]*: I really thought this is exactly what it's all about. I am so uncomfortable writing in this genre. I'm so uncomfortable about inserting myself in any way and thinking that I actually can tell a good, interesting story, one that's about real life and not about the classroom or my experience as a graduate student.

Tanya *[narrator]*: I learned what I knew, what I needed to know, and what I didn't know. I also learned an awful lot about myself both as a thinker and a writer. And then it occurred to me: This is the kind of learning I want my students to do. I'm a rhetoric teacher; I'm not a journalism teacher. I'm working primarily with English majors, high school teachers, and people studying to be high school teachers. I want them to learn about rhetoric and writing in general, sonic rhetoric in particular, sonic composing processes, and perhaps most importantly, how one goes about learning something entirely new and composing in a foreign mode, and possibly in a foreign genre. So it made sense to craft a flexible soundwriting assignment that emphasizes the process of writing and then to create an assessment mechanism that measures learning. So I gave this assignment to graduate students in a one-week intensive soundwriting class that asked them to compose a project plan, alphabetic or aural process notes, a reflection essay about their writerly choices, and an audio project in any genre for any audience. This assignment is flexible, and it can really be used in any undergraduate or graduate course that has a soundwriting unit or focuses on sound writing.

[Blue Dot Sessions's (2020) "Kilkerrin," a folk song that features a mandolin, fades in.]

Analyzing my students' process notes, they taught me a lot—more than I have time to talk about in this reflection. But let me offer some initial observations here.

[Music fades out.]

I initially thought the students would be annoyed at the emphasis on process rather than product. After all, it takes a lot of time, a lot of energy and focus and persistence, and the end product is what you have to show for this tremendous amount of effort and work. With that said, though, there was a general sense of relief among the first-time audio composers in my class.

> **Student 1** *[female voice; sounds of wind in the background]*: This is something that I've never done before. So it's hard not to be a little intimidated by it and feel pressure to produce something like really good. I mean, obviously, I'm going to do my best and try really hard to make a good product. But that being said, the guidelines for it are focused on the process of it, which I think is kind of reassuring to myself and the other people in the class just because I think this is the first time a lot of us have done anything like this. English majors, I think, we're so used to writing and getting our ideas down on paper as opposed to just speaking them aloud.

Tanya *[narrator]*: We all know that stress has a negative impact on someone's ability to write. So I think the low-stakes aspect of this assignment was really key to student engagement and buy-in and investment in the project. Interestingly, my students were divided in choosing to compose audio process notes or alphabetic notes or a combo of the two. In both the audio and alphabetic notes, people talked about their methods, the strategies they used, the challenges they faced, the decisions they made, or what decisions they needed to make, yet the audio notes, for some reason, they welcomed more macro-conceptual learning than the alphabetic notes. So for example, several students explored the similarities and differences between alphabetic writing and soundwriting in their recordings. And through this talk, they were working toward a more sophisticated understanding of modes, their affordances, their constraints, their composing processes, and how to write in them.

> **Student 2** *[female voice]*: Using Audacity was challenging, but at the same time, really awesome. And I enjoyed that as a writer.

So I liked being able to plan out what I was going to do first, and then kind of checking off my story plans like a checklist: "This is how I want to start, do that sound effect, moving on. This interview, moving on." And then kind of filling in with my narration in between. So it was writing because it's just like building brainstorming, um, kind of doing a graphic organizer type deal, for sure: It is writing. And you don't think about it until you're actually doing it. It's like oh, okay, here I am making my first draft, essentially. And then as I go in and edit things, here's my next draft. . . . [fades out]

Tanya [narrator]: Also, these first-time composers tended to elaborate much more on their ideas in the audio process notes than their alphabetic notes. So, for example, in an alphabetic process note, a student might simply write one or two sentences about how they felt frustrated or how they were working through a particular idea. In an audio note, students said much more. And they also allowed themselves to digress and move into talking about something either tangentially related or not at all related. I noticed that some of the most interesting moments—some of that really rich invention work in my students' audio process notes—occurred both in the digressions and also when people took the time to work through and grapple with ideas. It seemed like the longer people talked, the more meaning-making and invention occurred. Take a listen to the very end of this 8-minute audio process note.

Student 3 [female voice; static in background]: And I could call St. Elizabeth's, but they didn't see her till after the fact. And she had cardiac arrest. But! Oh, her death certificate could determine how . . . who? Well, basically, if Mark is lying, I don't think I don't believe at all that my parents are lying, but it would be like the ultimate proof, so maybe I could try again to get a copy of her death certificate and use that as the ending. But that could be an idea. Okay, I'm going to look into the death certificate idea. And play around with that and then see where it leads me.

Tanya [narrator]: After listening to my students' process notes, I realized I did the same thing in my car audio recordings: I would just sit in the car and blab on and on; I would stumble and fumble and then I'd hit on something, something that was good or insightful, or something that was awful and horrible. But whatever it was, I couldn't get there in any other way. This "freespeaking," if you will, this freedom to use language without constraints and limitations, it is no doubt valuable for student learning. And no doubt valuable for teaching students how to write effectively in any mode, but especially in the aural mode.

[Blue Dot Sessions's (2020) "Kilkerrin" plays again in the background.]

So this is all to say that a soundwriting assignment that focuses on process and the learning and the doing of soundwriting is incredibly valuable for students, especially first-time audio composers.

[Music. Car recording fades in.]

Child: Who are you talking to?
Tanya: I'm recording myself. So when I set out to write this story. . . .

[Car recording continues to faintly play in the background, words inaudible.]

Tanya *[narrator]:* I'm Tanya Rodrigue, an associate professor in English at Salem State University in Massachusetts. A big shoutout to the students in my Composing with Sound graduate class back in the summer of 2017. And a big thank you to Blue Dot Sessions for the music used in this reflection.

References

Blue Dot Sessions. (2020). Kilkerrin (Song). https://app.sessions.blue/browse/track /obda9cef-aef4-4691-a7c5-88ecd1e69c85.

The Council of Writing Program Administrators, the National Council of Teachers of English, and the National Writing Project. (2011). *Framework for success in postsecondary writing.* http://wpacouncil.org/aws/CWPA/asset_manager/get _file/350201?ver=7548.

Elbow, P. (2012). *Vernacular eloquence: What speech can bring to writing.* Oxford University Press.

Rodrigue, T. K. (2017, June 12). Peaceful warriors (No. 50) [Audio podcast episode]. On *Rocky Mountain revival: An audio art journal.* https://rockymtnrevival.libsyn .com/50-peaceful-warriors.

Rodrigue, T. K., Artz, K., Bennett, J., Carver, M. P., Grandmont, M., Harris, D., Hashem, D., Mooney, A., Rand, M. & Zimmerman, A. (2016). Navigating the soundscape, composing with audio. *Kairos: A Journal of Rhetoric, Technology, and Pedagogy, 21*(1). http://kairos.technorhetoric.net/21.1/praxis/rodrigue/index.html.

Contributors

Editors

Amplifying Soundwriting is the third open-access collection edited by this team on the topic of teaching with sound in rhetoric and writing classes. It is preceded by *Soundwriting Pedagogies* (Computers and Composition Digital Press/ Utah State University Press, 2018) and *Tuning in to Soundwriting* (Intermezzo/ enculturation, 2021).

Michael J. Faris (he/him) is Associate Professor of Technical Communication and Rhetoric in the English Department at Texas Tech University. His research areas are in digital literacies and rhetorics, queer rhetorics, and writing program administration. His work has appeared in *College Composition and Communication, Kairos: A Journal of Rhetoric, Technology, and Pedagogy, Journal of Business and Technical Communication, Composition Forum, Peitho,* and *WPA: Writing Program Administration.*

Courtney S. Danforth (she/her) teaches courses in writing and humanities, including first-year composition, creative nonfiction, poetry, and ancient literature, among other areas.

Kyle D. Stedman (he/him) is Associate Professor of English at Rockford University, where he teaches composition, rhetoric, and creative writing courses. His sonic and written work has been published in the journals *Technoculture, Composition Forum, Harlot, Memoir Magazine,* and *Computers and Composition,* as well as several edited collections. His podcasts are *Plugs, Play, Pedagogy* and the audio version of *Bad Ideas about Writing* (edited by Cheryl E. Ball and Drew M. Loewe, West Virginia University Libraries, 2017), and he co-authored the textbook *Soundwriting: A Guide to Making Audio Projects* with Tanya K. Rodrigue (Broadview Press, 2023).

Authors

Averi Ager (they/them) was a fourth-year undergraduate student studying English language and literature at the University of Maryland. They focused their studies in digital rhetoric and hoped to persist in exploring sonic rhetoric as they continue their studies post-graduation.

Timothy R. Amidon (he/him) is Associate Professor at Colorado State University, where he directs the graduate M.A. program in writing, rhetoric, and social change and teaches courses that examine the design and practice of digital rhetorics, histories of rhetoric, multimodal composing, and science writing. His scholarship, which explores the interrelationships of texts, technologies, and agency, has appeared in *Kairos: A Journal of Rhetoric, Technology, and Pedagogy, Journal of Business and Technical Communication, Hybrid Pedagogy, Communication Design Quarterly,* and edited collections including *The Routledge Companion* *to Media Education, Copyright, and Fair Use* (Routledge, 2011) and *Cultures of Copyright: Contemporary Intellectual Property* (Peter Lang, 2014).

Dorian Blue (they/them) was a fourth-year English major at the University of Maryland. They are an independent filmmaker and Head Storyteller at CoFED (Cooperative Food Empowerment Directive), where they seek to tell unconventional stories through the mediums of video and sound.

Jennifer J. Buckner (she/her) is Associate Dean of the College of Arts and Sciences and Professor of English at Gardner-Webb University. She teaches courses in writing studies and new media and learns alongside undergraduate and graduate students, where they dialogue about multimodality, language, semiotics, and composition. Her scholarship addresses intersections between writing studies and rhetorics of sound.

Helen J. Burgess (she/her) is Professor of English and core faculty in the communication, rhetoric and digital media Ph.D. program at North Carolina State University. She is editor of the journal *Hyperrhiz: New Media Cultures* and coeditor of the Hyperrhiz Electric series for strange digital humanities projects. Her most recent project is *Intimate Fields*, with Margaret Simon, published by the Maker Lab in the Humanities (MLab) at the University of Victoria as part of their Kits for Cultural History series.

Chris Burton (he/him) was a senior at University of South Florida St. Petersburg, where he was an English writing studies major and now holds a master of liberal arts degree as well as a certificate in creative writing. He is a member of Sigma Tau Delta English Honor Society and also blogs for their Alpha Xi Phi chapter. Chris has enjoyed stories all his life and published a piece of short fiction in *Papercut Literary Journal*. After graduation, he continues to pursue writing with plans to publish short fiction stories and novels and work with a publishing firm as an editor.

Steph Ceraso (she/her) is Associate Professor of Digital Writing and Rhetoric at the University of Virginia. Her 2018 book, *Sounding Composition: Multimodal Pedagogies for Embodied Listening* (University of Pittsburgh Press), proposes an expansive approach to teaching with sound in the composition classroom. Ceraso has published scholarship in journals such as *Rhetoric Society Quarterly*, *College English, Composition Studies, enculturation*, and *Peitho*. Her 2019 ebook, *Sound Never Tasted So Good* (Intermezzo), is an exploration of writing, sound, rhetoric, and food.

Madison Cissell (she/her) was a sophomore minoring in Jewish studies and a Jewish Heritage Fund for Excellence Scholar and Presidential Scholar at the University of Kentucky. She presented at the 2018 Kentucky Jewish History Symposium. Madison has always had a passion for studying religion, and under the Jewish Heritage Fund for Excellence Oral History Project, she learned more about Judaism and the Jewish community within and outside Kentucky. In 2020, she was invited to attend the Israel Institute Honors Symposium in New York. She studied abroad in Israel in spring 2020 and presented "An Undergraduate's

Experience with Audio Composition" at a virtual Interdisciplinary Day on Audio and Video Collections hosted by The Open University in Ra'anana, Israel. She graduated from the University of Kentucky in 2021, and in 2022, she will be enrolled in graduate school for folklore and library science at Indiana University Bloomington.

Trey Conner (he/him) is Associate Professor at the University of South Florida St. Petersburg, where he forms community partnerships that empower youth and provide service learning opportunities for USFSP students, facilitates a welcoming classroom space for students to learn rituals of writing ranging from contemplative practices to distributed authorship, and writes about the function of chanting, song, and rhythm in diverse rhetorical and poetic traditions. Recent publications include chapters in the edited volumes *The Routledge Handbook of Comparative World Rhetorics* (Routledge, 2020), *Responding to the Sacred: An Inquiry into the Limits of Rhetoric* (Penn State Press, 2021), and *Global Rhetorical Traditions* (Parlor Press, 2022). Trey remains always already engaged in a nourishing process of "infinite rehearsal" of collaboration with friends, family, students, and colleagues, and is currently at work on *Everything Worth Doing Now.*

Todd Craig (he/him) is Associate Professor of English at the Graduate Center of the City University of New York, Medgar Evers College (CUNY), and teaches in the African American Studies Department at New York City College of Technology (CUNY). His research explores the hip-hop DJ as 21st-century new media reader and writer. Craig's publications include the multimodal novel *tor'cha*, a short story in *Staten Island Noir*, and essays in scholarly journals including *Fiction International, Radical Teacher, Changing English, Modern Language Studies, Sounding Out!, Kairos*, and *Composition Studies*. He teaches courses in writing, rhetoric, and hip-hop studies while decrying that his cup runneth over the brim (Earl Sweatshirt).

Lance Cummings (he/him) is Associate Professor of English in the professional writing program at the University of North Carolina Wilmington. In addition to researching histories of rhetoric, Lance explores rhetoric and writing in technologically and linguistically diverse contexts in both his research and teaching. He has published chapters on rhetoric and multimodality in the edited volumes *Making Space: Writing Instruction, Infrastructure, and Multiliteracies* (University of Michigan Press and Sweetland Digital Collaborative, 2017) and *President Donald Trump and His Political Discourse* (Routledge, 2018). His work has also been published in *Rhetoric, Professional Communication, and Globalization, Business and Professional Communication Quarterly*, and *Res Rhetorica*.

Brandee Easter (she/her) is Assistant Professor of Writing at York University. Her research and teaching focus on digital rhetoric, feminist rhetoric, and 21st-century literacies. Her work has appeared in *Rhetoric Review* and *Feminist Media Studies*.

Janice W. Fernheimer (she/her) is Professor of Writing, Rhetoric, and Digital Studies and the Zantker Charitable Foundation Professor and Director of Jewish

Studies and a James B. Beam Institute for Kentucky Spirits Faculty Fellow at the University of Kentucky. She is the author of *Stepping Into Zion: Hatzaad Harishon, Black, Jews and the Remaking of Jewish Identity* (University of Alabama Press, 2014) and coeditor with Michael Bernard-Donals of *Jewish Rhetorics: History, Theory, Practice* (Brandeis University Press, 2014). She has published in *Rhetoric Society Quarterly, College English, Journal of Communication and Religion, Computers and Composition Online, Argumentation and Advocacy, Journal of Business and Technical Communication, Technical Communication*, and *Oral History Review*. She is cofounder with Dr. Beth L. Goldstein of the Jewish Heritage Fund for Excellence Jewish Kentucky Oral History Project and co-author with JT Waldman of *America's Chosen Spirit*, a transmedia project about the influence of Jews, African Americans, women, immigrants, and other "others" on the Kentucky bourbon industry. She is the founder of the Women in Bourbon Oral History Project.

Benjamin Flournoy (he/him) is an alumnus of Gardner-Webb University with a major in English with a concentration in literature and a minor in philosophy and ethics. He was active with the honors program and was co-president of the university's Sigma Tau Delta chapter. He plans on continuing his journey as an author and exploring career paths of book publication and editing.

Katie Furr (she/her) is majoring in English and minoring in education at Gardner-Webb University, preparing to teach at the high school level. She is a member of the honors program. She was interested in studying a college wrestling team because it is an often overlooked and misunderstood sport, so she thought it would be eye-opening to hear firsthand accounts about life in this community.

Thomas M. Geary (he/him) is Professor of English at the Virginia Beach campus of Tidewater Community College. He regularly teaches composition, rhetoric, technical writing, developmental writing, and humanities courses. Tom serves as the editor of *Inquiry*, the peer-reviewed journal for faculty, staff, and administrators in Virginia's community colleges.

Jennifer Geraci (she/her) is Lecturer in the composition program at the University of California, Irvine. Her research focuses on 21st century Latina life writing, diaspora theory, and literary genealogies.

Mariana Grohowski (she/her) is founder and editor of the *Journal of Veterans Studies*. She is currently an adjunct lecturer of veterans studies at the University of California, Irvine and writing and research at Sofia University.

Ashley Hall (she/her) is an independent scholar and researcher. She studies digital media and emerging technologies.

Emma Hamilton (she/her) graduated from the University of South Florida St. Petersburg in fall 2018 with a BA in English writing studies. She was a member of the Alpha Xi Phi chapter of the Sigma Tau Delta English honor society and an editor of *Papercut Literary Journal*. She is currently working toward her MA in English with a concentration in professional writing and rhetoric at Western Carolina University. Her creative writing has been published in *Papercut Literary Journal, 30 N*, and *Yonder Magazine*.

Ben Harley (he/him) is Assistant Professor in the Department of Languages, Literature, and Communication Studies at Northern State University in Aberdeen, South Dakota, where he also serves as the director of the Center for Excellence in Teaching and Learning. His pedagogy foregrounds accessibility, diversity, and inclusivity—inviting students to engage in collaborative high-impact assignments and active learning classroom activities. His scholarship predominantly focuses on the embodied, affective, and communal effects of sound, though he is currently researching instructor experiences with HyFlex course design and critical thinking assignments. His work has been published in *Rhetoric Society Quarterly, Textshop Experiments, The Journal of Multimodal Rhetorics,* and *Hybrid Pedagogy.*

Alyssa Harmon (she/her) graduated from the University of South Florida St. Petersburg in spring 2019 with a bachelor's degree in English writing studies and a minor in mass communications. She was the senior editor for the USFSP Her Campus chapter, the 2017–2018 president for the Alpha Xi Phi chapter of Sigma Tau Delta, and the editor-in-chief of *Papercut Literary Journal.* Now, she is working on her Master of Arts in English creative writing at University of West Florida. Her poems have been published in several print and online publications, including *Merrimack Review, Minerva Rising, Torrid Literary Journal, The Wild Word,* and *Odet Journal.*

Travis Harrington (he/him) graduated from North Carolina State University in summer 2020 with a bachelor's degree in English, concentrating in creative writing. He wrote poems, was published in the school's literary magazine *Windhover,* and taught himself how to handset type by sneaking into the university's design lab. Since graduating, he spends the majority of his time pursuing a career in music composition and performance with his band, Truth Club.

Chad Iwertz Duffy (he/him) is Assistant Professor of English at Pepperdine University. His research focuses on the framing of disability in technologies of accommodation, access/accessibility in composition classrooms, and *mētis,* the rhetorical concept of embodied wisdom and cunning. His other work can be found in *Computers and Composition, Peitho, HASTAC, Teaching with Writing, Willamette Valley Voices,* and *The Sigma Tau Delta Review.*

Sarah Johnson (she/her) is pursuing a double major in missiology and ESL at Gardner-Webb University. She is a member of the honors program and Alpha Chi. She plans to work in a local school as an ESL teacher after graduation while gathering support for mission work. Her long-term goal is to be a missionary teaching English in another country. She chose to do her soundwriting project on an inductive Bible study group because of the different perspectives provided and her passion for Bible study.

Ivan Jones (he/him) is an aspiring higher education instructor who holds a bachelor's in English rhetoric and master's in digital journalism. He has diverse professional experience in the audio field, including highlights such as touring as a front of house engineer, DJing for a live crowd of 2,000+ at Bullstock, and releasing his original album of bass music titled *DO4H*. He loves skiing and snowboarding and dreams of untouched alpine slopes.

Hannah Lane Kendrick (she/her) graduated from the University of North Carolina Wilmington in December 2017 with a bachelor's of science in business administration with a concentration in marketing. She also completed two minors in journalism and leadership studies. After graduation, she moved to Cary, North Carolina, to pursue a job opportunity with Kerridge Commercial Systems, a software company, where she currently works as a marketing assistant. During her time at UNCW, she participated in many writing workshops and projects that cultivated within her a deep passion to someday become a published writer alongside her career in marketing.

Doyuen Ko (he/him) is Associate Professor of Audio Engineering Technology at Belmont University in Nashville, Tennessee, where he teaches courses in critical listening, acoustics and classical music recording. He received his master's and Ph.D. from McGill University, Canada, and he has published his research in several international conferences and journals including Institute of Electrical and Electronics Engineers (IEEE), Acoustic Society of America (ASA), and Audio Engineering Society (AES).

L. Jill Lamberton (she/her) is the Special Assistant to the President for Diversity, Equity, and Inclusion and Associate Professor of English at Wabash College in Crawfordsville, Indiana. Her academic interests include women's rhetorical activism in the 19th century and access to higher education in the 21st century. Her essays have appeared in *College Composition and Communication* and *College English*, and she is a coauthor of *Public Speaking and Democratic Participation: Speaking, Listening, and Deliberation in the Civic Realm* from Oxford University Press (2015). She traces her love of audio to the hours she spent as a child listening to radio programs on long family car trips through the Pacific Northwest. Her belief in the unique power of audio storytelling to build connections among people and across borders led her to create a popular course in soundwriting at Wabash, where her students regularly astound her with their own stories.

Jasmine Lee (she/her) is Assistant Professor of English at California State University, San Bernardino. Her research interests include rhetorical education, political economy, affect theory, and pop culture, especially young adult fiction.

Katie Lewis (she/her) is majoring in English with teacher licensure at Gardner-Webb University. After graduation, she hopes to teach high school English in her hometown so that she can continue living near her family. She has volunteered with a breast cancer class in her community called Be Your Own Beautiful (BYOB) and loves the unique bonds created within the community. Soundwriting is something that she truly enjoyed, and she hopes to incorporate it in her own classroom one day.

Scott Lunsford (he/him) is Professor of Writing, Rhetoric, and Technical Communication at James Madison University. His research focuses on the intersections of sonic rhetorics, genre, and embodied knowledge. He has published in *Rhetorics Change/Rhetoric's Change* (enculturation/Intermezzo, 2018), *Present Tense, Writing on the Edge, Rhetoric Review,* and *The Journal of Multimodal Rhetorics.* He co-produces the podcast *Hidden Language.*

Jason Luther (he/him) is Assistant Professor of Writing Arts at Rowan University in Glassboro, New Jersey, where he teaches courses on digital rhetoric, publishing, and writing about pop culture. His research focuses on multimodal (counter)publics and DIY participatory media, especially zines. His work has most recently appeared in *Community Literacy Journal, SoundEffects,* and *Reflections.* He is also the co-founder of Syracuse in Print, curator of the Factsheet Five Archive Project, advisor to *Halftone Magazine* at Rowan, and is a public scholar for the New Jersey Council for the Humanities.

Meg M. Marquardt (she/her) is Assistant Professor of English in the composition and rhetoric program at Mississippi State University. Her research interests include historiography and the rhetoricity of science practices, materials, and methods. Her work has been published in *Rhetoric Review* and has appeared in the *Digital Rhetoric Collaborative.*

Angela Meade (she/her) is an ESL teacher in Gaston County Schools. She studied Spanish and ESL at Gardner-Webb University, where she graduated in 2018.

Logan Middleton (he/him) is Teaching Assistant Professor in the University Writing Program at the University of Denver. His research focuses on the ties and tensions between literacy, higher education in prison, and abolition in the 21st-century carceral state. His work has appeared in *Reflections: A Journal of Community-Engaged Writing and Rhetoric, Literacy in Composition Studies, Journal of Academic Freedom,* and the edited collection *Multimodal Composition: Faculty Development Programs and Institutional Change.*

D'Arcee Charington Neal (he/they) is a professional storyteller and doctoral candidate at The Ohio State University in English and disability studies, focusing on the intersections of Black digital media and disabled erasure within Afrofuturism. With a double master's in creative writing and rhetorical composition, through the lens of audionarratology, he works to tell stories of the Afrophantasmic, or Black disabled people who exist as phantoms within the community as both a power and a problem; critically analyzing digital blackface and ableism across popular culture. When not theorizing about Black techno-agency, he works as a disability and writing consultant for clients like Conde Nast, Uber, NASA, The World Bank, The Ford Foundation, and many nonprofits. As a queer disabled digital griot, he believes that the future can and should be both accessible and in Wakanda, forever.

Hannah Newberry (she/her) was a junior biology major, minoring in Jewish studies and a Jewish Heritage Fund for Excellence Scholar at the University of Kentucky. She presented at the 2018 Kentucky Jewish History Symposium. A Paducah native, She received a 2018 Jewish Studies Undergraduate Research

Award to conduct oral history interviews documenting the Jewish heritage of her hometown. She completed an independent research study on Preserving Paducah's Jewish History and Heritage and presented her research to the Commonwealth of Kentucky at the 2019 Posters at the Capitol Symposium in Frankfort, Kentucky. She now attends the University of Louisville School of Medicine and hopes to practice in Paducah one day.

Amber L. Nicol (she/her) is singer-songwriter and practicing attorney in St. Petersburg, FL. She plays live shows with her band and loves to write and record original music. She studied English at University of South Florida St. Petersburg and received her J.D. from Stetson University College of Law. In her free time, she enjoys practicing banjo, paddle boarding, and gardening.

Kathleen A. Olinger (she/her), a BA graduate of English, specializes in the written variances of rhetorical; creative and creative nonfiction; environmental and surrealistic writing, just to name a few. Her essay "In the Essence of Booker Creek" is published in the book *Voices of Booker Creek*.

Joel Overall (he/him) is Associate Professor of English at Belmont University in Nashville, Tennessee, where he teaches courses in writing, digital rhetoric, and sound and persuasion. He received his Ph.D. from Texas Christian University, and his work has appeared in *Rhetoric Society Quarterly* and *Rhetoric Review*. Readers can view his scholarly portfolio at https://joeloverall.com.

Devon Peterson (she/her) is a graduate from the University of North Carolina Wilmington's undergraduate English program. She began her academic career at the University of North Carolina Asheville in literary studies. Upon transfer to UNCW, Peterson maintained her major in English but shifted her focus to professional writing. Her participation in a graduate course on communicating with global and cross-cultural audiences culminated in the development of surveys and promotional materials for an emerging Polish energy company. She continues to use her education in rhetoric and professional writing for free-lance projects.

Hannah Ray (she/her) is an alumna English major of Gardner-Webb University. She is the product of two English-major parentsm and as a homeschool student, she was forced to label parts of speech and diagram sentences every day. Her majoring in and passion for the English language was perhaps inevitable; however, She has also dabbled in Spanish and linguistic classes during her time in college. She is a member of Sigma Tau Delta and Alpha Chi. She hopes to one day work as a feature writer or journalist for a missions agency or nonprofit to remind people globally that every word, language, and story matters.

Daniel P. Richards (he/him) is Associate Professor of English at Old Dominion University, where he teaches courses in technical communication, rhetoric, and pedagogy in the department's undergraduate and doctoral programs. His research currently focuses on the intersection of risk communication, user experience, and the public understanding of science. He has published in *Technical Communication Quarterly*, *Journal of Business and Technical Communication*, *Communication Design Quarterly*, and *Intercom*, as well as several scholarly

collections. His coedited collection *Posthuman Praxis in Technical Communication* (Routledge, 2018) explores the value of posthuman and new materialist theories in facilitating better communication practices in a broad array of public,
governmental, and scientific workspaces.

Tanya K. Rodrigue (she/her) is Associate Professor in English and coordi-
nator of the Writing Intensive Curriculum (WIC) program at Salem State University. She teaches courses in writing and rhetoric at the undergraduate and
graduate level. Her scholarly work has been published in *Computers and Composition*; *Kairos: A Journal of Rhetoric, Technology, and Pedagogy*; *Pedagogy*; *Across
the Disciplines*; *Teaching/Writing: The Journal of Writing Teacher Education*; and
Composition Forum. Her audio work has been played on local and national radio
including *PRX Remix* and NPR's *All Things Considered* as well as podcasts. She
recently coauthored the textbook *Soundwriting: A Guide to Making Audio Projects* with Kyle D. Stedman (Broadview Press, 2023).

Rich Shivener (he/him) is Assistant Professor in the writing department at
York University. His latest research investigates the composing practices and
affective work of digital media, including webtexts that embrace the sonic. Before
his academic journey began, he covered music and pop culture for newspapers
and magazines. His spare time includes playing guitar for his young son.

Garrett Simpson (he/him) is an alumnus of Gardner-Webb University,
majoring in English and minoring in business administration. During his academic tenure, he was involved in the GWU Pre-Law Society, the Student Government Association, and Sigma Tau Delta. He plans on attending law school and
practicing corporate law.

Hannah Thompson (she/her) was a junior biology major with minors in cognitive science and writing, rhetoric, and digital studies at the University of Kentucky. She presented research at the 2018 Kentucky Jewish History Symposium.
Supported by a 2018 Jewish Studies Undergraduate Research Award, she conducted additional oral histories and completed an independent research study
titled Maintaining the Legacy of American Jewish Hospitals and presented her
research to the Commonwealth of Kentucky at the Posters on the Capitol Symposium in Frankfort, Kentucky on February 21, 2019. She now attends the Liberty
University College of Osteopathic Medicine in Virginia and hopes to provide
medical care to underserved communities in the future.

Crystal VanKooten (she/her) is Associate Professor of Writing and Rhetoric
at Oakland University in Rochester, Michigan, where she teaches courses in writing for digital media and first-year composition. Her research interests include
composition pedagogy, multimodal and digital rhetoric, and methodologies for
research in digital writing.

Kate Vriesema (she/her) is majoring in English with an emphasis in creative writing and a psychology minor at Gardner-Webb University. There, she
is a member of the Alpha Chi National Honors Society and the Sigma Tau
Delta English Honor Society. She aspires to become an editor at a renowned

publishing agency in New York City and to have one of her young adult fiction books published.

Ally Ward (she/her) is majoring in English with a concentration in literature at Gardner-Webb University. She is a member of the honor society and is a peer leader to incoming first-year students. After graduation, she plans to pursue a doctorate degree in English studies with a concentration in British literature. Once she obtains this degree, she plans to teach English courses at a college or university.

Jennifer Ware (she/her) is an independent research and scholar. Her research interests include digital media and UX.

Sara Wilder (she/her) is Assistant Professor of English at the University of Maryland. Her teaching and research interests include rhetoric and composition, writing pedagogies, and writing center studies. Her current research project examines student learning in multidisciplinary writing groups.

Laura Will (she/her) is a sophomore accounting and finance major, a Social Enterprise Scholar, a Gatton Ambassador, and a Presidential Scholarship recipient at the University of Kentucky. She presented at the 2018 Kentucky Jewish History Symposium.

Justin Young (he/him) is Professor of English at Eastern Washington University, where he directs the English Composition Program and Writers' Center. His research interests include multimodal composing practices, critical pedagogies, and disability studies. He is also involved in statewide and national efforts to improve students' successful transitions to college, focusing on how writing instruction can better prepare students across the K–16 continuum to communicate effectively in both print and in digital environments.